Transboundary Environmental Governance in Asia

Practice and Prospects with the UNECE Agreements

Simon Marsden

Professor, School of Law, Flinders University, Australia

Elizabeth Brandon

Visiting Assistant Professor, School of Law, City University of Hong Kong

Edward Elgar PUBLISHING

Cheltenham, UK • Northampton, MA, USA

Published by
Edward Elgar Publishing Limited
The Lypiatts
15 Lansdown Road
Cheltenham
Glos GL50 2JA
UK

Edward Elgar Publishing, Inc.
William Pratt House
9 Dewey Court
Northampton
Massachusetts 01060
USA

A catalogue record for this book
is available from the British Library

Library of Congress Control Number: 2014954957

This book is available electronically in the **Elgar**online
Law subject collection
DOI 10.4337/9781782547129

MIX
Paper from responsible sources
FSC® C013056
FSC
www.fsc.org

ISBN 978 1 78254 711 2 (cased)
ISBN 978 1 78254 712 9 (eBook)

Typeset by Columns Design XML Ltd, Reading
Printed and bound in Great Britain by T.J. International Ltd, Padstow

Contents

Preface and Acknowledgements

This book grew from shared interests in international and regional law, global governance and environmental regimes. Each of us had recently completed a book project: *Transboundary Environmental Governance: Inland, Coastal and Marine Perspectives* (Marsden, with Warner, Ashgate Publishing, 2012); *Global Approaches to Site Contamination Law* (Brandon, Springer, 2013); and we wanted to collaborate on another, building on and developing this work.

Before commencing the book, Marsden had experience with several of the United Nations Economic Commission for Europe (UNECE) agreements (Environmental Impact Assessment (*EIA*), Strategic Environmental Assessment (*SEA*), and *Public Participation*, and developing interests in the *Water*, and *Water and Health* agreements); Brandon had experience with pollution and contamination regulation, which made enquiry into the remaining agreements very practical (*Pollutant Release and Transfer Registers*, *Industrial Accidents*, *Civil Liability*, and *Air Pollution*). The division of labour was therefore logical and straightforward, with collaboration on the remaining chapters to pull it all together.

It became apparent early on that, other than consideration of the relationship between two of the agreements (typically the *EIA* and *Public Participation* treaties), there had been no scholarly work on the combined effect of all of the agreements. The majority of existing research was also Europe focused, where most of the members of the UNECE are located. The focus on Asia came from the interests of each of us in the region in general and previous research. It became a practical prospect given UNECE membership of states in the Caucasus and central Asia, other UNECE Asian members with involvement in the development of one or more of the agreements (Turkey), or indeed those who had perhaps signed if not ratified the various agreements (Russia). The fact that Turkey and Russia are both European and Asian states is furthermore illustrative of the Eurasian dimensions of the UNECE.

The specific focus on practice made excellent sense given that implementation and compliance is the weakest part of environmental law, whether internationally or domestically. The fact that almost all of the agreements had provision for – either in the treaty text or as a result of decisions of the meetings or conferences of the Parties – periodic reporting of implementation together with a non-compliance procedure, also indicated the potential for comparative analysis. Central Asia was suggested by one of the reviewers of the proposal as a case study for the combined effect of the agreements, which, as a fast-developing region emerging from the former Soviet Union, could potentially highlight challenges applicable elsewhere.

As to prospects, the global opening of the *Water* and *EIA* conventions in 2013 and 2014, and interest shown in these by non-UNECE Asian states suggested there was significant potential to give consideration to the broader application of the agreements, both in parts of Asia not part of the UNECE and globally. The absence of treaty-making efforts by the other four United Nations regional commissions, the interest shown by other states in some of the agreements (particularly the *EIA*, *SEA*, *Public Participation* and *Water* agreements); and the clear need for improved transboundary environmental governance in relation to the others (*Air Pollution* and *Industrial Accidents*) not open to global membership, suggested this should also form a key part of the deliberations.

We would like to thank the Elgar team (Ben Booth in particular), for support, encouragement and patience with respect to the book project, which has been delayed due to work, family and health issues. We are particularly grateful to the reviewers of the original and revised proposal for their consideration and wisdom which improved the focus. We are indebted to our key supporters and mentors: Mr Nick Bonvoisin, who as Secretary to three of the five treaties (currently the *Water Convention*), and their linked protocols, has willingly shared invaluable experience; Research Professor Timo Koivurova, Arctic Centre, University of Lapland, whose knowledge of international environmental law is matched only by his ability to explain its intricacies in simple terms, and is always a source of ongoing help; Professor Susan Breau, Law School, University of Reading, for her guidance in connection with global law and governance; and Adjunct Professor Rob Fowler, formerly Chair of the IUCN Academy of Environmental Law, who has assisted us both at various stages of our academic careers.

The manuscript was completed in September 2014 in Adelaide and Hong Kong and is dedicated to our parents:

Edward and Sylvia Marsden, and Trevor and Jan Brandon.

Abbreviations

ADB	Asian Development Bank
APELL	Awareness and Preparedness for Emergencies at Local Level
ASEAN	Association of South East Asian Nations
Bvos	Basin water organisations
CBD	Convention on Biological Diversity
CC	Compliance Committee
CEP	Committee on Environmental Policy
CITES	Convention on International Trade in Endangered Species
CLRTAP	Convention on Long-Range Transboundary Air Pollution
CoE	Council of Europe
COP	Conference of the Parties
CSCE	Conference on Security and Cooperation in Europe
CSS	Country Safeguards System
EBRD	European Bank for Reconstruction and Development
EC	European Community
ECJ	European Court of Justice
EEC	Eurasian Economic Community
EECCA	Eastern Europe, the Caucasus and Central Asia
EIA	Environmental impact assessment
EMEP	European Monitoring [and] Evaluation Programme
EMMP	Environmental Mitigation and Management Plan
ESM	Environmentally sound management
EU	European Union
GAP	Global air pollution
GIZ	German International Cooperation
GMO	Genetically modified organism
GTI	Greater Tumen Initiative
IANS	Industrial Accident Notification System
IC	Implementation Committee

ICJ	International Court of Justice
ICP	International Cooperative Programme
ICSD	Interstate Commission on Sustainable Development
iCwC	Interstate Commission for Water Coordination
IEEP	Institute for European Environmental Policy
IFAS	International Fund for Saving the Aral Sea
IFI	International financial institution
IGO	Intergovernmental organisation
IUCN	International Union for the Conservation of Nature
IWGCL	Intergovernmental Working Group on Civil Liability
IWRM	Integrated water resources management
JC	Joint Committee
LRTAP	Long-Range Transboundary Air Pollution
MDB	Multilateral development bank
MDG	Millennium Development Goal
MEA	Multilateral environmental agreement
MOP	Meeting of the Parties
MoU	Memorandum of understanding
MRC	Mekong River Commission
NATO	North Atlantic Treaty Organisation
NCP	Non-compliance procedure
NEASPEC	Northeast Asia Subregional Programme on Environmental Cooperation
NEPA	National Environmental Policy Act
NIR	National implementation report
NOx	Nitrogen oxide
NPD	National Policy Dialogue
OECD	Organisation for Economic Cooperation and Development
OSCE	Organisation for Security and Cooperation in Europe
OVOS	Assessment of environmental impacts
PIC	Prior informed consent
POP	Persistent Organic Pollutant
PRTR	Pollutant Release and Transfer Registers
REC	Regional Environment Centre (for Eastern and Central Europe)
SEA	Strategic environmental assessment

SER	State Environmental Review
TC	Transnational corporation
UK	United Kingdom (of Great Britain and Northern Ireland)
UN	United Nations
UNCED	United Nations Conference on Environment and Development
UNCHE	United Nations Conference on the Human Environment
UNDP	United Nations Development Programme
UNECA	United Nations Economic Commission for Africa
UNECE	United Nations Economic Commission for Europe
UNECLAC	United Nations Economic Commission for Latin America and the Caribbean
UNEP	United Nations Environment Programme
UNESCAP	United Nations Economic and Social Commission for Asia and the Pacific
UNESCO	United Nations Educational, Scientific and Cultural Organisation
UNESCWA	United Nations Economic and Social Commission for Western Asia
UNFCCC	United Nations Framework Convention on Climate Change
UNITAR	United Nations Institute for Training and Research
UNSD	United Nations Conference on Sustainable Development
USA	United States of America
VOC	Volatile Organic Compound
WB	World Bank
WG	Working Group
WGD	Working Group on Development
WGE	Working Group on Effects
WGI	Working Group on Implementation
WGSR	Working Group on Strategies and Review
WHO	World Health Organization
WSSD	World Summit on Sustainable Development

Table of international cases, treaties and other international instruments

International Cases

International Treaties and Other International Instruments

European Union Legislation

PART I

Transboundary environmental governance

1. Introduction

I. OVERVIEW

Interest in global environmental governance has grown significantly in recent years, demonstrating its practical interest to scholars of international law and relations in particular,[1] as attempts are made to overcome largely state-based entrenched problems that have been recognised for some time.[2] Global environmental governance is therefore concerned with regulation in national as well as international contexts,[3] and responds and relates furthermore to issues of transnational environmental law which have also gained support.[4] This book is concerned with a related concept to global environmental governance and transnational environmental law, known as transboundary environmental governance. It examines this concept in practice in Asia, specifically with respect to matters of treaty implementation and compliance. Concerned mainly with governance across borders, examples in southeast Asia include the regulation of haze and other transboundary pollutants, water management (for instance in the Mekong river basin), trade in environmental

[1] See for example Jean-Frédéric Morin and Amandine Orsini (eds), *Essential Concepts of Global Environmental Governance* (Routledge, Abingdon, UK and New York, USA 2015).

[2] In a national context, problems experienced in the USA have been found globally by other nations also. See *Breaking the Logjam: An Environmental Law for the 21st Century, Background of the Breaking the Logjam Project*, accessed 22 November 2014 at http://www.law.yale.edu/documents/pdf/Alumni_Affairs/Esty_Breaking_the_Logjam_414.pdf.

[3] As to globalisation and the importance of context in connection with global environmental governance, see Robert Lee and Ellen Stokes, 'Environmental Governance: Reconnecting the Global and Local' (2009) 36(1) *Journal of Law and Society* 1.

[4] For examples, see *Transnational Environmental Law* (Cambridge Journals), accessed 12 November 2014 at http://journals.cambridge.org/action/display Journal?jid=TEL.

resources, and resolution of environment related issues in the South China Sea.[5]

In other parts of Asia, many of these issues are also present, with water quality issues dominant in international rivers and lakes (for instance the Caspian and Aral Seas), and the need to manage related pressures for infrastructure development, such as hydroelectricity. Coastal and marine issues, often involving disputed sovereignty claims,[6] are not discussed. This is mainly because they are beyond the scope of the five United Nations Economic Commission for Europe (UNECE) treaties,[7] which are the core focus of the book.[8] Until recently, the primary application of these agreements has been to European states, so it is important to be aware of the different regional contexts to environmental regulation between Europe and Asia, as well as the motivation for involvement of Asian states, which is essentially linked with social and economic development as well as environmental protection. However the possibility, and in some cases, reality, of accession to these five treaties by all United Nations (UN) member states furthermore emphasises the global

---

5 Antonio P Contreras, 'Transboundary Environmental Governance in Southeast Asia', in Amit Pandya and Ellen Laipson (eds), *Transnational Trends: Middle Eastern and Asian Trends* (The Henry L Stimson Center, Washington DC 2008), 156–9; see also Nathan Badenoch, *Transboundary Environmental Governance: Principles and Practice in Mainland Southeast Asia* (World Resources Institute, Washington DC 2002).

6 For current discussion in an Asian context, see S Jayakumar, Tommy Koh and Robert Beckman, *The South China Sea Disputes And Law Of The Sea* (Edward Elgar, Cheltenham, UK and Northampton, MA, USA 2014); and Stefan Talmon and Bing Bing Jia (eds), *The South China Sea Arbitration: A Chinese Perspective* (Hart Publishing, Oxford 2014).

7 In chapter order, see Convention on Access to Information, Public Participation in Decision-Making and Access to Justice in Environmental Matters (Aarhus, 25 June 1998) 2161 UNTS 447, in force 30 October 2001 (*Public Participation Convention*, Chapter 3); Convention on Environmental Impact Assessment in a Transboundary Context (Espoo, 25 February 1991), 30 ILM (1991) 802, in force 27 June 1997 (*EIA Convention*, Chapter 4); Convention on the Transboundary Effects of Industrial Accidents (Helsinki, 17 March 1992), 2105 UNTS 457, in force 19 April 2000 (*Industrial Accidents Convention*, Chapter 5); Convention on the Protection and Use of Transboundary Watercourses and Lakes (Helsinki, 17 March 1992), 31 ILM (1992) 1312, in force 6 October 1996 (*Water Convention*, Chapter 6); and the Convention on Long-range Transboundary Air Pollution (Geneva, 13 November 1979), 1302 UNTS 217, in force 16 March 1983 (*Air Pollution Convention*, Chapter 7).

8 Coastal issues are, however, noted to some degree in connection with the *Water Convention*.

aspect of environmental governance as well as the transboundary dimension, which is also discussed at length in the book.

There are three parts to the book. Part I concerns transboundary environmental governance, and contains the first two chapters. Chapter 1 will provide an overview of transboundary environmental governance in Asia and the role of the UNECE, before Chapter 2 considers institutions and regimes outside the UNECE to put the subject matter in context. It will first set out the objectives, research questions and approach; second, define transboundary environmental governance; third, consider the role of the UNECE in environmental policy making and capacity building; fourth, examine questions of implementation and compliance; and fifth, provide chapter summaries for what follows. Part II contains the substantive chapters on the UNECE agreements, Chapters 3–7. These examine each of the five environmental treaties and 12 related protocols in an Asian context, with a detailed common framework for the chapters enabling comparisons to be easily made wherever possible. Part III considers the combined effect and outlook for the UNECE agreements, and contains the final two chapters. Chapter 8 is a case study analysing the combined significance of the five agreements in central Asia,[9] where together with the Caucasus (considered in each of Chapters 3–7), application beyond Europe has been the greatest to date. Conclusions follow in Chapter 9 in relation to both this key question, together with thoughts on current (drawn from the other chapters) and prospective (based on discussion of existing experience) development in other parts of Asia.

[9] Central Asia consists of the five former Soviet states of Kazakhstan, Kyrgyzstan, Tajikistan, Turkmenistan and Uzbekistan. It should be noted that geographical terminology in relation to Asia is a source of some confusion, with the 'Middle East' also a common descriptor for the Islamic states of western Asia, and China's self-description as the 'Middle Kingdom' – despite some claims to geographical accuracy in an Asian continent in relation to the latter – where the Russian 'Far East' situates China very centrally in Asia, adding to the confusion.

II. OBJECTIVES, RESEARCH QUESTIONS AND APPROACH

The primary objective of this book is to analyse the contribution made to the development of transboundary environmental governance[10] in Asia by the UNECE. The book is focused on both transboundary governance and transboundary environmental governance in the context of these treaties, as the first examined, the *Public Participation Convention*, extends beyond environmental matters to also address, and link, human rights issues with environmental concerns. Similarly, a number of the agreements have a related focus on health as well as environmental protection, notably the *SEA Protocol*,[11] and *Water and Health Protocol*.[12] The book therefore potentially contributes to the discourse of both transboundary governance and transboundary environmental governance, as well as the related concepts of global/international environmental governance and transnational environmental law.

Asia has received minimal scholarly analysis in the area of transboundary governance or transboundary environmental governance,[13] particularly in comparison to European discussion,[14] and the book aims to

---

[10] As indicated in the text above, an extensive literature exists on global governance in general, and on transboundary environmental governance in particular. Additional recent examples of each are: Gráinne de Búrca, Claire Kilpatrick and Joanne Scott (eds), *Critical Legal Perspectives on Global Governance* (Hart Publishing, Oxford 2013); and Robin Warner and Simon Marsden (eds), *Transboundary Environmental Governance: Inland, Coastal and Marine Perspectives* (Ashgate Publishing, Farnham 2012).

[11] Protocol on Strategic Environmental Assessment to the Convention on Environmental Impact Assessment in a Transboundary Context (Kiev, 21 May 2003) unreported, in force 11 July 2010.

[12] Protocol on Water and Health to the Convention on the Protection and Use of Transboundary Watercourses and Lakes (London, 17 June 1999), UNTS 2331, 202, in force 4 August 2005.

[13] Although now dated, early examples are Kazu Kato and Wakana Takahashi, *Regional/Subregional Environmental Cooperation in Asia* (Institute for Global Environmental Strategies, Kanagawa 2001), which considers northeast, southeast and south Asia; and Badenoch, above n. 5, who emphasises the role of the Mekong River Commission in the southeast Asia subregion.

[14] See Simon Marsden and Timo Koivurova (eds), *Transboundary Environmental Impact Assessment in the European Union: The Espoo Convention and its Kiev Protocol on Strategic Environmental Assessment* (Earthscan/Routledge, Abingdon, UK and New York, USA 2011). In relation to comparing domestic environmental governance generally between these two regions, see Jona Razzaque, *Environmental Governance in Europe and Asia: A Comparative Study of*

(re-)address this imbalance as well as consider links between these regions.[15] The UNECE is one of five regional commissions of the UN,[16] whose treaty-making efforts uniquely intersect Europe with parts of Asia, because of its membership, in particular central Asia and the Caucasus.[17] The focused analysis in the book is especially concerned with questions of implementation and compliance (the 'practice' aspect in the subtitle),[18] which may help identify resource and capacity needs of developing states in Asia and its subregions. Implementation and compliance have for some time been recognised as the weak link in international environmental law.[19] In relation to compliance especially, the UN Environment Programme (UNEP) developed an influential guidance document over a decade ago to assist Parties and other stakeholders with this.[20] A secondary objective of the book is therefore to examine the operation of

---

Institutional and Legislative Frameworks (Routledge, Abingdon, UK and New York, USA 2013).

[15] Although focused on pollution, see S Jayakumar, Tommy Koh, Robert Beckman and Hao Duy Phan (eds), *Transboundary Pollution: Evolving Issues of International Law and Policy* (Edward Elgar, Cheltenham, UK and Northampton, MA, USA forthcoming).

[16] In addition to the UNECE (established in 1947), these are UN Economic and Social Commission for Asia and the Pacific (UNESCAP, 1947), UN Economic and Social Commission for Western Asia (UNESCWA, 1973), the UN Economic Commission for Latin America and the Caribbean (UNECLAC, 1948), and the Economic Commission for Africa (UNECA, 1958).

[17] The latter, consisting of Georgia, Armenia and Azerbaijan, and named after a mountain range, is often regarded to be part of the border dividing the combined continents of Europe and Asia known as 'Eurasia'. To the north the Europe/Asia boundary is found in the Ural Mountains of Russia. Other states have strong claims to both parts of Eurasia, in particular Turkey, to the west of the Caucasus, with Europe and Asia separated by the Bosphorus.

[18] A distinction has been made between the 'facilitative' and the 'enforcement' schools of thought on how states' compliance with international environmental law can be improved. The former is focused on assisting states to comply and the latter punishment. In both cases, non-compliance procedures have an important role to play in the process. See Timo Koivurova, *Introduction to International Environmental Law* (Routledge, Abingdon, UK and New York, USA 2014) 20.

[19] In relation to enforcement by courts and tribunals, see Philippe Sands and Jacqueline Peel, *Principles of International Environmental Law* (Cambridge University Press, New York 2012) 15–16.

[20] United Nations Environment Programme, *Manual on Compliance with and Enforcement of Multilateral Environmental Agreements* (UNEP 2001).

the processes for implementation and compliance in the UNECE agreements with a view to learning valuable lessons for similar processes operating under other international and regional agreements.

Finally, the book also recognises that the UNECE environmental treaties and related protocols are increasingly of global interest, with many potentially capable of accession by all UN member states and others likely to be so in the near future. As such, a third objective is to highlight this application (the 'prospects' in the subtitle), drawing on the experience in the Asian context specifically, and the UNECE context more broadly, to encourage UN states to introduce and/or develop existing transboundary governance mechanisms in other parts of the world. The potential for these agreements to contribute to the development of customary international law has also been noted by jurists and scholars, with the principle of transboundary environmental impact assessment (EIA) as established by the *EIA Convention* in particular, cited in cases before international courts and tribunals.[21] Based on state practice and judicial opinion, the development of customary international law is more than possible in relation to the content of these treaties – such as the procedure as well as the principle of the *EIA Convention* – in the future.

The central research question is similar to and related to these three objectives and asks: What is the current and potential combined contribution of the UNECE environmental agreements to the development of transboundary environmental governance in Asia and globally? Only after distinguishing the UNECE role from other institutions and regimes in Chapter 2, careful analysis of the application of the provisions of the agreements in Chapters 3–7 (particularly concerning implementation and compliance), and evaluating the application of each in the test subregion of central Asia, may it be possible to provide a tentative answer to this complex question in the conclusions at the end of the book. A recent study however provides an example of the potential combined effect of the UNECE agreements in specifically addressing water issues in another part of Asia, the Himalayas, and whether this experience is capable of transfer. The authors comment:

---

21 For examples, see International Court of Justice, *Case Concerning Pulp Mills on the River Uruguay (Argentina v. Uruguay)*, Judgment of 20 April 2010; and, in relation to discussion on the multiplicity of jurisprudence, see Simon Marsden, '*MOX Plant* and the Espoo Convention: Can Member State Disputes Concerning Mixed Environmental Agreements be Resolved outside EC Law?' (2009) 18(3) *Review of European Community and International Environmental Law* 312, 321.

> Assessing the normative and institutional relationship between the UNECE Water Convention and other UNECE environmental legal instruments is vital to understanding the potential role of the UNECE water regime as a whole, and thus to its transferability beyond the UNECE region.[22]

First it may be helpful to modestly and briefly consider three related questions: Why is Asia the focus? Why is the UNECE role in Asia of significance? And why is implementation and compliance so important? Second, transboundary environmental governance must also be defined and explained in the Asian context, the role of the UNECE in relation to it must be carefully explained, and the importance of implementation and compliance considered in a little more detail. The remainder of this chapter therefore briefly answers these three questions, and provides these definitions and explanations to set the scene for the rest of the book.

First, why is Asia the subject of this book? It is the largest continent, comprising 30 per cent of the land area of the globe, and it has the greatest population, amounting to 60 per cent of the world's total. Not including dependent and other territories, it is also ranked a very close third place for continents with the largest number of states (49), just behind Africa (54) and Europe (50). Geographically it is also home to the third largest number of international rivers and lakes (57), behind Europe (69) and Africa (59). The protection of international rivers and lakes is either a direct or indirect focus of three of the five UNECE treaties,[23] and several of the subregional agreements are also focused upon them.[24] Asia is also subject to rapid development to meet the needs of a population

---

22 Ruby Moynihan and Bjørn-Oliver Magsig, 'The Rising Role of Regional Approaches to International Water Law: Lessons from the UNECE Water Regime and Himalayan Asia for Strengthening Transboundary Water Cooperation' (2014) *Review of European, Comparative and International Environmental Law* 43.

23 Directly, note the *Water*, and indirectly the *Industrial Accidents*, and *EIA Conventions*.

24 See Framework Convention for the Protection of the Marine Environment of the Caspian Sea (Tehran, 4 November 2003), unreported, in force 12 August 2006; Agreement on the Cooperation for the Sustainable Development of the Mekong River Basin (Chiang Rai, 5 April 1995), unreported, in force 5 April 1995; and Agreement on the Establishment of the Tumen River Area Development Coordination Committee (New York, 6 December 1995), unreported, in force 6 December 1995; and Agreement on the Establishment of the Consultative Commission for the Development of the Tumen River Economic Development Area and Northeast Asia (New York, 6 December 1995), unreported, in force 6 December 1995.

that has quadrupled in the last century. Linked with the increased chance of industrial accidents impacting the environment, all of these factors highlight the potential for significant cross border impacts upon air and watersheds, with the consequent need to be matched by effective regimes for transboundary environmental governance.

Second, why is the role of the UNECE in Asia the subject of this book? The UNECE is the only one of the UN regional commissions to have produced any environmental treaties, and the subject matter of these treaties matches the concerns raised in the previous paragraph. It has also been actively involved in Asia, especially in the Caucasus and central Asia since the breakup of former Soviet Union. The need for its work in western Europe has additionally diminished since the European Union (EU) has developed and expanded. The following comment in relation to the *Industrial Accidents Convention* explains this as follows:

> From my point of view the problem is that the Convention serves primarily countries in [South-Eastern Europe, Eastern Europe, the Caucasus and Central Asia]. It does not serve so much EU member countries. So [the countries of South-Eastern Europe, Eastern Europe, the Caucasus and Central Asia] are the ones that really benefit from the Convention and its activities. They should identify their real needs and how they can improve. I would say it is up to them to develop the Convention further.[25]

Third, why is implementation and compliance the focus of the analysis? As noted, enforcement is the weakest link in regard to international environmental law in general, and in relation to the UNECE treaties and related protocols in Asia by the Parties in particular. Implementation is concerned with the transposition of the treaty obligations into domestic law,[26] and compliance means the practical fulfilment of the treaty obligations. Reporting mechanisms under the treaties are a means of evaluating the former, and non-compliance procedures (NCPs) respond to failings concerning the latter. NCPs are, however, distinct from the

---

[25] Wolfgang Gierke, in United Nations Economic Commission for Europe, *The Convention on the Transboundary Effects of Industrial Accidents: Twenty Years of Prevention, Preparedness and Response* (United Nations undated) 23, see http://www.unece.org/fileadmin/DAM/env/teia/doc/IA_Publications/TEIA-2October-final.pdf accessed 12 November 2014.

[26] This is to be distinguished from implementation by the treaty bodies themselves of workplan activities. See for example, Meeting of the Parties (Convention and Protocol), Working Group on Environmental Impact Assessment and Strategic Environmental Assessment, Third meeting, Geneva 11–15 November 2013, Implementation of the workplan activities, note by the secretariat, ECE/MP.EIA/WG.2/2013/INF.6, 16 October 2013.

dispute resolution procedures typified by the International Court of Justice (ICJ), which are considered in Chapter 2.

Chapter 2 provides an overview of applicable institutions and regimes in Asia outside the UNECE. The framework for analysis in Chapters 3–7 that follow is a documentary evaluation of the history and procedural effectiveness of the agreements themselves, Asian membership and potential membership of the agreements, Asian states' implementation of and compliance with their procedures, and the capacity building efforts of the UNECE and other public and private bodies. Extensive reference is made to UNECE documents as well as secondary sources where available. As Chapter 8 is focused on central Asia, examples of implementation and compliance in Chapters 3–7 will be focused on other Asian states, either current Parties (such as the Caucasian states) or those interested in joining the UNECE regimes. The remainder of this chapter will define transboundary environmental governance generally and in Asia specifically, explain the role of the UNECE broadly and in this region in particular, and individually summarise the purpose, content and significance of the remaining chapters very briefly.

III. TRANSBOUNDARY ENVIRONMENTAL GOVERNANCE IN ASIA

'Governance' is a system of control or management of human activities and is concerned generally with law, policy and institutions. The emphasis on the 'will of the people' as 'the basis of the authority of government' in the relationship between institutions, individuals and groups, as identified in Article 21(3) of the *Universal Declaration of Human Rights*,[27] has also been stressed by Suzuki, who comments significantly in a little more detail:

> Governance covers both the compatibility of substantive goals of institutions with expectations of authority that support the institutions and the appropriateness of broader processes of decision making of these institutions in carrying out their mandates entrusted to them. The question of governance hinges on the quality of the empowering relationship between authoritative

---

[27] Article 21(3), Universal Declaration of Human Rights (1948) GA res. 217A (III), UN Doc A/810 at 71, accessed 12 November 2014 at http://www.un.org/en/documents/udhr/.

> decision makers on one hand, and those aggregate individuals and groups that are subject to the former's decisions.[28]

'International environmental governance' has been defined as part of a management review of environmental governance within the UN system, as consisting of the following elements:

> (a) coherent decision-making and objective-setting for international environmental policies, among different environmental agreements and institutions; (b) institutional architecture to implement and coordinate environmental policies and decisions; (c) management and operationalization of the policies and decisions; and (d) coordination of the effective implementation of international environmental governance decisions at the country level.[29]

'Transboundary' primarily refers to the crossing of legal borders and boundaries, between sovereign nations, dependent and other territories, and within federations.[30] Transboundary governance includes formal and informal regulatory processes which may assess, mitigate and compensate significant impacts of human activities on the natural environment. EIA and strategic environmental assessment (SEA), NCPs and judicial enforcement are examples.[31] Government institutions, non-governmental organisations (NGOs) and the public – including indigenous people residing in areas of concern and which decide, input and implement these processes – are all key stakeholders and rightsholders.[32]

The transboundary aspect can also relate to activities which cross the boundary between areas within national jurisdiction and interactions with and between the global marine commons – such as the high seas, outer

---

[28] Eisuke Suzuki, 'Global Governance and International Financial Institutions' (2011) 19(1) *Asia Pacific Law Review* 13, 17.

[29] Inomata, Tadanori, *Management Review of Environmental Governance within the United Nations System* (United Nations Joint Inspection Unit 2008), JIU/REP/2008/3, 1. For details on environmental governance within the UN system generally, see Part II.

[30] Belgium, Canada, the USA and Russia are examples of the latter.

[31] See Robin Warner and Simon Marsden, 'Perspectives on Transboundary Environmental Governance', in Robin Warner and Simon Marsden (eds), *Transboundary Environmental Governance: Inland, Coastal and Marine Perspectives* (Ashgate Publishing, Farnham 2012) 1, 3.

[32] In relation to the latter, note the role of the *UN Declaration on the Rights of Indigenous People*; see Simon Marsden, 'The World Heritage Convention in the Arctic and Indigenous People: Time to Reform?' (2014) 6 *Yearbook of Polar Law* in press. The Declaration can be found at: http://www.un.org/esa/socdev/unpfii/documents/DRIPS_en.pdf, accessed 12 November 2014.

space and Antarctica – each of which is subject to a detailed regulatory regime.[33] Environmental issues that cross borders include air, water and soil pollution, transit of waste, protected areas and trade in flora and fauna. Some of these issues have international regulatory frameworks and some are regulated at the regional level, including the efforts of the UNECE and sub-regional bodies as will be seen in Chapter 2. For others there has been minimal or no regulation and there is regulatory space for this in the future.[34]

Transboundary environmental governance can include the relationship between international and domestic law, between law and policy, and between institutions of government within a state. More flexibly, learning across disciplines such as international law and international relations, and the relationship between environment, economy and society in exploring sustainable development can be included in the notion of transboundary environmental governance. Although it typically involves states acting through and with global and regional organisations, as noted, non-state actors are also important players.[35] NGOs perform a critical role in advocating, developing, and sometimes implementing transboundary environmental governance.[36] Finally, as indicated above,

---

[33] Above n. 31, 3–4.

[34] A notable example is historical pollution, or site contamination. For detailed analysis of the current situation and future options, see Elizabeth Brandon, *Global Approaches to Site Contamination Law* (Springer, Dordrecht 2013).

[35] See Bob Reinalda (ed.), *Non-State Actors in the International System of States* (Ashgate Research Companion, Ashgate Publishing, Farnham 2011). This recognises three types of non-state actor: non-governmental organisations (NGOs), intergovernmental organisations (IGOs) and transnational corporations (TNCs), which all play roles alongside nation-states (represented by governments). The UNECE is an example of an IGO. While environmental governance is typically public in nature, TNCs operate in the sphere of *private* environmental governance, with corporations lobbying states in relation to multilateral environmental agreements. See Robert Falkner, 'Private Environmental Governance and International Relations: Exploring the Links' (2003) 3(2) *Global Environmental Politics* 72.

[36] See Lars Gulbrandsen, Steinar Andresen and Jon Birgir Skjærseth, 'Non-State Actors and Environmental Governance: Comparing Multinational, Supranational and Transnational Rule Making', in Reinalda above n. 35, 463, who argue that the role of NGOs in environmental governance is strongly related to the authority and competence of states. Their three models of rule making (multinational, supranational and transnational) show a declining role for states and an increasing one for NGOs when moving from multinational to supranational and transnational rule making.

individuals and local and indigenous communities are essential to its development.[37] As an example in the context of the UNECE and its environmental treaties, the most recent EIA/SEA Meeting of the Parties (MOP) was attended by representatives not just of intergovernmental organisations such as UN bodies and multilateral development banks (MDBs)/international financial institutions (IFIs), but also some 15 NGOs.[38]

In the Asian context, the development of transboundary environmental governance was considered over a decade ago by Kato and Takahashi in relation to environmental cooperation efforts in northeast, southeast and south Asia.[39] They acknowledged the significance of the subsidiarity principle in contending with environmental challenges at the levels closest to the source rather than at the global level. However, they also recognised the importance of cooperative efforts at the international level, especially the role for regional and subregional approaches to address these challenges. As examples, they pointed to the work of UNEP – discussed in Chapter 2 – which has recognised the importance of a regional approach in establishing regional offices in the different parts of the world including the Asia-Pacific region. They also noted the establishment of a 'Regional Strategy for Environmentally Sound and Sustainable Development' as perhaps the initiation of transboundary environmental governance efforts in the Asian region as a whole.[40]

Kato and Takahashi finally acknowledged efforts in the Asian subregions as largely preceding this work. This began with the adoption of the Association of South East Asian Nations (ASEAN),[41] Subregional Environment Programme in 1977, followed by the establishment of the South Asia Cooperative Environment Programme in 1981 and the Northeast Asia Subregional Programme on Environmental Cooperation (NEASPEC) in 1992.[42] These are other governance mechanisms – including several subregional treaties that establish institutions to ensure

---

[37] Above n. 31, 4.

[38] Meeting of the Parties Sixth session (Convention), Second session (Protocol), Geneva, 2–5 June 2014, Report of the Meeting of the Parties, ECE/MP.EIA/20–ECE/MP.EIA/SEA/4, 15 July 2014, para. 4.

[39] Above n. 13, i.

[40] This was adopted at the second Ministerial Conference by one of the other UN regional commissions, UNESCAP in 1991, which is also considered in Chapter 2.

[41] http://www.asean.org/, accessed 12 November 2014.

[42] http://www.neaspec.org/, accessed 12 November 2014.

cooperation on environmental issues – which are explored in Chapter 2 of this book.

IV. ROLE OF THE UNITED NATIONS ECONOMIC COMMISSION FOR EUROPE

Geographically the UNECE region is more than 47 million square kilometres in size, and is home to 20 per cent of the world population.[43] It includes high-income developed states, as well as those with a relatively low level of development. States include the countries of Europe, Canada and the United States of America (USA), the central Asian states, the Caucasus, Turkey and Israel. In 1991 there were 34 member states, but as a result of the disintegration of the Soviet Union, Yugoslavia and Czechoslovakia, numbers increased significantly, and today there are 56 member states. The diverse nature of the Commission's membership has its source in history. When established, the UNECE included all participants in the reconstruction of post-war Europe: all European countries, from east and west, and North America. Israel was added to the list in 1991 followed by the former Soviet states and those from the Balkans and central Europe.[44]

The UNECE is one of the five regional commissions of the UN.[45] Its main aim is to promote pan-European economic integration,[46] and cooperation in environment, forests, housing and land management, statistics, energy, trade and transport.[47] It was established as a key UN organisation for ongoing dialogue and improved relationships among eastern and western European countries, Canada and the USA at a time

---

[43] http://www.unece.org/oes/nutshell/region.html, accessed 12 November 2014, from which this section is drafted.

[44] See generally, Yves Berthelot and Paul Rayment, *Looking Back and Peering Forward – A Short History of the United Nations Economic Commission for Europe, 1947–2007* (United Nations Economic Commission for Europe, Geneva 2007).

[45] For the others see above n. 16 and Chapter 2, with the work of UNESCAP and UNESCWA – which operate in Asia specifically – explained.

[46] http://www.unece.org/termsofreferenceandrulesofprocedureoftheunece.html, accessed 12 November 2014.

[47] For detailed general background, see http://www.unece.org/oes/history/history.html, accessed 12 November 2014.

of high political tension.[48] The signature of the Final Act of the Conference on Security and Cooperation in Europe (CSCE) in 1975,[49] with two references to the environment therein, led to a referral to the UNECE of an examination of two transboundary environmental issues, long-range transmission of air pollutants and the concept of EIA, including its later application to policies, plans and programmes, the proposals targeted by SEA.[50] The former was motivated by concerns about acid rain, the latter in part as a result of the US promulgation of the National Environmental Policy Act in 1969[51] – which led to the development of EIA globally thereafter – and also with Principle 21 of the *Stockholm Declaration*.[52]

Environmental policy is a significant part of the UNECE's work.[53] The broad aim of UNECE's environment activities is to safeguard the environment and human health, and to promote sustainable development in its member countries in line with *Agenda 21*.[54] The practical aim is to reduce pollution so as to minimise environmental damage and avoid compromising environmental conditions for future generations. The Committee on Environmental Policy (CEP) works to support countries to enhance their environmental governance and transboundary cooperation as well as strengthen implementation of the UNECE regional environmental commitments and advance sustainable development. It meets annually with special sessions convened as necessary. Organisations of the UN system as well as IGOs[55] and NGOs active in the UNECE region

---

48 Robert G Connelly, 'The UN Convention on EIA in a Transboundary Context: A Historical Perspective' (1999) 19(1) *Environmental Impact Assessment Review* 37, 38.

49 See http://www.osce.org/who/timeline, accessed 12 November 2014.

50 See UNECE, *Policies and Systems of Environmental Impact Assessment* (United Nations 1991), and UNECE, *Application of Environmental Impact Assessment Principles to Policies, Plans and Programmes* (United Nations 1992).

51 National Environmental Policy Act of 1969 [42 U.S.C. 4321].

52 See 11 ILM 1416 (1972).

53 See http://www.unece.org/env/welcome.html, accessed 12 November 2014. See also United Nations Economic and Social Council, Economic Commission for Europe, Committee on Environmental Policy, Tenth session (Geneva, 20–22 October 2003) (Item 8 of the provisional agenda), Future UNECE Strategic Directions for the Environment, CEP/2003/25, 23 July 2003, in particular 11–13 'UNECE conventions and environmental policy'.

54 See http://sustainabledevelopment.un.org/content/documents/Agenda21.pdf accessed 12 November 2014.

55 See above n. 35.

are invited to participate in CEP meetings as observers. Its main aim is to assess countries' efforts to reduce their overall pollution burden and manage their natural resources, to integrate environmental and socio-economic policies, to strengthen cooperation with the international community, to harmonise environmental conditions and policies throughout the region and to stimulate greater involvement of the public and environmental discussions and decision making.

The UNECE has adopted a five-pronged approach. First, the CEP brings together governments to formulate environmental policy and support its implementation. Intergovernmental meetings, seminars, workshops and advisory missions are organised under the Committee and its subsidiary bodies, providing a platform for environmental decision making as well as a forum for networking, sharing experiences and good practices. Second, the UNECE has an active role in regional and cross-sectoral processes, in particular the 'Environment for Europe' ministerial process, environment, transport and health, and education for sustainable development. Third, through its environmental performance reviews, the UNECE assesses individual countries' efforts to bring down pollution levels and manage their natural resources, and makes recommendations to improve their environmental performance. Fourth, the UNECE's work on environmental monitoring and assessment continues to help strengthen the environmental information and observation capacity in the countries of eastern Europe, the Caucasus and central Asia (EECCA) and Russia, as well as in interested countries of southeast Europe.

Reflecting its original purpose, the UNECE has since been responsible for a significant amount of treaty development in a transboundary context, notably the five environmental agreements that are the subject of this book, which in order of the date of adoption are: the Convention on Long-Range Transboundary Air Pollution (*Air Pollution Convention*); the Convention on EIA in a Transboundary Context (*EIA Convention*); the Convention on the Protection and Use of Transboundary Watercourses and International Lakes (*Water Convention*); the Convention on the Transboundary Effects of Industrial Accidents (*Industrial Accidents Convention*); and the Convention on Access to Information, Public Participation in Decision-Making and Access to Justice in Environmental Matters (*Public Participation Convention*). All are examples of procedural environmental law, so called because they focus on contributing to the prevention of harm and transboundary cooperation rather than substantive obligations of attributing liability resulting from harm and resolving claims for damage.[56] The focus on transboundary cooperation brings an additional benefit, consistent with a UN body: the prevention of conflict which can often arise in relation to natural resources.[57]

In relation to the protocols, excluding the eight associated with the *Air Pollution Convention*,[58] there are four of these. The first is the *Water and Health Protocol*, adopted in 1999 under the *Water Convention*. The other three were all adopted in Kiev in 2003, and are the Protocol on Pollutant Release and Transfer Registers (*PRTR Protocol*),[59] adopted under the *Public Participation Convention*; the *SEA Protocol* adopted under the *EIA Convention*; and the Protocol on Civil Liability and Compensation for Damage Caused by the Transboundary Effects of Industrial Accidents on Transboundary Waters (*Civil Liability Protocol*),[60] adopted under both the *Industrial Accidents Convention* and *Water Convention*. Unlike the five treaties and all of the other protocols, the *Civil Liability Protocol* – in addressing issues of responsibility and compensation – goes beyond the procedural obligations of the other agreements; this largely explains

---

56 See Simon Marsden, *Strategic Environmental Assessment in International and European Law: A Practitioner's Guide* (Earthscan/Routledge, Abingdon, UK and New York, USA 2008), ch. 4 in relation to the *EIA* and *Public Participation Conventions*.

57 See Branko Bošnjaković, 'The UNECE Environmental Conventions: Their Role and Potential to Promote Conflict Prevention and Settlement of Disputes in Transboundary Environmental Issues' in Eileen Petzold-Bradley, Alexander Carius and Arpád Vincze (eds), *Responding to Environmental Conflicts: Implications for Theory and Practice* (Kluwer, Dordrecht 2001) 263.

58 See Chapter 7 for full adoption, ratification and citation details. In summary these are the: Protocol on Long-term Financing of the Cooperative Programme for Monitoring and Evaluation of the Long-range Transmission of Air Pollutants in Europe (*EMEP Protocol*), the Protocol on the Reduction of Sulphur Emissions or their Transboundary Fluxes by at least 30 Per Cent (*Sulphur Protocol*), the Protocol on the Control of Emissions of Nitrogen Oxides or their Transboundary Fluxes (*NOx Protocol*), the Protocol on the Control of Emissions of Volatile Organic Compounds or their Transboundary Fluxes (*VOCs Protocol*), the Protocol on Further Reduction of Sulphur Emissions (*Second Sulphur Protocol*), the Protocol on Heavy Metals (*Heavy Metals Protocol*), the Protocol on Persistent Organic Pollutants (*POPs Protocol*), and the Protocol to Abate Acidification, Eutrophication and Ground-level Ozone (*AEO Protocol*).

59 Protocol on Pollutant Release and Transfer Registers to the Convention on Access to Information, Public Participation in Decision-Making and Access to Justice in Environmental Matters (Kiev, 21 May 2003), unreported, in force 8 October 2009.

60 Protocol on Civil Liability and Compensation for Damage Caused by the Transboundary Effects of Industrial Accidents on Transboundary Waters (Kiev, 21 May 2003) unreported, not in force.

why it has yet to obtain support from the members of the UNECE, and is therefore the only one of any of the agreements not yet in force.

V. IMPLEMENTATION AND COMPLIANCE

As noted in Part II above, implementation and compliance are traditionally the weak elements of international environmental law. There is a close relationship between implementation and compliance as noted in connection with Parties in EECCA, which have a shared history of former occupation by the Soviet Union. For example the *EIA Convention* MOP has noted that: 'compliance concerns both legal implementation and practical application'.[61] NCPs have grown hugely in recent years resulting in considerable scholarly comment,[62] and operate with a large degree of autonomy.[63] There is also an increasing trend towards the judicialisation of such procedures.[64] Implementation and compliance in central Asia is used as case study in this book, for the achievements

[61] ECE/MP.EIA/10, decision IV/2 (review of compliance), annex III, para. 24.

[62] See for example Tullio Treves, Attila Tanzi, Cesare Pitea, Chiara Ragni, and Laura Pineschi (eds), *Non Compliance Procedures and Mechanisms and the Effectiveness of International Environmental Agreements* (TMC Asser Press, The Hague 2009); Karen Scott, 'Non-compliance Procedures and the Resolution of Disputes under International Environmental Agreements', in Duncan French and Nigel White (eds), *International Law and Dispute Settlement: New Problems and Techniques* (Hart Publishing, Oxford 2010) 225. Note compliance mechanisms are also found in human rights regimes.

[63] Together with MOPs and other arrangements, NCPs are an example of an 'autonomous institutional arrangement'; they are, however, no longer a 'little-noticed phenomenon'. See Robin Churchill and Geir Ulfstein, 'Autonomous Institutional Arrangements in Multilateral Environmental Agreements: a Little-Noticed Phenomenon in International Law' (2000) 94 *American Journal of International Law* 623; and more recently, Nils Goeteyn and Frank Maes, 'Compliance Mechanisms in Multilateral Environmental Agreements: An Effective Way to Improve Compliance?' (2011) 10(4) *Chinese Journal of International Law* 791.

[64] Neil Craik and Timo Koivurova, 'Subsidiary Decision Making under the Espoo Convention: Legal Status and Legitimacy' (2011) 20 *Review of European Community and International Environmental Law* 258.

under the five treaties and related protocols to date,[65] and to enable consideration of the potential to expand to other parts of Asia and globally.

In recognition of this, the UNECE has therefore developed five modern treaties and (including the *Air Pollution Convention* protocols) 12 protocols, which overwhelmingly put these matters at the core of its environmental protection regime. Apart from the *Water Convention*, each of the agreements contains a reporting procedure to consider implementation. Similarly, apart from the *Industrial Accidents Convention*, each of the treaties contains a NCP and, other than the *Civil Liability Protocol*, the other 11 protocols each have a NCP included within its arrangements or applying to it. There is therefore significant experience dealing with implementation and compliance in the UNECE environmental regime as a whole, and the new NCP in the *Water Convention* has learnt from this experience in developing its own procedure. An informal network of the chairs of the bodies administering these NCPs furthermore operates to explore ways to improve implementation and compliance across states Parties to the treaties and protocols.[66]

In the central Asian context – as will be seen in Chapter 8 – the different contextual arrangements of post Soviet independence has left a legacy of a different approach to significant procedural matters that are the core of the *Public Participation Convention* and *EIA Convention*, and also concern procedures for EIA and assessment under both the *Industrial Accidents Convention* and *Water Convention*. The reporting processes and NCPs have had to contend with these different approaches in evaluating implementation and compliance, which has implications for the legal systems of these states as well as the specific environmental law affected by the UNECE treaties. While monist states allowing for direct application of international law into the central Asian domestic legal systems, the NCPs have, despite this, maintained a need for implementation by domestic law in order to effectively implement the UNECE agreements. Without this, it is not deemed possible to comply with the law in question.

---

[65] For background and examples of the role of various organisations in this fast changing region, see Emilian Kavalski (ed.), *The New Central Asia: The Regional Impact of International Actors* (World Scientific, Singapore 2010).

[66] Economic Commission for Europe/Environment, Informal Network of the Chairs of Compliance/Implementation Bodies under the Multilateral Environmental Agreements, First Meeting, Geneva, 25 March 2013, Note Prepared by the Chair of the Aarhus Convention Compliance Committee with the Assistance of the Secretariat.

Clearly, implementation of and compliance with the UNECE environmental treaties in Asia is a very different matter to implementation of and compliance with them in western Europe, notably in the EU. The reason for this is that the EU benefits from a strong governance framework with harmonised environmental regulation across the member states.[67] For the most part implementing the UNECE agreements has therefore been much easier in the EU. In addition, in some instances the UNECE agreements have been developed from existing EU legislation, for example the *SEA Protocol* which followed experience with developing the *SEA Directive*.[68]

The added value of this book to the existing literature therefore emphasises that in Asia different approaches to transboundary governance may be in place, derived largely from existing domestic contexts. Whether this is because of religion, state ecological expertise systems, or due to different attitudes towards key human rights known as the 'Asian values',[69] or the 'Asian way',[70] it nonetheless makes it much harder to ensure implementation and compliance. From the Islamic states of the Middle East/western Asia, to the post Soviet states of the Caucasus and central Asia, across to the states belonging to ASEAN, or indeed within the economic powerhouse of China, approaches to governance and the rule of law are very different to those in the west.

As access to information, public participation and access to justice – the three pillars of the *Public Participation Convention* – are a key part of the success of the other treaties, the application of this treaty in particular is likely to be more of a challenge to achieve than the procedural provisions of the other agreements, at least where the three pillar requirements are not also a part of the other agreements. In practice, given overlapping membership and cross-fertilisation of procedures,

---

[67] See for example Maria Lee, *EU Environmental Law, Governance and Decision-Making* (Hart Publishing, Oxford 2014).

[68] Directive 2001/42/EC of the European Parliament and of the Council of 27 June 2001 on the assessment of the effects of certain plans and programmes on the environment, [2001] OJ L197/30–37.

[69] See for example M Jacobsen and O Brun (eds), *Human Rights and Asian Values. Contesting National Identities and Cultural Representations in Asia* (Curzon Press, Abingdon 2000); and more recently, in summary, accessed 12 November 2014 at http://therightsfuture.com/wp-content/uploads/2010/11/The_Rights_Future_CT5_Asian_Values.pdf.

[70] For a positive outlook on this, see Asian Human Rights Commission, *Asian Human Rights Charter, a People's Charter*, 17 May 1998: accessed 12 November 2014 at http://www.refworld.org/pdfid/452678304.pdf. See also http://www.theguardian.com/commentisfree/2010/mar/04/global-problem-solving-asian-way, accessed 12 November 2014.

many of these issues, however, also pertain to the implementation and compliance of the other agreements.

VI. CHAPTER SUMMARIES

A brief overview of the book is set out as follows. As noted above, the common framework for Chapters 3–7 explains the status, membership and institutions in an introductory section, before turning to historical background and legal development, examining the objectives and main procedural provisions, evaluating practice, and examining prospects in Asia and globally. Conclusions from each of these chapters will be further analysed and synthesised with the conclusions from Chapter 2 – which concerns other institutions and regimes – in Chapter 8, with its focus on central Asia. As emphasised, implementation of and compliance with each of the agreements is examined in particular detail in Chapter 8 as this is the part of Asia where – beyond the Caucasus – the greatest take-up of the agreements has been.

Chapter 2 concerns institutions and regimes and aims to distinguish the UNECE from other organisations and its environmental treaties from other agreements. Four types of institutions are identified. These are first UN global institutions: UNEP, UN Development Programme (UNDP), Global Environment Facility (GEF), World Health Organisation (WHO) and the ICJ. They are second, other UN regional commissions operating in Asia: the UN Economic and Social Commission for Asia and the Pacific (UNESCAP), and the UN Economic and Social Commission for Western Asia (UNESCWA). Third, they are MDBs/IFIs, in particular the World Bank (WB, which is also part of the UN system); the European Bank for Reconstruction and Development (EBRD), and the Asian Development Bank (ADB). Finally, they are specialist environmental organisations operating globally or regionally, in particular, the International Union for the Conservation of Nature (IUCN). The multilateral regimes identified include the numerous conservation, waste, and climate/ozone protection conventions which also apply in Asia. The subregional regimes include those based on treaties operating in southwest and central Asia, southeast and northeast Asia.

Chapter 3 concerns the first of the UNECE treaties, the *Public Participation Convention*, and its related *PRTR Protocol*. This is dealt with first because it can be distinguished from the other UNECE treaties by focusing on a domestic rather than a transboundary context. Transboundary processes are, however, affected by this treaty, which links environmental and human rights. For example, it incorporates more detailed procedures for access to information, public participation in decision making and access to justice in environmental matters than any of the other treaties, is a benchmark for these to the extent to which these matters are taken into account in domestic contexts globally, and furthermore promotes the application of information, participation and access principles to decision making in international organisations more broadly, which includes those considered in Chapter 2. The Protocol pursues the same goal of public access to information, specifically through the establishment of national inventories of pollution from industrial sites and other sources. Being an 'open' global agreement, any country may accede to it, whether or not they are a party to the Convention, which is also, however, of this nature.

Chapter 4 explains the role of the *EIA Convention* and its related *SEA Protocol*, the latter which like the *Public Participation Convention* also operates primarily in a domestic context. It follows Chapter 3, since the principles of this agreement have also been raised in international institutional contexts, notably recent jurisprudence of the ICJ. The *EIA Convention* is also considered after the *Public Participation Convention*, as there has traditionally been a close relationship between the two. Public participation requirements under the second pillar of the latter treaty have been applied in a transboundary context in relation to the *EIA Convention* for example. Another illustration of the close relationship is that the *SEA Protocol* under the *EIA Convention* was initially considered as a joint instrument to both the *Public Participation* and *EIA Conventions*. Subject to further ratification and entry into force of an amendment, the *EIA Convention* will also become a global treaty; the *SEA Protocol* is already potentially open to accession by all UN members.

Chapter 5 concerns the *Industrial Accidents Convention*, which has a close relationship with the *Water Convention*, the subject of Chapter 6. Both were adopted at the same time in the Finnish capital city. The *Industrial Accidents Convention* is discussed after the *EIA Convention* in part since it also contains a transboundary EIA procedure applicable to hazardous domestic activities that may have serious transboundary effects. Notification and consultation provisions in the *Industrial Accidents Convention* require assessments to be carried out by the country in which the hazardous activity occurs, and specific information on effects to be provided to the affected country. Public participation is part of the notification and consultation process. Chapter 5 also includes discussion of the *Civil Liability Protocol*, which requires a significant number of ratifications before its entry into force. Although discussed in Chapter 5, it is also relevant to Chapter 6 as it is a joint legal instrument to both the *Industrial Accidents* and *Water Conventions*.

Chapter 6 analyses the *Water Convention*, the second of the two treaties – after the *Air Pollution Convention*, discussed in Chapter 7 – to focus on a specific environmental medium rather than a process (like the *Public Participation* or *EIA Conventions*) or address an issue of concern (*Industrial Accidents Convention*). The *Water Convention* will shortly be available for accession by all UN member states and contains provisions relevant to all Parties and those applicable to riparian Parties. A *Protocol on Water and Health* to the *Water Convention* is also in force and is furthermore analysed in this Chapter; as mentioned above the *Protocol on Civil Liability* – a joint legal instrument with the *Industrial Accidents Convention* which is yet to enter into force – is considered in Chapter 5.

Chapter 7 explores the well-established *Air Pollution Convention*, the first of the UNECE treaties adopted, together with its eight protocols. This treaty sets out a framework for scientific, technical and policy measures to be introduced at the domestic level, as well as for international collaboration measures, to reduce and prevent air pollution. The protocols contain specific measures and targets for the reduction of certain pollutant emissions. There is currently an emphasis on assisting central Asian countries to implement the treaty and key protocols, as well as the possibility that membership of the Convention could in future be expanded from regional to global. Given the serious, ongoing transboundary air pollution issues in some parts of Asia, it is opportune to ask whether the *Air Pollution Convention* and protocols may offer an appropriate regime in response.

Chapter 8 draws together examples of implementation of and compliance with each of the legal instruments in central Asia, the part of Asia with the greatest uptake of the treaties and related protocols. Central Asia is first considered as a distinct geo-political sub-region, environmental issues are outlined, and the UNECE role there is addressed. Explanation of the different approach to EIA – known as 'state ecological expertise' – is provided to set the frame of reference for why practice with the legal agreements has posed particular challenges. Chapter 9, in concluding the book, draws lessons from the central Asian experience for other parts of Asia and globally in addressing the central and related research questions asked in Chapter 1.

2. Institutions and regimes

I. INTRODUCTION

This chapter provides an overview of applicable institutions and regimes in Asia outside the UNECE,[1] and its five environmental treaties and numerous related protocols, which are the specific focus of the chapters that follow. In relation to institutions, these include other UN institutions, other UN regional commissions, MDBs/IFIs, and specialist environmental bodies. In relation to regimes these are based on either global multilateral or sub-regional environmental agreements in Asia,[2] the latter which are supported by a specific institutional structure. The reason for considering other institutions and regimes is to enable comparisons between them and the UNECE. As noted in Chapter 1, other than the regulation of inland seas (particularly the Caspian and Aral Seas), the focus is upon terrestrial agreements. Marine agreements are not considered, as this has not been an aspect of UNECE governance to date.[3]

In relation to other institutions, there are a large number that are of relevance. Chapter 2 groups these into a number of different categories. The first have a global focus and are the relevant UN institutions: UNEP, UNDP, GEF, WHO and the ICJ. The second are the other UN regional commissions operating in Asia, specifically UNESCAP, which has a division concerned with Environment and Development, and UNESCWA.

---

1 This is considered generally in Chapter 1, and specifically with respect to central Asia in Chapter 8. For definitions and theory of governance regimes, see Roda Mushkat, 'Creating Regional Environmental Governance Regimes: Implications of Southeast Asian Responses to Transboundary Haze Pollution' (2013) 4 *Washington and Lee Journal of Energy, Climate and Environment* 103, 105–8 with extensive references cited.

2 There is no environmental agreement that specifically applies to the entire Asian region.

3 For examples of transboundary environmental agreements in a marine context, see Robin Warner and Simon Marsden, 'Perspectives on Transboundary Environmental Governance', in Robin Warner and Simon Marsden (eds), *Transboundary Environmental Governance: Inland, Coastal and Marine Perspectives* (Ashgate Publishing, Farnham 2012) 1–20.

The third are the MDBs/IFIs operating at the global and regional levels, the WB (also part of the UN system), EBRD and, specifically, the ADB. Finally, the fourth are specialist environmental bodies and major environmental NGOs, the former including the IUCN, which is the brief focus.

There are also numerous environmental regimes that apply to Asia, several with transboundary dimensions or with a cross-border focus. The chapter groups these into two: multilateral environmental agreements (MEAs), and sub-regional transboundary environmental agreements. In regard to MEAs, these apply globally, and Asia is just one area of application. A few have already achieved, or are close to achieving universal ratification by all UN member states.[4] The intention is not to outline the detail of all of these treaties, as many of them are not specifically focused on transboundary environmental governance. Rather, where there is a transboundary focus or dimension, this will be briefly explained or noted, with examples of Asia application. For those focused on regulation in a national context, any transboundary relevance will be emphasised, particularly new cross border developments. In relation to the sub-regional agreements, these are focused on transboundary environmental governance, and are applicable in and to specific parts of Asia to address particular problems; the provisions focused on transboundary environmental governance will be briefly analysed. In the case of both MEAs and sub-regional agreements, a detailed institutional structure is in place, the level of detail in part dependent upon the age of the regime, to ensure that implementation and compliance are effectively dealt with.

Institutional structures for global agreements may furthermore have a broader structure, concerned with matters unconnected with the agreement in question, such as the UN Educational, Scientific and Cultural Organisation (UNESCO),[5] which while responsible for the *World Heritage Convention*,[6] is also concerned with many other matters within its broader remit. Similarly, institutional structures for the Asian agreements may provide a broader framework for development of treaties and

---

[4] See https://treaties.un.org/doc/source/events/2014/Treaties/list_global_english.pdf, accessed 13 November 2014.

[5] In 1947 UNESCO instructed the first Director-General to convene an international technical conference for the protection of nature which led UNESCO to host, with others, the meeting in 1948 that created what became the IUCN. See Stanley Johnson, *UNEP – The First 40 Years: A Narrative* (United Nations Environment Programme 2012).

[6] Convention Concerning the Protection of the World Cultural and Natural Heritage (Paris, 16 November 1972) 1037 UNTS 151, in force 17 December 1975.

associated matters, such as ASEAN, which while responsible for two transboundary environmental agreements is responsible for many other areas beyond environmental protection also. Alternatively, institutions may be focused upon the governance needs of the particular treaty, which is the case for the other sub-regional environmental agreements discussed in this chapter. In the case of the institutions with a broader focus (UNESCO and ASEAN), there are similarities with the broader role of the UNECE, which was considered generally in Chapter 1.

The conservation or biodiversity conventions are excellent examples of transboundary cooperation in a multilateral context.[7] These are concerned with protecting species and places, and include the *Convention on Biological Diversity*,[8] the *World Heritage Convention*, the *Wetlands Convention*,[9] the *Convention on International Trade in Endangered Species*,[10] and the *Convention on Migratory Species*.[11] The waste conventions are also strong examples, and include the *Hazardous Wastes Convention*,[12] the *Persistent Organic Pollutants (POPs) Convention*,[13] and the *Chemicals and Pesticides Convention*.[14] Furthermore the *Climate Change Convention*[15] and its *Protocol*[16] are of clear relevance in a transboundary context in addressing cross-cutting issues relating to

---

[7] The Convention on Biological Diversity (below n. 8) also makes reference to another conservation convention, the International Treaty on Plant Genetic Resources for Food and Agriculture (Rome, 3 November 2001), in force 29 June 2004.

[8] Convention on Biological Diversity (Rio de Janeiro, 22 May 1992), 31 ILM 822, in force 29 December 1993.

[9] Convention on Wetlands of International Importance, especially as Waterfowl Habitat (Ramsar, 2 February 1971), 11 ILM 963, in force 21 December 1975.

[10] Convention on International Trade in Endangered Species of Wild Fauna and Flora (Washington DC, 3 March 1973), 993 UNTS 243, in force 1 July 1975.

[11] Convention on the Conservation of Migratory Species of Wild Animals (Bonn, 23 June 1979), 19 ILM 15, in force 1 November 1983.

[12] Convention on the Control of Transboundary Movements of Hazardous Wastes and their Disposal (Basel, 22 March 1989), 28 ILM 657, in force 5 May 1992.

[13] Convention on Persistent Organic Pollutants (Stockholm, 22 May 2001), 40 ILM 532, in force 17 May 2004.

[14] Convention on the Prior Informed Consent Procedure for Certain Hazardous Chemicals and Pesticides in International Trade (Rotterdam, 10 September 1998), 38 ILM 1, in force 24 February 2004.

[15] United Nations Framework Convention on Climate Change (Rio de Janeiro, 9 May 1992), 1771 UNTS 107, in force 21 March 1994.

conservation and waste/pollution. These are examined in a sub-section which also includes the ozone protection regime of the *Ozone Convention*,[17] and its *Protocol*.[18]

In relation to the sub-regional agreements, the first is the *Caspian Sea Convention*.[19] This applies to the 'Caspian Littoral States' of Azerbaijan, Iran, Kazakhstan, Turkmenistan and Russia; all of these are southwest[20] or central Asian states or have territory that extends into northern or eastern Asia (Russia). The second is the *Mekong Agreement*,[21] which is made up of the southeast Asian states of Cambodia, Laos, Thailand and Vietnam; China and Myanmar additionally became Dialogue Partners in 1996. The third are the ASEAN *Conservation*,[22] and *Haze Pollution Agreements*.[23] The fourth are the *Tumen Agreements*,[24] which were originally signed by North Korea, China and Russia, and later by South Korea and Mongolia.

---

[16] Protocol to the United Nations Framework Convention on Climate Change (Kyoto, 11 December 1997), 37 ILM 22, in force 16 February 2005.

[17] Convention for the Protection of the Ozone Layer (Vienna, 22 March 1985), 1513 UNTS 323, in force 22 August 1988.

[18] Protocol on Substances that Deplete the Ozone Layer (Montreal, 16 August 1987), 1522 UNTS 3, in force 1 January 1989.

[19] Framework Convention for the Protection of the Marine Environment of the Caspian Sea (Tehran, 4 November 2003), unreported, in force 12 August 2006.

[20] The geography of the Middle East has connections both with Africa and Asia, and appears unsettled.

[21] Agreement on the Cooperation for the Sustainable Development of the Mekong River Basin (Chiang Rai, 5 April 1995), unreported, in force 5 April 1995.

[22] Association of South East Asian Nations, Agreement on the Conservation of Nature and Natural Resources, opened for signature 9 July 1985, 15 EPL 64 (1985), not yet in force.

[23] Association of South East Asian Nations, Agreement on Transboundary Haze Pollution (Kuala Lumpur, 10 June 2002), unreported, in force 2003. See Mushkat, above n. 1.

[24] Agreement on the Establishment of the Tumen River Area Development Coordination Committee (New York, 6 December 1995), unreported, in force 6 December 1995; and Agreement on the Establishment of the Consultative Commission for the Development of the Tumen River Economic Development Area and Northeast Asia (New York, 6 December 1995), unreported, in force 6 December 1995.

II. INSTITUTIONS

A number of institutions operate in relation to transboundary environmental governance in Asia as noted in the introduction above. These are UN institutions with a global focus, UN regional commissions, MDBs and specialist institutions with an environmental focus. In relation to the UN, among other important findings a recent review has noted that 'the current framework of international environmental governance is weakened by institutional fragmentation and specialization and the lack of a holistic approach to environmental issues and sustainable development.'[25] The role of civil society, although not an institution as such, is considerable and interacts with several of the UN institutions discussed below in significant ways.[26] As indicated, the purpose of this section is to outline their role in relation to transboundary environmental governance so that comparisons can be drawn with the role of the UNECE.

II.1 United Nations Global Institutions

The management review of environmental governance within the UN system also finds that environmental governance will be enhanced if the General Assembly (comprised of all UN states), 'establishes a clear division of labour among developmental agencies, UNEP and the MEAs'.[27] Focusing on UNEP first,[28] this was established in 1972 at the UN Conference on the Human Environment (UNCHE) in Stockholm; its role is to promote the wise use and sustainable development of the global environment. To achieve this it is involved with assessing environmental conditions and trends at global, regional and national levels, developing global and municipal instruments, and strengthening institutions. Examples of its work in the area of transboundary environmental governance include advocacy and support for the *Ozone Convention*, and its *Protocol*,[29] the launch of the Intergovernmental Panel on Climate Change and

---

25 Tadanori Inomata, *Management Review of Environmental Governance within the United Nations System* (United Nations Joint Inspection Unit 2008), JIU/REP/2008/3, iii.

26 See for example, Lauren Eastwood, *Negotiating the Environment: Civil Society, Globalisation and the UN* (Routledge, Abingdon, UK and New York, USA 2015).

27 Above n. 25, iii.

28 See http://www.unep.org/, accessed 13 November 2014; note also Johnson, above n. 5, 111.

29 See also Johnson, above n. 5, 65–80.

input to the *Climate Change Convention*,[30] contributions to the development of the *Hazardous Wastes Convention*,[31] secretariat support for the *Convention on Migratory Species*,[32] and the primary source of inputs for the UN Conference on Environment and Development (UNCED) in Rio de Janeiro in 1992.[33] The following comment effectively summarises some of these contributions:

> As we have seen, the list of UNEP's achievements by the end of the 1980s was impressive. Regional seas, ozone, climate change, toxic waste, biodiversity: in each and every one of these vital areas UNEP had made a major impact. The substantive agenda of UNCED, as finally envisaged by the General Assembly, followed almost word for word the text submitted by UNEP.[34]

Other areas of focus have included: resource efficiency, disasters and conflicts, environmental governance[35] and ecosystem management. In an Asian context, UNEP works in Asia and the Pacific to reduce atmospheric brown haze and adverse impacts of environmental deterioration on human health.[36] In west Asia improving information for decision making has been prioritised.[37] As an example of recent engagement in Asia, a China-UNEP Agreement in relation to climate change adaptation has recently been signed.[38]

The UNDP is the second of the global institutions, which since 1966 has collaborated with all levels of society to help build nations capable of withstanding crises, and driving and sustaining growth to improve the

---

30 Johnson, above n. 5, 81–94.

31 This was in fact the work of the Organisation for Economic Cooperation and Development's (OECD) Environment Committee and environment directorate, which predated the Stockholm Conference and the establishment of UNEP. Its programme in the field of chemicals is acknowledged as especially strong. See Johnson, above n. 5, 102.

32 Johnson, above n. 5, 116.

33 Johnson, above n. 5, 128.

34 Johnson, above n. 5, 130.

35 See UNEP, *Environmental Governance*, Factsheet (UNEP undated).

36 http://www.unep.org/environmentalgovernance/UNEPintheRegions/AsiaandthePacific/tabid/482/Default.aspx, accessed 13 November 2014.

37 http://www.unep.org/environmentalgovernance/UNEPintheRegions/WestAsia/tabid/479/Default.aspx, accessed 13 November 2014.

38 UNEP, 'New China-UNEP Agreement to Boost South-South Cooperation on Climate Change Adaptation', press release, 10 May 2014, accessed 13 November 2014 at http://www.unep.org/newscentre/Default.aspx?DocumentID=2788&ArticleID=10854&l=en#sthash.8zbzERix.dpuf.

quality of life. In 2004, it signed a MoU with UNEP establishing a cooperation framework in relation to environmental capacity development.[39] Guided by the Millennium Development Goals (MDGs)[40] – especially the overarching goal of halving poverty by 2015 – its network links and coordinates global and national efforts to reach these goals.[41] Four main areas are the focus: poverty reduction and achievement of the MDGs, democratic governance, crisis prevention and recovery, and environment and energy for sustainable development. Given the areas it shares in common with UNEP, it is no surprise that the UNDP collaborates extensively with it and other institutions with common objectives.[42]

The GEF is the third of these bodies, which is jointly managed by the WB (below), UNEP and the UNDP. It has been called the 'largest multipurpose facility to provide funding for the implementation of MEAs, in particular to support the *Convention on Biological Diversity* and the climate change conventions'.[43] It is legally and practically separate from the treaties it serves, and issues have arisen in connection with this resulting in recent recommendations to review the adequacy and effectiveness of current funding arrangements.[44]

The WHO is the fourth of these bodies, which is the coordinating authority for health within the UN system. It is responsible for 'providing leadership on global health matters, shaping the health research agenda, setting norms and standards, articulating evidence-based policy options, providing technical support to countries and monitoring and assessing health trends'.[45] The Assembly is the key decision-making body, meeting annually in Geneva and attended by delegations from all 194 member states. Health is a key part of several of the UNECE agreements that are the focus of this book, particularly the *SEA Protocol* (Chapter 4)[46] and

---

39 Above n. 25, 17; more coordination between them is however recommended by the Inspector in the management review report.

40 http://www.un.org/millenniumgoals/, accessed 13 November 2014.

41 In relation to the application of these goals in central Asia, see http://www.unece.org/fileadmin/DAM/publications/oes/UNECE_MDG_Report_2012.pdf, accessed 13 November 2014.

42 UNDP also collaborates extensively with the MDBs discussed in the next section, which account for a large amount of the earmarked, project-specific funding of UNDP.

43 Above n. 25, 23.

44 Above n. 25, 25.

45 See generally http://www.who.int/about/en/, accessed 13 November 2014.

46 Protocol on Strategic Environmental Assessment to the Convention on Environmental Impact Assessment in a Transboundary Context (Kiev, 21 May 2003), unreported, in force 11 July 2010. See Article 1 generally and requirement

Protocol on Water and Health (Chapter 6),[47] the latter of which is a collaborative effort of both the UNECE and WHO Regional Office for Europe.[48] The typical anthropocentric focus of environmental treaties is also true of the UNECE treaties in general, with the *Air Pollution Convention* in particular (Chapter 7),[49] addressing public health concerns. Furthermore in the Asian context, it is also significant that the WHO has a Regional Office for southeast Asia.[50]

The ICJ is the fifth of these bodies of relevance, particularly because as the 'World Court' of the UN it is responsible for, among other things, determining the outcome of disputes between UN member states, many of which are over resources or borders.[51] In the last 20 years therefore disputes between states in Europe,[52] Latin America,[53] and the Asia Pacific[54] have been brought before the ICJ for resolution, most of which are directly concerned with transboundary environmental governance. While access to the ICJ by individuals and NGOs has remained a problem, and the environment has often not been adequately considered by the ICJ,[55] nonetheless the initiation of litigation has been influenced

---

to consult health authorities, Articles 5(2) and 6(2); health effects are to also be included in the environmental report in accordance with Article 7(2).

47 Protocol on Water and Health to the Convention on the Protection and Use of Transboundary Watercourses and Lakes (London, 17 June 1999), UNTS 2331, 202, in force 4 August 2005.

48 For an overview, see WHO, *The Protocol on Water and Health: Making a Difference* (WHO 2006), accessed 13 November 2014 at http://www.euro.who.int/__data/assets/pdf_file/0003/97833/WaterProtocol_2006upd_web.pdf.

49 Convention on Long-Range Transboundary Air Pollution (Geneva, 13 November 1979) 1302 UNTS 217, entered into force 16 March 1983.

50 See http://www.searo.who.int/en/, accessed 13 November 2014.

51 See generally, Tim Stephens, *International Courts and Environmental Protection* (Cambridge University Press, Cambridge 2009) and Malgosia Fitzmaurice, 'The International Court of Justice and Environmental Disputes', in Duncan French, Matthew Saul and Nigel White (eds), *International Law and Dispute Settlement* (Hart Publishing, Oxford 2010) 17, 54–5, for a discussion of the (now defunct) ICJ's Chamber for Environmental Matters.

52 ICJ, *Case Concerning Gabčíkovo-Nagymaros Project (Hungary v. Slovakia)*, decision of 25 September 1997 (ICJ Reports 1997, 7).

53 ICJ, *Case Concerning Pulp Mills on the River Uruguay (Argentina v. Uruguay)*, Judgment of 20 April 2010.

54 ICJ, *Whaling in the Antarctic (Australia v. Japan: New Zealand intervening)*, 2010; and *Advisory Opinion on the Legality of the Threat or Use of Nuclear Weapons opinion of 8 July 1996* (ICJ Reports 1996, 226).

55 Ole W Pederson, 'An International Environmental Court and International Legalism' (2012) 24 *Journal of Environmental Law* 547, 550.

by the advocacy of these non-state actors,[56] which have played a much greater role in recent times.

While several other environmental or related regimes establish their own dispute settlement mechanisms,[57] neither the global agreements above, subregional Asian agreements nor the UNECE agreements have a dedicated mechanism. In such instances, while the opportunity to take disputes to the ICJ is likely to be a feature of each regime, in other instances NCPs may have a particular role to play in avoiding disputes before they escalate. This is the case for almost all of the UNECE agreements examined in this book and hence why the focus on compliance alongside implementation is a fundamental feature.

II.2 United Nations Regional Commissions

Five regional commissions were created by the UN in order to fulfil the economic and social goals set out in the UN Charter by promoting cooperation and integration between the countries in each region of the world.[58] They have also signed a MoU with the UNDP to enhance cooperation.[59] The regional commissions contributed to the UN Conference on Sustainable Development (UNCSD) in 2012,[60] which was intended to renew commitments made to sustainable development, assess progress, consider implementation gaps and address new challenges. In

---

[56] Karen Alter, *The New Terrain of International Courts: Courts, Politics, Rights* (Princeton University Press, Princeton, NJ 2014) 7.

[57] Such as that under the United Nations Convention on the Law of the Sea (Montego Bay, 10 December 1982), 1833 UNTS 3, in force 16 November 1994. Note the connection between this treaty and the *EIA Convention*, see David Langlet, 'Transboundary Transit Pipelines: Reflections on the Balancing of Rights and Interests in Light of the Nord Stream Project' (2014) September *International and Comparative Law Quarterly* 1, DOI: 10.1017/S00205893 14000232.

[58] http://www.regionalcommissions.org/, accessed 13 November 2014.

[59] See Cooperation Between the Regional Commissions and the United Nations Development Programme (UNDP), New York, 24 October 2007, accessed 13 November 2014 at http://www.unece.org/fileadmin/DAM/operact/Technical_Cooperation/Item8_UNDPsigned.pdf.

[60] The earlier UNCED called on the regional commissions to promote the integration of environmental concerns in regional and sub-regional development policies and consider improving consultation processes to facilitate the implementation of Agenda 21. The World Summit on Sustainable Development (WSSD) – the UNCSD – subsequently tasked the commissions to facilitate and promote balanced integration of the economic, social and environmental dimensions into their work.

particular, contributions were made to the green economy in the context of sustainable development and to the institutional framework for sustainable development. Climate change has also been a recent focus.[61] After considering the role of the UNECE in Chapter 1, this section focuses on the regional commissions that are specifically relevant to Asia,[62] UNESCAP and UNESCWA. The UN Secretary-General reported on regional cooperation efforts including those by UNESCAP and UNESCWA in 2012.[63]

Unlike the UNECE, UNESCAP, which was established in 1947, has not sponsored any environmental treaties of its own.[64] It consists of 53 members and nine associate members.[65] Three of the members are states located outside the Asia Pacific – the United Kingdom (UK), France and the Netherlands – who have historical interests in the region. It has a mandate to convene a Ministerial Conference on Environment and Development and to promote a 'Green Growth' approach.[66] Sustainable development is also a focus of its work.[67] Although it has not produced any environmental treaties, it was the first initiator of the basin programme for the Mekong River (see below), and is the secretariat of NEASPEC (see Chapter 1 and below); the secretariat is also promoting transboundary energy cooperation in northeast Asia and promoting dialogue in central Asia to develop programmes on energy and water,[68] within the framework of the Special Programme for Economies in

---

61 http://www.regionalcommissions.org/CCchallenges.pdf, accessed 13 November 2014.

62 The UN Economic Commission for Latin America and the Caribbean (UNECLAC, 1948), and the UN Economic Commission for Africa (UNECA, 1958), make up the other two regional commissions, which operate in their respective parts of the world. Again, neither has produced any environmental treaties.

63 United Nations Economic and Social Council, Substantive session of 2012, New York, 2–27 July 2012. Item 10 of the provisional agenda, Regional cooperation. Regional cooperation in the economic, social and related fields, Report of the Secretary-General. E/2012/15, 16 April 2012, 11–12 (ESCAP), 14–15 (ESCWA).

64 http://www.unescap.org/, accessed 13 November 2014.

65 http://www.unescap.org/about/member-states, accessed 13 November 2014.

66 http://www.unescap.org/our-work/environment-development, accessed 13 November 2014.

67 http://www.unescap.org/sustainable-development, accessed 13 November 2014.

68 World Water Assessment Programme, *The World Water Development Report 2014: Water and Energy* (2014).

Central Asia.[69] Finally, it has also closely cooperated with UNEP and the League of Arab States via a joint technical secretariat established to follow-up on the Johannesburg Plan of Implementation.[70]

UNESCWA was established in 1973, and has also not sponsored any environmental treaties of its own.[71] It comprises the 17 Arab states of western Asia (and Africa).[72] Consideration of environmental issues is limited to sustainable development – via the Sustainable Development Policies Division[73] – which has sections on energy, water resources and food and environment, and in relation to productivity matters. The Council of Arab Ministers Responsible for the Environment is the regional coordination and cooperation mechanism, with recommendations of the Joint Committee on Environment and Development considered by the Council and used to guide sustainable development in the region. The League of Arab States is the secretariat for the Council which is supported by UNESCWA and UNEP in its tasks.[74] Other regional initiatives supported by UNESCWA include the Arab Ministerial Council for Water, with major challenges in this area to meet.[75]

---

69 See for example, http://www.unescap.org/news/un-office-almaty-strengthens-inclusive-and-sustainable-growth-north-and-central-asia, accessed 13 November 2014.

70 See generally, Author unknown, 'Towards a More Coherent Institutional Framework for the UN System's Environmental Activities: Views and Roles of the Regional Commissions' (May 2006) and Author unknown, 'Note on the Regional Dimension of Development within the UN' (15 June 2006). These are available at http://www.regionalcommissions.org/RCs%20views%20on%20Instituional%20Framework%20for%20UN%20Environmental%20activities-%20Note,%20Final%208%20May%2006.pdf and http://www.regionalcommissions.org/newsletter/Joint.note.Coherence%20panel.pdf, both accessed 13 November 2014.

71 http://www.escwa.un.org/, accessed 13 November 2014.

72 http://www.escwa.un.org/about/members_8_2012.pdf, accessed 13 November 2014.

73 http://www.escwa.un.org/divisions/main.asp?division=sdpd, accessed 13 November 2014.

74 Report of the UN Secretary-General, above n. 63, 14.

75 Author unknown, 'Timely water solutions need of the hour: PM', *Gulf Times* 28 May 2014, available 13 November 2014 at http://www.gulf-times.com/qatar/178/details/393810/timely-water-solutions-need-of-the-hour%3a-pm.

II.3 Multilateral Development Banks/International Financial Institutions

The WB, EBRD and ADB are all involved in the Asian region and have their own lending requirements for Asian borrower states involved with transboundary environmental governance, such as projects with cross-border effects.[76] The WB for example, also part of the UN system as noted, and which actually consists of five organisations,[77] integrates EIA into its funding procedures to governments of developing countries, which includes transboundary EIA. Sectoral environmental assessments or country environmental assessments are often required.[78] The WB explains these requirements in its Operational Policy 4.01 as follows:

> **Environmental Assessment**, one of ten Safeguard Policies, is used in the Bank to examine the potential environmental risks and benefits associated with Bank investment lending operations. It is an essential tool for integrating environmental and social concerns into development policies, programs and projects by providing the minimum requirements that all Bank-supported operations must meet.[79]

The EBRD also plays a prominent role in this area, and committed itself to amending its environmental policy to ensure compliance with the *EIA Convention*,[80] (see Chapter 4).[81] The EBRD's 2014 Environmental and

---

[76] See generally, Sanae Fujita, *The World Bank, Asian Development Bank and Human Rights – Developing Standards of Transparency, Participation and Accountability* (Edward Elgar, Cheltenham, UK and Northampton, MA, USA 2013).

[77] The International Bank for Reconstruction and Development, the International Development Association, the International Finance Corporation, the Multilateral Investment Guarantee Agency, and the International Centre for Settlement of Investment Disputes. See http://www.worldbank.org/en/about, accessed 13 November 2014.

[78] Jean-Roger Mercier, 'The World Bank and Environmental Impact Assessment', in Kees Bastmeijer and Timo Koivurova (eds), *Theory and Practice of Transboundary Environmental Impact Assessment* (Martinus Nijhoff, Leiden 2008) 291.

[79] http://web.worldbank.org/WBSITE/EXTERNAL/TOPICS/ENVIRONMENT/EXTENVASS/0,,menuPK:407994~pagePK:149018~piPK:149093~theSitePK:407988,00.html, accessed 30 July 2014.

[80] Convention on Environmental Impact Assessment in a Transboundary Context (Espoo, 25 February 1991), 30 ILM (1991) 802, in force 27 June 1997.

[81] Elizabeth Smith, 'Implementing the Espoo Convention: An International Financial Institutions Perspective', in Kees Bastmeijer and Timo Koivurova

Social Policy therefore contains a number of performance requirements to ensure that EIA is implemented as part of any financing by the bank, particularly in central Asia, its main area of Asian operation. Performance requirement 1 concerns 'Assessment and Management of Environmental and Social Impacts and Issues', and 6 relates to 'Biodiversity Conservation and Sustainable Management of Living Natural Resources'.[82] Where the *EIA Convention* or other international treaties do not bind states because they are not Parties, the requirements of the WB, EBRD or ADB may hence be an important means of ensuring compliance with transboundary EIA and related provisions indirectly by requiring adherence to international best practice.

Similarly, the ADB operates a comprehensive Country Safeguards System (CSS) to determine the suitability of borrower countries.[83] Within a sustainable development framework, the focus of the CSS on the legal and institutional framework of potential borrower countries raises the prospect of legal reform in relation to EIA, and requirements to mitigate involuntary resettlement additionally require the application of social impact assessment.[84] Again the focus on ensuring international best practice is met because where the *EIA Convention* does not bind states in the region, the requirements of these lenders are the only way to ensure compliance.[85]

(eds), *Theory and Practice of Transboundary Environmental Impact Assessment* (Martinus Nijhoff, Leiden 2008) 313.

[82] Document of the European Bank for Reconstruction and Development, *Environmental and Social Policy*, 7 May 2014, accessed 13 November 2014 at http://www.ebrd.com/downloads/research/policies/esp-english.pdf.

[83] http://www.adb.org/site/safeguards/main, accessed 3 November 2014.

[84] Asian Development Bank, *Safeguard Policy Statement* (Asian Development Bank 2009), see appendix 1 (environment). See also Asian Development Bank, *Operations Manual: Bank Policies*, 1 October 2013, which is based on the *Safeguard Policy Statement*.

[85] See Meeting of the Parties Sixth session (Convention), Second session (Protocol), Geneva, 2–5 June 2014, Item 6 of the provisional agenda, Seminar on the globalization of the Convention and the Protocol and the role of international financial institutions, Information on the seminar on the globalization of the Convention and the Protocol and the role of international financial institutions, ECE/MP.EIA/2014/INF.8, 28 May 2014.

II.4 Specialist Environmental Organisations Operating Globally or Regionally

The IUCN is the most significant of these bodies.[86] It was founded in 1948 as the first global environmental organisation and is the largest professional conservation network and a leading authority on the environment and sustainable development. Its experts are grouped into six commissions, which include the World Commission on Environmental Law and the World Commission on Protected Areas. It is a neutral forum for governments, NGOs, scientists, business and local communities to find solutions to conservation and development challenges, and is governed by a Council elected every four years at the World Conservation Congress. It is funded by governments, bilateral and multilateral agencies, foundations, member organisations and corporations, and has official observer status at the UN General Assembly.

III. MULTILATERAL REGIMES IN ASIA

As outlined in the Introduction to this chapter, there are many MEAs that are applicable to Asia.[87] While membership is not uniform across the region, there are significant numbers of Asian states Parties to each of these agreements to merit brief commentary upon them. Those of greatest relevance are grouped in this section into the conservation, waste and climate change/ozone protection conventions. Where regimes are focused on transboundary environmental governance, requirements will be briefly explained. Where regimes have a national focus, new developments in relation to transboundary application will be summarised.

III.1 Conservation Conventions

Each of the conservation or biodiversity-related conventions below is focused on action at the national, regional and international levels, to reach the shared goals of conservation and sustainable use.[88] Supported

---

[86] See generally http://www.iucn.org/about/, accessed 13 November 2014.

[87] For information on these, see the UN Information Portal on Multilateral Environmental Agreements, accessed 13 November 2014 at http://www.informea.org/.

[88] Since entering into force following the ratification of Vietnam in mid-2014, the *International Water Convention* can perhaps be added to the list of conservation conventions operating at the global level. This is considered in

by institutions with law-making powers, the regime of each of the conventions has over time either enhanced existing transboundary-focused application (*Convention on International Trade in Endangered Species* and *Convention on Migratory Species*), or applied and developed existing provisions in a transboundary context (*Convention on Biological Diversity*, *World Heritage Convention*, and *Wetlands Convention*). Each regime has also developed complementary approaches (site, species, genetic resources and/or ecosystem-based) and operational tools (programmes of work, trade permits and certificates, multilateral system for access and benefit-sharing, regional agreements, site listings, and funds). While each therefore operates independently, these links between them provide a basis for enhanced cooperation.[89]

The *Convention on Biological Diversity* is the first of these regimes, which is focused upon the conservation of biological diversity, the sustainable use of its components, and the fair and equitable sharing of benefits arising from the use of genetic resources. Article 5 states: 'Each Contracting Party shall, as far as possible and as appropriate, cooperate with other Contracting Parties, directly or, where appropriate, through competent international organizations, in respect of areas beyond national jurisdiction and on other matters of mutual interest, for the conservation and sustainable use of biological diversity.' This provides impetus for transboundary cooperation in environmental management,[90] with Goal 1.3 intended to establish and strengthen regional networks, transboundary protected areas and collaboration between neighbouring protected areas across national boundaries.[91] Two examples of such cooperation relate to the Himalayas and southeast Asia.

Chapter 6. See Convention on the Law of Non-Navigable Uses of International Watercourses (New York, 21 May 1997, by UNGA Res. 51/229), 36 ILM (1997) 700, in force August 2014.

[89] See above n. 25, 20, where the management review report refers to this coordination as being 'best practice'.

[90] See Louis J Kotze and Thilo Marauhn (eds), *Transboundary Biodiversity Governance* (Brill/Nijhoff, Leiden 2014); and Sabine Brels, David Coates and Flavia Loures, *Transboundary Water Resources Management: The Role of International Watercourse Agreements in Implementation of the CBD* (CBD/UNEP/WWF 2008).

[91] See *Convention on Biological Diversity (CBD) Handbook*, 3rd edn, which also covers the *Protocol on Biosafety*, accessed 13 November 2014 at http://www.cbd.int/convention/refrhandbook.shtml.

The first is demonstrated by an event in 2012 organised by the International Centre for Integrated Mountain Development in collaboration with GB Pant Institute of Himalayan Environment and Development and other partners, entitled 'Managing Biodiversity in Transboundary Landscape in the Hindu Kush-Himalaya Region'.[92] This was a side event to the 11th Conference of the Parties (COP11), the purpose of which was to share experiences and lessons learnt on managing biodiversity with an 'ecosystem approach' in the transboundary landscapes in the region, raise awareness among communities about the prospect of regional cooperation, and highlights transboundary initiatives and lesson learnt.

The second is another side event to COP11, which was organised by the Wildlife Enforcement Network, and entitled 'Managing Biodiversity Conservation and Wildlife Protection at Landscape and Transboundary Scales in South Asia'.[93] Since several biodiversity rich protected areas are located over international boundaries between countries in south Asia, applying a landscape approach is the best way of achieving long term conservation outcomes and human well-being. Poaching and illegal trade in wildlife is an imminent threat to a number of species in south Asia, so cooperation and collaboration amongst countries with shared borders is essential and this side event showcased two ongoing externally funded WB projects, one in India and the other a regional project (Bangladesh, Bhutan, India and Nepal), that provide the scale and opportunity to influence conservation for positive outcomes.

The related *Cartagena Protocol on Biosafety*[94] is part of the above regime. At COP2 in November 1995, an Open-ended Ad Hoc Working Group on Biosafety was established to develop the draft protocol, focusing specifically on transboundary movement of any living modified organism resulting from modern biotechnology that may have adverse effect on the conservation and sustainable use of biological diversity. After several years of negotiations, the *Protocol* was finalised at an extraordinary meeting of the COP.

The *World Heritage Convention* is the second of the conservation regimes operating at the global level. The Convention facilitates the inscription of natural, cultural and mixed properties on the World

---

92 http://www.cbd.int/kb/record/sideEvent/2541?RecordType=sideEvent, accessed 13 November 2014.

93 http://www.cbd.int/kb/record/sideEvent/2948?RecordType=sideEvent, accessed 13 November 2014.

94 Protocol on Biosafety to the Convention on Biological Diversity (Cartagena, 29 January 2000), 2226 UNTS 208, in force 11 September 2003.

Heritage List and imposes requirements on states that have proposed those properties for inscription, for the protection and conservation of their outstanding universal value.[95] While it is focused on properties in a national context, there is currently one transboundary Asian property on the List of World Heritage, the Uvs Nuur Basin,[96] which is shared between Russia and Mongolia. This is the northernmost of the enclosed basins of central Asia and is a large, shallow and very saline lake, important for migrating birds, waterfowl and seabirds. It comprises 12 protected areas representing the major biomes of eastern Eurasia. A transboundary extension of another listing of Russia has also been recommended, to the Golden Mountains of Altai.[97] These mountains in southern Siberia form the major mountain range in the western Siberia biogeographic region and provide the source of its greatest rivers – the Ob and the Irtysh. The region represents the most complete sequence of altitudinal vegetation zones in central Siberia, from steppe, forest-steppe, mixed forest, subalpine vegetation to alpine vegetation. Another potential transboundary property is on the tentative list, the Western Tien-Shan.[98]

As a follow-up to a project which highlighted the international significance of the cultural heritage of the Altai Mountains – extending over China, Kazakhstan, Mongolia and Russia – and the need for transboundary cooperation for conservation, the World Heritage Centre (the key administrative body) initiated a similar exercise for the Golden Mountains of Altai, whose Russian part was inscribed on the World Heritage List in 1998. The Subregional World Heritage Consultative Workshop for Promotion of Transboundary Cooperation involved the four states Parties in discussing cultural value and management arrangements for a possible transboundary nomination.[99]

A final very significant example under the *World Heritage Convention* was formalised by the Ashgabat Agreement. Under this, representatives of 12 Asian countries outlined the Silk Roads Heritage Corridors

---

[95] See UNESCO World Heritage Centre, *Operational Guidelines for the Implementation of the World Heritage Convention* (UNESCO 2013).

[96] http://whc.unesco.org/en/list/769, accessed 13 November 2014.

[97] http://whc.unesco.org/en/list/768, accessed 13 November 2014.

[98] This is a serial transboundary nomination including protected nature areas in this mountainous country in three states: Kazakhstan, Kyrgyzstan and Uzbekistan. The tentative list is used by states Parties to propose properties for potential inscription on the World Heritage List.

[99] http://whc.unesco.org/en/events/513, accessed 13 November 2014.

approach for a future serial and transboundary World Heritage nomination.[100] Fifty potential Silk Roads Heritage Corridors have been identified, with three corridors within the central Asian countries and China recommended as a top priority for the first phase of the nomination of the Silk Roads at the second meeting of the Coordinating Committee of the Serial World Heritage Nomination of the Silk Roads in 2011. In 2014 at the 38th Session of the World Heritage Committee in Doha, the Routes Network of Chang'an-Tianshan Corridor (a China, Kazakhstan and Kyrgyzstan joint nomination) was inscribed on the List of World Heritage as part of this process.[101]

The *Wetlands Convention* is the third of the conservation regimes operating at the global level that is of relevance to Asia. Although like the *Convention on Biological Diversity* and *World Heritage Convention* the *Wetlands Convention* is also focused on domestic application within a single state, increasingly collaborative international management of adjacent wetlands (often known as Ramsar sites after the city of adoption) in more than one state is taking place. This operates pursuant to Article 5 of the Convention and Resolution VII.19 (1999) on international cooperation, the latter of which states:

> Increasingly, Ramsar Contracting Parties are designating their new and existing Ramsar Sites also as **Transboundary Ramsar Sites**, meaning that an ecologically coherent wetland extends across national borders and the Ramsar Site authorities on both or all sides of the border have formally agreed to collaborate in its management, and have notified the Secretariat of this intent.[102]

This is a cooperative management arrangement and not a distinct legal status for the sites involved. There are 16 transboundary wetland sites, all of which are, however, currently in Europe except one in Africa. The treaty also encourages transboundary species conservation under Article 5 and further to Recommendation 4.12 (1990).[103] A number of cooperative flyway programmes have been developed to manage shared wetland species or to conserve individual species. In an Asian context these include the African Eurasian Migratory Waterbird Agreement established under the *Convention on Migratory Species* (below), the Asia-Pacific Migratory Waterbird Conservation Strategy, the Central Asian Action

---

100 http://whc.unesco.org/en/news/751, accessed 13 November 2014.

101 http://whc.unesco.org/en/list/1442, accessed 13 November 2014.

102 See the Ramsar Convention Secretariat, *The Ramsar Convention Manual: A Guide to the Convention on Wetlands (Ramsar, Iran, 1971)*, (6th edn, 2013) 61.

103 Ibid, 62–63.

Plan for Migratory Waterbirds and their Habitats, and the East Asian-Australasian Flyway.[104] Collaborative arrangements furthermore exist between the *Wetlands Convention* and the most relevant of the UNECE treaties, the *Water Convention* (Chapter 6).[105] The Working Group on Monitoring and Assessment under the *Water Convention* for example is attended by representatives of the *Wetlands Convention* secretariat. This secretariat has also supported several regional initiatives in Asia to encourage collaboration further.[106]

The *Convention on International Trade in Endangered Species* (often abbreviated as CITES) is the fourth relevant global conservation treaty operating in Asia. Drafted as a result of a resolution adopted in 1963 at a meeting of members of the IUCN, the aim is to ensure that international trade in specimens of wild animals and plants does not threaten their survival.[107] It subjects international trade in selected species to certain controls. All import, export, re-export and introduction of species covered must be authorised through a licensing system. Each Party must designate one or more Management Authorities responsible for administering the licensing system and one or more Scientific Authorities to advise them on the effects of trade on the status of the species. A number of resolutions have been passed by the COP for cooperation with other related regimes including the biodiversity related conventions generally and specifically the *Convention on Migratory Species* (below).[108] MoU between these regimes have also been concluded.[109]

The relevance of this treaty in Asia is without question, either because many of the species are located there or because much of the trade in threatened species operates there or via there. There are a number of particularly notable species on which efforts have been focused. Decisions have been passed in relation to these, which include the Asian big

---

[104] Ibid.

[105] Convention on the Protection and Use of Transboundary Watercourses and Lakes (Helsinki, 17 March 1992), 31 ILM (1992) 1312, in force 6 October 1996.

[106] See Ramsar Regional Center for Training and Research on Wetlands in Western and Central Asia in Iran (RRC-CWA), and the Ramsar Regional Center for East Asia in Changwon, Republic of Korea. These are all noted in the Ramsar Manual, above n. 102, 63.

[107] Willem Wijnstekers, *The Evolution of CITES: A Reference to the Convention on International Trade in Endangered Species of Wild Fauna and Flora* (9th edn, International Council for Game and Wildlife Conservation 2011).

[108] See Resolutions 16.4 and 13.3.

[109] http://www.cites.org/eng/disc/coop.php, accessed 13 November 2014.

cats.[110] Recent developments include the first destruction of confiscated elephant ivory in Hong Kong which contains the largest stockpiles of seized ivory in the world.[111] Other recent activities include the work of the Global Snow Leopard Conservation Forum held recently in Kyrgyzstan. The Forum aims to protect a species which is under severe threat from the poaching and illegal trade in fur and other body parts.[112]

The *Convention on Migratory Species* is the fifth relevant global conservation treaty operating in Asia. Operating under the guidance of UNEP, it aims to ensure the conservation and sustainable use of migratory animals and their habitats.[113] It brings together the states through which migratory species pass, which are known as the Range States, and it provides a legal foundation for internationally coordinated conservation measures throughout the migratory range of the listed species. Migratory species threatened with extinction are listed on Appendix I of the Convention and those that need or would significantly benefit from international co-operation are listed in Appendix II. As the only global convention specialising in the conservation of migratory species, their habitats and migration routes, it complements and cooperates with a number of other international organisations, NGOs and other stakeholders.

Examples of Asian migratory species protected are Saiga antelopes, wild camels, Mongolian gazelles and Asiatic wild asses which need to be able to roam freely across open plains in central Asia. Further to Recommendations 9.1 (Central Eurasian Aridland Mammals and Resolution) and 10.3 (the Role of Ecological Networks in the Conservation of Migratory Species), the treaty mandate is to coordinate activities to conserve this unique ecological network in the Central Asian steppes. At a conference in Vilm, Germany, government officials from Germany, Mongolia, Kazakhstan and Kyrgyzstan, the treaty and a panel of experts

---

110 See Decision 16.70, and note also Resolution 12.5, which concerns tigers especially. http://www.cites.org/eng/disc/coop.php, accessed 13 November 2014.

111 http://www.cites.org/eng/CITES-secretary-general-remarks-at-first-destruction-confiscated-elephant-ivory-Hong_Kong-China, accessed 13 November 2014.

112 http://www.cites.org/eng/news/sg/2013/20131024_snow_leopard.php, accessed 13 November 2014.

113 Various publications can be located at: http://www.cms.int/, accessed 13 November 2014.

have adopted an action plan to mitigate the impacts on migratory wildlife of the rapidly growing infrastructure development due to mining activities.[114]

III.2 Waste Conventions

The waste conventions are also a collection of regimes with similar objectives that have collaborated with one another, and again operate in the Asian context as well as globally. More recent in origin than the majority of the conservation conventions, they address the problems of hazardous wastes, chemicals and pesticides, and POPs, primarily in a transboundary context. The notion of 'prior informed consent' (PIC) is a keystone of the first two of these regimes and the closeness of all three is indicated by a shared Secretariat and coordination of COPs.[115]

The *Hazardous Wastes Convention* is the first of the relevant waste conventions, adopted in response to a public outcry following the discovery in the 1980s in the developing world of deposits of toxic wastes imported from abroad. The problem had been caused by public resistance to local disposal of hazardous wastes which led operators to seek cheap disposal options where environmental awareness was less developed and regulations and enforcement were lacking. The overarching objective is therefore to protect human health and the environment against the adverse effects of hazardous wastes.[116] Wastes are defined as hazardous based on their origin and/or composition and their characteristics. The regulatory system is based on the concept of PIC, and requires notification by the exporting to the importing state with the provision of detailed information on the intended movement. The movement may only proceed if and when all states concerned have given their written consent (Articles 6 and 7).

---

114 http://biodiversity-l.iisd.org/news/central-asian-countries-adopt-cms-action-plan-on-migratory-species-and-impacts-of-mining/, accessed 13 November 2014.

115 The sixth ordinary meeting of the COP to the *Chemicals and Pesticides Convention* was held in coordination with the eleventh ordinary meeting of the COP to the *Hazardous Wastes Convention* and the sixth ordinary meeting of the COP to the *POPs Convention*. This has been heralded as a major improvement for the governance of MEAs under the UN system; see above n. 25, 10. The economies of scale of the UNECE regime are also commented on favourably in connection with this.

116 UNEP, Secretariat of the Basel Convention, *The Basel Convention Mechanism for Promoting Implementation and Compliance: Celebrating a Decade of Assistance to Parties* (UNEP 2011).

In an Asian context, bilateral agreements have been concluded between Malaysia and the Philippines and the USA, and between East Timor and Australia.[117] Asia is a key area for implementation and compliance, hosting a Regional Centre for Southeast Asia and a recent key event in Indonesia, the Second meeting of the Expert Working Group on Environmentally Sound Management (ESM). This established a common understanding of what ESM encompasses, and identified tools and strategies to promote the implementation of ESM.[118] Indonesia itself has been an important focus of efforts in recent years, with significant programmes established to improve compliance with the Convention.[119] Another example is the Programme on the Environmentally Sound Management of Electrical and Electronic Wastes for the Asia-Pacific Region, with the goal of enhancing the capacity of Parties in this region to manage electrical and electronic wastes in an environmentally sound manner through the establishment of public-private partnerships, and the prevention of illegal traffic.[120]

The *Chemical and Pesticides Convention* is the second relevant waste convention operating in Asia. This has the objectives of promoting shared responsibility and cooperative efforts in the international trade of certain hazardous chemicals in order to protect human health and the environment, and to contribute to the environmentally sound use of those hazardous chemicals, by facilitating information exchange about them.[121] Like the *Hazardous Wastes Convention*, it creates legally binding obligations for the implementation of a PIC procedure, initially a voluntary procedure. It covers pesticides and industrial chemicals that have been banned or severely restricted for health or environmental reasons by Parties and which have been notified for inclusion in the PIC procedure.

[117] http://www.basel.int/Countries/Agreements/BilateralAgreements/tabid/1517/Default.aspx, accessed 13 November 2014.

[118] http://www.basel.int/Implementation/CountryLedInitiative/Meetings/SecondmeetingoftheExpertWorkingGrouponESM/tabid/3710/mctl/ViewDetails/EventModID/8495/EventID/498/xmid/11706/Default.aspx, accessed 13 November 2014.

[119] http://www.basel.int/Portals/4/Basel%20Convention/docs/convention/XX%20Anniversary/Press%20kit/Indonesia%20Project%20leaflet.pdf, accessed 13 November 2014.

[120] See http://www.basel.int/Portals/4/Basel%20Convention/docs/pub/leaflets/leaflet01012011-1.pdf, accessed 13 November 2014.

[121] See UNEP, *Introduction to the Resource Kit: A Stepwise Guide – Rotterdam Convention, Share Responsibility* (UNEP 2009), accessed 13 November 2014 at http://www.pic.int/Portals/5/ResourceKit/0_Introduction/stepwiseE-09.pdf.

Parties have nine months to prepare a response concerning the future import of the chemical. Asia has also been a key focus of its work.

The *POPs Convention* is the third relevant waste convention operating in Asia. This is a global treaty to protect human health and the environment from chemicals that remain intact in the environment for long periods, become widely distributed geographically, accumulate in the fatty tissue of humans and wildlife, and have harmful impacts on human health or the environment.[122] It requires Parties to take measures to eliminate or reduce the release of POPs into the environment, and promotes the use of best available techniques and best environmental practices for preventing releases of POPs into the environment. Asia has again been a key focus of its work.

III.3 Climate Change/Ozone Protection Conventions

The third series of MEAs of relevance to Asia concern climate change and ozone protection. As noted these are cross cutting with conservation and waste since they aim to limit, reduce or end the production of polluting substances which impact significantly upon the natural environment. The regulation of climate change is a major concern for the international community and has resulted in a significant amount of scholarly endeavour in recent years as academic lawyers and others contribute to the debate from multifarious perspectives.[123]

The first of these is the *Climate Change Convention* and its associated *Protocol*. The purpose of the *Climate Change Convention* is to bring states together to cooperatively consider what can be done to limit average global temperature increases and resulting climate change, and to

---

[122] See UNEP, Secretariat of the Stockholm Convention, *Ridding the World of POPs: A Guide to the Stockholm Convention on POPs* (UNEP 2010).

[123] For examples, see Alexander Zahar, *International Climate Change Law and State Compliance* (Routledge, Abingdon, UK and New York, USA 2015); Thoko Kaime (ed.), *International Climate Change Law and Policy: Cultural Legitimacy in Adaptation and Mitigation* (Routledge, Abingdon, UK and New York, USA 2014); Harro van Asselt, *The Fragmentation of Global Climate Governance: Consequences and Management of Regime Interactions* (Edward Elgar, Cheltenham, UK and Northampton, MA, USA 2014); Peter Lawrence, *Justice For Future Generations: Climate Change and International Law* (Edward Elgar, Cheltenham, UK and Northampton, MA, USA 2014); Stephen Farrall, Tawhida Ahmed and Duncan French (eds), *Criminological and Legal Consequences of Climate Change* (Hart Publishing, Oxford 2012).

cope with impacts from that change.[124] The purpose of the *Protocol* to the Convention was driven by the subsequent realisation that the emission reductions provisions in the Convention were inadequate and the global response needed to be strengthened.[125] The *Protocol* therefore legally binds developed countries to emission reduction targets, with the first commitment period between 2008 and 2012, and the second between 2013 and 2020. At the 2012 COP in Doha, governments consolidated the gains of the previous three years of negotiations and 'opened a gateway to necessary greater ambition and action on all levels'.[126] Among the decisions taken, governments strengthened their resolve and elaborated a timetable to adopt a universal climate agreement for all developed and developing states by 2015, which would come into effect in 2020.

The second of these regimes is the *Ozone Convention*, and its related *Protocol*. In 2009, the *Ozone Convention* became the first of any kind to achieve universal ratification.[127] The objectives are for Parties to promote cooperation by systematic observations, research and information exchange on the effects of human activities on the ozone layer. They are also to adopt legislative or administrative measures to address activities likely to have adverse effects upon it. As with the *Climate Change Convention*, the *Ozone Convention* also did not require countries to take concrete action, so the *Protocol* was needed to advance that goal.[128]

What is noteworthy from the above is that the UN lacks 'an overarching authority' for global environmental governance; UNEP has been criticised as having 'fallen short in exercising effectively its original mandate to coordinate all environmental initiatives', responses to challenges have been 'sector specific, specialized and fragmented' despite some noted improvements, including the sharing of secretarial support in connection with the waste conventions and under the UNECE regime.

---

124 See UN Framework Convention on Climate Change, *Uniting on Climate: A Guide to the Climate Change Convention and the Kyoto Protocol* (UNFCCC 2007).

125 See UN Framework Convention on Climate Change, *The Kyoto Protocol Mechanisms: International Emissions Trading Clean Development Mechanism Joint Implementation* (UNFCCC 2010).

126 http://unfccc.int/key_steps/doha_climate_gateway/items/7389.php, accessed 13 November 2014.

127 See UNEP, *Handbook for the Vienna Convention for the Protection of the Ozone Layer* (9th edn, Ozone Secretariat UNEP 2012) for discussion of the text, decisions and rules of procedure.

128 See UNEP, *Handbook for the Montreal Protocol on Substances that Deplete the Ozone Layer* (9th edn, Ozone Secretariat UNEP 2012) for discussion of the text, decisions and rules of procedure.

UNEP's role is also considered to have become 'dwarfed compared to other institutions dealing with major environmental concerns such as climate change'.[129] This lack of an 'overarching authority' also includes the absence of an international court to specifically address environmental issues.[130]

IV. SUBREGIONAL REGIMES IN ASIA

Four sub-regional regimes have been identified in Asia, which are outlined in this section and have guiding legal instruments: the *Caspian Sea Convention*, the *Mekong Agreement*, the *ASEAN Agreements* and the *Tumen Agreements*. Most of them are focused on protection and conservation of watercourses and surrounding environments and related issues.

IV.1 The Caspian Sea Convention (Southwest and Central Asia)

The Caspian Sea is the largest inland body of water on earth. Economic development, especially oil and gas exploration and exploitation, is a particular threat to the environment. After the 1994 adoption of the *Almaty Declaration on Cooperation of the Environmental Protection of the Caspian Sea Region*, in 2003 Azerbaijan, Iran, Kazakhstan, Russia and Turkmenistan (the 'Caspian Littoral States') signed the Convention.[131] The combined efforts of UNEP, UNDP, the WB, and others[132] contributed to this, reflecting its strategic importance.

The Convention has the stated objective in Article 2 of 'the protection of the Caspian environment from all sources of pollution including the protection, preservation, restoration and sustainable and rational use of the biological resources of the Caspian Sea'. General obligations are found in Article 4 and include taking measures to prevent, reduce and control pollution; and to protect, preserve and restore the environment.

---

129 Above nn. 25, 30 and 10 (in relation to the waste conventions and UNECE).

130 Above nn. 51 and 55.

131 Shirin Akiner, 'Ten years on: Achievements, Prospects, New Concerns', in Shirin Akiner (ed.), *The Caspian: Politics, Energy and Security* (Routledge, Abingdon, UK and New York, USA 2004) 337.

132 Although focused on the Eastern part of the region, for detailed background and analysis of the recent situation, see UNEP, UNECE, UNDP, North Atlantic Treaty Organisation (NATO), Regional Environment Centre (REC), OSCE, *Environment and Security in Europe, Transforming Risks into Cooperation: The Case of the Eastern Caspian Region* (2008).

Principles guiding action include the precautionary principle, the polluter pays principle and the principle of access to information (Article 5). Parties also have a duty to cooperate in the development of protocols and other measures to implement the Convention (Article 6).

Procedures for EIA are briefly enumerated in the Convention, with *Guidelines on Environmental Impact Assessment in a Transboundary Context* providing more detail.[133] These contain the obligation of Article 13, which deals with environmental emergencies and requires EIA in relation to hazardous activities, and also Article 17(1), for 'any planned activity that are likely to cause significant adverse effect on the marine environment'.[134]

IV.2 The Mekong Agreement (Southeast Asia)

The *Mekong Agreement* obliges the Mekong River Commission (MRC) to adopt framework rules and procedures and carry out its work through a Joint Committee (JC).[135] Key activities include the formulation of a Basin Development Plan (Article 2), a programme for the protection of the environment and ecosystems (Article 3), and reasonable and equitable programming, utilisation and protection of water resources and the environment for the member countries (Article 5). Funded by the GEF, and executed by the WB, in 1999 the MRC and member states adopted a Water Utilisation Programme to develop rules for water utilisation.

Procedures for Notification, Prior Consultation and Agreement ('the Procedures'), have also been established in relation to development

---

[133] UNEP and Caspian Environment Programme, *Guidelines on Environmental Impact Assessment in a Transboundary Context in the Caspian Sea Region: Step by Step Procedures* (UNEP 2003).

[134] For detailed discussion of these provisions, their development, practice and law reform, see Simon Marsden, 'Developing Agreements for Transboundary Environmental Impact Assessment and Strategic Environmental Assessment in Asia', in Robin Warner and Simon Marsden (eds), *Transboundary Environmental Governance: Inland, Coastal and Marine Perspectives* (Ashgate Publishing, Farnham 2012) 141, 159–60.

[135] The Mekong regime has been extensively studied. See for example Tun Myint, *Governing International Rivers: Polycentric Politics in the Mekong and the Rhine* (Edward Elgar, Cheltenham, UK and Northampton, MA, USA 2012); and 'Case Study 1: The Mekong River Basin', in Ariel Dinar, Shlomi Dinar, Stephen McCaffrey and Daene McKinney, *Bridges over Water: Understanding Transboundary Water Conflict, Negotiation and Cooperation*, (2nd edn, World Scientific, Singapore 2013) 273–98.

activity.[136] Chapter III of the Agreement, entitled 'Objectives and Principles of Cooperation' contains the substantive operative provisions. Article 1 outlines the areas of cooperation 'in all fields of sustainable development, utilization, management and conservation of the water and related resources of the Mekong River Basin … to optimize the multiple-use and mutual benefits of all riparians and to minimize the harmful effects that might result …'. Article 7 is concerned with the prevention and cessation of harmful effects.

The *Procedures* are explained in related *Guidelines on Implementation,*[137] which provide practical assistance as to their content and application. The objectives of the *Procedures* are to, 'provide steps for the MRC member States to support the establishment of the Rules for Water Utilization and Inter-Basin Diversions' (Article 26) and to 'promote better understanding and cooperation among the MRC member countries …'. With respect to notification, intra-basin use or diversion on the tributaries or mainstream during the wet season, these require notification to the MRC JC in a timely manner (Section 4).[138]

IV.3 The ASEAN Agreements (Southeast Asia)

ASEAN comprises Vietnam, Cambodia, Laos, Thailand, Indonesia, Malaysia, Singapore, Brunei, Myanmar and the Philippines. Although it has been involved with environmental governance since 1997, 'there has been an admittedly slow and often uneven trajectory of institutionalization of environmental governance arrangements'.[139] In 1985, it adopted the *Conservation Agreement.* This is a non-binding instrument containing

[136] Approved pursuant to the MRC Council Resolution of 18 October 1999, on the Water Utilization Programme and its subsequent approval by the Joint Committee on 13 November 2003 at its 10th Meeting. For a general overview see Worawan Sukaroek, 'The MRC Policy Framework on Transboundary EIA: A Better Cooperation will be Enhanced in the Lower Mekong Basin', paper presented to conference entitled *Role of Water Sciences in Transboundary River Basin Management,* Thailand, 2005; and J Horberry, 'Transboundary Environmental Assessment: The Experience of the Mekong River Commission', presentation to the third MOP to the Espoo Convention, 2004.

[137] http://www.mrcmekong.org/assets/Publications/policies/Guidelines-on-implementation-of-the-PNPCA.pdf, accessed 13 November 2014.

[138] These procedures have also been elaborated in detail elsewhere. See Marsden above n. 134, 153–6, which also discusses recent practice.

[139] Lorraine Elliott, 'ASEAN and Environmental Governance: Rethinking Networked Regionalism in Southeast Asia' (2011) 14 *Procedia Social and Behavioural Sciences* 61.

many broad environmental objectives and obligations. The fundamental principle (Article 1) is that Parties agree to adopt the necessary measures to maintain essential ecological processes and life-support systems, to preserve genetic diversity, and to ensure the sustainable utilisation of natural resources. In accordance with Article 1(2), national conservation strategies are to be developed in support of these measures and coordinated within a regional conservation policy framework.

The *Conservation Agreement* includes specific provisions on conserving genetic diversity, endangered and endemic species, vegetation cover and forest resources, soil, water and air. It also has provisions on conserving ecological processes (by minimising environmental degradation and pollution); using environmental planning measures (through land use planning and protected areas); conducting impact assessments; and introducing national support measures (for example scientific research and public participation). Under Article 19, Parties with shared natural resources are to cooperate concerning their conservation and harmonious utilisation, so as to avoid adverse environmental effects on each other. Environmental assessments, advance notification, and appropriate consultation should all be undertaken prior to any proposed utilisation of the shared resources by one of the Parties (Article 19(2)). It refers specifically to 'transfrontier environmental effects', reminding Parties of the international legal principle of state responsibility and calling on them to avoid 'to the maximum extent possible' causing adverse environmental effects beyond their national boundaries (Article 20). The Agreement is not in force, as it has not yet attained the six ratifications it requires under Article 33 to do so.

In 2002, ASEAN negotiated the *Haze Agreement*, which entered into force the following year.[140] According to ASEAN, it is the 'first regional arrangement in the world that binds a group of contiguous states to tackle transboundary haze pollution resulting from land and forest fires'.[141] Under Article 2, the primary aim is to prevent, monitor and mitigate transboundary haze pollution arising from land and forest fires through 'concerted national efforts and intensified regional and international co-operation'.

Specifically, Article 4(1) requires Parties to cooperate in developing and implementing measures to minimise and monitor transboundary haze

---

140 Nine countries have now ratified the Agreement: Brunei, Cambodia, Laos, Malaysia, Myanmar, Philippines, Singapore, Thailand and Vietnam.

141 ASEAN, 'Haze Action Online – ASEAN Agreement on Transboundary Haze Pollution', available 13 November 2014 at http://haze.asean.org/?page_id=185.

pollution. These include control of the sources of fires; development of monitoring, assessment and early warning systems; exchange of information and technology; and provision of mutual assistance. Article 4(2) requires Parties to respond promptly to a request for relevant information made by any state that may be affected by transboundary haze pollution, so as to minimise any adverse effects. Article 4(3) states that legal, administrative and other appropriate measures must be taken by Parties to implement their obligations.

Further to Article 5(1), the ASEAN Co-ordinating Centre for Transboundary Haze Pollution Control was established to facilitate cooperation between the Parties in managing the impacts of haze pollution. However, although it has been lauded by ASEAN as a 'global role model for the tackling of transboundary issues',[142] the effectiveness of the *Haze Agreement* is significantly undermined by the lack of participation by Indonesia.[143] Indonesia is the largest source of forest fires within the region, and transboundary haze pollution therefore continues to present a challenge for ASEAN.[144]

IV.4 The Tumen Agreements (Northeast Asia)

The Greater Tumen Initiative (GTI) is the name given to the intergovernmental co-operation mechanism under the *Tumen Agreements*. The Consultative Commission is the core decision-making institution. At its eighth meeting the governments of the Parties to these agreements (China, Russia, Mongolia and South Korea), agreed to extend the 1995 Agreements for a decade.[145] The role of the Coordination Committee is to consult and coordinate in relation to social, legal, environmental and economic issues raised by any of the Parties.

A MoU was agreed between the Parties, which was signed by all five contracting parties at the same time as the original two agreements.[146] This affirms the overall goal: 'to attain environmentally sound and

---

142 Ibid.

143 David Jerger, 'Indonesia's role in realizing the goals of ASEAN's Agreement on Transboundary Haze Pollution' (2014) 14(1) *Sustainable Development Law and Policy* 35–45.

144 For example Singapore suffered its worst haze episode in 2013; see National Environment Agency, 'Factsheet on Transboundary Haze Pollution' (Government of Singapore 2014) 1. For further comment, see Mushkat, n. 1.

145 North Korea, also an original Party, chose not to participate in 2010.

146 *Memorandum of Understanding on Environmental Principles Governing the Tumen River Economic Development Area and North East Asia*, 1995.

sustainable development of Northeast Asia and the Tumen River Economic Development Area', in accordance with '(b) the international consensus reached at the United Nations Conference on Environment and Development; (c) the requirements of national laws and regulations and of bilateral and multilateral environmental agreements; and (d) the environmental requirements of the multilateral development banks of which the Contracting Parties are members'. The Contracting Parties also 'affirm their intention to cooperate and coordinate with each other to protect and enhance the environment of the Region and to conduct all development activities in the Region in a manner that does not damage the environment of any Contracting Party, of any other State or of areas beyond the limits of national jurisdiction'.[147]

In relation to procedure, the first section of the MoU is entitled 'Environmental Assessment, Mitigation and Management'. Article 1.3 states that Contracting Parties will prepare and adopt national laws and policies and bilateral and multi-lateral environmental agreements where 'required to attain environmentally sound and sustainable development of the Region'. Article 1.5 contains the EIA obligation for environmentally significant national and transboundary projects, although it fails to detail this other than requiring an EIA report and an Environmental Mitigation and Management Plan (EMMP) to deal with any anticipated effects. Participation by experts in the affected state is also a specific requirement, but not public participation.[148]

V. CONCLUSIONS

Chapter 2 highlights the breadth of international institutions and regimes operating in the Asian region. These include numerous UN bodies, and MDBs/IFIs funded by states with interests in the region; they also include many MEAs that apply to Asia, some of which have a transboundary dimension to their work; additionally, there are a handful of subregional environmental regimes that apply specifically to certain parts of the continent. Although some of the institutions are focused on Asia – such as two of the UN regional commissions and the ADB – only the latter

[147] For further discussion, see Simon Marsden, 'Developing Approaches to Transboundary Environmental Impact Assessment in China: Cooperation through the Greater Tumen Initiative and in the Pearl River Delta Region' (2010) 9(2) *Chinese Journal of International Law* 393–414.

[148] For further detail on these obligations, see Marsden, above n. 134, which again discusses recent practice.

operates specifically across the entire Asian region, and its remit is not concerned in particular with treaty implementation and compliance.

In Part II.1 it was also seen that although certain contributions have been made to addressing Asian environmental problems by UN global bodies – in particular UNEP in relation to haze and climate change adaptation, and the WHO in establishing a regional office for southeast Asia – no particular efforts have focused on developing environmental agreements in the Asian context. In regard to the regional commissions, the outline of the work of UNESCAP and UNESCWA in Part II.2 emphasises the absence of any treaty making efforts by either of these bodies in contrast to the work of the UNECE as outlined in Chapter 1; the specific application of the work of the UNECE in central Asia will also be analysed in Chapter 8.

Finally, Chapter 2 illustrates that while certain environmental issues and processes are currently regulated in certain parts of Asia, they are typically not addressed as comprehensively in geographical scope, nor in as much depth or subject to the same degree of obligation as the UNECE agreements, as will be seen in Chapters 3–7 that follow. While the application of EIA to decision making is required by some of the subregional agreements, and as a matter of policy and practice by MDBs/IFIs; and water and air pollution matters are also addressed by some of the subregional regimes (in harmony with the focus of the *EIA*, *Water* and *Air Pollution Conventions*); other issues and processes regulated by the UNECE treaties and protocols are not dealt with at all. There is therefore nothing comparable to the regulatory framework to meet the challenge of industrial accidents, nor a comprehensive regime dealing with access to information, public participation and access to justice. Given that these are the focus of two of the other UNECE agreements (*Industrial Accidents* and *Public Participation*), this additionally evidences the value of these two treaties. Similarly, there is nothing comparable to the *SEA*, *Water and Health* and *Civil Liability Protocols* in the Asian context. Each of these agreements are comprehensively analysed in the Asian context in the chapters that follow.

PART II

Treaties and Protocols

3. The Public Participation Convention and Pollutant Release and Transfer Registers Protocol

I. INTRODUCTION: STATUS, MEMBERSHIP AND INSTITUTIONS (CONVENTION AND PROTOCOL)

The Convention on Access to Information, Public Participation in Decision-Making and Access to Justice in Environmental Matters (*Public Participation Convention*) was adopted on 25 June 1998, and entered into force on 30 October 2001, following ratification by the required number of states.[1] There are currently 47 Parties. It is open to member states of the UN beyond the UNECE Region, subject to the approval of the existing Parties,[2] and is hence open to Asian states.[3] It has had a major influence on the development of both the *EIA Convention*[4] and *SEA*

[1] Convention on Access to Information, Public Participation in Decision-Making and Access to Justice in Environmental Matters (Aarhus, 25 June 1998) 2161 UNTS 447, in force on 30 October 2001. This is often known as the 'Aarhus Convention'.

[2] Article 19(3). See Meeting of the Parties, Fourth session Chisinau 29 June–1 July 2011, Item 6(a) of the provisional agenda, Promotion of the Convention and relevant development and interlinkages: accession to the Convention by States from outside the United Nations Economic Commission for Europe region, Decision IV/5 on accession to the Convention by non-United Nations Economic Commission for Europe member states, as adopted on 1 July 2011, ECE/MP.PP/2011/CRP.3. The *Water Convention* and *EIA Convention* are also global treaties, and the *SEA Protocol* furthermore shares this significant feature.

[3] For background, see Jona Razzaque, 'Information, Public Participation and Access to Justice in Environmental Matters: Rio+20 Appraisal', in S Alam, J H Bhuyian, T M Chowdhury and E J Techera (eds), *Routledge Handbook of International Environmental Law* (Routledge, Abingdon, UK and New York, USA 2012) 137–54.

[4] Convention on Environmental Impact Assessment in a Transboundary Context (Espoo, 25 February 1991) 30 ILM (1991) 802, in force 27 June 1997.

Protocol,[5] particularly in the area of public participation. It has also been influential in contributing to the development of democratic and constitutional principles in the countries of the EECCA, and beyond the nation state, and it has served to link the environment and human rights in international law.[6] These are all significant claims and resonate in the Asian context where democratic traditions may be unfamiliar or emerging.[7]

Unlike the other UNECE agreements analysed in this book, the focus of the *Public Participation Convention* is upon the domestic,[8] rather than the transboundary context,[9] although transboundary process and decision making may also be affected by the Convention, particularly in relation to the *EIA Convention* (examined in Chapter 4).[10] Despite a domestic focus, it is nonetheless the case that the Convention is a contributor to improving international environmental governance, as confirmed by the

---

[5] Protocol on Strategic Environmental Assessment to the Convention on Environmental Impact Assessment in a Transboundary Context (Kiev, 21 May 2003) unreported, in force 11 July 2010.

[6] Elisa Morgera, 'An Update on the Aarhus Convention and its Continued Global Relevance' (2005) 14 *Review of European Community and International Environmental Law* 138, 139.

[7] Stephen Stec, 'EU Enlargement, Neighbourhood Policy and Environmental Democracy', in Marc Pallemaerts (ed.), *The Aarhus Convention at Ten: Interactions and Tensions between Conventional International Law and EU Environmental Law* (Europa Law Publishing, Groningen 2011) 35.

[8] As such it has spurned scholarship focused on practice in states Parties, see for example Charles Banner (ed.), *The Aarhus Convention: A Guide for UK Lawyers* (Hart Publishing, Oxford 2015) in press. For other examples (UK, Belgium and Germany), see Marc Pallemaerts (ed.), *The Aarhus Convention at Ten: Interactions and Tensions between Conventional International Law and EU Environmental Law* (Europa Law Publishing, Groningen 2011).

[9] The *SEA Protocol* (Chapter 4) and the *Protocol on Water and Health* (Chapter 6) also operate mainly domestically.

[10] Jonas Ebbesson, 'A Modest Contribution to Environmental Democracy and Justice in Transboundary Contexts: The Combined Impact of the Espoo Convention and the Aarhus Convention' (2011) 20 *Review of European Community and International Environmental Law* 248; and Simon Marsden, 'Enforcing Non-Discrimination in Transboundary Environmental Impact Assessment: Advantages for EU Citizens from the Transposition of the Espoo and Aarhus Conventions?' (2009) 6 *Journal for European Environmental and Planning Law* 437.

MOP at the fourth session.[11] Given the focus of the book on transboundary governance, this chapter will emphasise the transboundary context. Because of the link between environmental and human rights, and the focus on government accountability, transparency and responsiveness, this agreement is arguably the most difficult for Asian states to adopt, as many do not have a background of democratic governance. This is the case in respect of the former states of the Soviet Union in the EECCA for example, where a culture of secrecy and experts makes access to information and public participation a challenge in particular.

Nevertheless, just after the fifth session of the MOP,[12] seven states in southwest and central Asia are currently Parties (Armenia, Azerbaijan, Georgia, Kazakhstan, Kyrgyzstan, Tajikistan and Turkmenistan), and the MOP has, through strategic goal II prioritised increasing the impact of the Convention in the UNECE region and beyond.[13] Other Asian states have for example expressed an interest in becoming Parties recently, both members of the UNECE (Russia[14]), and member states of the UN (Mongolia,[15] and Myanmar[16]).

The main institutions under the Convention are the MOP,[17] Bureau,[18] Working Group (WG),[19] and Compliance Committee (CC).[20] Each is

---

[11] Meeting of the Parties, Fourth session Chisinau, 29 June–1 July 2011, Report of the fourth session of the Meeting of the Parties, ECE/MP.PP/2011/2, 19 August 2011, para. 12.

[12] The fifth session of the MOP met in Maastricht from 30 June–4 July 2014; the sixth is due in 2017.

[13] Meeting of the Parties, Fifth session Maastricht, 30 June and 1 July 2014, Item 7(b) of the provisional agenda, Programme of work and operation of the Convention: Strategic Plan for 2015–2020, Draft decision V/5 on the Strategic Plan for 2015–2020, in particular Objective II.3: 'States in other regions of the world effectively exercise their right to accede to the Convention. Parties actively encourage accession to the Convention by States of other regions of the world.'

[14] Press release: UNECE welcomes the Russian Federation's intention to ratify the Aarhus and Espoo environmental conventions, 23 June 2011. See: http://www.unece.org/press/pr2011/11env_p26e.html, accessed 14 November 2014.

[15] Above n. 11, para. 34.

[16] Meeting of the Parties, Fifth session Maastricht, 30 June–4 July 2014, Agenda item 6, Promotion of the Convention and relevant developments and interlinkages, Myanmar's Statement (Ms Khin Thida Tin), 1 July 2014.

[17] See Article 10.

[18] See thirty-fourth meeting of the Bureau, *Report of the Meeting*, Palais de Nations, Geneva, 29 June 2014.

[19] The eighteenth meeting of the WG met in Geneva from 29 June 2014.

[20] The forty-fifth meeting of the CC met in Geneva from 29 June–2 July 2014.

supported by the Secretariat.[21] The MOP is the main governance body, comprising all Parties, and meets every few years to keep under continuous review the implementation of the Convention. The MOP is also responsible for the establishment of subsidiary bodies, which include the WG – also comprising all Parties – meeting regularly to oversee implementation of the workplan between the MOPs. The Bureau has a small membership elected to meet very frequently to consider items of strategic significance and report to the MOP on these.[22] There are also task forces concerned with each of the three pillars of the Convention (access to information, public participation and access to justice[23]) which are subsidiary bodies appointed by the MOP. The CC has prepared a summary document of its case law,[24] which has been incorporated into the *Implementation Guide*[25] in respect of authoritative interpretation of the Convention.

The Protocol on Pollutant Release and Transfer Registers (*PRTR Protocol*) was adopted in 2003, under the auspices of the Convention. The Protocol is the first legally binding international instrument on PRTRs, which are inventories of pollution from industrial sites and other sources. It is open to all states, whether or not they are Parties to the Convention or members of the UNECE. In 2009, the Protocol attained sufficient ratifications to enter into force.[26] By 2014, there were 33 Parties, including the EU. The Protocol has also been signed by three Asian states (Armenia, Georgia and Tajikistan), although it has been

---

[21] Article 11.

[22] See thirty-second meeting of the Bureau of the Meeting of the Parties to the Convention on Access to Information, Public Participation in Decision-Making and Access to Justice in Environmental Matters, *Report of the Meeting*, Palais de Nations, Geneva, 2–3 December 2013, ACB 32 Report, 13 January 2014.

[23] The seventh meeting of the Task Force on Access to Justice met in Geneva from 24–25 February 2014.

[24] A Andrusevych, T Alge and C Konrad (eds), *Case Law of the Aarhus Convention Compliance Committee (2004–2011)*, (2nd edn, RACSE, Lviv 2011).

[25] See United Nations Economic Commission for Europe, *The Aarhus Convention: An Implementation Guide* (2nd edn, United Nations 2014). The original edition was published in 2000, prior to the entry into force of the Convention. The updated edition takes into account the considerable experience with the Convention since.

[26] Protocol on Pollutant Release and Transfer Registers to the Convention on Access to Information, Public Participation in Decision-Making and Access to Justice in Environmental Matters (Kiev, 21 May 2003), unreported, in force 8 October 2009.

ratified by none of them. It is, however, in force for one western Asian state (Israel). The preparation of the Protocol was the responsibility of the MOP.

The main institutions under the Protocol are the MOP,[27] Bureau,[28] WG,[29] and CC.[30] These bodies are specific to the Protocol although meetings of the Convention and Protocol MOPs are arranged at the same time. The role of the MOP, as the governing body of the Protocol, is to take the measures required to achieve its purposes, as well as to review implementation by the Parties. The Bureau consists of seven members, elected at each MOP session to serve a term up until the following MOP session.[31] The role of Secretariat is performed by the Executive Secretary of the UNECE. The WG of the Parties meets on a regular basis and oversees the implementation of the work programme for the Protocol between MOP sessions. The CC comprises nine representatives selected from Signatories or Parties, who meet at least once a year to review progress in implementation and compliance. In practice, as a result of a heavy workload, it has met four times each year. It has recently established a close relationship with other NCPs operating across the UNECE treaties and protocols, which adds to the combined effect of the agreements.[32]

The chapter will first provide some historical background to the legal development of the Convention and Protocol, before outlining the general procedural provisions of both. In relation to practice, specific questions of legal implementation and compliance of each instrument will then be analysed, particularly in the western Asian context (the Caucasus).

---

27 The second session of the Protocol MOP was held at the same time as the Convention MOP, from June–July 2014.

28 See Meeting of the Parties, Report on the Fifth meeting of the Bureau of the Meeting of the Parties to the Protocol on Pollutant Release and Transfer Registers, Madrid, 2–3 July 2013.

29 The third meeting of the WG of the Parties to the PRTR Protocol was held from 20–21 November 2013 in Geneva.

30 The first meeting of the CC was held from 27–28 January 2011 in Geneva.

31 Established under Rule 22 of the Rules of Procedure of the Meeting of the Parties to the PRTR Protocol, ECE/MP.PRTR/2010 (Annex). The Bureau has met on seven occasions to date.

32 Economic Commission for Europe/Environment, Informal Network of the Chairs of compliance/implementation bodies under the Multilateral Environmental Agreements, First Meeting, Geneva, 25 March 2013, Note prepared by the Chair of the Aarhus Convention Compliance Committee with the assistance of the secretariat.

Prospective membership and application in other parts of Asia and globally will also be considered based on experience to date, and conclusions will follow at the end. As with the other chapters on the five agreements, examples of practical implementation in central Asia are examined in Chapter 8.

II. HISTORICAL BACKGROUND AND LEGAL DEVELOPMENT

II.1 Convention

Public participation drove the development of EIA in the USA, where greater involvement in political decisions was demanded by the environment movement in the 1960s and 1970s, and which was a strong contributor to the development of the National Environmental Policy Act in 1969.[33] Demands for public participation were motivated by redefinitions of the concept of democracy, widespread education, greater access to information through the expansion of the media, and the growth of bureaucracy. International and European developments took the concept further in the 1980s and 1990s, with Principle 10 of the *Rio Declaration* 1992,[34] and the *Fifth Environmental Action Plan (1993–2000): Towards Sustainability*,[35] for example, recognising the importance of information, participation and justice and their links with sustainable development.

In 1991 the Environment for Europe Process was begun in Dobris, which eventually led to the Convention.[36] The Process was established with the objective of agreeing on ways to improve the environment at the pan-European level. The second meeting in Lucerne in 1993 resulted in the *Lucerne Declaration* which called for proposals by the UNECE for legal, regulatory and administrative mechanisms to encourage public participation. The third Ministerial Conference in Sofia in 1995 endorsed *Guidelines on Public Participation in Environmental Decision Making*.[37]

33 National Environmental Policy Act 1969 (NEPA) [42 U.S.C. 4321 et seq].

34 *United Nations Declaration on Environment and Development,* Rio de Janeiro, 1992. UN Doc A/CONF.151/5/Rev.1 (1992).

35 European Commission, *Fifth Environmental Action Plan (1993–2000): Towards Sustainability.*

36 David Stanners and Philippe Bordeau (eds), *Europe's Environment: The Dobris Assessment* (European Environment Agency 1995).

37 United Nations Economic Commission for Europe, *Guidelines on Public Participation in Environmental Decision Making* (UNECE 1996).

The negotiation process for these *Sofia Guidelines* lasted several years. From 1996 to 1998, there were ten meetings at which NGOs were involved from the start until the finish, when the final text was ready for signature. At the fourth conference, in Aarhus, the Convention was finally adopted by 36 countries and the European Community (EC).[38]

The tenth session of the working group in 1998 responsible for the draft included seven Asian states: Armenia, Azerbaijan, Kazakhstan, Kyrgyzstan, Russia, Turkey and Uzbekistan. Georgia, Israel, Tajikistan and Turkmenistan – the other Asian members of the UNECE – were not present.[39] Various changes to the draft convention were made by both Russia and Turkey, yet despite this neither of these two UNECE members has adopted the *Public Participation Convention* or has ratified it since.[40] Of particular note in the tenth final session was the position of the Environmental NGO Coalition, who advocated strongly for a compliance provision of equivalence to that found in international human rights regimes. The report comments as follows:

> The Environmental NGOs Coalition expressed the view that this convention linked international human rights law and environmental law, and that it was therefore regrettable that the convention should have a provision on compliance which fell short of minimal international human rights standards established over more than 20 years. It gave all delegates a copy of a background paper prepared on its behalf and pointed out that the three rights guaranteed in the draft convention had equivalents in at least six international human rights instruments, which all, or at least virtually all, of the Governments present had ratified, in addition to the European Convention on Human Rights and its right of individual redress, which had been similarly ratified. It deplored the dilution of earlier proposals and the resulting text, which the United Kingdom described as the weakest compliance provision of any international environmental law instrument.

The relationship between the *Public Participation Convention* and international human rights treaties is an area worthy of further exploration,[41] with the Strategic Plan for 2015–2020 including an objective for the achievement of synergies between the Convention and other international

---

[38] For more detail, see *Implementation Guide* 1–4, 9 and 85.

[39] Committee on Environmental Policy, Working Group for the preparation of a draft convention on access to environmental information and public participation in environmental decision-making, Report of the tenth session, CEP/AC.3/20, 19 March 1998.

[40] See above n. 14 however, in respect of Russia.

[41] See Alan Boyle, 'Human Rights or Environmental Rights – A Reassessment' (2006–2007) 8 *Fordham Environmental Law Review* 471, and p. 10 of the

environmental and human rights agreements.[42] This is also important given the recent focus of the CC on monitoring the follow-up of its decisions.[43] The range of remedies available to the CC for recommendation to the MOP are an area for future consideration if the conclusion reached is that they are not adequate, or indeed there are other failures in procedure which could be strengthened by amendment. There is of course also some irony in the fact that the United Kingdom has generated some 30 communications from members of its own public to the CC – not far short of a third of the current total – which indicates that it has perhaps benefited the most from any weaknesses in the provision to which it draws attention.[44]

II.2 Protocol

The origins of the Protocol lie in a recommendation made by the Signatories to the Convention, at their first meeting in 1999, to establish a task force on PRTRs. A formal commitment was made to develop a *PRTR Protocol* in the *Lucca Declaration*, adopted at the first MOP to the Convention in October 2002.[45] The legal basis for this commitment was contained in Article 5(9) of the *Public Participation Convention*. Shortly after the decision was taken, the WG on PRTR convened for the first time to begin drafting the Protocol. The open-ended, ad hoc WG on PRTR replaced an earlier body of the same name, which had been established by the CEP and had already begun working towards the same goal.[46]

---

following updated paper; note also 26–29 which discusses transboundary application of human rights treaties, including under the *Public Participation Convention*, accessed 14 November 2014 at: http://www.unep.org/environmentalgovernance/Portals/8/documents/Events/HumanRightsEnvironmentRev.pdf.

[42] Above n. 13, Objective II.6.

[43] Meeting of the Parties Fifth session, Maastricht, the Netherlands, 30 June and 1 July 2014. Item 5(b) of the provisional agenda, Procedures and mechanisms facilitating the implementation of the Convention: compliance mechanism, Report of the Compliance Committee, ECE/MP.PP/2014/9 (paras 18–24), 23 April 2014.

[44] See Banner, above n. 8 for discussion of these cases.

[45] Report of the First Meeting of the Parties to the Aarhus Convention, Addendum – Lucca Declaration, ECE/MP.PP/2/Add.1 (Section IV, para 24), 21–23 October 2002.

[46] The first WG, established by the Committee on Environmental Policy, was itself a replacement for the original task force on PRTR formed by the Signatories to the *Public Participation Convention*.

The first session of the WG, in November 2002, made good progress on the draft Protocol, but various substantive issues remained unresolved. Sub-groups were formed to work, in parallel with the WG, on technical, scientific and legal issues relating to the draft Protocol over the following few months. In line with the objectives of the Convention, the negotiating process for the Protocol is said to have been 'enriched by the active involvement of representatives of environmental citizens' organizations and industry'.[47] The second and final meeting of the WG took place in January 2003, at which all outstanding substantive issues were resolved. The Protocol was then adopted at an extraordinary MOP to the Convention in May 2003, held to coincide with the fifth 'Environment for Europe' Ministerial Conference.[48]

At the extraordinary MOP, the Chair highlighted some of the most significant features of the Protocol. Among these was the openness of its membership to all states, which was based on the perceived need to share public information on pollutants as widely as possible. According to the Chair, another important feature of the new Protocol was its 'implicit recognition of the need to adapt to the present situation while ensuring enough flexibility for further evolution'. In addition, the cohesion of the Protocol with the *Hazardous Wastes Convention* would 'contribute to the improvement of international environmental governance'.[49]

Simultaneously with the adoption of the Protocol on 21 May 2003, a resolution by the signatories to the *PRTR Protocol* and a mandate for further work on PRTRs were approved by the Convention MOP. The Resolution provided that a new WG on PRTRs be established as a subsidiary body to the MOP, to prepare for the entry into force of the Protocol. The functions of the WG were to identify the necessary steps to be taken, prepare guidance documents, share information, and periodically report on progress to the MOP to the Convention.[50] The WG held five meetings between 2003–2008, ceasing to operate when the first MOP to the Protocol took place in April 2010 and new subsidiary bodies were formally appointed.

In 2005, at the second meeting of the WG, it was noted that proposed regulatory measures by the EC to establish a Europe-wide PRTR system

---

[47] Report of the First Extraordinary Meeting of the Parties, ECE/MP.PP/4, 3 (per Mr Blaha), 21 May 2003.

[48] Ibid.

[49] Above n. 47, 2 (per Mr Gauer). For details on the *Hazardous Wastes Convention*, see Chapter 2.

[50] Resolution of the Signatories to the Protocol on Pollutant Release and Transfer Registers, ECE/MP.PP/2003/1/Add.1/Rev.1, 21 August 2003.

could accelerate the ratification process of the *PRTR Protocol*.[51] At this meeting, support was also given to the concept of adopting separate rules of procedure and a separate compliance mechanism, using those under the Convention as a starting point. At subsequent meetings in 2006 and 2007, the WG also discussed capacity-building activities and proposals for subsidiary bodies, financial arrangements and a reporting mechanism.[52] A key guidance document on implementation of the Protocol was adopted,[53] and draft decisions to establish a WG of the Parties were considered, together with a proposed work programme under the Protocol.[54] At the sixth (and final) meeting of the WG, in 2008, all of the issues considered at previous meetings were discussed and finalised further, with a view to the first MOP to the Protocol in due course.

The third MOP to the Convention, held in June 2008, adopted a statement urging signatories that had not yet ratified or implemented the Protocol, and other states intending to accede to it, to do so as soon as possible.[55] The MOP acknowledged the need for technical assistance to be given to some countries, particularly in the Caucasus and central Asian subregions, to overcome difficulties in implementing the Protocol.[56] Efforts to sustain the momentum towards a prompt entry into force of the Protocol, such as through high-level meetings and declarations, were endorsed by the third MOP.

In 2008, the Protocol Bureau was mandated by the WG on PRTRs to prepare a declaration for adoption by the MOP to the Protocol.[57] The *Geneva Declaration*, as it became called, affirmed the need for Parties to ensure full implementation of the Protocol and called on Signatories to

---

[51] Report of the Second Meeting of the Working Group on PRTRs, ECE/MP.PP/AC.1/2005/2, 13–15 April 2005.

[52] These were the third meeting (17–19 May 2006) and the fourth meeting (14–16 February 2007), respectively.

[53] United Nations, *Guidance to Implementation of the Protocol on Pollutant Release and Transfer Registers* (2007); adopted at the Fifth Meeting of the Working Group on PRTRs, ECE/MP.PP/AC.1/2007/4, 22–24 October 2007.

[54] Report of Fifth Meeting of the Working Group on PRTRs, ECE/MP.PP/AC.1/2007/4, 22–24 October 2007.

[55] Report of the Third Meeting of the Parties – Addendum: Statement on Pollutant Release and Transfer Registers, ECE/MP.PP/2008/2/Add.2, 11–13 June 2008.

[56] Ibid, 22.

[57] Report of the Sixth Meeting of the Working Group on PRTRs, ECE/MP.PP/AC.1/2008/2, 6, 24–26 November 2008.

ratify the instrument at the earliest opportunity.[58] It also invited all other interested states to accede to the Protocol and participate actively in its work, to ensure that 'the standards contained in the Protocol are recognized and applied by as many states as possible and widely reflected in effective rules and regulations at the national level'.[59] It was ultimately adopted at the first MOP to the Protocol, in April 2010. Since then, a further eight states have become Parties.[60]

By July 2009, the Protocol had attained sufficient ratifications to enter into force, which occurred in October the same year. The following year, at the first MOP to the *PRTR Protocol*, several key decisions were made. The CC and the WG of the Parties were established, with new members also being elected for both of those bodies and the Bureau.[61] A formal process for the review of compliance matters was adopted.[62] Rules of procedure for MOP sessions, financial arrangements for Protocol-related activities, implementation reporting requirements, and a work programme for the period 2011–2014 were also adopted.[63]

III. OBJECTIVES AND GENERAL PROCEDURAL PROVISIONS

III.1 Convention

As indicated by its title, the Convention is concerned above all with three pillars: access to information, public participation in decision making and access to justice in environmental matters. It gives special attention to genetically modified organisms (GMOs), which has links with the

---

[58] Report of the First session of the Meeting of the Parties to the Protocol on Pollutant Release and Transfer Registers – Addendum: Declaration and Decisions adopted by the Meeting of the Parties, ECE/MP.PRTR/2010/2/Add.1, 20–22 April 2010.

[59] Ibid, Section I, para. 4.

[60] Namely, Cyprus, Ireland, Israel, Poland, Moldova, Serbia, Slovenia, and FYR Macedonia.

[61] Decision I/2, Annex on the Structure and Functions of the Compliance Committee and Procedures for the Review of Compliance, and Decision I/4, Annex on the Establishment of the Working Group of the Parties to the Protocol.

[62] Ibid, Decision I/2.

[63] Decision I/1, Rules of Procedure; Decision I/3, Financial Arrangements; Decision I/5, Reporting on Implementation of the Protocol; and Decision I/6, Annex I – Work Programme for 2011–2014.

Cartagena Protocol on Biosafety.[64] GMOs are subject to an amendment to the Convention, which is awaiting sufficient ratifications before entry into force.[65] This will amend Article 6(11) and introduce a new Article 6(bis) providing for public participation on decisions on the deliberate release into the environment and placing on the market of GMOs. The lengthy preamble is made up of some 23 paragraphs recognising earlier legal and policy developments relating to environmental protection and the procedural rights enshrined in the Convention.[66] As noted, the UNECE has prepared an *Implementation Guide* on the Convention which is an authoritative manual to its implementation and compliance. It has recently been updated as a second edition and will be referred to extensively in the text that follows.

Article 1 indicates that the objective of the Convention is to guarantee procedural rights in order to contribute to protection of the right of current and future generations to live in an environment adequate for health and well-being.[67] Article 2 contains the definition section, with terms such as 'Party', 'public authority', 'environmental information', 'the public' and 'the public concerned' set out.[68] The *Implementation Guide* also helpfully considers terms not defined in the Convention, which include 'within the framework of its national legislation', which may permit flexibility in implementation.[69] In regard to Article 2(5) which includes NGOs within the category of the interested public so long as they meet 'any requirements under national law', this does not allow unlimited discretion to the state Party, and the CC has emphasised that NGOs 'generally have greater ability to effectively exercise their rights under the Convention than individual members of the public'.[70]

---

[64] *Implementation Guide*, 25. The *Cartagena Protocol* was briefly considered in Chapter 2. See also Meeting of the Parties, Fourth session Chisinau, 29 June–1 July 2011, Report of the Fourth session of the Meeting of the Parties, ECE/MP.PP/2011/2, 19 August 2011, para. 38, which notes that all Parties to the *Public Participation Convention* at that time were also Parties to the *Cartagena Protocol*, providing 'a unique opportunity for joint implementation'.

[65] See Report of the Second Meeting of the Parties, Addendum Decision II/1 Genetically Modified Organisms, adopted at the second meeting of the Parties held in Almaty, Kazakhstan, on 25–27 May 2005, ECE/MP.PP/2005/2/Add.2, 20 June 2005. The number of Parties to the amendment was 28 in July 2014.

[66] *Implementation Guide*, 11–29.

[67] *Implementation Guide*, 30–32.

[68] *Implementation Guide*, 32–49.

[69] *Implementation Guide*, 33–34.

[70] *Implementation Guide*, 48, 58 (Turkmenistan).

Article 3 contains general provisions which apply to the Convention as a whole. Of particular importance is the need for a 'clear, transparent and consistent framework to implement the Convention' (Article 3(1)). The CC has found that this requirement has often been breached by Parties at the same time as other obligations, that it includes the need to produce domestic law despite under the monist legal systems of some Parties this not being a constitutional requirement, and the independence of the judiciary being no excuse for not having domestic implementing law.[71] An effective means of increasing understanding of public authority obligations under Article 3(1) has been found to be the establishment of inter-agency coordination mechanisms, including multi-stakeholder participation.[72] In contrast, a specific example of non-compliance with Article 3(1) was the failure to establish legislation on public associations which did not limit the participation rights of environmental NGOs.[73]

Other requirements are for public authorities to assist and guide the public (Article 3(2)), that environmental education and awareness be promoted (Article 3(3)),[74] that environmental NGOs should be supported and recognised (Article 3(4)), that Parties have the right to introduce more stringent measures (Article 3(5)) and should not derogate from existing rights (Article 3(6)), and that the Convention should be promoted in the international arena (Article 3(7)).[75] Anti-harassment and anti-discrimination provisions are also an important part of the Convention scheme (Articles 3(8) and 3(9)).

Article 3(7) is a significant broad-ranging obligation to promote the application of the principles of the Convention in international decision-making processes and within the framework of international organisations where relating to the environment, including UNEP, or in the key decision-making bodies of other treaties, such as the MOP. Following a preliminary study prepared by the WG of the Parties, it was found that

---

[71] *Implementation Guide*, 51–52.

[72] *Implementation Guide*, 53 (Armenia).

[73] *Implementation Guide*, 51 (Turkmenistan).

[74] Note the establishment of 'Aarhus Centres' in a number of countries in the Caucasus and central Asia, which have become important tools for promoting environmental education and venues to discuss topical issues. See *Implementation Guide*, 57.

[75] At its second session the MOP adopted the *Almaty Guidelines on Promoting the Application of the Principles of the Aarhus Convention in International Forums*. See *Implementation Guide*, 61–63, which notes that the negotiation of the *Protocol on Water and Health* to the *Water Convention* was an example of the principles of the *Public Participation Convention* being applied in this way.

there was a need for improved access to fair and transparent proceedings, allowing the public to review access to information and for public participation and the review of the rules of international organisations in this regard. An ad hoc working group was subsequently established, and in May 2005 the resulting *Almaty Guidelines* on the issue were due to be discussed at the MOP.[76]

Most recently, the fifth session of the MOP adopted Decision V/4 on promoting the application of the principles of the Convention in international forums.[77] This reaffirmed the commitment to continue to apply the *Almaty Guidelines* (contained in Decision II/4) within the activities and subsidiary bodies under the Convention.[78] The Parties also decided to continue to promote the application of the principles of the Convention in international forums,[79] among other things requesting the WG to regularly convene a thematic session on promoting the principles of the Convention in international forums as an item on the agenda with a view to providing opportunities for Parties, Signatories and stakeholders to exchange experiences.[80]

Finally, Article 16 deals with settlement of disputes between Parties in relation to the interpretation or application of the Convention. Such disputes are very rare and as such, although they may follow the failure to avoid a dispute via a NCP, they are not a focus of this book. For completeness, however, Article 16 provides for resolution by negotiation or by any other means of dispute settlement acceptable to the Parties in dispute. If disputes are not to be resolved in this way Parties can declare in advance whether they accept compulsory dispute resolution via the ICJ or arbitration in accordance with the procedure set out in Annex II of the Convention. If both are accepted, the dispute will proceed to the ICJ unless the Parties stipulate otherwise. The *Implementation Guide*[81] explains the role of arbitration in relation to the dispute settlement

---

[76] Ibid, and see also Morgera, above n. 6, 145–6.

[77] Meeting of the Parties Fifth session, Maastricht, the Netherlands, 30 June and 1 July 2014. Item 6(b) of the provisional agenda Promotion of the Convention and relevant developments and interlinkages: promotion of the Convention's principles in international forums. This was adopted as Decision V/4, ECE/MP.PP/2014/CRP.2.

[78] Ibid, para. 3.

[79] Ibid, para. 4.

[80] Ibid, para. 6(a).

[81] *Implementation Guide*, 239.

provision in the Convention, which is almost identical to that found in the *EIA Convention*.[82]

a. Access to information

The first pillar of the Convention concerns access to information, provisions for which are located in Articles 4 and 5. The purpose of this pillar 'ensures that members of the public are able to know and understand what is happening in the environment around them. It also ensures that the public is able to participate in an informed manner'.[83] Article 4 outlines the general right to gain access to existing information, known as 'passive access', and Article 5 outlines governmental duties to collect and disseminate information on its own initiative, known as 'active access'. The *Implementation Guide* highlights other UNECE treaties discussed in this book with similar requirements, notably the *Industrial Accidents Convention* (Article 9(1)), *Water Convention* (Article 16), and *Protocol on Water and Health* (Article 10).[84] This is an example of the combined contribution of the agreements to environmental governance.

Article 4(1) therefore requires public authorities to make information available upon request,[85] Article 4(2) sets time limits for public authorities to respond and provide the information, Article 4(3) indicates optional grounds for refusing requests,[86] and Article 4(4), additional optional grounds where disclosure would adversely affect listed interests, which indicate how to interpret the exceptions, including reference to the *Sofia Guidelines*.[87] Article 4(5) obliges public authorities that do not hold the information requested to inform the applicant which authority does or

---

[82] Article 16 is limited to disputes between the Parties, so disputes with third parties, such as NGOs, are not covered. Parties remain free to enter into arbitration with third parties; it is just that the arbitration provision is not automatically applicable in such instances.

[83] *Implementation Guide*, 67.

[84] *Implementation Guide*, 68.

[85] There is no requirement for applicants to state the reasons for their requests, see *Implementation Guide*, 73–74 (Georgia and Kazakhstan).

[86] These include the confidentiality of public authority proceedings; international relations, national defence or public security; the course of justice, the ability of a person to receive a fair trial or an authority to conduct an inquiry of a criminal or disciplinary nature; the confidentiality of commercial and industrial information; intellectual property rights; personal data; third party interests; and the environment to which the information relates, such as breeding sites for rare species.

[87] *Implementation Guide*, 85.

transfer the request to that authority, and Article 4(6) requires information which is not exempt to be disclosed wherever possible. Finally, Article 4(7) outlines the procedure for refusing an information request and Article 4(8) sets boundaries for optional charges for information.

Article 5(1) obliges public authorities to collect, possess and disseminate various types of environmental information; Article 5(1)(c) for instance requires public authorities to inform the public of environmental emergencies, which is similar to the *Industrial Accidents Convention* requirement (Article 9). Article 5(2) requires information to be made available in a transparent way and to be effectively accessible. Article 5(3) requires each Party to ensure that environmental information progressively becomes available in electronic databases, which are easily accessible to the public through public telecommunications networks. Information in this form should include texts of legislation on or relating to the environment (Article 5(3)(b)), and, 'as appropriate', plans or programmes on or relating to the environment and environmental agreements (Article 5(3)(c)). The *Implementation Guide* comments on the latter that:

> In this case 'as appropriate' means that Parties have additional flexibility in determining which policies, plans and programmes would be most usefully accessible through electronic databases because of a public interest in assessing them. For example, this can be a useful tool for implementing article 7 on public participation in decisions concerning plans, programmes and policies. It is very important for the public and for public authorities to have easy access to existing plans, programmes and policies when commenting on proposals.[88]

Article 5(4) contains an obligation to produce national state of the environment reports, including information on the quality of the environment and the pressures upon it. Such reports must be published and disseminated at regular intervals. Article 5(5)(a) contains measures for the dissemination of legislation and policy documents, such as strategies, policies, programmes and action plans relating to the environment, and progress reports on their implementation, prepared at various levels of government. There are extensive information disclosure and reporting obligations contained in this section, as Parties must develop a legal system to disseminate legislation and policy documents that concern the environment.

---

88 *Implementation Guide*, 103–4.

This provision should be considered also in the context of Articles 7 and 8 (public participation in plans, programmes, policies, law-making and rule making) discussed below. Parties are required to actively disseminate the texts of strategies, policies, programmes and action plans relating to the environment. In addition to the texts of these law and policy documents, the Convention requires Parties to disseminate progress reports on their implementation. The term 'relating to the environment' is used here instead of 'environmental information'. 'Relating to the environment' arguably includes a broader range of information such as policies on transport, energy, agriculture or mining as these relate to the environment through their impacts or otherwise.

Article 5(6) obliges operators to regularly inform the public of the environmental impact of their activities. Article 5(7) requires Parties to publish information that will help the public, public authorities and other Parties understand the content of government decisions, monitor their implementation and make more effective contributions to decision making. Article 5(7)(a) requires publication of the facts and analyses of facts 'which it considers relevant and important' in framing major environmental policy proposals. Although there is discretion given to the state Party here, the *Implementation Guide* states that: 'Since article 7 provides for public participation during the preparation of policies ... the publication of facts and analyses of facts under article 5, paragraph 7(a), will help to ensure that the public has the relevant information it needs to make its participation in policymaking as effective as possible.'[89]

Finally, Article 5(8) requires the development of mechanisms to disseminate environment-related product information for consumers, Article 5(9) obliges the progressive establishment of a publicly accessible nationwide system of pollution registers, and Article 5(10) sets out optional exceptions from disclosure in Article 4(3) and (4). Article 5(9) is particularly significant, as since the adoption of the Convention the expression PRTR has become the standard term to describe such inventories. In 2003, as noted above and described below, the *PRTR Protocol* was adopted.[90]

At the fifth session of the MOP, the Parties adopted Decision V/1 on access to information.[91] This recognises the need to further the

[89] *Implementation Guide*, 109.

[90] *Implementation Guide*, 111–13.

[91] Meeting of the Parties Fifth session, Maastricht, the Netherlands, 30 June and 1 July 2014. Item 4(a) of the provisional agenda, Substantive issues: access to information, including electronic information tools Draft decision V/1 on access to information, ECE/MP.PP/2014/L.1 4 April 2014.

implementation of the first pillar (Articles 4 and 5) to provide effective public access to environmental information and actively disseminate it to the public, including through electronic information tools. It also underlined the importance of the Aarhus Clearinghouse for Environmental Democracy,[92] as an effective global mechanism to share knowledge and practices related to principle 10 of the *Rio Declaration*.

b. Public participation

The second pillar concerns public participation as related to specific activities (especially but not exclusively linked with EIA), plans and programmes, and policies and legislation. There is no express definition of public participation, although the preamble emphasises some of the values and considerations to be taken account of.[93] Provisions in other treaties, especially the related *EIA* and *Industrial Accidents Conventions*, and *SEA* and *Water and Health Protocols*, have also been inspired by the *Public Participation Convention* requirements. This is another example of the combined contribution of the agreements to environmental governance.

Specific activities are considered in Article 6;[94] policies, plans and programmes in Article 7;[95] and executive regulations and/or generally applicable legally binding normative instruments in Article 8, meaning environmental legislation. There is no definition of policies, plans or programmes in the Convention, but the *Implementation Guide* indicates that the meaning is likely to be the same as when considered under the other UNECE legal instruments, the *EIA Convention* and *SEA Protocol*.[96] It also indicates that the experience of the EIA MOP 'may be relevant in interpreting the meanings of "plans, programmes and policies"'.[97]

---

92 http://aarhusclearinghouse.unece.org/resources/?c=1000094, accessed 14 November 2014. Case summaries posted by the Task Force on Access to Justice and decisions of domestic courts can be located here; for Armenia these include the *Dolphynarium*, *Teghout Mine* and *Armenian Sewerage Company* cases for example.

93 *Implementation Guide*, 116.

94 In addition to *Implementation Guide*, note also the UNECE guidance on public participation, above n. 37.

95 Jerzy Jendrośka, 'Public Participation in the Preparation of Plans and Programs: Some Reflections on the Scope of Obligations under Article 7 of the Aarhus Convention' (2009) 6 *Journal for European Environmental and Planning Law* 495.

96 *Implementation Guide*, 113.

97 Ibid.

The *Implementation Guide* indicates at length that whether public participation during decision making on specific activities is required depends on whether the decision making itself may have a potentially significant impact on the environment, not on whether the procedure requires EIA. The Convention does not require EIA, but if either EIA or SEA are carried out the public participation provisions must be given effect to. It comments: 'Even if the Aarhus Convention does not establish an EIA regime per se, its article 6 does establish a kind of review of the environmental impacts of particular activities, where decision making in relation to them takes place.'[98] Identifying whether a decision relates to specific activities (Article 6) or plans or programmes (Article 7) must be considered in context and labels given by national authorities are not conclusive, as the CC has found.[99]

Article 6(1) requires public participation for permit decisions if proposed activities are listed in Annex I of the Convention.[100] These include decisions related to energy, waste management, industrial plants, and water resources. For activities which are not listed, public participation is required where activities are likely to have a significant effect on the environment.[101] Information to enable participation must be made available of the proposed activity, decisions, responsible authorities and procedures (including EIA and transboundary EIA) 'in an adequate, timely and effective manner' (Article 6(2)).[102] Reasonable timeframes must be established (Article 6(3)), when all options are open (Article 6(4)).

Permit applicants are encouraged to identify and engage the public concerned before permit applications (Article 6(5)). All information

---

[98] At 125. Note also the discussion on the relationship between the Convention and EIA and SEA, 117–19, 124–7, which includes consideration between western approaches to EIA which have been taken up by most of the globe, and the OVOS/expertise system in former Soviet states, as outlined in more detail in Chapter 8.

[99] *Implementation Guide*, 119–20.

[100] Although it is not defined in the *Public Participation Convention*, 'proposed activity' is defined in the *EIA Convention* (Article 1(v)); see *Implementation Guide*, 129. This is another example of the combined contribution of the agreements to environmental governance.

[101] For guidance on 'significance' Parties can also look to Appendix III of the *EIA Convention* for assistance; see *Implementation Guide*, 131.

[102] This obligation to inform the public concerned in a transboundary context must be considered in the light of the non-discrimination provision in Article 3(9); see Marsden, above n. 10. On transboundary EIA and the relationship with the *EIA Convention*, see *Implementation Guide*, 141–3.

relevant to the decision must be made available by responsible authorities, including physical descriptions and effects, and measures to prevent or reduce them (Article 6(6)). Procedures must allow for the public to comment (Article 6(7)), and Parties must ensure that due account is taken of public participation in the decision (Article 6(8)),[103] and the public is properly informed of it (Article 6(9)). Decisions on whether to permit the deliberate release of GMOs into the environment must ('if feasible and appropriate' under national law) also be subject to public participation (Article 6(11)).[104] As noted above, the Almaty (GMO) amendment was adopted by the MOP to insert a new Article 6(11),[105] so that the provision would not apply to decisions on whether to permit the deliberate release into the environment and placing on the market of GMOs.[106]

Article 7 concerns policies, plans and programmes; with policies as the highest order decisions treated differently to plans and programmes. The *Implementation Guide* notes that: 'While the Convention does not oblige Parties to undertake assessments, a legal basis for the consideration of the environmental aspects of plans, programmes and policies is a prerequisite for the application of article 7 … Proper public participation procedures in the context of SEA are a valuable tool to assist in the implementation of article 7.'[107] The *Implementation Guide* justifies this by indicating that since due account must be taken of the outcome of public participation there is an implication that there must be a legal basis to take environmental considerations into account in policies, plans and programmes.[108]

---

[103] The understanding of 'due account' is particularly important and has been considered by the Compliance Committee on a number of occasions. See for example, *Implementation Guide*, 158–60.

[104] This is discussed in detail in the *Implementation Guide*, 165–77.

[105] Meeting of the Parties, Report of the Second Meeting of the Parties, Addendum, Decision II/I Genetically Modified Organisms, adopted at the second Meeting of the Parties held in Almaty, Kazakhstan on 25–27 May 2005, ECE/MP.PP/2005/2/Add.2, 20 June 2005.

[106] This is subject to Article 3(5) so that the more extensive requirements of Article 6 can still be applied. See *Implementation Guide*, 167. Note that the *Almaty* amendment is to date the only one to be adopted by the MOP under Article 10(e). See *Implementation Guide*, 225.

[107] *Implementation Guide*, 180.

[108] During its sixth meeting in April 2006, the Working Group agreed to hold a workshop on public participation in strategic decision making, which would focus on participation in policies, plans and programmes and also laws with environmental impact (i.e. covering both Articles 7 and 8 of the Convention). The workshop was aimed at providing an opportunity for a broad exchange of

Furthermore, the obligations in Article 7 are capable of enforcement through the access to justice provisions in Article 9, provided states already have guarantees of such rights (in which case they cannot go back on them as a result of the principles in Article 3(5) and (6), or because they decide to adopt such guarantees).

Article 7 distinguishes between plans and programmes on one hand, and policies on the other; hence the more specific the decision, the greater the procedural guarantees that are available. Articles 6(3), (4) and (8) apply to plans and programmes, which set time-frames, require participation at an early stage in decision making, and ensure that due account is taken of the participation in the decision.[109] With respect to plans and programmes therefore, Article 7 states:

> Each party shall make appropriate practical and/or other provisions for the public to participate during the preparation of plans and programmes relating to the environment, within a transparent and fair framework, having provided the necessary information to the public. Within this framework, article 6, paragraphs 3, 4 and 8, shall be applied. The public which may participate shall be identified by the relevant public authority, taking into account the objectives of this Convention …

With respect to policies, there is no express incorporation of the provisions of Article 6, although a state is free to include those provisions in domestic law if it wishes. Although 'policies' are not defined in the Convention, this does not mean that Parties lack an understanding of what they mean or that preparation of policies should not also be subject to public input. Article 7 therefore suggests that 'to the extent appropriate' each Party 'shall endeavour' to provide opportunities for public participation in the preparation of policies relating to the environment.

In similar fashion, Article 8 in providing that the public shall be involved in the law making process, uses the wording that a state should 'promote', or use its best efforts to allow public input, establishing elements of participation procedures, (such as appropriate timeframes and publication of draft rules), and requiring Parties to ensure that participation is taken account of in decision making. The relationship between SEA and the strategic decision making on policies, plans and

---

views amongst experts involved with the *Public Participation* and *EIA Conventions* and the *SEA Protocol*.

[109] Clearly, certain paragraphs of Article 6 are not applicable to the implementation of Article 7. The *Implementation Guide* (117) discusses these and the reasons why they are not applicable in the case of policies, plans and programmes.

programmes is, like the relationship between EIA and specific, project-level, decision making, a close one, and the *SEA Protocol* is referenced in the *Implementation Guide* as a useful source in this respect.[110]

At the fifth session of the MOP, the Parties adopted Decision V/2 on public participation in decision making.[111] This notes that following the 2011 cycle of national implementation reports (NIRs), the findings of the CC and the work carried out by the Task Force on Public Participation in Decision-making have collectively shown that challenges remain to the full implementation of the second pillar of the Convention across the region. Because of this it decided to extend the mandate of the Task Force to carry out further work as inputted by that undertaken by Parties, Signatories and other stakeholders. This should identify the main obstacles to effective public participation in all types of decision making under Articles 6, 7 and 8, and to continue to exchange good practices to identify best practices in areas of high priority.[112]

c. Access to justice

Given the focus of this book on implementation and compliance, the access to justice provisions in the *Public Participation Convention*, are particularly inspirational and the CC, the procedures of which are considered in the next section, is kept extremely busy. The third pillar deals with three situations: where the right of access to environmental information is impaired (Article 9(1)), where the right to public participation is impaired (Article 9(2)), and access to justice where acts and omissions of public authorities or private persons are in breach of the law (Article 9(3)). As such the public can therefore defend the rights and interests under the first two pillars of the Convention, and these rights are independent of rights to administrative proceedings under domestic law.[113] The *Implementation Guide* comments further that:

---

[110] See Chapter 4 and note the *Implementation Guide*, 180–92. This is another example of the combined contribution of the agreements to environmental governance.

[111] Meeting of the Parties Fifth session, Maastricht, the Netherlands, 30 June and 1 July 2014. Item 4(b) of the provisional agenda, Substantive issues, public participation in decision-making, ECE/MP.PP/2014/CRP.1.

[112] These include decision making for sustainable development; climate-change related decision making; energy-related planning; and, if resources allow, decision making on the extractive sector, chemicals; emerging technologies (for example nanotechnology) and product-related decision making. Ibid, para. 11(f).

[113] *Implementation Guide*, 129, 193.

> Access to justice helps to create a level playing field for the public seeking to enforce these rights. It also helps to strengthen the Parties' implementation of, and compliance with, the Convention as well as the effective application of national laws relating to the environment. The public's ability to help enforce environmental law adds important resources to government efforts.[114]

The *Implementation Guide* could add that access to justice also helps strengthen the implementation of, and compliance with, the other four UNECE treaties and protocols that are the subject of this book. As will be seen, most have a NCP, and for Parties to these treaties that are also Party to the *Public Participation Convention*, there is a powerful incentive to ensure access to justice meets the Aarhus standard. The same is also true of Parties who are EU member states, as noted by this author and others following non-compliant jurisprudence by the European Court of Justice (ECJ), an organ of a Party to the *Public Participation Convention*, the EU.[115] In a similar manner, compliance with the third pillar by Asian state Parties to the Convention, is based on very high expectations, not dissimilar to the standards expected by the EU of potential member states, who must meet human rights norms prior to accession.[116]

Article 9 refers specifically to the provisions on access to information found in Article 4 and public participation in decisions on specific activities in Article 6. However, other decisions, acts and omissions related to the environment must be subject to review by the access to

---

114 *Implementation Guide*, 193.

115 Simon Marsden, 'Direct Public Access to EU Courts: Upholding Public International Law via the Aarhus Convention Compliance Committee' (2012) 81(2) *Nordic Journal of International Law* 175; Charles Poncelet, 'Access to Justice in Environmental Matters – Does the European Union Comply with its Obligations?' (2012) 24(2) *Journal of Environmental Law* 287.

116 Turkey is a good example here, which like Russia, is an Asian as well as a European state. Unlike Russia, however (which has no interest in joining the EU), potential membership of the EU is likely to continue to be a much more difficult prospect for Turkey than membership of the *Public Participation Convention*. In the case of the latter, as noted Russia has expressed a willingness to ratify this. As a member of the UNECE, Turkey currently participates as an observer in the MOP in relation to the Convention, but following events in 2013, the European Environment Bureau has called on Turkey to take the necessary steps to become a Party and ensure its prompt implementation. See EEB AGM, Resolution on Turkey and the Aarhus Convention, Brussels, 19–20 October 2013, available 14 November 2014 at http://www.eeb.org/EEB/?LinkServID=0221C9E1-5056-B741-DB4DA9F842D25CF4&showMeta=0. See also *Implementation Guide*, 194–5.

justice provisions which 'essentially apply to all matters of environmental law'.[117] However, different criteria apply and different degrees of flexibility are allowed to the Parties dependent on which category of decisions, acts and omissions is applicable. The first is refusals and inadequate handling of requests for information from authorities (Article 9(1)); the second is where decisions, acts and omissions concern permits, related procedures and decision making for specific activities (Article 9(2)); and the third, other acts and omissions that may have broken domestic law (Article 9(3)). Wide access to justice in all cases is however the norm.[118]

For the first two categories a review procedure before a court or court-like body established by law is required, and for the last category administrative or judicial procedures are possible. The distinction is that judicial/court procedures are typically independent of the administrative function of the state, the executive branch. For court procedures the question of standing is very important, with Article 9(2) referring to 'members of the public concerned' being entitled to use the review procedures, provided they have a 'sufficient interest',[119] or maintain the 'impairment of a right'.[120] While it is for Parties to decide further to domestic law whether these criteria are met, 'wide access to justice' is required in all cases.

Article 9(2) also provides that Parties may establish preliminary review procedures as noted. These are not intended to replace the judicature, but where these procedures are in place (and they potentially provide for a 'timely' resolution of the issues), they must be utilised first before litigation commences; in both cases decisions based on either procedural or substantive grounds are capable of challenge.[121] In all circumstances procedures must be 'fair, equitable, timely and not prohibitively expensive' (Article 9(4));[122] they must provide 'adequate and effective remedies' including injunctive relief (Article 9(4));[123] decisions must be

117 *Implementation Guide*, 193.

118 *Implementation Guide*, 193–4.

119 This is the case for NGOs if they meet the requirements of Article 2(5). See *Implementation Guide*, 203–4.

120 *Implementation Guide*, 199–200 (Kazakhstan), 202, 207, 209, and see the references in n. 115 above for the restrictive standing position of the ECJ.

121 *Implementation Guide*, 205.

122 *Implementation Guide*, 212–16.

123 *Implementation Guide*, 209–12.

recorded in writing and publicly accessible (Article 9(4));[124] and information on the procedures must be disseminated to the public and assistance to remove financial and other barriers provided (Article 9(5)).[125]

At the fifth session, the MOP adopted Decision V/3 on promoting effective access to justice.[126] This decided to extend in time the mandate of the Task Force on Access to Justice, under the authority of the WG of the Parties to the Convention, to carry out further work in relation to the implementation of the Convention, taking into consideration the relevant activities being undertaken by Parties, Signatories and other stakeholders in order to do various things. These include promoting the exchange of information, experiences, challenges and good practices relating to implementation, on such issues as costs, remedies, scope of review, timeliness, protection against persecution and harassment. They also included identifying priority needs with respect to public access to justice, taking stock of capacity-building initiatives taking place in the region and beyond, and promoting the involvement of associations of judges, public interest lawyers and other legal professionals in these initiatives. Finally, they included preparing analytical, guidance and training materials to support this work, and promoting an understanding and the use of relevant findings of the CC of a systemic nature.[127]

III.2 Protocol

The main objective in Article 1 is to enhance public access to information through the establishment of coherent, integrated, nationwide pollutant release and transfer registers. The broader aims of creating such registers as indicated in the Preamble are to help prevent and reduce pollution, facilitate public participation in environmental decision making, increase corporate accountability and promote sustainable development.[128] The Preamble puts specific emphasis on:

---

[124] *Implementation Guide*, 216.

[125] *Implementation Guide*, 216–18.

[126] Meeting of the Parties, Fifth session Maastricht, the Netherlands, 30 June and 1 July 2014. Item 4(c) of the provisional agenda, Substantive issues access to justice, ECE/MP.PP/2014/L.3 7 April 2014.

[127] Ibid, para. 13.

[128] These objectives were identified in the *Lucca Declaration*, adopted at the First MOP to the Convention, ECE/MP.PP/2/Add.1, 21–23 October 2002.

> … the value of pollutant release and transfer registers as a cost-effective tool for encouraging improvements in environmental performance, for providing public access to information on pollutants released into and transferred in and through communities, and for use by Governments in tracking trends, demonstrating progress in pollution reduction, monitoring compliance with certain international agreements, setting priorities and evaluating progress achieved through environmental policies and programmes.

The potential applications of the information obtained through the PRTR process are manifold, as acknowledged. The Preamble notes that there are 'opportunities for using data from pollutant release and transfer registers, combined with health, environmental, demographic, economic or other types of relevant information, for the purpose of gaining a better understanding of potential problems, identifying "hot spots", taking preventive and mitigating measures, and setting environmental management priorities'.

General provisions in Article 3 include a requirement that each Party take the necessary legislative, regulatory and other measures to implement and enforce provisions under the Protocol;[129] that each Party take the necessary measures to require that individuals[130] who report a violation of relevant national law by a facility to public authorities, are not punished for doing so; that each Party shall be guided by the precautionary approach when implementing provisions; that PRTR systems be integrated with existing information sources wherever practicable, to avoid duplication of reporting; and that Parties aim to achieve convergence among national PRTRs.

The key elements of a national PRTR set out in Article 4, are that it is publicly accessible, coherent and user-friendly; is facility-specific with respect to reporting on point sources; allows for reporting on diffuse sources (for example, transport and agriculture); is pollutant-specific or waste-specific (as appropriate); distinguishes between releases to land, water and air; includes information on transfers; is based on mandatory, periodic reporting; includes standardised and timely data, with only limited provision (if any) for confidentiality; allows for public input into its development and modification; and comprises a structured, computerised database (or several linked databases) maintained by the competent authority. Parties should also provide links in their registers to other

---

[129] A Party is not prevented from maintaining or introducing a more extensive or publicly accessible PRTR than is required by the Protocol as set out in Article 3(2).

[130] For instance employees of the facility and members of the public.

publicly accessible databases relating to environmental protection, as well as to PRTRs in other countries, wherever feasible (Articles 5(5) and 5(6)).

Articles 6(1) and 7(2) require that a national PRTR must include information on all releases and transfers involving certain pollutants stipulated by the Protocol. There are currently 86 listed in Annex II, ranging from greenhouse gases, acid rain pollutants, ozone-depleting substances and heavy metals, to certain carcinogens, such as dioxins. A 'pollutant' is defined in Article 2(6) as a substance or a group of substances that may be harmful to the environment or to human health on account of its properties and of its introduction into the environment. A 'release' is defined in Article 2(7) as any introduction of pollutants into the environment as a result of any human activity, whether deliberate or accidental, routine or non-routine, including spilling, emitting, discharging, injecting, disposing or dumping, or through sewer systems without final waste-water treatment.

A national PRTR must also cover releases and transfers from certain types of major point sources (listed in Annex I), such as oil and gas refineries, thermal power stations, mining and metallurgical industries, chemical plants, waste and waste-water treatment plants, timber processing industries, intensive livestock production and other specified activities. Article 5(1) provides that each PRTR database should be searchable by reference to a facility and its geographical location; an activity; an owner, operator or company; a type of pollutant or waste; each of the environmental media into which a pollutant is released; the destination of a transfer; and the disposal or recovery operation for waste.

Under Article 7(1) and 7(2), each Party is required to impose reporting requirements on the owners or operators of two broad types of facility: those that undertake one or more Annex I activities above a certain threshold, and release or transfer off-site an Annex II pollutant, hazardous waste or other waste above specified quantities; and those that undertake an Annex I activity and manufacture, process or use any Annex II pollutants above specified quantities. Owners and operators must submit information regarding the pollutant(s) or waste(s) involved to the competent authority for inclusion in the national register.

Finally, the Protocol contains the same standard procedure for dispute settlements as most other MEAs. Under Article 23(1) any dispute between Parties regarding the interpretation or application of the Protocol should be resolved either through negotiation or any other peaceful method acceptable to the Parties. Where the matter is not resolved through the negotiation process, Article 23(2) requires that it be referred to either the ICJ or an arbitration procedure, if the Parties involved have formally accepted one or both of those methods of dispute settlement. Dispute settlement mechanisms such as this are very rarely used, as the emphasis of environmental agreements is primarily on avoiding disputes through the application of their compliance mechanisms.[131]

IV. PRACTICE

IV.1 Convention

a. Implementation

Article 10(2) contains the requirement for the reporting procedure, which like most of the other treaties is based on NIRs submitted by the Parties, and potentially others. Article 10(2)(a) also requires a review of policies for, and legal and methodological approaches to, the three pillars with a view to further improving them. At the first session in 2002, the MOP adopted Decision I/8 outlining the main reporting process.[132] There have been three reporting cycles completed since then, in 2005, 2008 and 2011. At its fourth session in Chisinau in 2011 where the reports from the third cycle were considered, the MOP adopted Decision IV/4 which endorsed the reporting format applicable in the current (2014) reporting cycle.[133]

Key features of the reporting regime identified based on the 2011 reports are that: all reports should be prepared via a transparent and consultative process involving the public, that Parties follow methodology for preparing and submitting them in guidance on reporting prepared by the CC,[134] that signatories and other non Parties submit reports, that a

---

[131] G Ulfstein, T Marauhn and A Zimmermann (eds), *Making Treaties Work: Human Rights, Environment and Arms Control* (Cambridge University Press, Cambridge 2007) 189.

[132] Meeting of the Parties, First session, Report of the first session of the Meeting of the Parties, Addendum, Decision I/8, Reporting Requirements, adopted at the first Meeting of the Parties held in Lucca, Italy on 21–22 October 2002, ECE/MP.PP/2/Add.9, 2 April 2004. See also Decision I/7, Review of Compliance, adopted at the same MOP and contained in the same document, which established the CC.

[133] Meeting of the Parties, Fourth session Chisinau 29 June–1 July 2011, Report of the fourth session of the Meeting of the Parties, Addendum, Chisinau Declaration and decisions adopted by the Meeting of the Parties, IV/4 Reporting requirements, ECE/MP.PP/2011/2/Add.1.

[134] Meeting of the Parties, Working Group of the Parties to the Convention Seventh meeting Geneva, 2–4 May 2007 Item 9 of the provisional agenda

synthesis report for each session of the MOP should summarise progress and identify significant trends, and that other organisations (including NGOs) providing support to Parties and/or other states in the implementation provide reports on their programmes or activities and lessons learned.[135]

As a general example of application in an Asian state, the 2014 NIR for Georgia, a Eurasian state in the Caucasus, is instructive.[136] This report built on previous NIRs and was prepared in collaboration with a range of government departments, published on a government website and incorporated public feedback prior to a public hearing. In common with other states in the Caucasus and central Asia (see Chapter 8), Georgia notes that the Convention applies directly without the need for domestic implementing law, although effective implementation requires revision of municipal law.[137] Georgia cites provisions in a range of specific domestic statutes as evidence of compliance with various provisions in the Convention; these include the *Law of Georgia on the Protection of Environment.*[138] It notes throughout the report, in response to 'obstacles encountered in the implementation of section x', matters yet to be dealt with to ensure full compliance with the Convention. In Chapter 8, more detailed examples of responses are outlined in relation to Kazakhstan and Tajikistan.

Experience with the previous reporting mechanism was recently commented on by the Secretariat.[139] This found that overall experience was positive, with valuable information provided and positive developments in law and practice highlighted. It however identified difficulties in implementation, with some reports being late. Practical challenges were also indicated, the main one being involving the public from the start, suggesting two public consultations be held during the process. The first should be a scoping exercise on the possible content, and the second for comments to be incorporated into the draft. Practical information on

---

Reporting requirements, Guidance on Reporting Requirements prepared by the Compliance Committee, ECE/MP.PP/WG.1/2007/L.4, 20 February 2007.

[135] http://www.unece.org/env/pp/guidelines_nir_2014.html, accessed 14 November 2014.

[136] Ministry of Environment and Natural Resources Protection of Georgia, *Implementation Report*, 7 December 2013.

[137] Ibid, 3.

[138] Ibid, 6.

[139] Aarhus Convention Secretariat, *The Aarhus Convention Reporting Mechanism National Implementation Reports: Experiences and Lessons Learned*, Geneva, 19 June 2013.

implementation and practice was also lacking in many reports, and some failed to follow the required format and answer the questions.

It also emphasised that compliance with the fourth MOP recommendations on issues arising from compliance matters, considered by the CC,[140] needed to be included in NIRs for the 2014 MOP. It reminded Parties of Decision I/7, para 13(c) on Review of Compliance,[141] that a function of the CC is to 'monitor, assess and facilitate the implementation of and compliance with the reporting requirements under article 10, paragraph 2, of the Convention'. The reporting deadline for the sixth session of the MOP in 2014 closed in December 2013, with detailed requirements and timeframes outlined.

At the fifth session of the MOP Decision V/8 on reporting requirements was adopted.[142] Further to considering reports from the Parties, the CC, the secretariat, NGOs and other matters, the MOP noted that NIRs had been submitted by more than three-quarters of the Parties, considering 'that these reports provide a valuable overview of the status of implementation of the Convention, as well as help to identify significant trends in and challenges to implementation, which will help to guide future activities'.[143] Some states, however, including Turkmenistan, failed to provide reports. At the fifth session the CC also noted the inadequacies of state Parties reporting obligations, and recommended the MOP to 'underline the importance of complying with the reporting requirements and to initiate the process for the national implementation reports well in advance of the upcoming session of the MOP …'.[144]

b. Compliance

Article 15 is concerned with the review of compliance, which is to be 'non-confrontational, non-judicial and consultative'. This provision is of notable interest in examining implementation and compliance with the Convention to date.[145] A detailed guidance document indicates the composition, election and functions of the CC and its modus operandi. It provides helpful assistance to NGOs, the public generally and the Party

---

140 Ibid.

141 See above n. 132.

142 Meeting of the Parties, Fifth session Maastricht, the Netherlands, 30 June and 1 July 2014. Item 5(a) of the provisional agenda, Procedure and mechanisms facilitating the implementation of the Convention: reports on the status of implementation of the Convention, ECE/MP.PP/2014/L.8 4 April 2014.

143 Ibid, para. 4.

144 Above n. 43, para. 101.

145 *Implementation Guide*, 234.

concerned.[146] The CC has a developing quasi-jurisprudence, sometimes referred to as 'case law'.[147] An electronic database furthermore contains decisions of national and regional courts and those of the CC itself to assist its work, and for those wishing to access its procedures.[148] Some are referred to in the commentary that follows.

The work of the CC can be triggered in four ways: a Party may make a submission about compliance by another Party; a Party may make a submission concerning its own compliance; the secretariat may make a referral to the CC; and, of greatest significance, members of the public may make communications concerning a Party's compliance with the Convention. The CC cannot issue binding decisions, but can make recommendations to the MOP, and in some cases, directly to the Parties. It is for the MOP to decide what action to take, including issuing declarations of non-compliance, cautions or suspensions of special rights and privileges to Parties.[149] Additionally, the CC can examine compliance issues itself and make recommendations; prepare reports on implementation or compliance at the request of the MOP; and monitor, assess and facilitate implementation of and compliance with reporting requirements.[150]

The public communications heard by the CC frequently consider the link between environmental and human rights. The CC is the most advanced of these bodies in providing public access, with almost 100 communications to date from individuals and NGOs. It is therefore perhaps not surprisingly heralded as a precedent for other comparable bodies, with recent consideration given to transplanting some aspects of the procedure into a more complex global context.[151] Early reviews of the

---

[146] United Nations Economic Commission for Europe, *Guidance Document on the Aarhus Convention Compliance Mechanism* (United Nations undated).

[147] Above n. 24.

[148] See Aarhus Clearing House for Environmental Democracy, which in mid 2014 contained 76 resources, accessed 14 November 2014 at http://aarhus clearinghouse.unece.org/resources/?c=1000094.

[149] *Implementation Guide*, 237.

[150] Above n. 132 (Decision I/7), 2.

[151] Antonio Cardesa-Salzmann, 'Constitutionalising Secondary Rules in Global Environmental Regimes: Non-Compliance Procedures and the Enforcement of Multilateral Environmental Agreements' (2012) 24 *Journal of Environmental Law* 103; and Simon Marsden, 'Public Participation in Transboundary Environmental Impact Assessment – Closing the Gap between International and Public Law?', in Brad Jessup and Kim Rubenstein (eds), *Environmental Discourses in Public and International Law* (Cambridge University Press, Cambridge 2012) 238.

CC by its first chair indicated key features.[152] As noted above, at the first MOP in October 2002, a decision on review of compliance was adopted,[153] which established the Committee, later to hold its first meeting in March 2003.

The procedures adopted are innovative, permitting wide access to meetings and documentation. In its work it has addressed a number of interpretative issues relating to the Convention, and therefore has contributed significantly to its developing jurisprudence; it has also made recommendations to the MOP, which may result in changes to the Convention in the future.[154] Most of the cases have related to Article 6 or 9, although one case found a provision of Article 7 not to be complied with, and also considered a potential breach of Article 8. The developing jurisprudence of the CC is significant as it increasingly clarifies terms of relevance in the Convention, and indeed, the other agreements, for example rulings in relation to the direct application of international treaties. This is an example of the combined effect of the agreements to transboundary environmental governance. The MOP has adopted most of the recommendations made by the CC, although: 'It still remains to be seen to what extent recommendations will be implemented [by the state Party] in practice.'[155]

At the fifth session of the MOP Decision V/9 on general issues of compliance was adopted.[156] Under this the Parties decided that the implementation of measures to bring legislation or practice of a Party

---

[152] Veit Koester, 'Review of Compliance under the Aarhus Convention: A Rather Unique Compliance Mechanism', (2005) 2(1) *Journal for European Environmental and Planning Law* 33; Veit Koester, 'The Compliance Committee of the Aarhus Convention – An Overview of Procedures and Jurisprudence' (2007) 37(2) *Environmental Policy and Law* 83–96; see also Morgera, above n. 6, 140–3.

[153] See above n. 132.

[154] Morgera, above n. 6, 141, emphasises that the MOP is ultimately responsible for deciding upon issues of compliance and may take appropriate measures to ensure the Convention is complied with. This includes assistance to individual parties, recommendations, declarations of non-compliance and cautions. It can also request a party to submit to the CC a time-limited strategy on the achievement of compliance and to report on the implementation of the strategy.

[155] Koester (2007), above n. 152, 93.

[156] Meeting of the Parties, Fifth session Maastricht, the Netherlands, 30 June and 1 July 2014. Item 5(b) of the provisional agenda Procedures and mechanisms facilitating the implementation of the Convention: compliance mechanism, ECE/MP.PP/2014/CRP.3.

into compliance with the Convention should commence as soon as possible once specific problems with compliance have been identified, with a view to already bringing about full compliance.[157] It notes the need for the CC to ensure transparency and due process for both communicants and the Parties concerned in respect of communications received from members of the public (including informing the Party concerned, at an early stage, of the receipt of a communication by the CC); and that the CC ensure that where domestic remedies have not been utilised and exhausted, it takes account of such remedies, in accordance with paragraph 21 of the Annex to Decision I/7.[158]

There have been no submissions by Parties or referrals by the Secretariat in relation to Asian states. However claims against Armenia, Kazakhstan and Turkmenistan have been made by public communications, the latter two which are considered in Chapter 8. In relation to Armenia, the CC reviewed the progress made in the intersessional period in implementing Decision IV/9a in a report presented to the MOP in advance of the fifth session.[159] This reviewed the three communications made against Armenia,[160] and found that Armenia had still not met the requirements of Decision IV/9a, remaining non-compliant with Article 6 on public participation and Article 3(1) in respect of a clear, transparent and consistent framework to implement the Convention.

The content of, and considerable delay in finalising, a new law on EIA (to add to a new framework law on environmental policy) was the primary concern of the Armenian NGOs in relation to the follow-up process.[161] It was as a consequence unclear when the draft legislation would be adopted, and whether the final texts would implement Decision IV/9a.[162] The MOP subsequently endorsed draft Decision V/9a prepared

---

[157] Ibid, para. 3.

[158] Ibid, para. 5(bis).

[159] Meeting of the Parties Fifth session, Maastricht, the Netherlands, 30 June and 1 July 2014. Item 5(b) of the provisional agenda, Procedures and mechanisms facilitating the implementation of the Convention: compliance mechanism, Compliance by Armenia with its obligations under the Convention, Report of the Compliance Committee, ECE/MP.PP/2014/10.

[160] ACCC/C/2004/8, decision-making on the modification of land use designation and zoning, and leasing plots of agricultural land; ACCC/C/2009/43, issuance and renewal of licenses to a developer for the exploitation of copper and molybdenum deposits; and ACCC/C/2011/62, access to justice.

[161] See Save Teghut Civic Initiative, Statement on the 5th meeting of the Parties to the Aarhus Convention, Maastricht, 1 July 2014, where the NGO suggests the MOP issue a caution to Armenia in respect of its failings.

[162] Above n. 159, para. 30.

by the Bureau based on the recommendations of the CC. This reiterated Decision IV/9a and invited Armenia to provide the text of the draft EIA law by September 2014, and evidence that it meets the requirements of the earlier decision, together with annual progress reports in the lead-up to a review for the sixth session of the MOP in 2017.[163]

IV.2 Protocol

a. Implementation

Article 17(2) of the Protocol requires the MOP to 'keep under continuous review the implementation and development' of the Protocol on the basis of regular reporting by the Parties. Parties are therefore required to submit a NIR prior to each MOP session, keep the Secretariat updated with any relevant developments between sessions, and make their reports publicly available.[164] The NIR is to provide details of the necessary legislative, regulatory or other measures that the relevant Party has taken to implement the provisions of the Protocol, as well as the practical application of those measures.[165] The CC is tasked with monitoring, assessing, facilitating and reporting to the MOP on the implementation of Protocol provisions by the Parties.[166] The WG of the Parties is broadly responsible for overseeing implementation.

The first reporting round for the *PRTR Protocol* was conducted prior to the Second MOP session in July 2014. All but five of the Parties submitted NIRs, and the CC compiled a synthesis report of those received, for the purposes of review by the Second MOP.[167] The synthesis report indicated that, in most cases, PRTRs were integrated into existing laws and regulations, rather than being introduced through new,

---

[163] Meeting of the Parties Fifth session, Maastricht, the Netherlands, 30 June and 1 July 2014. Item 5(b) of the provisional agenda, Procedures and mechanisms facilitating the implementation of the Convention: compliance mechanism, Draft decision V/9a concerning compliance by Armenia with its obligations under the Convention, ECE/MP.PP/2014/L.10, 7 May 2014.

[164] Meeting of the Parties, First session, Geneva, 20–22 April 2010, Decision I/5: Reporting on Implementation of the Protocol, ECE/MP.PRTR/2010/2/Add.1.

[165] Ibid.

[166] Meeting of the Parties, First session, Geneva, 20–22 April 2010, Decision I/2: Review of Compliance, Annex – Structure and functions of the Compliance Committee and procedures for the review of compliance, ECE/MP.PRTR/2010/2/Add.1.

[167] Synthesis report on the implementation of the Protocol on Pollutant Release and Transfer Registers, ECE/MP.PRTR/2014/5 (at 4), 23 May 2014.

specific PRTR legislation.[168] Almost all of the Parties had legislative and regulatory measures that were more extensive than the minimum requirements of the *PRTR Protocol* (for example, by covering more activities and setting lower thresholds).[169] Although enforcement measures were envisaged by some Parties against facility owners and operators, either enforcement had not yet actually occurred or the Parties were unwilling to disclose details.[170]

In western Asia/the Near East, Israel prepared for its accession to the *PRTR Protocol* by enacting the *Environmental Protection Law* in 2012.[171] Following accession in 2013, the Ministry of Environmental Protection established the national PRTR, which is known as 'Miflas'.[172] According to the NIR submitted by Israel in 2014, the *Environmental Protection Law* applies the provisions of the Protocol, 'with the full intention of complying with [those] provisions'.[173] In fact, the national legislation appears to go further and be more stringent than the minimum requirements of the Protocol, particularly regarding the types of activities covered and reporting thresholds for pollutants.[174]

Several challenges to national implementation of the *PRTR Protocol* were identified in the synthesis report.[175] These included the need to minimise duplicative reporting by analysing relevant legislation; raise awareness among stakeholders as to the availability of PRTR data; ensure the confidentiality of information received from whistle-blowers; and promote harmonisation where minimum standards are exceeded.[176] The report also identified some gaps in the data kept by national PRTRs, and recognised the need for some Parties to complete or revise their relevant

---

168 Ibid, 27.

169 Ibid, 5. This is primarily due to many of the EU-based Parties also having to implement the similar provisions of the European Pollutant Release and Transfer Register; see Regulation (EC) No. 166/2006 of the European Parliament and of the Council of 18 January 2006 concerning the establishment of a European Pollutant Release and Transfer Register, [2006] OJ L33/1, 1–17.

170 Ibid, 4 and 27.

171 *Environmental Protection Law (Releases and Transfers to the Environment – Reporting and Recording Duties)* 2012.

172 Israel Ministry of Environmental Protection, 'Pollutant Release and Transfer Register (PRTR)', undated.

173 Implementation Report for Israel regarding the PRTR Protocol, 29 January 2014, 2.

174 Ibid, 6.

175 Above n. 167, 27–8.

176 Above n. 167, 27–8.

legislation so as to fully implement the Protocol provisions.[177] The *Maastricht Declaration*, adopted by the MOPs to both the Convention and Protocol in 2014, noted that 'improvement of the quality and the completeness of data reported and the effective access to information by the public in relation to the pollutants that are released into the environment remain important tasks to be fulfilled'.[178]

Implementation of the Protocol was acknowledged as particularly challenging for Parties with economies in transition, due to financial constraints and a lack of human resources and technical facilities.[179] The CC therefore recommended that 'substantial and continuing international cooperation with, assistance to and support for such countries [should be] a priority in order to deliver full compliance with the Protocol'.[180] In 2014, the CC was given a more active role in facilitating implementation by Parties and non-Parties, based on the high level of knowledge it had gained in such matters by preparing the synthesis report.[181]

The Second MOP to the Protocol took place in July 2014 and adopted decisions on reporting requirements, a strategic plan for 2015–2020, a work programme for 2015–2017, and financial arrangements. It also endorsed a document on promotion of the *PRTR Protocol* in the EECCA countries,[182] as an overall framework for possible areas of bilateral and multilateral cooperation.[183] In addition, a high-level meeting was held jointly by the MOPs to both the Convention and Protocol to discuss and adopt the *Maastricht Declaration*.[184] The Declaration emphasises that the Convention and Protocol provide:

---

[177] Above n. 167, 28.

[178] Maastricht Declaration – Transparency as a driving force for democracy, ECE/MP.PRTR/2014/CRP.1, Maastricht, 2 July 2014, 4.

[179] Ibid, 33.

[180] Ibid, 33.

[181] Third Meeting of the Compliance Committee, Possible role of the Compliance Committee in facilitating implementation of the Protocol on Pollutant Release and Transfer Registers, PRTR/C.1/2014/Inf.1 (11 June 2014); Decisions and Major Outcomes [as adopted by the Meeting of the Parties at its second session], ECE/MP.PRTR/2014/CRP.3, 4 July 2014, 4.

[182] UNECE, Promotion of the Protocol on Pollutant Release and Transfer Registers in countries in Eastern Europe, the Caucasus and Central Asia, ECE/MP.PRTR/2014/L.6.

[183] Decisions and Major Outcomes [as adopted by the Meeting of the Parties at its second session], ECE/MP.PRTR/2014/CRP.3, 3.

[184] Above n. 178.

> effective tools for furthering environmental democracy, through encouraging the active participation of all interested stakeholders in processes that contribute to better decision-making, planning and implementation of policies and programmes at all levels [...][185]

It calls on the Protocol's Parties to work towards full implementation, and for countries within the UNECE region that are not yet Parties, to ratify or accede to the Protocol at the earliest opportunity.[186] The Declaration also recognises the need for Parties to streamline their national pollutant reporting system, and to enhance consistency with other relevant reporting obligations (for example under other MEAs).[187] Potential synergies with other such agreements are to be explored further.[188]

The Strategic Plan for 2015–2020 is intended to guide the implementation and further development of the Protocol over the next several years, until the MOP fourth session. The Strategic Plan contains broad, long-term goals as well as more specific focal points, which use indicators and targets to assess progress.[189] Specific goals include achieving implementation of the Protocol by each Party; removing barriers to ratification and expansion beyond the UNECE region; developing the Protocol in terms of possible improvements to Annexes I and II; and emphasising the roles and responsibilities of the Parties, stakeholders and Secretariat in promoting, facilitating and supporting implementation of the Protocol. The Strategic Plan also contains a Framework for Implementation, setting out how and when these specific goals should be achieved.[190]

b. Compliance

The Protocol MOP established the CC at its First Session in April 2010 (Decision I/2), in accordance with Article 22 of the Protocol.[191] The functions of the CC are to consider submissions, referrals and communications on compliance issues; prepare compliance and implementation reports upon request by the MOP; ensure compliance by Parties with the

---

185 Above n. 178, 2.

186 Above n. 178, 4.

187 Above n. 178, 3.

188 Above n. 178, 3.

189 Meeting of the Parties, Second session: Draft Decision II/2 on the strategic plan for 2015–2020 for the Protocol on Pollutant Release and Transfer Registers (Annex), ECE/MP.PRTR/2014/L.2, 2–4 July 2014.

190 Ibid.

191 Meeting of the Parties, First session, Geneva, 20–22 April 2010, Decision I/2: Review of Compliance, ECE/MP.PRTR/2010.

Protocol's reporting requirements; take appropriate measures to secure compliance by individual Parties; and carry out any other functions assigned to it by the MOP.[192] The CC has broad powers to gather appropriate information when considering cases of possible non-compliance, which extend to holding hearings and seeking expert opinions.[193] The CC is required to report on its activities to each MOP session and 'make such recommendations as it considers appropriate'.[194]

The Protocol stipulates the circumstances in which a compliance issue may be raised. Where a Party is concerned about another Party's compliance with the Protocol, it can make a submission to the Secretariat, which forwards the submission to the CC and other relevant Party.[195] The submission must be supported by corroborating information, and the relevant Party is given three months to respond, after which the CC must consider the matter 'as soon as practicable'.[196] Alternatively, a case of possible non-compliance may be referred by the Secretariat if it becomes aware of a potential issue arising from the national implementation and compliance reports.[197] First, the Secretariat must request the potentially non-complying Party to provide the necessary information. If there is no response, or the matter is unresolved after three months, the Secretariat will refer the matter to the CC for consideration.[198]

There are two other circumstances in which a submission can be made regarding non-compliance. A submission may be made by a Party when it is unable to comply fully with its own obligations under the Protocol, despite its best efforts. In such case, the Party must explain the specific reasons why full compliance is not possible.[199] The CC may also consider communications from members of the public regarding possible non-compliance by a Party, unless that Party has specifically notified the CC that it will not accept such communications.[200] The communication

---

192 Decision I/2 on Review of Compliance, Annex – Structure and functions of the Compliance Committee and procedures for the review of compliance (Section III), ECE/MP.PRTR/2010/2/Add.1.

193 Ibid, Section VII, 25.

194 Ibid, Section XI, 39.

195 Ibid, Section IV, 15.

196 The three month limit can be extended to a maximum of six months if necessary: ibid, Section IV 15.

197 Above n. 192, Section V, 17.

198 Ibid, Section V, 17.

199 Ibid, Section IV, 16.

200 Ibid, Section VI, 18. Notification periods can be for up to 4 years.

must initially be made through the Secretariat, and supported by corroborating evidence.[201] The CC can refuse to consider a communication on several grounds, for example when it is manifestly unreasonable or ill-founded.[202] Where the communication is accepted, the Party alleged to be non-complying is given the opportunity to respond.

No formal submissions regarding non-compliance with the Protocol have been made to date. However, as mentioned above, several Parties did not comply with their obligation to provide a NIR prior to the Second MOP in 2014.[203] This clearly constituted non-compliance with the reporting requirement under the Protocol in accordance with Article 17(2). In response, the Second MOP noted 'with regret' that they had failed to submit NIRs, and urged them to do so by an extended deadline.[204] No further action appears to have been taken to date, but the CC has a range of options at its disposal to address instances of ongoing non-compliance such as this.[205]

V. PROSPECTS

V.1 Asia

As noted in Part I above, the *Public Participation Convention* has generated interest among a number of Asian states. Whether the membership aspirations of the non-UNECE states intending to join the Convention are matched by positive action remains to be seen. An encouragement to the efforts of current Parties in central Asia was a recent joint report by the UNECE, UNDP, UNEP and other relevant UN institutions. Whether matched by practice on the ground or not, this commented on changes to governance for sustainable development in the central Asian region – a significant focus of this book – many of which were without doubt inspired by the Convention, in the following positive terms:

> … there clearly has been important progress in reforming governance structures in the region in the last two decades. Electoral bodies, national human rights institutions and anticorruption agencies have been created;

---

[201] Ibid, Section VI, 19.

[202] Ibid, Section VI, 20.

[203] See Decisions and Major Outcomes [as adopted by the Meeting of the Parties at its second session], ECE/MP.PRTR/2014/CRP.3, 4 July 2014, 4.

[204] Ibid.

[205] Above n. 192, 25.

> public administrations have been modernized; administrative procedures have been streamlined; more effective social protection has been delivered; the rights and responsibilities of subnational governments have been clarified; and legal frameworks for civic engagement have been put in place.[206]

In other parts of Asia there are similar issues with states joining, notably the different attitudes to democracy and human rights that have been expressed in the past via the notion of the 'Asian way' or 'Asian values' that was raised in Chapter 1. It appears that the main stimulation for the Asian values perspective was the World Conference on Human Rights, held in Vienna in 1993,[207] and, in preparation, the earlier adoption by Asian states of the *Bangkok Declaration*, containing 'the aspirations and commitments of the Asian region' with regard to human rights.[208] NGOs saw this as involving a high degree of underlying hostility to human rights.[209] In southeast Asia, environmental governance was subsequently considered in practice in relation to transparency and access to information, involvement of the public, and accountability to affected stakeholders.[210]

As noted earlier, participation in the Protocol by Asian countries is very low, despite the fact that membership has been open to all countries since its inception over a decade ago. However, there have been other initiatives by international organisations to promote the use of PRTRs across Asia. At least one of these initiatives pre-dates the Protocol and continues to wield significant influence in the region, possibly also enhancing the prospect of some countries implementing the Protocol itself.

The OECD has been actively promoting PRTRs among its member states since 1993, primarily through its Task Force on PRTRs. In 1996,

---

[206] United Nations, *Building More Inclusive, Sustainable and Prosperous Societies in Europe and Central Asia: A Common United Nations Vision for the Post-2015 Development Agenda* (United Nations 2013), 58.

[207] See: http://www.ohchr.org/EN/ABOUTUS/Pages/ViennaWC.aspx, accessed 14 November 2014.

[208] For a critique, see Catherine Shanahan Renshaw, 'The ASEAN Human Rights Declaration – Cause for Celebration?', 25 January 2013, available 14 November 2014 at http://asiapacific.anu.edu.au/regarding-rights/2013/01/25/the-asean-human-rights-declaration-cause-for-celebration/.

[209] See http://therightsfuture.com/wp-content/uploads/2010/11/The_Rights_Future_CT5_Asian_Values.pdf, accessed 14 November 2014.

[210] Nathan Badenoch, *Transboundary Environmental Governance: Principles and Practice in Mainland Southeast Asia* (World Resources Institute, Washington DC 2002) 15–21.

the OECD Council adopted the *Recommendation on Implementing Pollutant Release and Transfer Registers*,[211] calling on member states to establish a PRTR scheme. The OECD also published a guidance manual to assist governments in developing and implementing a PRTR scheme.[212] All OECD member states, including Japan and South Korea, have now adopted a PRTR scheme.[213] If the PRTRs adopted by Japan and South Korea are substantially compatible with requirements under the *PRTR Protocol*, it may not be difficult for those countries to then accede to the Protocol.[214] If Japan and South Korea took this step, other Asian countries may be alerted to the benefits of the Protocol and be encouraged to follow suit.[215]

Another international organisation, the UN Institute for Training and Research (UNITAR), in collaboration with UNEP has also been proactive in encouraging some Asian countries to adopt PRTR schemes, although mainly in the context of managing certain chemicals under the POPs Convention.[216] Cambodia, Thailand and Kazakhstan were among the countries that were selected as pilots for the Global PRTR Project on POPs monitoring, reporting and information dissemination using PRTRs. The first phase of the pilot project, completed in 2012, involved designing a national PRTR system and using it as a tool to obtain data on POPs emissions. A second phase that would assist these countries to implement their national PRTRs has been proposed.[217] The PRTRs that have been developed through this project, although currently somewhat narrow in scope, could conceivably be extended to all chemicals covered

---

211 C/(96)41/Final, as amended in 2003 C(2003)87.

212 Organisation for Economic Co-operation and Development, 'The PRTR Guidance Manual for Governments' (1996), OECD/GD(96)32.

213 Organisation for Economic Co-operation and Development, 'OECD and Pollutant Release and Transfer Registers (PRTRs)', available 14 November 2014 at http://www.oecd.org/chemicalsafety/pollutant-release-transfer-register/.

214 The OECD has already produced technical guidance for its member states on achieving harmonisation with the PRTR Protocol requirements.

215 Cambodia, Thailand, Tajikistan and Georgia have also already laid foundations for a national PRTR, either by signing the Protocol, designing a draft national PRTR, or putting a PRTR scheme in place pursuant to OECD requirements.

216 See Chapter 2. Article 10 of this Convention explicitly acknowledges the value of PRTRs in assisting Parties to meet their compliance requirements.

217 Final Meeting of the Steering Committee for the GEF Medium-sized project on POPs Monitoring, Reporting and Information Dissemination using Pollutant Release and Transfer Registers (PRTRs) – Possible elements of a second phase proposal on POPs-PRTRs, Geneva, 29–31 August 2012.

by the PRTR Protocol in the future. Similarly to the OECD project countries, this would make eventual accession to the Protocol a viable prospect.

In 2013 representatives of governments, NGOs and other stakeholders released the *Jakarta Declaration*,[218] advocating the implementation of PRTRs in Asia as part of a broader effort to improve access to environmental information.[219] It recognised that access to corporate, facility and state-owned enterprise information that reveals pollutant discharges and its impact on the environment is limited in many countries in the region,[220] and demanded that emissions data be provided by companies to governments to allow adequate environmental monitoring. The Declaration stated that:

> Stronger Legislative frameworks must be enacted that require the proactive release of information of pollutant discharge, stored and transfered [sic] information. Creating mandatory environmental information disclosure programs such as pollutant release transfer registers are a priority for the region. Pollution data should be linked to government enforcement, and in addition it should communicate risk to public health and the environment. Where companies proactively disclosed pollutant discharge information this can strengthen corporate social responsibility.[221]

V.2 Global

In relation to the *Public Participation Convention* globally, prospects may be bright. A former Secretary to the Convention, after reviewing the achievements of the first decade of operation, considered the future for the treaty in the next decade.[222] His comments make particular reference to the Strategic Plan for 2009–2014, part of which was concerned to encourage states outside as well as inside the UNECE region to accede to the treaty. Concerning the former, Russia and Turkey are singled out for

---

[218] The Jakarta Declaration for Strengthening the Right to Environmental Information for People and the Environment, 1 May 2013, available 14 November 2014 at http://pdf.wri.org/jakarta_declaration_for_strengthening_right_to_environmental_information.pdf.

[219] Representatives from China, Indonesia, Japan, Mongolia, Philippines and Thailand signed the Jakarta Declaration on 1 May 2013.

[220] Para. 15.

[221] Para. 16.

[222] Jeremy Wates, 'The Future of the Aarhus Convention', in Marc Pallemaerts (ed.), *The Aarhus Convention at Ten: Interactions and Tensions between Conventional International Law and EU Environmental Law* (Europa Law Publishing, Groningen 2011) 383.

attention as, although they both played an active role in the negotiating process, they have yet to ratify. Russia has since indicated a willingness to do so,[223] but progress has stalled, and Turkey's position is closely linked with its wish to join the EU, and meeting the criteria for membership.[224]

Beyond Europe and Asia, there does not appear to have been much practical interest, despite the work of scholars.[225] The USA and Canada, despite being member states of the UNECE, decided not to participate in the Convention process on the basis that their own processes were adequate, with Canada also raising the challenge of compliance given its federal structure. Nonetheless, there has been some progress since. The UNEP guidelines for the development of national legislation in relation to the three pillars under the Convention, have, however, been one notable development to encourage global activity[226] – whether these are subsequently applied or not. Nonetheless, Wates is positive about prospects globally, as despite the failure of many states to implement Principle 10 of the *Rio Declaration*, and the absence of efforts by other UN regional commissions, this may in fact be an advantage for greater uptake of the Convention:

> Given the lack of any early prospect of other regions having their own legally binding instruments on principle 10, or of the global guidelines being followed up in the near future with a global convention with provisions similar to those of the Aarhus Convention, the option of accession to the Aarhus Convention might be seen by some non-ECE states as a practical and low-cost option for joining with a larger group of countries working on environmental democracy issues.[227]

---

[223] Above n. 14. The events leading up to the Sochi Winter Olympics, and circumstances in Ukraine in 2014 (in the Crimea, and eastern Ukraine including the downing of a Malaysian airliner), have not helped this process. See http://www.hrw.org/russias-olympian-abuses, accessed 14 November 2014 in relation to the former.

[224] Above n. 222, 399–400.

[225] See for example, Victoria Lambropoulos, 'What can Australia Learn from the Europeans about Public Participation? – Article 6 of the Aarhus Convention and Environmental Impact Statements' (2010) 27(4) *Environmental and Planning Law Journal* 272.

[226] UNEP Governing Council, Decision SS.XI/5: Environmental law, part A. Available 14 November 2014 at http://www.unep.org/civil-society/Portals/24105/documents/Guidelines/GUIDELINES_TO_ACCESS_TO_ENV_INFO_2.pdf.

[227] Above n. 222, 403.

The *PRTR Protocol*'s Strategic Plan for 2015–2020 identifies one key objective as the removal of barriers to global expansion of the Protocol.[228] This objective is to be attained through the translation of guidance material into other languages, regional workshops on PRTRs, training sessions and capacity-building activities for officials, and promotion of the Protocol at events outside the ECE region and through international and bilateral cooperation, the International PRTR Coordinating Group, and joint activities with other multilateral environmental agreements.[229]

The Global Round Table on PRTRs – hosted jointly in 2013 by the UNECE and OECD – emphasised the growing need for global use of PRTRs.[230] Importantly, the Global Round Table Report noted that the *PRTR Protocol* is 'the only legally binding instrument on PRTRs to ensure minimum standards for equal rights and transparency in the use of environmental data'.[231] As such, it is the preferred model on which national PRTR schemes should be based, and it makes non-compliance by individual countries a politically unattractive option. As the Global Round Table recognised, the *PRTR Protocol* provides 'a solid legal framework for enhancing public access to information and moving towards sustainable and environmentally sound development, thereby protecting the health of present and future generations'.[232] A valuable feature of a national PRTR implemented under the Protocol is that it can serve as a 'single window' for the relevant country to meet all of its environmental reporting obligations under various international and regional schemes.[233] The UNECE has also been proactive in promoting the *PRTR Protocol* to the rest of the world. The *Maastricht Declaration*, adopted at the Second MOP to the Protocol in 2014, states:

> We warmly welcome [...] the establishment of PRTR systems around the globe. We encourage similar initiatives intending to replicate the achievements of the Aarhus Convention and its Protocol and we stand ready to

---

228 Second Session of the Meeting of the Parties to the Protocol on Pollutant Release and Transfer Registers: Draft Decision II/2 on the strategic plan for 2015–2020 for the Protocol on Pollutant Release and Transfer Registers (Annex), ECE/MP.PRTR/2014/L.2, 2–4 July 2014, 5.

229 Ibid, 8.

230 Global round table on PRTRs held in Geneva on 19 November 2013 – Joint report by the secretariat of the Protocol on Pollutant Release and Transfer Registers and the Organisation for Economic Co-operation and Development, ECE/MP.PRTR/2014/7, 5.

231 Ibid, 3.

232 Ibid, 3.

233 Ibid, 6.

> support these initiatives. We also call upon countries that are interested in doing so to join the Aarhus family, since the Aarhus Convention and its Protocol are open to accession by countries outside the ECE region, and express our renewed commitment to encouraging such accessions.[234]

Support for the global promotion of the Protocol was reaffirmed by the Bureau at the Joint Global Round Table on PRTRs in 2013,[235] and in 2014 the Second MOP mandated the Bureau and Secretariat to continue work in this regard.[236]

VI. CONCLUSIONS

Despite not being focused primarily on transboundary governance, the *Public Participation Convention* is in many ways the most significant of all of the UNECE agreements. These include the connections it makes between domestic procedures and public international law, and linking environmental and human rights. Given the focus of this book on Asia – which contains many developing nations – the latter consideration is particularly important. It is also notable that it was mainly the ratifications of the countries of EECCA that brought about the entry into force of the Convention. The adoption of the *PRTR Protocol* was also a development of some significance, occurring on target in Kiev in 2003, and introducing a focus on the private sector to the main attention on the public sector of the Convention. The adoption of the *GMO Guidelines*, and first amendment to strengthen public participation in respect to GMOs, were also notable early achievements.

In relation to international activity, the obligation to promote the application of Convention principles in international decision-making processes, and within the framework of international organisations, emphasises the importance of participatory approaches to global governance more broadly. The subsequent adoption of the *Almaty Guidelines* brought about extensive outreach activity which has enhanced the potential of the Convention to gain acceptance as a global treaty. Given that the *Water Convention* (Chapter 6), and *EIA Convention* (Chapter 4), are potentially now global treaties, the *Public Participation Convention* sits

---

234 Above n. 178.

235 Report on the Sixth Meeting of the Bureau of the Meeting of the Parties to the Protocol on Pollutant Release and Transfer Registers, Geneva, 21 November 2013, 2.

236 Above n. 203, 2.

squarely with these as having this fundamental feature; as does the *PRTR Protocol*, along with the *SEA Protocol* (Chapter 4).

The compliance procedure of the *Public Participation Convention* is particularly important in the context of this book and has been considered at length. Steered by an influential CC and following and applying a developing and recorded 'jurisprudence' to matters under consideration, it has not only made findings which have been accepted by the MOP and which have largely been implemented by the Parties, but it has also made major contributions to the development of the Convention itself, and increasingly to the other UNECE agreements. This has been seen in respect of its guiding role in liaising with the other NCPs in developing their 'case law' in the scope of the overall UNECE regime, with its many synergies between the five treaties and 12 protocols that constitute it.

4. The Environmental Impact Assessment Convention and Strategic Environmental Assessment Protocol

I. INTRODUCTION: STATUS, MEMBERSHIP AND INSTITUTIONS (CONVENTION AND PROTOCOL)

The Convention on Environmental Impact Assessment in a Transboundary Context (*EIA Convention*) came into force on 27 June 1997 after adoption in Espoo, Finland on 25 February 1991 with 30 signatory countries and the EC, the first major treaty to specify in detailed terms, transboundary EIA procedures.[1] There are currently 45 Parties, and since the entry into force of an amendment, the treaty is now potentially open to all members of the UN beyond the UNECE region.[2] It is hence very relevant to Asian states beyond the current members of the UNECE, including those in western and central Asia.

Since then, although other treaties have also provided for transboundary EIA,[3] the *EIA Convention* remains the most significant of any of

[1] Convention on Environmental Impact Assessment in a Transboundary Context (Espoo, 25 February 1991), 30 ILM (1991) 802, in force 27 June 1997. This is often known as the 'Espoo Convention'.

[2] 'UNECE Espoo Convention on Environmental Impact Assessment becomes a global instrument', press release 27 August 2014; see http://www.unece.org/index.php?id=36354 accessed 17 November 2014. For related discussion, see Timo Koivurova, 'Could the Espoo Convention become a Global Regime for Environmental Impact Assessment and Strategic Environmental Assessment?' in Robin Warner and Simon Marsden (eds), *Transboundary Environmental Governance: Inland, Coastal and Marine Perspectives* (Ashgate Publishing, Farnham 2012) 323.

[3] See Neil Craik, *The International Law of Environmental Impact Assessment: Process, Substance and Integration* (Cambridge University Press, Cambridge 2008); Kees Bastmeijer and Timo Koivurova (eds), *Theory and Practice of Transboundary Environmental Impact Assessment* (Martinus Nijhoff, Leiden

these agreements because of the large number of Parties that have ratified the Convention.[4] These include most of the member states of the UNECE and the EU, as well as members of the European Economic Area. Current Parties include four western and central Asian states (Armenia, Azerbaijan, Kazakhstan and Kyrgyzstan). As noted in the previous chapter, the *Public Participation Convention*[5] has a particularly close relationship with the *EIA Convention*. Russia (as a northern and eastern Asian, as well as a European state) announced its intention to ratify both of these treaties in 2011, although it is yet to do so.[6] Other states have also indicated an interest in joining the *EIA Convention*, as indicated below.

The Strategic Environmental Assessment Protocol (*SEA Protocol*) is also in force with 38 signatories and 26 Parties.[7] Although it is mainly applicable in a domestic context, it contains a provision for transboundary application.[8] Armenia is currently the only Asian Party to the

---

2008); and Simon Marsden and Timo Koivurova (eds), *Transboundary Environmental Impact Assessment in the European Union: The Espoo Convention and its Kiev Protocol on Strategic Environmental Assessment* (Earthscan/Routledge, Abingdon, UK and New York, USA 2011).

[4] Another example with provisions for this (as explained in Chapter 7) is the *Industrial Accidents Convention*. See Convention on the Transboundary Effects of Industrial Accidents (Helsinki, 1992), 31 ILM (1992) 1333, in force 19 April 2000. Specific Asian examples containing transboundary EIA provisions are the *Caspian Sea Convention* and the *Mekong Agreement*, which were briefly analysed in Chapter 2.

[5] Convention on Access to Information, Public Participation in Decision-Making and Access to Justice in Environmental Matters (Aarhus, 25 June 1998), 38 ILM (1999) 517, in force 30 October 2001. In addition to the same states Parties to the *EIA Convention*, Tajikistan and Turkmenistan are also Parties to this treaty.

[6] UNECE, 'UNECE welcomes the Russian Federation's intention to ratify the Aarhus and Espoo environmental conventions', UNECE Weekly, issue 432, 27 June–1 July 2011.

[7] Protocol on Strategic Environmental Assessment to the Convention on Environmental Impact Assessment in a Transboundary Context (Kiev, 21 May 2003), unreported, in force 11 July 2010. This is sometimes known as the 'Kiev Protocol'.

[8] Simon Marsden, *Strategic Environmental Assessment in International and European Law: A Practitioner's Guide* (Earthscan, Abingdon 2008); and Jan de Mulder, 'The Protocol on Strategic Environmental Assessment: A Matter of Good Governance' (2011) 20 *Review of European Community and International Environmental Law* 232.

Protocol and there are no other Asian signatories.[9] The need to expand the application of the Protocol is therefore significant in the Asian region, although interest has already been expressed by some non-UNECE countries in joining.[10] This is already possible as the Protocol is also open to accession by all UN members upon approval by existing members.[11]

The main institutional bodies under both the Convention and Protocol are the MOP (meeting every few years), Bureau, WG on EIA and SEA, inquiry commission (applicable only to the Convention) and the Implementation Committee (IC). Other than the non-permanent inquiry commission, the others provide assistance to both the agreements. The MOP is the main decision-making body and its principal role is to keep the implementation of the agreements under continuous review.[12] The Bureau provides high level input into the MOP, with a focus upon ratification status, implementation and compliance, sub-regional cooperation and capacity building, and preparations for the next sessions of the MOP.[13]

The WG was established to assist in the implementation of the Convention and the Protocol and the management of the workplan, which is both forward looking and also, in examining the completion of past activities, backward looking. The success of the implementation of the workplan is in large part dependent upon the availability of adequate financial resources; this is especially important for the capacity building activities, many of which relate to the Caucasus and central Asia.[14] The

---

[9] Note, however, as an example of the current relevance of this treaty to Asia, see 'Workshop on Environmental Impact Assessment in a Transboundary Context in Eastern Asia' held between 13 and 15 June 2012 in Seoul, Republic of Korea.

[10] Korea has expressed an interest following the workshop hosted in 2012, and has been supportive of capacity building activities in central Asia, pledging financial assistance.

[11] Article 23(3).

[12] The MOP therefore held its sixth session (Convention) in conjunction with its second session (Protocol) between 2 and 5 June 2014 in Geneva.

[13] The most recent meeting of the Bureau was held in January 2014 in Athens.

[14] The third meeting of the Working Group was held in November 2013 in Geneva. This examined implementation of workplan activities to date. See Meeting of the Parties, Working Group on Environmental Impact Assessment and Strategic Environmental Assessment, Third meeting, Geneva 11–15 November 2013, Implementation of the workplan activities, note by the secretariat, ECE/MP.EIA/WG.2/2013/INF.6, 16 October 2013.

inquiry commission is a means of determining whether there are significant adverse environmental effects from development proposals where this is contested; it has been established only once to date. The IC manages the compliance procedure, and has compiled its opinions (*Committee Opinions*) on compliance matters to assist Parties with their obligations.[15]

The chapter will first provide some historical background to, and explain the legal development of, the Convention and Protocol, before outlining the objectives and general procedural provisions of each. In relation to practice, it will then consider questions of legal implementation and compliance with reference to Asia where possible, including an analysis of future prospects in this region and globally. As with the other chapters on the five agreements, while other Asian examples are given – particularly in western Asia – implementation in central Asia is examined in Chapter 8 with examples from each of the treaties.

II. HISTORICAL BACKGROUND AND LEGAL DEVELOPMENT (CONVENTION AND PROTOCOL)

The *EIA Convention* has one of the longest histories of all of the UNECE treaties, building upon other international and European law with transboundary procedures, in particular the 1974 *Nordic Convention*[16] and the 1985 *EIA Directive*.[17] Principle 21 of the *Stockholm Declaration* was also an important influence,[18] together with the elaboration of principles of transboundary EIA in 1987 under the auspices of the UNEP Group of Experts on Environmental Law. The Brundtland Report, *Our Common*

---

[15] The thirty-second session was held in December 2014 in Geneva. See Economic Commission for Europe, Convention on Environmental Impact Assessment in a Transboundary Context, *Opinions of the Implementation Committee (2001–2010)* (United Nations 2011) (*Committee Opinions*).

[16] Nordic Environmental Protection Convention (Stockholm, 19 February 1974), UNE EPL, Vol 1, 1975–1976 p. 44, entered into force 5 October 1976. This was the first international agreement on transboundary EIA.

[17] Council Directive 85/337/EEC of 27 June 1985 on the assessment of the effects of certain public and private projects on the environment [1985] OJ L175/40; note Jonas Ebbesson, 'Innovative Elements and Expected Effectiveness of the 1991 EIA Convention' (1999) 19 *Environmental Impact Assessment Review* 47, 49, who draws attention both to the *Nordic Convention* and also the 1977 OECD Recommendation on the Implementation of a Regime of Equal Right of Access and Non-Discrimination in Relation to Transfrontier Pollution.

[18] See 11 ILM 1416 (1972).

Future, furthermore recommended that governments support the development of regional and subregional cooperative arrangements for the protection and sustained use of transboundary ecological systems, with joint action programmes to combat common problems.[19] However, the *Nordic Convention* and *EIA Directive* undoubtedly were major influences on the work of the UNECE in the development of the *EIA Convention* and subsequent *SEA Protocol*, and in relation to the latter, the SEA Directive.[20]

A Working Group was responsible for the preparation of the text that would form the basis of the adopted Convention. Connelly discusses the debate over the provisions included, and indicates that at the third meeting the document 'began to bear the resemblance of an international agreement'.[21] He makes the following important observations and conclusions on the significance of the *EIA Convention*, which are each relevant to its development in the Asian context:

- The political environment was conducive to the development of the Convention, giving the attention being paid internationally to environmental issues and the growing desire for cooperation between eastern and western countries …
- The Convention was innovative and far from the 'lowest common denominator' – the content and obligations were, in many instances, beyond what was in existence in many countries at the time and its reference to the possible application to policies, plans and program[s] was forward looking;
- The Convention has influenced the development of EIA legislation in a number of countries through the content and nature of its obligations;
- The Convention has served as a model in the development of regional and bilateral agreements on EIA in a transboundary context …[22]

---

[19] For discussion of these influences, see Robert G Connelly, 'The UN Convention on EIA in a Transboundary Context: A Historical Perspective' (1999) 19 *Environmental Impact Assessment Review* 37.

[20] Directive 2001/42/EC of the European Parliament and of the Council of 27 June 2001 on the assessment of the effects of certain plans and programmes on the environment [2001] OJ L197/30–37. For discussion, see Gregory Jones and Eloise Scotford (eds), *The Strategic Environmental Assessment Directive: A Plan for Success?* (Hart Publishing, Oxford 2015); also Simon Marsden, 'The Espoo Convention and Kiev Protocol in the European Union: Implementation, Compliance, Enforcement and Reform (2011) 20(3) *Review of European Community and International Environmental Law* 267.

[21] Above n. 19, 41–42

[22] Above n. 19, 44–46

Of particular note here is the need for a welcoming political environment, provision of a model to take such matters forward, and the Convention's influence on other legislative developments including its transposition. The reach of the *EIA Convention* has therefore been seen with respect to other international legal developments outlined and analysed in this book, such as the *Industrial Accidents Convention* (Chapter 7), and the *Mekong* and *Tumen Agreements* and the *Caspian Sea Convention* (all in Chapter 2). In Asia, these agreements have responded to the success of the *EIA Convention* in enhancing transboundary consultation and decision making, and as will be seen, opening up the treaty to all UN member states beyond the UNECE region will enable other non-UNECE Asian states to join.[23]

After its adoption in 1991 and entry into force in 1997 there have been several important developments in the history of the Convention. Of particular relevance to Asia, the first was the adoption of Decision II/8 on strengthening subregional cooperation, at their second session of the MOP, held in Sofia in 2001. The objective was to accelerate ratification and practical application of the Convention, and one of the measures considered was to produce a guidance document to summarise experience gained and provide recommendations for further action. The resulting guidance document was based on three workshops held in the Balkan and Black Sea regions, in central and eastern Europe and in southeastern Europe.[24] At the third session of the MOP, held in Cavtat in 2003 Decision III/5 was also adopted, confirming that capacity building for the countries in EECCA would be included in the work plan.[25]

The second and perhaps most significant, however, was the adoption in Kiev in 2003, and final entry into force in 2010, of the Protocol, which achieved the forecast application of the Convention to policies, plans and programmes as noted above. Although the Convention encouraged Parties to apply EIA to these areas, it was not mandatory.[26] The Secretariat of the *EIA Convention* published a report on the application of EIA principles to policies, plans and programmes in 1992, following on from

---

[23] As noted in Chapter 1, the 11 Asian members of the UNECE are Armenia, Azerbaijan, Georgia, Israel, Kazakhstan, Kyrgyzstan, the Russian Federation, Tajikistan, Turkey, Turkmenistan and Uzbekistan, five of which are in central Asia.

[24] See http://www.unece.org/env/eia/pubs/subregional_coop.html#Guidance, accessed 17 November 2014.

[25] Ibid.

[26] Article 2(7).

another guide the previous year.[27] Incorporation of SEA provisions in other international treaties generated the necessary political will to develop the Protocol,[28] which began in 2001 and gave particular consideration to the need to incorporate requirements of the *Public Participation Convention*, which was also closely linked with the deliberations of the time.[29] De Mulder comments:

> Many NGOs regarded the SEA Protocol negotiation process as an opportunity to strengthen the Aarhus outcome in a specific instrument and strove for a comprehensive instrument that would provide for broad public participation and access to justice in strategic decision making.[30]

Prior to its adoption there were two preparatory meetings held in November 2003 and January 2004 prior to the first meeting of the signatories in June 2004 in Cavtat. This was followed by a second and later third meeting of the signatories (both in Geneva) in April 2005 and November 2010 respectively. The third and final session of the meeting of the signatories followed its entry into force in July 2010, attended by various signatories and Parties and other members of the UNECE, including Armenia, Azerbaijan, Kyrgyzstan, Tajikistan and Turkmenistan. Iraq and Vietnam, as UN member states, were also represented.[31]

The meeting agreed that the first session of the MOP to the Convention serving as the MOP to the Protocol would be held in Geneva, in the week from 20 to 24 June 2011, in conjunction with the fifth session of the

---

27 See UNECE, *Policies and Systems of Environmental Impact Assessment,* (United Nations 1991); UNECE, *Application of Environmental Impact Assessment Principles to Policies, Plans and Programmes,* ECE/ENVWA/27, (United Nations 1992).

28 These included the Convention on Biological Diversity, see Chapter 2 and Marsden above n. 8, 115.

29 See Jerzy Jendrośka and Stephen Stec, 'The Kyiv Protocol on Strategic Environmental Assessment' (2003) 33 *Environmental Policy and Law* 105, 106, where the possibility of the Protocol being allied with the *Public Participation Convention* is considered. For further comment on the link between the *EIA* and *Public Participation Conventions*, see references in n. 38 below.

30 See De Mulder, above n. 8, 235; for further background, see also Marsden, above n. 8.

31 Although there was no experience in Iraq to share, the delegate from Vietnam made a presentation on his country's national SEA system and practice that concluded with some key challenges, which some other delegates observed were shared by countries in the UNECE region, including the difficulties of gaining acceptance by planning authorities and of encouraging stakeholder participation. See n. 32 below, para. 13.

MOP to the Convention.[32] Capacity building efforts in central Asia were a key part of the initial deliberations on setting the path for the way forward:

> The Meeting took note of the report by the secretariat on preparations for a second national awareness-raising workshop on the Protocol and training using the draft resource manual to support application of the Protocol, originally expected to be held in Kyrgyzstan with the participation of Tajikistan. The secretariat reported on contacts with a possible donor to implement the planned workshop in Kyrgyzstan, while noting practical difficulties with holding the workshop in Bishkek at present. However, the secretariat was also arranging for a strategic environmental assessment (SEA) training workshop to be held in Almaty (Kazakhstan) in spring 2011 for the countries of Central Asia.[33]

A third development that was also particularly noteworthy was the adoption of the first and second amendments, the first of which as noted above has now obtained sufficient ratifications to enter into force, although more are still needed for non-UNECE states to accede. This therefore permits non-UNECE member states to potentially join the Convention, and hence it has now also effectively become a global treaty,[34] which since 2013 is also the case for the *Water Convention* (Chapter 6),[35] and has always been the case for the *Public Participation Convention* (Chapter 3); non-UNECE Asian states are now potentially able to join.[36] The first amendment also increases public participation in the procedures of the Convention,[37] which given its adoption prior to the *Public Participation Convention* has been more limited in this respect. Both Conventions nonetheless have a very close connection, which is a

---

[32] Meeting of the Signatories, Third session, Geneva, 22 and 23 November 2010, Report of the Meeting of the Signatories, ECE/MP.EIA/AC.3/2010/2 17 January 2011, para. 8.

[33] Ibid, para. 10. It was also noted at the third session by the secretary to the CEP that preparations were being made for the seventh 'Environment for Europe' Ministerial Conference, to be held in Astana from 21 to 23 September 2011; see above n. 32, para. 14. Delegates commented that the Astana Conference's outcome should reflect on the importance of SEA in both Conference themes, and that round tables on both themes should consider SEA.

[34] See Decision II/14, Amendment to the Convention on Environmental Impact Assessment in a Transboundary Context, Sofia, 27 February 2001.

[35] 'UNECE Water Convention goes global', press release, 6 February 2013.

[36] The Protocol already permits this, see Article 23(3).

[37] Although now quite dated, see UNECE, *Guidance on Public Participation in EIA in a Transboundary Context* (United Nations 2006), ECE/MP.EIA/7.

strong example of the combined contribution of the agreements to transboundary environmental governance.[38] As SEA is undertaken much earlier in the decision-making process than project level EIA, and is seen as a key tool for sustainable development, public participation in relation to SEA has also been a recent focus.[39] The second amendment, which is still awaiting sufficient ratifications to enter into force, is designed to formalise the compliance procedure to the Convention and Protocol to be based upon regular reporting and to extend the list of activities to which the Convention potentially applies.[40]

The details of the coming into force of the two amendments were clarified by the United Nations Legal Council in 2013, when, in line with an interpretation of the WG, this was confirmed as occurring upon ratification by at least three fourths of the number of Parties at the time of the adoption of the amendments. At that time, three further ratifications were needed for the first amendment, and ten for the second amendment.[41] To simplify the procedure for accession, the sixth session of the *EIA Convention* MOP adopted decision VI/5–II/5 giving blanket approval to any future request for accession to the Convention by countries outside the UNECE region.[42] However non-UNECE countries

---

38 See Jonas Ebbesson, 'A Modest Contribution to Environmental Democracy and Justice in Transboundary Contexts: The Combined Impact of the Espoo Convention and Aarhus Convention' (2011) 20(3) *Review of European Community and International Environmental Law* 248; Simon Marsden, 'Public Participation in Transboundary Environmental Impact Assessment: Closing the Gap Between International and Public Law?' in Brad Jessup and Kim Rubenstein (eds), *Environmental Discourses in Public and International Law* (Cambridge University Press, Cambridge 2012) 238; and Simon Marsden, 'Enforcing Non-Discrimination in Transboundary Environmental Impact Assessment: Advantages for EU Citizens from the Transposition of the Espoo and Aarhus Conventions?' (2009) 6(4) *Journal for European Environmental and Planning Law* 437.

39 Meeting of the Parties, Second session, Geneva 2–5 June 2014, item 11(b) of the provisional agenda, Adoption of decisions: decisions to be taken by the Meeting of the Parties, Good practice recommendations on public participation in strategic environmental assessment, Note by the secretariat, ECE/MP.EIA/SEA/2014/2* 19 March 2014.

40 See Decision III/7, Amendment to the Convention on Environmental Impact Assessment in a Transboundary Context, Cavtat, 4 June 2004.

41 See Meeting of the Parties, Report of the Working Group on Environmental Impact Assessment and Strategic Environmental Assessment on its second meeting, Geneva 27–30 May 2013, ECE/MP.EIA/WG.2/2013/2, 21 October 2013. Treaty Section of the Office of Legal Affairs, United Nations, *Treaty Handbook* (United Nations 2012).

42 ECE/MP.EIA/2014/L.2–ECE/MP.EIA/SEA/2014/L.2.

are still not able to accede to the Convention, until the amendment to Article 17 is in force for all the (31) Parties that were Parties at the time of the amendment's adoption (on 27 February 2001), which is being actively encouraged to expedite the process;[43] this is also the case with respect to the *Water Convention.*

III. OBJECTIVES AND GENERAL PROCEDURAL PROVISIONS

III.1 Convention

The preamble to the Convention emphasises the need to 'ensure environmentally sound and sustainable development', 'enhance international co-operation', 'develop anticipatory policies', and 'give explicit consideration to environmental factors at an early stage in the decision-making process'. Other than these aspirations, there are no specific objectives in the treaty. The following procedural provisions make up the *EIA Convention*, which deal primarily with prevention of harm and international cooperation. The main substantive provision in the Convention is the requirement for the state of origin to take 'due account' of the EIA and the comments received from the public and the affected state. There are, however, no requirements to prohibit proposed activities or minimise adverse transboundary effects, which have caused some to question its validity.[44]

Article 1 contains the definition section with terms such as 'Party of origin' and 'affected Party',[45] 'proposed activity', 'EIA', 'impact', 'transboundary impact', 'competent authority'[46] and 'public' explained. The

---

[43] Meeting of the Parties Sixth session (Convention), Second session (Protocol), Geneva, 2–5 June 2014 Item 2(e) of the provisional agenda, Organizational matters: Status of ratification of the Convention, its amendments and its Protocol – at 4 March 2014, with additions to date, Note by the secretariat.

[44] John Knox, 'The Myth and Reality of Transboundary Environmental Impact Assessment' (2002) 96 *American Journal of International Law* 291, 304. More recently, see also Charles Kersten, 'Rethinking Transboundary Environmental Impact Assessment' (2009) 34 *Yale Journal of International Law* 173; and Alexander Langshaw, 'Giving Substance to Form: Moving towards an Integrated Governance Model of Transboundary Environmental Impact Assessment' (2012) 81(1) *Nordic Journal of International Law* 21.

[45] These are collectively known as the 'concerned Parties'.

[46] This must be the national authority or authority with decision-making powers. This has been one of the challenges for Caucasian and central Asian

Party of origin is the state proposing the development, and the affected Party the state likely to be impacted by it. EIA is defined as a national procedure to evaluate likely environmental impacts, and transboundary impact refers to the impacts within the current jurisdiction when the source originates from another jurisdiction. Impacts include human health and safety and to cultural as well as natural heritage; climate impacts and change to socio-economic conditions are also included.

Article 2 contains general provisions for the management of effects, legal measures required, anticipation and notification, consultation and participation, reference to SEA, exemptions, and requirements for more stringent measures. Article 2(1) obliges the Parties to 'take all appropriate and effective measures to prevent, reduce and control significant adverse transboundary environmental impact from proposed activities'. Appendix I lists the proposed activities that are likely to cause impacts, and for which an EIA procedure is to be established in accordance with Article 2(2), including public participation and with the documentation required by Appendix II. Even where not listed in Appendix I, proposals which are considered by affected Parties to have potential significant adverse environmental effects must be treated as if they were (Article 2(4)). The EIA must be undertaken by the Party of origin prior to any authorising decision being taken (Article 2(3)), and the Party of origin must also provide an opportunity for the public to participate in the EIA procedure, whether they are in the origin or affected state(s) (Article 2(5)). These opportunities must be made available by the competent authority rather than the proponent, unless the proponent is the state.[47]

The detailed specific provisions of the agreement then follow: Article 3, notification[48]; Article 4, documentation[49]; Article 5, consultation[50]; Article 6, the final decision[51]; Article 7, post project analysis[52]; and Article 8, bilateral and multilateral cooperation.[53] Article 3(1) requires

---

Parties to date as noted in Chapter 8, given the different EIA system which has allowed proponents to take on this role.

[47] See *Committee Opinions*, para. 12, which emphasises the challenges faced by Parties who were formerly part of the Soviet Union. This is discussed further in Chapter 8 of this book in relation to the expertise system. Other decisions on public participation can be found in paras. 58–64.

[48] See *Committee Opinions,* paras. 30–45, which include comment on the importance of bilateral and multilateral agreements in addressing these issues.

[49] See *Committee Opinions,* paras. 46–55.

[50] See *Committee Opinions,* paras. 65–69.

[51] See *Committee Opinions,* paras. 70–77.

[52] This is yet to be addressed by the CC, see *Committee Opinions,* para. 78.

[53] See *Committee Opinions,* paras. 79–80.

the Party of origin to give notification of proposals to any affected Party or Parties as soon as possible, consistent with notifying its own public. Specific content requirements are set out in Article 3(2), concerning the proposed activity and potential transboundary impacts, the decision and response times. The CC has confirmed that even a low likelihood of such an impact should trigger the obligation to notify affected Parties in accordance with Article 3, which 'means that notification is necessary unless a significant adverse transboundary impact can be excluded'.[54]

If the affected Party wishes to participate, Article 3(5) obliges the Party of origin to provide relevant information. The affected Party is also required to provide information on the potentially affected environment in accordance with Article 3(6) to enable the Party of origin to prepare the EIA documentation. This must be provided promptly through a joint body if one exists.[55] If notification has not been given to a potentially affected Party which considers itself such, Article 3(7) provides that discussions should commence with the Party of origin which must be based on the exchange of sufficient information between the Parties. Failing a successful outcome, the Appendix IV inquiry procedure may be triggered to determine whether there are likely to be significant adverse environmental effects.[56] This has been used only once to date, in relation to the Danube-Black Sea Deep Water Navigation Canal in the Ukrainian Sector of the Danube Delta.[57] Parties are also free to decide on alternative means to determine such questions. The inquiry procedure has been subject to considerable comment by the IC. Although many of the opinions were expressed in the context of the submission by Romania

---

[54] *Committee Opinions*, para. 17.

[55] There is no definition of 'joint body', reference to which is also made in other requirements such as Article 4(2) and Article 5 below. Appendix VI concerning elements for bilateral and multilateral cooperation also does not refer to the establishment of such bodies, although para. 2(g) suggests joint EIA and joint monitoring programmes. Note the role of joint bodies under Article 9(2) of the *Water Convention*, discussed in Chapter 6 and the commentary of the *Implementation Guide* thereon, which may provide some assistance. This is another example of the combined contribution of the agreements to transboundary environmental governance.

[56] In relation to significance determinations, see http://www.unece.org/env/eia/pubs/cepwg3r6.html, accessed 17 November 2014.

[57] Espoo Inquiry Commission, *Report on the Likely Significant Adverse Transboundary Impacts of the Danube-Black Sea Navigation Route at the Border of Romania and the Ukraine*, July 2006, accessed 17 November 2014 at http://www.unece.org/fileadmin/DAM/env/eia/documents/inquiry/Final%20Report%2010%20July%202006.pdf.

against the Ukraine, several have broad potential application. These include that:

> The final opinion of an inquiry commission is a matter of fact and takes effect immediately; in particular the Convention does not provide for the Parties to 'study' such an opinion ... The final opinion of an inquiry commission cannot be challenged and should lead to notification if the opinion is that a significant adverse transboundary impact is likely.[58]

Article 3(8) contains the significant requirement imposed on the concerned Parties to inform the public of the proposed activity and of the right of the public to make comments to the competent authority of the Party of origin.[59] Article 4(1) requires the EIA documentation to comprise the minimum information specified in Appendix II, which must be submitted to the competent authority of the Party of origin. The affected Party must be forwarded this information via a joint body, again if one exists, under Article 4(2), and the concerned Parties must then distribute the documentation to the public and competent authorities of the affected Parties in the area likely to be affected. Any comments must also be submitted within a reasonable time before any final decision is taken.

After the EIA documentation is complete, Article 5 requires the Party of origin to enter into consultations with the affected Party without delay. These must include the potential transboundary impact of the proposed activity and measures to reduce or eliminate it. Alternatives, monitoring and other measures should also be included in the consultations. Reasonable time frames must be agreed on and consultations held via a joint body if one exists.

Article 6 contains detailed obligations concerning the final decision taken, which, as noted below in relation to Caucasia and in Chapter 8 in relation to central Asia, has been a cause of some concern to date. Under Article 6(1), due account must be taken of the EIA,[60] including the

---

[58] *Committee Opinions*, para. 21. Other comments are located in paras. 20–28. The *Industrial Accidents Convention* also has provision for an inquiry procedure to be established, and this opinion would very likely be persuasive in relation to findings of that body.

[59] The importance of public participation has been confirmed by several decisions of the IC, see *Committee Opinions*, paras. 13 (domestic regulatory framework needed), 11 (to be included in primary rather than secondary legislation), and 12 (for the competent authority not the proponent unless the proponent is also the state).

[60] 'Due account' is not defined under the Convention, but as with the information and public participation provisions (such as timeframes), reference

documentation, comments received and consultation outcomes. Article 6(2) requires the final decision be transmitted to the affected Party together with the reasons and considerations on which it is based. Article 6(3) importantly provides that if additional information on the significant adverse transboundary impact comes to light before the project commences – and which would have affected the decision to allow it – consultations must begin immediately between the concerned Parties with a view to changing the decision if one of them requests it.

Article 7(1) provides that the concerned Parties shall decide if monitoring is required of the impacts of an approved activity, with a view to achieving the objectives listed in Appendix V. If following the post-project analysis a Party has reasons to believe there are significant adverse transboundary impacts, the other Party must be informed. Consultations with the objective of reducing or eliminating the impact must then begin. Enhancing cooperation between the concerned Parties is the subject of Article 8, which provides for the continuance or establishment of bilateral and multilateral cooperation. Appendix VI provides further information in relation to such cooperation, and reference to other UNECE treaties with similar provisions, particularly where Parties are also Parties to those treaties, may provide additional assistance.[61] Article 9 provides for the establishment or intensification of research programmes to aid further cooperation in relation to the procedures and science of EIA.[62]

Article 15(1) permits the application of any method of dispute settlement, but Parties who ratify and fail to reach agreement (under the non-judicial means of settlement), are obliged to submit the dispute either to the ICJ or to arbitration, depending on their stated wishes, and in accordance with the procedure set out in Appendix VII of the Convention. The same dispute settlement mechanisms apply under the Protocol.[63] A related provision is Article 2(10) which states 'the provisions of this Convention shall not prejudice any obligations of the Parties under international law with regard to activities which have or are

to the *Public Participation Convention* and its *Implementation Guide* (see Chapter 3) – especially for Parties to both treaties – is of considerable assistance. Article 6(8) elaborates on 'due account' to include the reasons and considerations on which the decision was taken.

[61] See the *Water Convention*, Article 9, and the *Implementation Guide* thereon analysed in Chapter 6.

[62] See *Committee Opinions,* paras. 80–83.

[63] See Article 20.

likely to have a transboundary impact'.[64] This indicates that other causes of action that may be available to states (such as any customary rules of international law relating to environmental harm, international cooperation or liability, and/or other treaty obligations), remain applicable despite the requirements – or absence thereof – in the *EIA Convention*.[65]

The *EIA Convention* therefore contains a number of innovative substantive elements. Attention has focused upon detailed information to be submitted to the competent authority of the party of origin for onward transmission to the affected party, provisions for post-project analysis and follow-up/monitoring, and concern for human health and safety, the former of which is also included in the *SEA Protocol*. While many previous treaties have made provision for transboundary assessment, it has been emphasised that the *EIA Convention* also operates to change the behaviour of 'non-state actors' as well as states, that formal compliance is dependent upon the establishment of implementing provisions in domestic law, and that it provides the right of the public in one state to participate in the administrative and judicial procedures established in another state, what is known as the principle of non-discrimination.[66] If the affected public is not given the opportunity to participate, 'the state in question does not comply with international law'.[67]

---

[64] This is not duplicated in the Protocol, presumably because it primarily operates in a domestic context.

[65] In regard to customary international law, see ICJ, *Case Concerning Pulp Mills on the River Uruguay (Argentina v. Uruguay)* (20 April 2010, Judgment), para. 204. For discussion, see Alan Boyle, 'Developments in the International Law of Environmental Impact Assessments and their Relation to the Espoo Convention' (2011) 20 *Review of European Community and International Environmental Law* 227; and Rachel Lorne Johnstone, 'Evaluating Espoo: What Protection does the Espoo Convention Offer the Arctic Marine Environment?' (2013) V *Yearbook of Polar Law* 337, 339–42. Note also *Committee Opinions*, para 29. For the prospects of transboundary SEA (in relation to the JARPA II programme), see Separate Opinion of Judge ad hoc Charlesworth (paras. 8–10) in ICJ, *Case Concerning Whaling in the Antarctic (Australia v. Japan: New Zealand Intervening)* (31 March 2014, Judgment).

[66] Simon Marsden, 'Enforcing Non-discrimination in Transboundary Environmental Impact Assessment: Advantages for EU citizens from the Transposition of the Espoo and Aarhus Conventions?' (2009) 6 *Journal for European Environmental and Planning Law* 437. See *Committee Opinions,* para. 53.

[67] Ebbesson, above n. 17, 50.

III.2 Protocol

Although the Protocol has a provision for the evaluation of transboundary environmental effects,[68] it focuses almost entirely on establishing SEA procedural requirements in a national context, whereas the Convention deals almost exclusively with procedural issues for EIA in a transboundary context.[69] This has some synergies with the *Protocol on Water and Health* to the *Water Convention* (Chapter 6), the former of which also has a large focus on the effectiveness of national measures.[70] The *SEA Protocol* has generated significant interest, regardless of its connection with the *EIA Convention*. To assist potential and existing members, a detailed *Resource Manual* provides guidance on its application.[71] In contrast to the absence of an objective for the *EIA Convention*, the objective of the *SEA Protocol* in Article 1 is to provide for a high level of protection of the environment, including health,[72] by:

(a) Ensuring that environmental, including health, considerations are thoroughly taken into account in the development of plans and programmes;
(b) Contributing to the consideration of environmental, including health, concerns in the preparation of policies and legislation;
(c) Establishing clear, transparent and effective procedures for strategic environmental assessment;

---

[68] Article 10.

[69] Jan de Mulder, 'The Expansion of Environmental Assessment in International Law: the Protocol on Strategic Environmental Assessment to the Espoo Convention' (2006) 18 *Environmental Law and Management* 269.

[70] See Chapter 6. See also Annex I, *Resource Manual* in n. 71 below.

[71] United Nations Economic Commission for Europe, *Resource Manual to Support Application of the UNECE Protocol on Strategic Environmental Assessment* (United Nations 2012) ECE/MP.EIA/17 ('*Resource Manual*'); Part A is concerned with the application of the Protocol and Part B is a trainers' guide. Unlike the Implementation Guides to the *Water Convention* and the *Public Participation Convention*, this is not, however, a formal guide, and although the other guides are authoritative legal interpretations, none are legally binding. A shorter version of this is also available as an aide memoir: United Nations Economic Commission for Europe, *Simplified Resource Manual to Support Application of the UNECE Protocol on Strategic Environmental Assessment* (United Nations 2012), ECE/MP.EIA/18 ('*Simplified Resource Manual*').

[72] The focus on health in the *SEA Protocol* builds on this focus in the *Protocol on Water and Health*, which is another example of the combined contribution of the agreements. For further discussion, see T B Fischer, 'Health and Strategic Environmental Assessment', in R Fehr, M Martuzzi, J Nowacki and F Viliani (eds), *Health in Impact Assessments* (WHO/EUPHA/IAIA, 2014).

(d) Providing for public participation in strategic environmental assessment;
(e) Integrating by these means environmental, including health, concerns into measures and instruments designed to further sustainable development.

Article 2 is the definition section and follows the definitions in the Convention wherever possible, including the definition of the public (Article 2(8)) which currently fails to accord with the definition of 'the public concerned' in the *Public Participation Convention*.[73] Plans and programmes (or modifications thereto) must be 'required by legislative, regulatory or administrative provisions' (Article 2(5)(a)), and 'subject to preparation and/or adoption by an authority or prepared by an authority for adoption, through a formal procedure, by a parliament or a government' (Article 2(5)(b)).[74] SEA is defined in Article 2(6) as:

> ... the evaluation of the likely environmental, including health, effects, which comprises the determination of the scope of an environmental report and its preparation, the carrying out of public participation and consultations, and the taking into account of the environmental report and the results of the public participation and consultations in a plan or programme.[75]

General provisions are outlined in Article 3, and require each Party to 'take the necessary legislative, regulatory and other appropriate measures to implement the provisions of this Protocol within a clear, transparent framework' (Article 3(1)). Assistance from authorities to the public (Article 3(2)), and support to NGOs (Article 3(3)) are also requirements of the Protocol, which is confirmed to introduce only minimum requirements, enabling Parties to do more if they wish (Article 3(4)). The expansive nature of the Protocol is such that, like the *Public Participation Convention* (see Chapter 3) Parties are to promote its objectives in international decision making and forums (Article 3(5)). Non-discrimination in relation to public participation regardless of citizenship, nationality or domicile is a clearly stated international norm confirmed by Article 3(7).

---

[73] This will be addressed now the first amendment has come into force, although for Parties who are also Party to the *Public Participation Convention*, the definition in that Convention must nonetheless be applied.

[74] To examine whether plans or programmes are subject to SEA under these provisions see Chapter A3, *Resource Manual*, which explains the legal obligations, tests applied and suggests some practical arrangements.

[75] See Chapter A1, *Resource Manual*, which explains this in more detail together with the benefits and costs, and guiding principles.

Article 4 establishes the field of application of the Protocol in relation to established sectors: agriculture, forestry, fisheries, energy, industry including mining, transport, regional development, waste management, water management, telecommunications, tourism, town and country planning or land use. For each of these sectors, SEA is to be carried out for plans and programmes which set the framework for future development consent of projects listed in annex I or II of the Protocol (EIA) (Article 4(2)).[76] This is strong evidence of the combined contribution of the UNECE agreements. For other plans and programmes not related to the established sectors, the state Party decides whether to carry out the assessment or not (Article 4(3)). This is also the case for those which do relate to these sectors but which determine the use of small areas at local level and for minor modifications to plans and programmes (Article 4(4)). In each of these cases, the Party decides whether the plan or programme is likely to have significant effects either on a case-by-case basis, by specifying types of plans and programmes, or by combining both approaches; the criteria in Annex III are to be taken into account in these cases (Article 5(1)). Environmental and health authorities (Article 5(2)) are to be consulted, the public provided with participation opportunities where possible (Article 5(3)),[77] and conclusions and reasons for deciding not to carry out SEA outlined (Article 5(4)).

Article 6(1) states that each Party shall establish arrangements for the determination of the relevant information to be included in the environmental report.[78] There is no obligation to prepare a scoping report which would set out the terms of reference. Environmental and health authorities are again to be consulted on what to include (Article 6(2)), and also the public where appropriate (Article 6(3)). The obligation to prepare the report is found in Article 7(1); they are to be prepared for plans and programmes subject to SEA. Article 7(2) requires that it 'identify,

---

[76] The integration of SEA into plan and programme making is the subject of Chapter A2 of the *Resource Manual*, which explains the links between them, practical approaches and options. Systems of plan and programme making have developed differently to those in western Europe, see Jiri Dusik, Aleh Cherp, Ausra Jurkeviciute, Henrieta Martonakova and Nick Bonvoisin, *SEA Protocol: Initial Capacity Development in Selected Countries of the Former Soviet Union* (REC/UNDP 2006), accessed 17 November 2014 at http://www.unece.org/env/eia/documents/SEA_CBNA/UNDP-REC-UNECE_SEAbulletin_no.2_en.pdf.

[77] This is another of the provisions of the Protocol not currently compliant with the *Public Participation Convention*, which the coming into force of the first amendment will change.

[78] Scoping and the environmental report are explained in Chapter A4.2 of the *Resource Manual*.

describe and evaluate the likely significant environmental, including health, effects of implementing the plan or programme and its reasonable alternatives'. Article 7(3) emphasises that reports must be 'of sufficient quality', with Annex IV stipulating the information that must be contained within.

Article 8(1) requires 'early, timely and effective opportunities for public participation, when all options are open'.[79] Article 8(2) contains an information provision, such that each Party shall ensure the 'timely public availability of the draft plan or programme and the environmental report'. The public concerned (including relevant NGOs) must be identified (Article 8(3)), and must have an opportunity to express its opinion on the draft plan or programme and the environmental report within a 'reasonable time frame' (Article 8(4)). The detailed arrangements for informing and consulting the public must be decided on and also made publicly available (Article 8(5)).

In accordance with Article 9(1) it is up to each Party to designate the authorities that must be consulted,[80] and to whom the draft plan or programme and environmental report shall be made available (Article 9(2)). Authorities must be given 'in an early, timely and effective manner, the opportunity to express their opinion on the draft plan or programme and the environmental report' (Article 9(3)). The detailed arrangements for informing and consulting these authorities are left to the state Party (Article 9(4)).

Article 10 draws a close link between the *SEA Protocol* and *EIA Convention*, requiring transboundary consultations between Parties of origin and affected Parties, at the initiation of either, 'as early as possible before the adoption of the plan or programme' (Article 10(1)).[81] Notifications are to include the draft plan or programme and the environmental report, and information on the decision-making procedure. The public concerned in either country are able to express their opinions within a reasonable timeframe, subject to agreement between each Party as to the detailed arrangements (Article 10(4)).

---

[79] Public participation is explained in Chapter A4.3 of the *Resource Manual*. See also good practice recommendations on public participation in SEA, above n. 37.

[80] Consultation with authorities is explained in Chapter A4.4 of the *Resource Manual*.

[81] Transboundary consultations are explained in Chapter A4.5 of the *Resource Manual*. See also good practice recommendations on public participation in SEA, above n. 37, paras. 47–50, with a UK/Ireland example of transboundary consultation.

When the decision is taken to adopt the plan or programme,[82] Parties must ensure that due account is taken of the conclusions of the environmental report, the measures to prevent, reduce or mitigate the adverse effects identified, and the comments received (Article 11(1)). In accordance with Article 11(2), notice of the decision must be given to the public and authorities (including any consulted affected Party), together with the adopted plan or programme, with a statement of how the environmental and health considerations and comments received have been integrated/taken into account, as well as the reasons for adopting it 'in the light of the reasonable alternatives considered'.[83]

Article 12(1) of the Protocol requires each Party to monitor effects 'to identify, at an early stage, unforeseen adverse effects and to be able to take appropriate remedial action'.[84] Monitoring measures must be stipulated in the environmental report in accordance with Annex IV(7), and results are to be made available to the authorities and the public in accordance with Article 12(2). Article 13 encourages Parties to ensure that environmental concerns are considered and integrated to the extent appropriate in the preparation of policy and legislative proposals likely to have significant effects on the environment, including health.[85]

IV. PRACTICE

IV.1 Convention

a. Implementation

In common with the other UNECE agreements, Parties to the Convention should introduce domestic implementing legislation to ensure compliance with its obligations.[86] This has been confirmed in relation to many Parties

---

[82] Decision making is explained in Chapter A4.6 of the *Resource Manual.*

[83] See Ainhoa Gonzalez and Riki Therivel, 'Alternatives in Strategic Environmental Assessment of Plans and Programs' (2014) 7 *FasTips,* International Association for Impact Assessment.

[84] Monitoring is explained in Chapter A4.7 of the *Resource Manual.*

[85] Chapter A6 of the *Resource Manual* explains this and sets out possible approaches. See also Barry Sadler, *Strategic Environmental Assessment at the Policy Level – Recent Progress, Current Status and Future Prospects* (Regional Environmental Center for Eastern and Central Europe, Prague 2005).

[86] The role of domestic courts in relation to international law is in large part related to whether a state requires implementation of treaty obligations into domestic legislation first ('dualism') or does not ('monism'). Incorporation of customary international law as well as treaties may also differ among dualist

whose constitutional frameworks allow for the direct application of international treaties.[87] Implementation of the Convention has been reviewed four times, following detailed reports submitted to the Secretariat by the Parties in response to a standard questionnaire. The MOP decided at its second meeting in Sofia, (from 26–27 February 1991), to adopt a work plan (Decision II/11), that included an activity on 'Reviews of the implementation of the Convention'.[88] The first review was up until mid-2003, and was primarily focused upon national legislation to implement the Convention; it included responses from both Armenia and Kyrgyzstan (see Chapter 8).[89] The structure of the first review, in considering the implementation of each of the Convention provisions in turn, was followed in subsequent reviews.

The second review of implementation was prepared for the period mid-2003 to the end of 2005.[90] The report for this period revealed a number of weaknesses, including deficiencies in information exchange, public participation and reporting obligations, and a lack of monitoring. Many of these are also common to the enforcement of other treaties.[91] There also remained a continuing need for bilateral and multilateral agreements to identify contacts, and address differences in procedural steps, timing of participation, the interpretation of certain terms, and the content of the report.

The third review was for the period from the start of 2006 to the end of 2009.[92] This found that while there had been a major improvement in application, development of national legislation and bilateral and multilateral agreements to support implementation in a number of areas were

---

states. For other aspects of the issue in an Asian comparative context see Veronika Fifak, 'International Law before English and Asian Courts: Finding the Judicial Role in the Separation of Powers' (2013) 3 *Asian Journal of International Law* 271.

[87] See for example, *Committee Opinions*, paras. 8 (Ukraine) and 9 (Armenia).

[88] The obligation to report was later confirmed by the IC, see *Committee Opinions,* paras. 84–86.

[89] Economic Commission for Europe, *Review of Implementation 2003,* Advance Copy, 30 August 2004.

[90] United Nations Economic Commission for Europe, *Review of Implementation of the Convention on Environmental Impact Assessment in a Transboundary Context* (United Nations 2008), ECE/MP.EIA/11.

[91] Above n. 69, 270.

[92] United Nations Economic Commission for Europe, *Review of Implementation of the Convention on Environmental Impact Assessment in a Transboundary Context (2006–2009)* (United Nations 2011), ECE/MP.EIA/16.

still of concern. These included confusion about functions of the contact point for notification and the focal point for administrative matters, that Appendix I (a list of activities) was not reflected in full by some, the lack of a definition of 'the public' was possibly leading to narrow interpretations, and there was a failure to understand that 'concerned Parties' are responsible for public participation opportunities. It also noted the failure to recognise that transboundary consultations are distinct, that there was a lack of experience in carrying out post-project analysis, and a continuing need for bilateral and multilateral agreements or other arrangements. Other issues raised were how to proceed when there is no response to a notification or disagreement about the need for notification, the interpretation of various terms, and the requirement for post-project analysis. The third review found that Armenia and Azerbaijan had yet to introduce domestic implementing legislation, with both recognising the need to either amend the current law (Armenia), or adopt new legislation and guidance (Azerbaijan).

The fourth review was based on the years 2010–2012, with a draft report prepared for the WG finalised by the IC for the sixth session of the MOP.[93] The findings were that again, despite improvements, several areas still needed attention. These included continuing definition problems ('promptly', 'due account', 'reasonably obtainable', 'final decision'). Responsibilities for public participation remained an issue, together with contact points for notification and focal points for administrative matters – all noted in the third review. Other matters still not understood were the distinct nature of transboundary consultations and lack of experience with post-project analysis. Development of bilateral and multilateral agreements to address some of these failings was widely recognised, together with an ongoing need to enhance awareness of and capacity in implementation by all stakeholders.

From the information it is clear that Armenia and Azerbaijan have now adopted domestic implementing legislation but it is not yet in force.[94] Armenia finds the formality of the obligations difficult in respect of its

---

[93] Meeting of the Parties, Sixth session, Geneva, 2–5 June 2014, Item 6 of the provisional agenda, Review of compliance, implementation and work done by the Implementation Committee, Draft fourth review of implementation of the Convention, note by the Secretariat, ECE/MP.EIA/2014/3, 20 March 2014.

[94] For detailed responses, see Ministry of Nature Protection, *Report of Armenia on the Implementation of the Convention on Environmental Impact Assessment in a Transboundary Context in the period 2010–2012*, informal translation, 27 March 2013; and Ministry of Ecology and Natural Resources, *Report of Azerbaijan on the Implementation of the Convention on Environmental*

non diplomatic relations with Azerbaijan, which acknowledges similar problems; this has necessitated the use of the Secretariat as a go between (discussed further below).[95] Detailed consideration by the other two Asian Parties to this Convention (Kazakhstan and Kyrgyzstan) is analysed in Chapter 8. Also in the Caucasus, a start-up workshop for the development of a new law on EIA and SEA in Georgia was held in August 2014 in Tbilisi.[96] This took account of the UNECE guidance on enhancing consistency between the Convention on one hand, and EIA within the framework of state ecological expertise in the countries of EECCA on the other.[97] This guidance is considered in detail in Chapter 8 in relation to central Asia but is applicable to all these countries.

b. Compliance

The objective of the IC is to review compliance with obligations under both the Convention and Protocol to assist them in meeting their commitments. The IC was established by the MOP in February 2001,[98] and has eight members who are nominated by Parties elected by the MOP, with alternates elected for Protocol matters.[99] The functions are to consider any submissions concerning possible non-compliance by a Party, examine compliance on the basis of information provided to the implementation reviews and elsewhere – and if needs be on its own initiative request further information and follow-up – and to prepare

Impact Assessment in a Transboundary Context in the period 2010–2012, 30 March 2013.

95 As seen above, the *EIA Convention* contains a provision for dispute settlement where Parties are unable to avoid disputes via a compliance procedure. In relation to dispute settlement in general terms, see Duncan French, Matthew Saul and Nigel White, *International Law and Dispute Settlement: New Problems and Techniques* (Hart Publishing, Oxford 2010).

96 http://www.unece.org/index.php?id=35879 accessed 17 November 2014.

97 Meeting of the Parties, Sixth session, Geneva, 2–5 June 2014, Item 11(a) of the provisional agenda, Adoption of decisions: decisions to be taken by the Meeting of the Parties to the Convention, General guidance on enhancing consistency between the Convention and environmental impact assessment within State ecological expertise in countries of Eastern Europe, the Caucasus and Central Asia, ECE/MP.EIA/2014/2, 20 March 2014.

98 See Decision II/4, later revised as Decision III/2 appendix, ECE/MP.EIA/6.

99 See United Nations Economic Commission for Europe, Convention on Environmental Impact Assessment in a Transboundary Context, *Structure and Functions of the Implementation Committee and Procedures for Review of Compliance/Operating Rules of the Implementation Committee* (United Nations 2011).

reports on compliance issues to the MOP. The MOP may decide what measures to take in relation to any non-compliance upon information being received from the IC. If a question is being considered by an inquiry commission it may not be the subject of a submission under the compliance procedure.

Koivurova distinguishes between the requirements for compliance control under the Convention and Protocol, the latter which imposes reporting obligations on the Parties and the former which will if amendment to the Convention is approved by the Parties.[100] The only existing requirement under the Convention is Article 11(2), which indirectly sets out the terms of reference of the MOP to require Parties to continuously review implementation in the ways stated. Further to the second amendment, a new Article 14 bis concerning review of compliance by regular reporting arrangements will be applicable to the Protocol (see Article 14(1)) and Convention if ratified.[101] Apart from these provisions, the current regime operates further to Decision II/4 in relation to the review of compliance, and Decisions I/6–V/6 which extend the application of the Convention compliance procedure to the Protocol.[102]

The IC notes that 'compliance concerns both legal implementation and practical application';[103] this is known in the impact assessment community as the distinction between procedural (the former) and substantive (the latter) effectiveness. As with those prepared by the *Public Participation Convention* CC, and the *Implementation Guides* for both the *Public Participation Convention* (Chapter 3) and *Water Convention* (Chapter 6) – and to some degree the *Resource Manual* for the *SEA Protocol* (discussed below) – the *Committee Opinions* are a persuasive legal source on the obligations in the Convention, and when updated, the

---

[100] Timo Koivurova, 'The Convention on Environmental Impact Assessment in a Transboundary Context' in G Ulfstein, T Marauhn and A Zimmermann (eds) *Making Treaties Work: Human Rights, Environment and Arms Control* (Cambridge University Press, Cambridge 2007) 227.

[101] Ibid, 228.

[102] Meeting of the Parties, Sixth session (Convention), Second session (Protocol), Geneva, 2–5 June 2014, Item 6 of the provisional agenda, Review of compliance, implementation and work done by the Implementation Committee, Adoption of decisions: decisions to be taken by the Meeting of the Parties to the Convention, Report on the activities of the Implementation Committee, Note by the Implementation Committee, ECE/MP.EIA/2014/4–ECE/MP.EIA/SEA/2014/4, 24 March 2014, para. 9.

[103] ECE/MP.EIA/10, decision IV/2 (review of compliance), annex II, para. 24.

Protocol.[104] The document mainly contains direct quotations of the opinions and recommendations of the IC in the period from 2001 to 2010 (the IC's first 19 sessions), as expressed in its session reports, in its report to the fourth session of the MOP, and in its findings and recommendations following either a submission or an IC initiative.

The most recent sessions of the MOP were held in June 2014, at which the IC gave its latest report. Of significance, the IC notes the follow up of Decisions V/4 (Armenia and Azerbaijan), which are discussed below,[105] and summarised in the report.[106] There have therefore been two submissions by Asian states Parties against others under the Convention, both by the same states. The IC has also on its own initiative considered a case of non-compliance against each of these Parties.[107] The first submission was by Azerbaijan on 5 May 2011 having concerns about Armenia's compliance, with respect to the planned building of a nuclear power station in Metsamor, Armenia.[108] The second was another submission by Armenia on 31 August 2011 having concerns about Azerbaijan's compliance, with respect to six named oil and gas projects developed in Azerbaijan.[109] As noted, both cases were complicated due to a lack of diplomatic relations between the states Parties and the need for the Secretariat to act as an intermediary.[110]

The first has since concluded, with the IC suggesting ways to deal with communication difficulties. These were informed by a seminar on sharing good practice and tools for communication, cooperation and conflict

[104] Above n. 15.

[105] Above n. 102, paras. 18–21 and 24–26.

[106] Above n 102, paras. 42–48 and 57–60.

[107] These concern the drafting of domestic implementing legislation in Armenia and Azerbaijan. See Meeting of the Parties, Implementation Committee, Seventeenth session, Geneva 14–18 September 2009, Report of the Implementation Committee on its Seventeenth session, ECE/MP.EIA/IC/2009/4, 22 October 2009.

[108] See EIA/IC/S/3: http://www.unece.org/env/eia/implementation/eia_ic_s_3.html, accessed 17 November 2014.

[109] This case concerns transit pipelines relating to the two states Parties. See http://www.unece.org/env/eia/implementation/eia_ic_s_5.html, accessed 17 November 2014.

[110] However the IC believes that there could still be ways to implement the Convention, in particular in relation to notification, exchange of information, public participation and consultations. Meeting of the Parties, Implementation Committee, Twenty-sixth session, Geneva 26–28 November 2012, Report of the Implementation Committee on its Twenty-sixth session, ECE/MP.EIA/IC/2012/6, 19 December 2012.

resolution for countries with no diplomatic relations.[111] Seminar presentations provided case studies from western Europe, Africa, east Asia and Latin America where co-management and environmental protection were possible despite political tensions. Asian examples included India and Pakistan, Iran and Iraq, and China, Japan and South Korea.[112] Preliminary lessons learnt were that environmental peacemaking efforts may begin with initiatives from NGOs and other bodies, that the environment can often be a catalyst for cooperation, that conflict resolution may be possible even in the absence of diplomatic relations, although ultimately, political will is the key.[113]

In the second, considered during the twenty-eighth session, the IC found that Azerbaijan was compliant with its obligations, although it was encouraged 'to continue monitoring and submitting monitoring reports to Armenia with a view to taking all appropriate and effective measures to control any significant adverse transboundary impact from the activities mentioned in the submission'.[114] Azerbaijan was also encouraged to continue improving the legal, administrative and other measures needed to comply with the Convention, including clearly designating in its legislation what decision constitutes a final decision. Another compliance issue arising from the first review of compliance concerned Kyrgyzstan, which is discussed in Chapter 8.[115]

---

[111] Meeting of the Parties, Working Group on Environmental Impact Assessment and Strategic Environmental Assessment, Third meeting Geneva, 11–15 November 2013, Item 4 of the provisional agenda, Exchange of good practices, Background paper on good practice on communication, cooperation and conflict resolution, Note by the Chair of the Implementation Committee and representatives of the European Commission and the International Association of Impact Assessment, ECE/MP.EIA/WG.2/2013/INF.11, 24 October 2013.

[112] Ibid, pp. 6–7.

[113] Ibid, p. 9.

[114] Meeting of the Parties, Implementation Committee, Twenty-eighth session, Geneva 10–12 September 2013, Report of the Implementation Committee on its Twenty-eighth session, ECE/MP.EIA/IC/2013/4, 1 November 2013, para. 78.

[115] This concerned clarification of a response to the questionnaire, which was dealt with, EIA/IC/SCI/1/3. See http://www.unece.org/env/eia/implementation/eia_ic_sci_1_3.html, accessed 17 November 2014.

IV.2 Protocol

The draft first review of implementation of the Protocol has also recently concluded, again for the period from 2010–2012.[116] It was based on responses from 19 of the 25 Parties in mid-July 2013, and was followed by a draft Decision on the review of compliance at the second session of the MOP in June 2014, which was designed to promote and improve compliance.[117] As a first review on an instrument not long in force, experience was not surprisingly found to be relatively limited, with no compliance issues to report. The main issues identified were confusion regarding definitions, difficulty identifying relevant plans and programmes, and concerning the content and level of detail of the environmental report. Other issues were confusion about the final decision and whether monitoring requirements should be included, and related requirements and responsibilities concerning monitoring. Finally, the need for bilateral and multilateral agreements was recognised, improving awareness and capacity to implement obligations, and the lack of a central registry or database which made sectoral reporting challenging.[118]

In relation to transboundary consultations, the review found that if the plan or programme was likely to have cross border effects, most Parties would inform the affected Party either during the scoping phase and/or when the draft plan or programme and report had been prepared. Armenia commented that although there was no practice or legislation as yet, it would include this within its legislative framework being prepared.[119] Most of the responding Parties indicated that they did not have any legislative requirements for the application of principles and elements of the Protocol to policies and legislation.[120] In relation to domestic SEA procedures, there were difficulties in reporting for most

---

[116] Meeting of the Parties, Second session, Geneva, 2–5 June 2014, Item 6 of the provisional agenda, Review of compliance, implementation and work done by the Implementation Committee, Draft first review of implementation of the Protocol, Note by the secretariat, ECE/MP.EIA/SEA/2014/3, 20 March 2014.

[117] Meeting of the Parties, Second session, Geneva, 2–5 June 2014, Item 11(b) of the provisional agenda, Adoption of decisions: decisions to be taken by the Meeting of the Parties to the Convention serving as the Meeting of the Parties to the Protocol, Draft decision on the review of compliance with the Protocol, Proposal by the Implementation Committee, ECE/MP.EIA/SEA/2014/L.3, 14 March 2014.

[118] Above n. 116, para. 8.

[119] Above n. 116, para. 36.

[120] Above n. 116, para. 47.

Parties due to decentralisation. Armenia reported that following ratification in 2011 it had begun about 50 domestic EIA procedures, with some also subject to SEA due to their nature and scale; these included the mining, agriculture and large-scale construction sectors.[121]

V. PROSPECTS

V.1 Asia

As stated at the beginning, although there are currently only four Asian Parties to the Convention in the Caucasus and central Asia (out of eight), there has been a considerable amount of capacity building activity in these subregions. In July 2013, a conference on EIA in central Asia and Azerbaijan was held, entitled 'Joining efforts on Environment Impact Assessment for Central Asia and Azerbaijan – the transition to Participation'.[122] Russia as a signatory has indicated its intention to ratify.[123] As also noted, a number of Asian states have indicated their wish to join the treaty when the first amendment comes into force (which has now occurred), although further ratifications are still needed for non-UNECE states to accede as indicated. A workshop on EIA in a transboundary context in eastern Asia was held in Korea in June 2012, at which most of these states were present.[124] In addition, the most recent MOP for the Convention and Protocol was attended by all Caucasian and central Asian states other than Turkmenistan, indicating the level of interest. Russia (as a signatory) and Mongolia, South Korea and Vietnam (as UN members) were also in attendance, together with various Asian environmental

---

[121] Above n. 116, para. 53.

[122] This was organised by the Tajik branch of CAREC and the Environmental Committee of the Parliament of the Republic of Tajikistan with the support of the Swiss Government, the University of Bern and the Secretariat of the Espoo Convention. See http://www.unece.org/index.php?id=33502, accessed 17 November 2014.

[123] Above n. 6.

[124] This was organised by the Korea Environment Institute and South Korean Ministry of Environment and included presentations on the Caspian Sea, Korea, Japan, Mongolia, northeast Asia, Vietnam, Indonesia and southeast Asia. See Korea Environment Institute, Ministry of Environment, UNECE Espoo Convention, *Workshop on Environmental Impact Assessment in a Transboundary Context in Eastern Asia*, May 2013, accessed 17 November 2014 at http://www.unece.org/index.php?id=29911.

NGOs.[125] Further to attendance by others at previous sessions (for instance Iraq), this is indicative of the continuing interest by Asian states, whether they are UNECE members or not.

National round-tables on legal implementation of the *SEA Protocol* are proposed for both Azerbaijan[126] and Armenia.[127] The purpose of these is to assist capacity building and national implementation efforts further to the difficulties with implementation and compliance discussed above. Furthermore in the other Caucasian state, Georgia, a start-up workshop for the development of a new law on SEA was also recently held.[128] Each of these developments emphasises the need to respond to the differences and difficulties imposed by the system of state ecological expertise in former Soviet countries, which compounds the implementation and compliance issues. This is considered in detail in Chapter 8 of this book in relation to central Asia, but is relevant to all states that were formerly part of the Soviet Union in the EECCA group.

Beyond the UNECE region in Asia, there is significant potential for the *SEA Protocol*. Despite systems and implementation falling behind countries in Europe and north America, and still being limited to a few jurisdictions, Hayashi et al comment that SEA 'is now widely recognised and increasingly applied in the Asian region'.[129] The experience of the most advanced jurisdictions is reported on, which are Hong Kong, China, South Korea, Japan, Vietnam and Indonesia. In a WB publication, Dusik and Xie also comment on experience in Malaysia, the Philippines, Thailand, Cambodia and Laos.[130] Although the Protocol is not referred to

---

125 Meeting of the Parties Sixth session (Convention), Second session (Protocol), Geneva, 2–5 June 2014, Report of the Meeting of the Parties, ECE/MP.EIA/20–ECE/MP.EIA/SEA/4, 15 July 2014, paras. 3 and 4.

126 Held on 28 August 2014 in Baku; see http://www.unece.org/index.php?id=35881, accessed 17 November 2014.

127 Held on 18 September 2014 in Yerevan; see http://www.unece.org/index.php?id=35882, accessed 17 November 2014. See also Dusik et al, above n. 76.

128 Held between 24–25 August 2014 in Tbilisi; see http://www.unece.org/index.php?id=35879, accessed 17 November 2014. See also Dusik et al, above n. 76.

129 Kiichiro Hayashi, Young-il Song, Elvis Au and Jiri Dusik, 'SEA in the Asia Region', in Barry Sadler, Ralf Aschemann, Jiri Dusik, Thomas B Fischer, Maria R Partidario and Rob Verheem, *Handbook of Strategic Environmental Assessment* (Earthscan, Abingdon, UK and New York, USA 2011).

130 Dusik, Jiri and Jian Xie, *Strategic Environmental Assessment in East and Southeast Asia: A Progress Review and Comparison of Country Systems and Cases* (World Bank, Washington, DC 2009).

as a reference point for either of these studies, there is clearly an opportunity for it to be used to harmonise procedures in the region and elsewhere.

V.2 Global

The global outlook for the *EIA Convention* is strong and encouraging. It is acknowledged as a global treaty on transboundary EIA in theory, and since the entry into force of the first amendment, it is also, subject to the additional ratifications needed by the MOP, also so in practice.[131] It is made reference to in international courts and tribunals,[132] and used as a precedent for the development of regional agreements for transboundary EIA.[133] The global outlook is therefore extremely positive, as confirmed by Koivurova, the most experienced scholar in the area, who adds valuable insights based on his significant understanding of the regime:

> On balance, there do seem to be good prospects for the Espoo Convention to spread as obstacles are lifted by the States Parties when the 1st amendment enters into force. This is very much related to the design of the Espoo regime, which builds both on sub-regional bottom-up practical co-operation but also on the treaty community being able to address issues related to capacity building and financial support, which are of vast importance to the developing world.[134]

As an indication of recent work in this area, which confirms a positive outlook for the Protocol as well as the Convention, the MOP incorporated a seminar on the globalisation and the role of IFIs as part of the sixth (Convention) and second (Protocol) sessions in mid-2014.[135] This brought together government representatives, NGOs, IFIs and others 'to provide insights on the practice, needs and expectations of non-ECE countries regarding the implementation of strategic environmental assessment (SEA) and transboundary environmental impact assessment (EIA)

---

[131] Above n. 2.

[132] Above n. 65.

[133] These include the regimes of the Caspian Sea, Tumen and Mekong agreements considered in Chapter 2.

[134] Above n. 2, 338.

[135] Meeting of the Parties Sixth session (Convention), Second session (Protocol), Geneva, 2–5 June 2014, Item 6 of the provisional agenda, Seminar on the globalization of the Convention and the Protocol and the role of international financial institutions, Information on the seminar on the globalization of the Convention and the Protocol and the role of international financial institutions, ECE/ MP.EIA/2014/INF.8, 28 May 2014.

procedures, including in view of their possible future accession to the Convention and the Protocol'.[136] With a focus on the role of IFIs, including on energy related projects,[137] the seminar engaged with a full and varied range of stakeholders in considering how best to globalise the agreements moving forward. It was followed by a draft Declaration proposed by the Bureau on the global application of the Convention and Protocol,[138] and Decision VI/5–II/5 on 'Accession by Member States of the United Nations nor members of the United Nations Economic Commission for Europe'.[139]

VI. CONCLUSIONS

The *EIA Convention* was the second of the UNECE treaties to be adopted, some 13 years after the *Air Pollution Convention*. It was undoubtedly a treaty of its time, with objectives of sustainable development, precaution and integration. While it was not the first agreement to provide for transboundary EIA, it has proven the most significant in procedural scope and geographical reach. Given the time lag since the *Air Pollution Convention* it also was able to incorporate a number of procedures which were particularly notable, especially for public participation. It was followed closely in time by the *Water* and *Industrial Accidents Conventions*, which were adopted the following year and incorporated similar provisions in the context of their more specific concerns.

---

136 Ibid, para. 2.

137 See Meeting of the Parties, Sixth session (Convention), Second session (Protocol), Geneva, 2–5 June 2014, Item 9 of the provisional agenda, Panel discussion on the application of the Convention and Protocol to energy-related issues, Informal summary of the panel discussion by the moderator. Available 17 November 2014 at http://www.unece.org/fileadmin/DAM/env/eia/documents/mop6/presentations/energy_panel/InformalSummaryModerator.pdf.

138 Meeting of the Parties, Sixth session (Convention), Second session (Protocol), Geneva, 2–5 June 2014, Items 3(d) and 12 of the provisional agenda, Outstanding issues: draft declaration, Adoption of the declaration, Draft declaration proposal by the Bureau, ECE/MP.EIA/2014/L.4–ECE/MP.EIA/SEA/2014/L.4, Part B, 19 March 2014.

139 Meeting of the Parties, Sixth session (Convention), Second session (Protocol), Geneva, 2–5 June 2014, Report of the Meeting of the Parties (Convention and Protocol), Addendum, Decisions and the Declaration adopted jointly by the Meeting of the Parties (Convention and Protocol), ECE/MP.EIA/20/Add.3–ECE/MP.EIA/SEA/4/Add.3, 15 July 2014, 31–32.

More recently, the adoption and coming into force of the *Public Participation Convention* has enabled cross-fertilisation of procedures for public participation, in effect updating the *EIA Convention* for states which are Parties to both, and since the coming into force of the first amendment, this is now also obligatory for Parties to the *EIA Convention*. The adoption and coming into force of the *SEA Protocol* thereafter, has further enhanced provisions for strategic proposals to undergo assessment, and has in turn been influenced by the public participation provisions in that Convention. Legal implementation of and compliance with the *EIA Convention* is, further to provisions for public participation, the added strength of this treaty, which will be enhanced significantly in legal terms when the second amendment also comes into force. The application of the review of implementation by the MOP and review of compliance by the IC are major benefits to the success of the EIA regime, which in time will benefit the Protocol also.

In an Asian context, it is hoped that the existing states Parties of both agreements will be added to by the other Asian UNECE members, especially Russia given its large number of neighbouring states. At present the four western and central Asian states Parties to the Convention are making progress, although it is impeded by the diplomatic relationship between Armenia and Azerbaijan and the introduction of domestic implementing legislation in both of these states. The central Asian states of Kazakhstan and Kyrgyzstan appear better placed due to the absence of such issues and the existence of specific guidance on the application of the Convention, which is discussed in Chapter 8. The influence in Asia more broadly has, however, been considerable, as the developments under the Caspian Sea, Tumen and Mekong agreements considered in Chapter 2 have shown with respect to transboundary EIA; capacity building efforts in relation to the Protocol also continue apace, which added to the experience with SEA in a considerable number of states in east and southeast Asia, has potential to harmonise procedures for states which choose to become members, subject to the agreement of the MOP.

5. The Industrial Accidents Convention and Civil Liability Protocol

I. INTRODUCTION: STATUS, MEMBERSHIP AND INSTITUTIONS (CONVENTION AND PROTOCOL)

The Convention on the Transboundary Effects of Industrial Accidents (*Industrial Accidents Convention*)[1] was signed by 27 UNECE member countries, as well as the EU, and entered into force in 2000. Both Canada and the USA signed the Convention but have yet to ratify it. There are currently 41 Parties, although Russia, Azerbaijan and Kazakhstan are the only Parties located in the Asian region. Unlike the *Public Participation Convention* (Chapter 3) and *EIA Convention* (Chapter 4), the *Industrial Accidents Convention* is not currently open to membership by non-UNECE member states, nor is there potential for this in the immediate future. The issue dealt with by the Convention is, however, particularly significant in the Asian region.

The Convention was a response by the CSCE and the UNECE to concerns raised by high-profile industrial accidents over the preceding two decades: dioxin releases from a chemical manufacturing plant near Seveso (1976), into the air and River Rhine from an agrochemical warehouse fire in Basel (1986), and the Chernobyl disaster in the same year. The Convention was adopted in Helsinki in 1992, at the same time as the *Water Convention*.[2] The signatories to both decided to cooperate on these interlinked issues, on the premise that major industrial accidents may have far-reaching transboundary effects and can lead to accidental water pollution.

Only months before its entry into force, the need for the Convention was further highlighted by another major industrial accident: a cyanide

---

[1] Convention on the Transboundary Effects of Industrial Accidents (Helsinki, 17 March 1992) 2105 UNTS 457, in force 19 April 2000.

[2] Convention on the Protection and Use of Transboundary Watercourses and Lakes (Helsinki, 17 March 1992), 31 ILM (1992) 1312, in force 6 October 1996.

spill from a mine tailings dam into a transboundary river at Baia Mare. This accident was also a catalyst for efforts to develop the Protocol on Civil Liability and Compensation for Damage Caused by the Transboundary Effects of Industrial Accidents on Transboundary Waters (*Civil Liability Protocol*) which was adopted at Kiev in 2003 and signed by 24 countries.[3] In the intervening decade, only one of these countries (Hungary) has ratified the Protocol, which requires 16 ratifications to enter into force. If the Protocol enters into force, it will, however, be open to all UN member states upon approval of the Protocol MOP.

The institutions of the Convention comprise the Conference of the Parties (COP), Bureau, Working Group on Implementation (WGI), Working Group on Development (WGD), Joint Expert Group on Water and Industrial Accidents (Joint Expert Group), and the Secretariat; there is also provision for a non-permanent inquiry commission to be established. The COP is the governing body of the Convention and meets every two years, with the most recent, the eighth session, being held in late 2014. The main tasks of the COP are to review implementation; advise countries on issues relating to prevention, preparedness and response to industrial accidents with transboundary consequences; create a work programme for activities; and establish the subsidiary bodies needed to address matters related to implementation and development.[4]

The Bureau is elected from representatives of countries at each COP, with 10 members, three of whom must be the COP Chairperson and COP officers.[5] The Bureau meets annually, and its primary roles are to undertake the tasks given to it by the COP, to lead efforts to improve implementation of the Convention, and to monitor the implementation of the work programme. The Bureau is assisted by the Secretariat in performing these tasks. The Executive Secretary of the UNECE carries out the functions of the Convention Secretariat.

One of the two subsidiary bodies of the Convention, the WGI has up to 10 members who are nominated representatives from UNECE member states. It must meet at least once before every COP session, but in

---

3 Protocol on Civil Liability and Compensation for Damage Caused by the Transboundary Effects of Industrial Accidents on Transboundary Waters (Kiev, 21 May 2003), not in force. This was adopted on the same occasion as the *SEA Protocol* (Chapter 4).

4 http://www.unece.org/env/teia/cop.html, accessed 18 November 2014.

5 A maximum of three other members may be drawn from non-Parties to the Convention; the remaining members are elected from among the representatives of the Convention Parties. The number of Bureau members was increased from eight to ten in 2006, to reflect a growing workload.

practice it may meet several times between these meetings.[6] The main tasks of the WGI are to monitor implementation and report to the COP; to review NIRs and prepare an implementation report; to assist the Bureau in facilitating ratification and/or implementation by UNECE member states; to monitor the Strategic Approach as part of the Assistance Programme, and to review countries' self-assessments and action plans.[7]

The second of the subsidiary bodies, the WGD, was established in 2004 to review developments in legal instruments in other international fora that are of relevance to the Convention, and in particular Annex I (Hazardous substances for the purposes of defining hazardous activities). Membership is open to representatives of all Parties, and it is convened whenever required by the COP. The WGD prepared amendments to Annex I in 2005–2006, which were subsequently adopted at the fourth session of the COP. More recently, in 2012, the COP requested the WGD to draft a revised Annex I to ensure consistency with both the UN Globally Harmonized System of Classification and Labelling of Chemicals,[8] and the corresponding EU legislation known as the *Seveso III Directive*.[9]

The Joint Expert Group was created in 1998 by the Parties to both the *Industrial Accidents* and *Water Conventions*. In 2000, its mandate was significantly extended and a future work plan was agreed upon by the Parties to both.[10] Since that time, the activities of the Joint Expert Group have included: supporting the drafting process of the *Civil Liability Protocol*; preparing guidelines for cross-border contingency plans; reviewing relevant criteria for the identification of hazardous activities under the *Industrial Accidents Convention*; developing an inventory of existing safety guidelines and good practices for the prevention of accidental transboundary water pollution; promoting international response exercises; developing safety guidelines for pipelines and tailing

---

[6] For example, it met on five occasions over the period from 2011 to early 2012.

[7] http://www.unece.org/env/teia/wgimplementation.html, accessed 18 November 2014.

[8] 4th Revision (2011).

[9] Directive 2012/18/EU of the European Parliament and of the Council of 4 July 2012 on the control of major-accident hazards involving dangerous substances, amending and subsequently repealing Council Directive 96/82/EC Text with EEA relevance, [2012] OJ L197/1–37.

[10] UNECE, Annex VI: Decision 2000/5 on the Prevention of Accidental Water Pollution, ECE/CP.TEIA/2.

dams; facilitating the exchange of information on the functioning of emergency notification systems; and developing a methodology for harmonised contingency planning.[11]

The institutions for the Protocol are the Protocol MOP, Intergovernmental Working Group on Civil Liability (IWGCL), and Secretariat. In relation to the Protocol MOP, ordinary meetings are held at dates to be determined and if appropriate in conjunction with a meeting of the COP of the *Industrial Accidents Convention* or the MOP of the *Water Convention*. The functions of the Protocol MOP in accordance with Article 21 are to review the implementation of and compliance with the Protocol, consider proposals for amendment and other action for the purposes of the Protocol. The IWGCL held its first meeting in November 2001; as noted its work has been supported by the Joint Expert Group to the *Industrial Accidents Convention* and *Water Convention* as part of the drafting process. The role of the Secretariat in accordance with Article 22 is performed by the Executive Secretary to the UNECE, convening and preparing meetings and associated documentation.

The chapter will, as with each of the other chapters 3–7, first provide some historical background to the legal development of the Convention and Protocol, before outlining the general procedural provisions of both. Legal implementation and compliance will then be analysed in relation to practice, particularly in the western Asian context (the Caucasus), with central Asian experience examined in Chapter 8. Prospective membership and application in other parts of Asia and globally will then be discussed, with conclusions at the end.

II. HISTORICAL BACKGROUND AND LEGAL DEVELOPMENT (CONVENTION AND PROTOCOL)

The issue of transboundary water pollution within the European context began to emerge in political dialogue in the early 1970s. A key document adopted in 1975 by the CSCE,[12] the 'Helsinki Final Act', identified water pollution as one of several environmental concerns. It called on CSCE participating states to cooperate proactively in 'the prevention and control

[11] http://www.unece.org/env/teia/jeg.html, accessed 18 November 2014. The Joint Expert Group last met in October 2011.

[12] The CSCE was established in the early 1970s to serve as 'a multilateral forum for dialogue between East and West', see http://www.osce.org/who/87, accessed 18 November 2014. The name was changed from the CSCE to the Organisation for Security and Cooperation in Europe (OSCE) in 1994.

of water pollution, in particular of transboundary rivers and international lakes'.[13] More generally, the states also agreed to tackle 'environmental problems which, by their nature, are of a multilateral, bilateral, regional or sub-regional dimension',[14] as well as to promote the development and implementation of international law on pollution caused by activities within their jurisdiction or control that affected other countries and regions.[15] These commitments were based on the principle that each state should ensure that activities carried out on its territory did not 'cause degradation of the environment in another State or in areas lying beyond the limits of national jurisdiction',[16] the 'no harm' rule.

However, it was another decade before formal discussions took place on specific measures to address the transboundary effects of industrial accidents. These discussions were provoked by the accident at the Chernobyl nuclear plant in April 1986[17] and the Sandoz chemical spill later the same year.[18] Shortly after the Sandoz accident, and reflecting the high level of concern over the issue, the CSCE stated that its member countries would:

> … cooperate bilaterally and multilaterally with a view to improving and co-ordinating their arrangements for prevention, early warning, exchange of information and mutual assistance in cases of industrial accidents likely to cause transboundary damage to the environment. They will also initiate the examination of key elements related to the transboundary character of industrial accidents, such as clean-up, restoration and liability.[19]

At the Meeting on the Protection of the Environment, convened in 1989 by the CSCE, the participating countries confirmed their commitment to

---

[13] Conference on Security and Co-operation in Europe – Final Act, Helsinki, 1975, 28.

[14] Ibid, 27.

[15] Ibid, 30.

[16] Ibid, 27.

[17] Ironically, nuclear accidents would later be expressly excluded from the scope of the *Industrial Accidents Convention*. See the work of the International Atomic Energy Agency in this regard: http://www.iaea.org/, accessed 18 November 2014.

[18] The Sandoz accident occurred on 1 November 1986 at an agrochemical storage facility in Schweizerhalle, near Basel.

[19] CSCE, *Concluding Document of the Vienna Meeting 1986 of Representatives of the Participating States of the Conference on Security and Co-operation in Europe*, Vienna, 1989, 11, para. 36.

undertaking these tasks.[20] On this basis, the Conference recommended that the UNECE 'elaborate an international convention, code of practice or other appropriate legal instruments on the prevention and control of the transboundary effects of industrial accidents'.[21] This referral of the matter to the UNECE was due to the separate but complementary roles of the two organisations at the time: whilst the CSCE was primarily a political organisation, the UNECE had expertise in developing international instruments, norms and standards.[22]

The formal negotiation phase for the Convention was remarkably brief, in comparison with most other MEAs. The draft text of the Convention was developed over five sessions, held between mid-1990 and late 1991.[23] It was finalised in time for adoption at the Meeting of Senior Advisers to UNECE Governments on Environmental and Water Problems in Helsinki on 17 March 1992. Concurrently to the preparation of the draft Convention, work continued on a non-binding instrument, the Code of Conduct on Accidental Pollution of Transboundary Inland Waters.[24] In 1990, at its 45th Session, the UNECE adopted the Code, which was hailed as 'the first collective response by ECE member Governments to the need to reinforce international co-operation in preventing and combating accidental pollution'.[25] Although the Code of Conduct was both non-binding and narrower in scope due to a focus on inland waters only,

---

[20] *The CSCE/OSCE and the Environment: 1975–2000, Working Paper 5*, Centre for OSCE Research, University of Hamburg, 37. The Meeting was held in Sofia from 16 October–3 November 1989. Discussion of the transboundary effects of industrial accidents was one of three key issues on the agenda.

[21] CSCE, *Report on Conclusions and Recommendations of the Meeting on the Protection of the Environment of the Conference on Security and Co-operation in Europe* (1990), 2–3. The instructions were that such a document should be based on several key objectives and principles that were specified in the Report of the Meeting.

[22] UNECE website, Economic and Environment Dimension of Security – Background, accessed 18 November 2014 at http://www.unece.org/eeds/welcome.html: 'UNECE and the OSCE have shared virtually the same membership of over 50 states. They have both operated on a consensus principle and they have both provided a neutral framework to discuss and resolve potential conflicts [...] As a result of [their] complementarities and shared goals, the two organizations have developed a close relationship.'

[23] Branko Bošnjaković, 'Negotiations in the Context of International Water-Related Agreements' (2003), 13.

[24] Decision C(45); E/ECE/1225; ECE/ENVWA/16.

[25] Foreword to the Code of Conduct, ibid, iii.

it was nevertheless a significant precursor to the *Industrial Accidents Convention* and influenced the preparations of the draft text.[26]

Despite adoption by 26 UNECE member countries (and the EU) in 1992, progress towards the entry into force was slow for several years. During this interval, various projects were commenced to assist with eventual implementation, such as developing a notification system and procedures for identifying hazardous activities, providing training courses and a manual for points of contact, and holding seminars on preventive measures.[27] Some of the signatories also began to put national measures in place to implement the provisions of the Convention. The Convention secured sufficient ratifications and accessions to enter into force in 2000, eight years after its initial adoption.

As mentioned above, the high-profile industrial accident at Baia Mare, Romania, in 2000 revealed a significant gap in international law in terms of allocating liability and providing compensation for the impacts of such accidents. The Institute for European Environmental Policy (IEEP) noted that 'no international legal instrument in force at the time of the accident provided specific rules governing liability for environmental harm and damage to persons and property resulting from transboundary water pollution'.[28] At the first Joint Special Session of the Parties to the *Industrial Accidents Convention* and the *Water Convention* in mid 2001, delegates identified the main shortcomings of existing regimes on civil liability: that they were lacking in specificity, and that they had failed to enter into force.[29] The UNECE explained the consequences of this as follows:

> Experience with industrial accidents causing damage to transboundary waters has shown how difficult it is to receive compensation in these situations. Civil claims very rarely succeed. If there is a settlement, it is usually made out of court. The compensation paid by the operator, if any, is usually much less than the amount of the damage, and the actual compensation paid to victims comes to less than 10 per cent of their claims. Clean-up costs are mostly

---

[26] Ibid, iii.

[27] UNECE, Committee on Environmental Policy, Report on the Sixth Session, 14 December 1999, ECE/CEP/69, 14, Annex I.

[28] Marc Pallemaerts, *Study on National Legislation Needed to Implement the Protocol on Civil Liability and Compensation for Damage Caused by the Transboundary Effects of Industrial Accidents on Transboundary Waters* (Institute for European Environmental Policy, London undated) 2.

[29] UNECE, Report of the Joint Special Session, held at Geneva on 2–3 July 2001, 11 October 2001, ECE/CP.TEIA/5, Annex, 6.

> borne by the State or municipality, and only partially by the operator causing the damage, and the restoration of the environment remains incomplete.[30]

In 2001 the Joint Special Session therefore recognised that there was a need for a binding instrument on civil liability for transboundary damage caused by hazardous activities, which would fit within the scope of both the *Industrial Accidents Convention* and the *Water Convention*.[31] Moreover, Article 13 of the *Industrial Accidents Convention* requires the Parties to 'support appropriate international efforts to elaborate rules, criteria and procedures in the field of responsibility and liability'. Accordingly, an open-ended intergovernmental working group was formed to begin negotiations for the draft *Civil Liability Protocol*.[32]

The negotiation process for the Protocol was unique at the time, as it involved a range of actors: not only governments, but also the private sector (including industry and insurance groups), IGOs and NGOs. The WG held its first meeting in late 2001. Following 15 months of negotiations, the draft agreement was finalised by early 2003, at the seventh meeting of the WG. It was then opened for signature at the 'Environment for Europe' Ministerial Conference in Kiev in May 2003, and subsequently in New York, attaining 24 signatures in total.[33] As was originally intended, the Protocol is a joint instrument to the *Industrial Accidents Convention* and the *Water Convention*. However, it is yet to attain sufficient signatures to enter into force.[34]

In accordance with Article 28(1) and (2) it is open for ratification or accession by Parties to either treaty, or both.[35] By 2006, it had become evident that progress on the ratification of the Protocol was proving to be

---

[30] UNECE, Challenges and Opportunities of Transboundary Accidental Water Pollution, Liability and Compensation – Progress Towards Ratification of the Civil Liability Protocol, ECE/BELGRADE.CONF/2007/INF/2, 15 August 2007, 2–3.

[31] UNECE, Report of the Joint Special Session, held at Geneva on 2–3 July 2001, 11 October 2001, ECE/CP.TEIA/5, Annex, 6.

[32] UNECE, Report of the Joint Special Session, held at Geneva on 2–3 July 2001, 11 October 2001, ECE/CP.TEIA/5.

[33] http://www.unece.org/env/civil-liability/welcome.html, accessed 18 November 2014. Two more countries (Austria and Poland) became signatories when the Protocol was subsequently opened for signature in New York.

[34] As noted earlier, entry into force for the Protocol requires 16 ratifications, but only Hungary has ratified it to date.

[35] Any other Member of the UN may accede to the Protocol once it enters into force, upon approval by the Meeting of the Parties to the Protocol: Article 28(3).

more difficult than expected, and a workshop on this specific issue was held in mid 2007.[36] A major factor that was identified as contributing to the failure of the Protocol to achieve sufficient ratifications so far was the implementation in the EU of the *Directive on Environmental Liability* in 2004.[37] There was an initial perception by some within the EU that the Protocol may be incompatible with the terms of this Directive.[38] Some of these apparent inconsistencies had been resolved by the 2007 workshop, and were further dispelled by the 2012 report of the IEEP, which concluded:

> There is no substantive incompatibility between the liability rules laid down in the Environmental Liability Directive and those set out in the Protocol. The respective liability regimes are complementary rather than contradictory.[39]

Accordingly, in recent years the UNECE has been urging the EU to take steps towards ratification and implementation of the Protocol.[40] However, the EU has steadfastly refused to ratify the Protocol, even though it expressly supports the work being done by the UNECE in this area.[41]

The EU *Environmental Liability Directive* does not apply to areas that are outside the EU borders but still within the UNECE, for instance transboundary waters shared by non-EU countries, and waters shared by

---

36 Above n. 30, 2–3.

37 Directive 2004/35/CE of the European Parliament and of the Council of 21 April 2004 on environmental liability with regard to the prevention and remedying of environmental damage, [2004] OJ L143/56–75.

38 Above n, 30, 4.

39 UNECE, Protocol on Civil Liability and Compensation for Damage Caused by the Transboundary Effects of Industrial Accidents on Transboundary Waters – Note by the Bureaux, 7th Meeting of the Conference of the Parties to the Industrial Accidents Convention, Stockholm, 14–16 November 2012, ECE/CP.TEIA/2012/7, 7.

40 Above n. 30, 3. Pallemaerts, above n. 28, 15–16, notes that 'there is no legal obstacle as a matter of either EU or international law that would prevent EU Member States from becoming Parties to the CLP [Civil Liability Protocol] and giving effect to its provisions in their internal law, while at the same time being bound to implement the provisions of the ELD [Environmental Liability Directive].'

41 At the 7th session of the COP to the *Industrial Accidents Convention* in 2012, the EU reported that 'it was not in a position to ratify the Protocol at that stage because of the complexity of some issues covered by the Protocol that touched upon a large number of interrelated EU laws and EU member State laws': Report of the Conference of the Parties on its Seventh Meeting, Stockholm, 14–16 November 2012, ECE/CP.TEIA/24, 14 (para. 62).

EU and non-EU countries. Civil liability for damage in either of these categories of transboundary waters would only arise if the Protocol were in force.[42] The UNECE is therefore particularly motivated to highlight to its members the importance of ratifying the Protocol for non-EU countries. As it stated in 2007, 'should a transboundary accident occur, there would be no suitable pan-European legal regime in place to cope with civil liability and compensation issues. In this regard, a much more active approach by UNECE member States is needed to create an efficient legal framework to address these issues.'[43]

Therefore, to better facilitate the ratification of the Protocol, the UNECE at that time encouraged its members to establish a national dialogue with all stakeholders potentially affected by its implementation.[44] Cooperation was needed between all relevant actors, particularly the private sector and the insurance industry.[45] Countries should also involve their insurance and financial sectors in assessing the current and future potential for, and limitations to, providing financial guarantees for the risks addressed by the Protocol.[46] Lastly, the UNECE identified a need to increase capacity-building activities to assist authorities and administrative bodies in various countries, particularly those with economies in transition. Such activities should assist with developing good administrative and legislative practice, and should encourage these countries to take the necessary steps to introduce appropriate liability regimes and to ratify the Protocol.[47]

Looking at the Convention in an Asian context, currently Kazakhstan, Russia, Azerbaijan, Armenia and Georgia are the only Parties in the region.[48] This low participation rate is partly due to inaction by the other UNECE member states located in central and western Asia, and partly because membership of the Convention and Protocol is not open to non-UNECE countries, so it does not extend to other parts of Asia. However, this may change in the future if the example of the UNECE *Water Convention* is followed, a matter which will be discussed further

---

[42] Above n. 30, 3.
[43] Above n. 30, 4.
[44] Above n. 30, 4.
[45] Above n. 30, 4.
[46] Above n. 30, 4.
[47] Above n. 30, 4.
[48] Georgia and Ukraine have also signed, but not ratified, the *Civil Liability Protocol*.

below.[49] Before exploring whether the *Industrial Accidents Convention* offers any benefits to Asian countries, it is important to consider whether there is a need for a legal regime to address the transboundary effects of industrial accidents in Asia. This is discussed below in the section on implementation and compliance, which follows an outline of the objectives and general procedural provisions of the Convention and Protocol.

III. OBJECTIVES AND GENERAL PROCEDURAL PROVISIONS

III.1 Convention

In accordance with the Preamble, the central aim of the Convention is to protect humans and the environment against industrial accidents. This is to be achieved by Parties taking measures to prevent industrial accidents as far as possible, reduce their frequency and severity and mitigate their effects. The Preamble also indicates that the Convention promotes active international cooperation between the relevant Parties before, during and after an industrial accident. It emphasises the need for Parties to enhance appropriate policies, and to reinforce and coordinate action at all appropriate levels in promoting prevention, preparedness and response measures for transboundary effects.

The scope of the Convention is clearly delineated in Article 2(1), which states that it applies to the prevention of, preparedness for, and response to, industrial accidents capable of causing transboundary effects, including the effects of such accidents caused by natural disasters. It also applies to international cooperation relating to mutual assistance, research and development, and the exchange of information and technology in the area of industrial accident prevention, preparedness and response. The Convention does not apply to nuclear accidents, accidents at military installations, dam failures,[50] land-based transport

[49] The decision to open the *Water Convention* to all members of the UN was adopted in 2003, and came into effect in early 2013: UNECE, Background Paper on Possible Amendments to the Convention – Note by the Secretariat, 25 June 2013, ECE/CP.TEIA/WG.1/2013/3, 8–10.

[50] However, a proposal has been made to extend the scope of the Convention to tailings dams: see the Working Group on the Development of the Convention, 'Background Paper on Possible Amendments to the Convention', 2014, Informal Doc. WG.1-2014.Inf.1, 24–25.

accidents (except for emergency responses to such accidents and transportation on the site of the hazardous activity), accidental releases of GMOs; accidents caused by activities in the marine environment (including seabed exploration or exploitation), or spills of oil or other harmful substances at sea (Article 2(2)). Other MEAs typically cover these matters or aspects of them as noted or seen to some extent in Chapter 2.

An 'industrial accident' is defined in the Convention as 'an event resulting from an uncontrolled development in the course of any activity involving hazardous substances', either in an installation (for example during manufacture, use, storage, handling or disposal) or during transportation (Article 1(a)). Threshold limits for hazardous substances are found in Annex I. 'Effects' are defined broadly under Article 1(c), as 'any direct or indirect, immediate or delayed adverse consequences caused by an industrial accident' on humans, flora, fauna, soil, water, air, landscape, material assets or cultural heritage. Under Article 1(d) the term 'transboundary effects' refers to 'serious effects within the jurisdiction of a Party as the result of an industrial accident occurring within the jurisdiction of another Party'.

General obligations of the Parties are set out in Article 3, requiring Parties to cooperate to protect humans and the environment, and to take 'appropriate measures' for the prevention and mitigation of, and response to, industrial accidents and their transboundary effects (Article 3(1)). Policies and strategies must be developed and implemented to reduce the risks of industrial accidents and improve preventive, preparedness and response measures (Article 3(2)).[51] Parties must also ensure that operators of industrial facilities are required to take all measures necessary for the safe performance of hazardous activities and for the prevention of industrial accidents (Article 3(3)). Appropriate legislative, regulatory, administrative and financial measures must be taken by Parties to implement the provisions of the Convention (Article 3(4)).

The Convention also contains several more specific obligations. Article 4 requires Parties to identify proposed and existing hazardous activities within their jurisdictions and ensure that any potentially affected Parties are notified and consulted in accordance with the procedures in Annex III (Articles 4(1) and (3)). Article 6 requires appropriate prevention measures to be taken based on Annex IV, including inducements for operators to reduce the risk of industrial accidents (Article 6(1)). Operators must be required to demonstrate the safety of their hazardous activities, in

---

[51] This should be done through exchange of information, consultation and other forms of cooperation with other Parties.

accordance with the minimum requirements in Annex V (Article 6(2)). Under Article 7, decisions on the location of any proposed new facilities or major modifications to existing facilities should be made so as to minimise the risk to the people and environment of all affected Parties.

Article 8(1) obliges Parties to establish and maintain adequate emergency preparedness to respond to industrial accidents, in line with Annex VII. Preparedness measures must be in place to mitigate the transboundary effects of accidents, with operators responsible for all on-site measures. On-site and off-site contingency plans are to be prepared (and, if necessary, implemented) by the Party of origin, which shall also provide information on these contingency plans to affected Parties (Articles 8(2) and (3)); the terminology here is of course the same as that under the *EIA Convention* in relation to the concerned Parties, illustrating the cross-fertilisation of procedures between the agreements and potential for combined effect. Where there are two or more affected Parties, they should collaborate in developing joint off-site contingency plans so as to facilitate adequate response measures. Contingency plans should be reviewed regularly (Article 8(4)). Article 9(1) requires Parties to ensure that adequate information is provided to the public in areas that could potentially be affected by an industrial accident, covering all of the elements in Annex VIII. Opportunities for public participation by those potentially affected must be provided by the Party of origin whenever possible and appropriate (Article 9(2)). For ECE states which are also Parties to the *Public Participation Convention*, its detailed obligations would also be required, adding to the combined effect.

One of the key requirements of the Convention is the establishment of an Industrial Accident Notification System (IANS) to ensure that all relevant Parties are promptly and adequately informed when an industrial accident occurs. Under Article 10(1), Parties are expected to create and operate compatible and efficient industrial accident notification systems at the appropriate levels. Under Article 10(2), a Party of origin must notify the affected Party or Parties without delay through the IANS in the event of an industrial accident (or the imminent threat of one) that causes, or is capable of causing, transboundary effects.[52] In this event, contingency plans are to be activated as soon as possible and 'to the extent appropriate in the circumstances' (Article 10(3)). The WGD has

---

[52] The notification must include the information stipulated in Annex IX.

recently proposed that Parties should also submit formal reports on individual industrial accidents to the Convention Secretariat.[53]

Article 11(1) obliges Parties to take adequate response measures as soon as possible after an industrial accident, or wherever there is an imminent threat of one. Response measures should employ the most efficient practices to contain and minimise effects. Under Article 11(2) where there are two or more affected Parties, they should jointly assess the effects of the actual or potential accident, and coordinate their responses to it. Under Article 12(1) in the event of an accident, a Party needing assistance can seek it from other Parties ('mutual assistance'). The requested Party should give a prompt answer as to whether it can provide assistance, and if so, how much and when. Mutual assistance is to be provided in accordance with Annex X, unless a bilateral or multilateral agreement already deals with such matters (Article 12(2)).

There are further requirements for Parties to undertake research and development relating to methods and technologies for prevention, preparedness and response (Article 14) and to exchange information and technology with other Parties (Articles 15 and 16 respectively). One important provision is the obligation on Parties to establish or designate at least one competent authority for the purposes of the Convention (Article 17(1)). Parties must also designate a point of contact for industrial accident notifications and mutual assistance requests (Article 17(2)). Details of both the competent authorities and the points of contact are to be given to the other Parties and the Convention Secretariat, and kept updated (Article 17(3)). The competent authorities and points of contact in each Party must remain operational at all times (Articles 17(5) and (6)).

An informal procedure for resolving specific lower-level disagreements between Parties is found in Articles 4(1) and (2). These require Parties of origin and affected Parties to enter into discussions on the identification of hazardous activities within the jurisdiction of the Party of origin that are reasonably capable of causing transboundary effects. If the Parties involved cannot agree on whether a particular activity falls into this category, and if they have not already agreed on another method of resolving the issue, they can submit the question to an inquiry commission in accordance with the provisions of Annex II for advice. This provision, which is similar to that established under the *EIA Convention* – that has itself only been used once – has not been utilised to date.

---

[53] Above n. 50, 31. This could be achieved through an amendment to Article 23 of the Convention.

An inquiry commission formed under Annex II would be comprised of three scientific and/or technical experts, including one nominated by each Party and one to be selected by the nominated experts to act as president. Any commission established has broad powers to 'take all appropriate measures in order to carry out its functions'.[54] The Parties involved must facilitate the work of the inquiry commission by providing all relevant documents, facilities and information, and allowing witnesses and experts to give evidence.[55] A final opinion must be made by the inquiry commission within two months, unless a further two-month extension is warranted.[56] The final opinion is to be 'based on scientific principles' and communicated to the relevant Parties and the Secretariat.[57] It is very likely that the views of the IC under the *EIA Convention* in relation to the inquiry commission there would be influential in relation to any determinations concerning any inquiry commission established under the *Industrial Accidents Convention* (see Chapter 4).

In relation to dispute settlement, Article 21(1) of the Convention provides that, where a dispute arises between two or more Parties over interpretation or application, the matter should be resolved either through negotiation or any other dispute settlement method acceptable to the Parties. Under Article 21(2) if one of these methods fails to resolve the matter, Parties may elect in writing to resort to the ICJ or the international arbitration procedures set out in Annex XIII to the Convention. Before the matter may proceed to the ICJ, consent is required from each Party involved. If arbitration is the preferred avenue, the Secretariat must be notified by the Parties that the dispute is to be submitted for arbitration.[58] A decision must be rendered by the arbitral tribunal within five months and is both final and binding on all Parties to the dispute.[59]

III.2 Protocol

Under Article 1, the main objective of the Protocol is to provide a comprehensive regime for civil liability, and through this to provide for 'adequate and prompt compensation' for damage caused by the transboundary effects of industrial accidents on transboundary waters. A key feature of the Protocol is that it actively promotes the 'polluter pays

---

54 Annex II, para. 6.
55 Annex II, para. 7.
56 Annex II, para. 13.
57 Annex II, para. 14.
58 Annex XIII, para. 1.
59 Annex XIII, paras. 16 and 17.

principle',[60] imposing strict liability on operators for damage caused by accidents at their industrial facilities (Article 4(1)). The Protocol uses the threat of liability as an incentive for operators of industrial facilities to minimise operational risks so as to avoid causing damage. The maximum limits on operators' financial liability depend on the level of toxicity of the hazardous substances involved in the relevant industrial accident.[61]

The Protocol also contains a clause on fault-based liability, providing that any person (for instance not only the operator) can be held liable for damage 'caused or contributed to by his or her wrongful, intentional, reckless or negligent acts or omissions' in accordance with applicable domestic law (Article 5).[62] There is no financial limit on liability under this provision (Article 9(3)). To cover their liability risks, operators are required to obtain adequate financial security through insurance, bonds or other guarantees (Article 11).[63] In the event of an industrial accident, operators are also required to take 'all reasonable response measures' (Article 6(1)). Under Article 4(2) there are several defences to liability, as well as partial exemptions to liability (Articles 4(3) and (4)), and a right of recourse for one liable party against another liable party (Article 7(1)).

The corollary of the liability regime under the Protocol is the availability of compensation to individuals and entities affected by industrial accidents on transboundary watercourses. According to the UNECE, the Protocol 'fills one of the major gaps in international environmental legislation by solving the problem of uncompensated damage in neighbouring countries'.[64] Liability under the Protocol is joint and several, meaning that where two or more operators are liable, claimants can seek full compensation from any or all of the operators (Article 4(4)).

'Damage' is defined broadly, to include loss of life or personal injury, property loss or damage, economic loss resulting directly from the impairment of a legally protected interest, reinstatement costs, and the costs of response measures (Article 2(2)(d)). The Protocol applies only to

---

[60] The Preamble expressly refers to the polluter pays principle as 'a general principle of international environmental law'.

[61] Annex II (Part 1 – Limits of Liability). These are divided into three categories, with a limit of 10 million units of account for Category A, and 40 million units of account for both Category B and Category C.

[62] The operator's strict liability is without prejudice to any fault-based liability than can alternatively be applied to the operator: see Pallemaerts, above n. 28, 2.

[63] State-owned operators may make a declaration of self-insurance to meet this obligation. The minimum amounts of financial security depend on the nature of the hazardous activity, and are set out in Annex II (Part 2).

[64] Above n. 30, 3.

damage suffered in a Party other than the Party where the industrial accident has occurred (Article 3(2)). Claims for compensation must be brought in the courts of a Party where the damage was suffered, where the industrial accident occurred, or where the defendant has their residence or principal place of business (Article 13(1)). The dispute settlement clause contained in the Protocol (Article 26) is the same as that found in the Convention.

IV. PRACTICE

IV.1 Convention

a. Implementation

Article 23 of the Convention requires Parties to report periodically on their implementation measures, and the COP is required by Article 18 to review progress in such implementation.[65] At the first COP in late 2000, the Parties agreed on procedures for reporting on implementation of the Convention, and established the WGI.[66] In the first reporting round after entry into force of the Convention (2000–2001), 17 out of the then 23 Parties submitted NIRs. The WGI commented that it was 'unsatisfactory that close to a third of the Parties had not submitted a report', and suggested that those Parties should be reminded of their obligations under the Convention.[67] There was a similar pattern in the second reporting round (2002–2003), with only 24 out of the then 30 Parties submitting reports.[68] The WGI once again expressed its concern and reminded the non-complying Parties of their obligations.[69] A few countries, particularly Russia, have failed to submit NIRs over subsequent reporting rounds in the past decade, although the proportion of non-complying Parties is smaller with each round.

Apart from ongoing non-reporting by Russia (discussed below in the section on non-compliance), implementation of the Convention by its

---

[65] The role of COP is to review the implementation of the Convention, to provide advisory support to Parties and facilitate technical assistance etc; and to establish relevant working groups and committees (Article 18).

[66] UNECE, Report of the First Meeting, 22 February 2001, ECE/CP.TEIA/2, Annex III, Decision 2000/2, para. 4 and appendix.

[67] UNECE, First Report on the Implementation of the Convention, 12 September 2002, CP.TEIA/2002/9, 3.

[68] Kazakhstan and Russia failed to submit reports.

[69] UNECE, Second Report on the Implementation of the Convention, 15 July 2004, CP.TEIA/2004/1, 3.

Parties generally appears to have proceeded satisfactorily. Both Azerbaijan and Armenia submitted NIRs in the latest round, but their reports appear to provide insufficient detail on relevant measures,[70] which makes it difficult to accurately assess the status of their implementation of the Convention. The individual NIRs that have been submitted over the six reporting rounds to date are also not publicly available, in accordance with a decision by the COP. However, a proposal has recently been made to amend Article 23, to make them so.[71] This would bring the Convention into line with most other MEAs, including other UNECE treaties, which already have public access provisions. In the meantime, the biennial Implementation Report compiled by the WGI provides an overview of progress being made in implementing the Convention, as well as a detailed analysis of NIRs. The most recent is the 6th Implementation Report, covering the period 2010–2011.[72] In this Report, the WGI concluded that, overall, the level of implementation of the Convention was 'steadily improving'.[73] The WGI has furthermore stated:

> With regard to an overall assessment, the Working Group concludes that, in general, the level of implementation of the Convention measured by the existence of relevant policies is satisfactory. Also, the difference between Western and Eastern countries of the region is less visible than in the past.[74]

However, the WGI still saw 'a need for more work to be carried out towards a better understanding of the contents and implications of the Convention, especially in the case of countries with economies in transition'.[75]

b. Compliance

Unlike many other MEAs, including several of the UNECE agreements, the *Industrial Accidents Convention* does not contain a NCP. A possible

---

70 UNECE, Sixth Report on the Implementation of the Convention (2010–2011), ECE/CP.TEIA/2012/3, 23 August 2012, 21.

71 Above n. 50, 31.

72 Above n. 70. For the 2013–2014 period, US$800,000 was earmarked by the UNECE for the Assistance Programme, compared to an estimated US$675,000 for the 'core activities' of the Convention: UNECE, Priorities, Workplan and Resources under the Convention for 2013–2014, ECE/CP.TEIA/2012/9, 2 (Table 1).

73 Above n. 70, 6.

74 UNECE, Fifth Report on the Implementation of the Convention (2008–2009), ECE/CP.TEIA/2010/3, 4 (para. 21).

75 Above n. 70, 5.

amendment to the Convention to introduce a compliance mechanism, as was done for the *Water Convention* in 2012, is currently under discussion by the WGD and will be considered at forthcoming COP meetings.[76] The WGD suggested that Article 23 of the *Industrial Accidents Convention* be amended to include the following:

> The Parties shall review the compliance of the Parties with the provisions of this Convention on the basis of, but not limited to, the reports referred to in paragraph 1 of this article. The Conference of the Parties [at their … meeting] shall establish multilateral arrangements of a non-confrontational, non-judicial and consultative nature for reviewing compliance. These arrangements shall allow for appropriate public involvement.[77]

The proposed amendment also provides that the NCP would be applicable to all protocols adopted under the Convention.[78] As with other UNECE environmental treaties, a compliance body would need to be established to administer the mechanism. Probably consisting of eight or nine members, it would be independent from other Convention bodies and would report to the COP.[79] The WGD has proposed that the relevant amendment to the Convention set out only the basic features of the NCP, and provide a mandate for the COP to elaborate the details of the mechanism.[80] Such details would include, for example, the circumstances in which the compliance procedure may be triggered, and by whom.

As indicated above, of the few Asian countries that are Parties to the *Industrial Accidents Convention*, Russia has shown a distinct pattern of non-compliance with the reporting obligations under the Convention. When it failed to submit the required NIR for the third reporting round, the WGI expressed 'serious concern', noting that this was the second consecutive time that Russia had not provided a report.[81] Russia's non-compliance continued into the fourth reporting round (2006–2007), in which it was the only Party to the Convention not to submit a report.[82]

---

[76] Above n. 50, 10–11.

[77] Above n. 50, 11.

[78] Above n. 50, 11.

[79] Above n. 50, 34.

[80] Above n. 50, 35.

[81] UNECE, Third Report on the Implementation of the Convention (2004–2005), 6 September 2006, ECE/CP.TEIA/2006/2, 3.

[82] Out of the then 37 Parties, 35 submitted reports; the EU was not required to do so, as all relevant EU member states submitted their own instead.

The WGI again 'expressed serious concern' and recommended that the Russian Government be reminded by the COP of its obligation to report.[83]

Once again, in the fifth reporting round (2008–2009), all Parties except Russia submitted a report, although the latter notified the Secretariat that their report was being prepared and would be submitted shortly. In response, the WGI invited the COP to 'stress the issue of timely reporting with the competent authority' of Russia.[84] In the most recent reporting round, for the period 2010–2011, Russia failed to submit its NIR on time.[85] This long-term pattern of non-compliance was 'noted with concern' by the WGI, especially in light of assurances made by the Russian delegation at the 6th COP Meeting.[86] At the 7th COP Meeting, the COP stated that it 'regretted the failure of the Russian Federation to report in compliance with its legal obligations under the Convention', and requested the UNECE Executive Secretary to write to the Russian foreign minister to express concern and ask for a report.[87]

These responses by the WGI to non-compliance by Russia highlight the limitations of the current provisions of the Convention. Whilst stern words were issued on many occasions over a period of several years, these failed to secure compliance by Russia with its international obligations. No other avenues or mechanisms were available to the WGI or any other Convention bodies to take action against Russia, and there appears to be little to deter either Russia, or any other Party, from future instances of non-compliance.

The consequences of repeated non-compliance with the Convention are yet to be discussed in more detail by either the WGD or COP. To date, the WGD has only recommended that remedies for non-compliance would be best addressed within an overarching compliance mechanism, rather than in one particular provision.[88] Currently, the preferred strategy for non-compliance is to issue reminders and support the non-complying Party in taking 'corrective action' to achieve compliance. Greater public

---

83 UNECE, Fourth Report on the Implementation of the Convention (2006–2007), 1 September 2008, ECE/CP.TEIA/2008/3, 3.

84 UNECE, Fifth Report on the Implementation of the Convention (2008–2009), 27 August 2010, ECE/CP.TEIA/2010/3, 3.

85 This time, it was not the only non-complying Party; Greece also submitted its report late, in May 2012.

86 See above n. 70; note also, UNECE, ECE/CP.TEIA/2010/3, 3.

87 UNECE, Report of the Conference of the Parties on its Seventh Meeting, Stockholm, 14–16 November 2012, ECE/CP.TEIA/24, 4 (para. 15).

88 Above n. 50, 10.

involvement in compliance matters, as proposed by the WGD, is seen as a potential motivation for countries to ensure future compliance.[89] However, the combined use of stern reminders, supportive measures and increased public participation may not provide an adequate incentive for Parties to achieve consistent compliance. The introduction of a wider range of non-compliance tools – as seen in the *Public Participation Convention* – may therefore be appropriate for the *Industrial Accidents Convention*.[90]

IV.2 Protocol

As the Protocol is not in force, this short section is limited to an outline of the relevant provision. Article 8(1) of the Protocol stipulates that Parties must adopt 'any legislative, regulatory and administrative measures that may be necessary to implement the Protocol'. Parties are to inform the Secretariat of these measures once they have been taken, and cooperate closely with other Parties to promote implementation (Articles 8(2) and (4)). There are no specific requirements that Parties submit NIRs or otherwise report on their compliance with the Protocol, although the review of implementation and compliance is one of the main functions of the MOP (Article 21(4)(a)). In the event that the Protocol enters into force, the first MOP will be held within 18 months, with later meetings to be held at agreed intervals, probably in conjunction with the COP Meeting of either the *Industrial Accidents Convention* or the *Water Convention* as noted above.

V. PROSPECTS

V.1 Asia

There have been transboundary industrial accidents across the Asian region over recent decades. One particularly high-profile example is the

[89] Above n. 50, 11 and 31.

[90] There are eight possible responses to non-compliance available under the *Public Participation Convention*, ranging from the provision of advice and recommendations, to the suspension of rights and privileges under the Convention: Addendum to the Report of the 1st Meeting of the Parties (2004), Decision I/7: Review of Compliance, Annex (Structure and Functions of the Compliance Committee and Procedures for the Review of Compliance), ECE/MP.PP/2/Add.8, Section XII, para. 37.

explosion at a petrochemical factory in Jilin, northeastern China, on 13 November 2005, which had downstream impacts on Russia. The accident resulted in the pollution of the Songhua River (known as the Sungari River in Russia), with an estimated 100 tonnes of benzene, aniline and nitrobenzene, which formed a contaminated plume 80 km long. The plume moved downriver and into the Amur River, along the border between China and Russia. It then entered the Russian far eastern region of Khabarovsk Krai, emerging into the Pacific Ocean. The effects of the river pollution on the Russian cities downstream were significant. Evidence of dying fish was widespread, and some contamination of the public water supply was inevitable. Russia itself had not been informed of the spill by China until over a week had passed.[91] Large-scale construction works were undertaken by both Chinese and Russian workers to divert the polluted water from city supplies.[92] The cost of cleaning up the effects of the benzene spill in Russia was estimated at around USD$7 million.[93]

In the interval between the accident occurring, and the plume reaching Russia, Chinese and Russian agencies were in communication. China was very concerned about the possible hazards to Russia, with the Chinese Foreign Minister stating that 'both [China and Russia] have pledged to cooperate closely to handle the pollution'.[94] China offered Russia water testing kits and purifying materials, including 1,000 tonnes of activated carbon.[95] It indicated that it was 'ready to increase contacts and consultations with the Russian side and take effective measures to minimize the impact of the pollution'.[96] In late November, Russian experts visited the Jilin site to carry out investigations, and joint monitoring of the Songhua River commenced in early December under

---

[91] Song Ying, 'International Legal Aspect of the Songhua River Incident', in Michael G Faure and Song Ying (eds), *China and International Environmental Liability: Legal Remedies for Transboundary Pollution* (Edward Elgar, Cheltenham, UK and Northampton, MA, USA 2008) 325.

[92] Lisa A Kirschner and Edward B Grandy, 'The Songhua River Spill: China's Pollution Crisis', *Natural Resources and Environment* (Spring 2006), American Bar Association.

[93] Sergei Blagov, 'Damage control for Russia and China after chemical spill', 23 January 2006, China Environmental News Digest.

[94] 'China pledges to minimize impact of river pollution on Russia', Xinhua News Agency, 24 November 2005.

[95] '2nd batch of water purifying materials offered to Russia', Xinhua News Agency, 16 December 2005.

[96] Ibid.

the China-Russia Joint Emergency Response Monitoring Plan on Water Quality of the Songhua River.[97]

Relations were not always positive, with Russian officials criticising China for being slow to notify Russia and to release relevant information.[98] Some also indicated that compensation would be sought from China in international courts,[99] which emphasises the relevance of the *Civil Liability Protocol* in both Asia, and globally (the prospects for which are considered further in the next section). The threat of legal action receded by the time the chemical plume reached Russia, perhaps due to a formal apology by the Chinese Government, combined with offers to assist with preventive, monitoring and clean-up measures. This may also be due to the lower than expected levels of benzene pollution that were detected.[100]

In early 2006, the authorities signed a five-year agreement to jointly monitor their transboundary waters for contamination.[101] Chinese officials also travelled to Russia to reassure their neighbours that only minimal benzene contamination would occur during the coming spring thaw. The Jilin accident served a useful purpose in revealing the weaknesses in China's emergency preparedness and response systems at the time:

> As the pollution slick from the 2005 spill moved from one administrative region to the next over a period of several weeks, local and national governments moved toward a degree of transparency that is often lacking in the many similar incidents that continue to occur in China. The Songhua spill exposed flaws in China's environmental regulation, including weak local enforcement of environmental laws, poor communication between state

---

[97] Above n. 91.

[98] It also took five days for the Chinese public to be informed of the spill: Elizabeth Wishnick, 'Why a Strategic Partnership?', in James Bellacqua (ed.), *The Future of China-Russia Relations* (University Press of Kentucky, Lexington 2010), 71.

[99] Above n. 93.

[100] Above n. 93.

[101] The Memorandum on Joint Monitoring of the Sino-Russian Border Waters, 21 February 2006; Environment News Service, 'China and Russia Sign River Monitoring Pact', 21 February 2006, accessed 18 November 2014 at http://www.ens-newswire.com/ens/feb2006/2006-02-21-02.asp.

agencies and officials, and poor emergency response capacity. Most importantly, the transboundary nature of the incident helped bring it unprecedented levels of international and domestic attention.[102]

As some have noted since the Jilin accident, the northeastern region has long been known as the 'industrial cradle of China', and that the Songhua River basin in particular is characterised by heavy and outdated industrial development.[103] Therefore, as Song Ying predicts, the Jilin accident is unlikely to be an isolated occurrence,[104] and indeed another chemical spill occurred into a tributary of the Songhua River in August 2006.[105] A report by UNEP on the Songhua River spill made important findings and recommendations on emergency preparedness in that part of China.[106] China had notified UNEP within approximately two weeks of the accident, and invited an expert team to carry out a field mission to the affected region.[107] The role of the UNEP team was to visit the polluted area, discuss with local and national experts and officials the details of the accident and relevant measures, and advise the Chinese Government on preventive measures against future accidents.[108] In its report, the UNEP team noted that the Songhua River spill was 'probably one of the largest transboundary chemical spill incidents in a river system in recent years' and that it was 'of major transboundary and international significance'.[109] The UNEP Report concluded that:

> It is clear that, during the initial response phase, government communication and information sharing with the general public was not adequate enough to ensure appropriate responses of the affected population. Further investigations are needed to clarify whether existing early warning systems and contingency plans were sufficient.[110]

The team provided suggestions on addressing the awareness, preparedness and response to environmental emergencies in a systematic manner.

---

[102] Nat Green, 'Positive Spillover? – Impact of the Songhua River Benzene Incident on China's Environmental Policy', March 2009, *China Environment Forum*, The Wilson Center, Washington DC.

[103] Ibid.

[104] Above n. 91, 330.

[105] However, this spill does not appear to have had transboundary effects.

[106] United Nations Environment Programme, *The Songhua River Spill, China, December 2005 – Field Mission Report* (2005).

[107] Ibid, 4.

[108] Ibid, 4.

[109] Ibid, 16.

[110] Ibid, 16.

In particular, it recommended the preparation of contingency plans and application of methodologies developed by UNEP, such as the 'APELL Programme' (Awareness and Preparedness for Emergencies at Local Level).[111] The APELL process is a methodological tool that is applied at the local level to help identify possible industrial hazards, raise awareness of these hazards, and build local capacity for immediate, multi-party response in the event of an emergency.[112]

Another area for improvement identified by the UNEP Report was the sampling procedure for transboundary river spills in the region. It appears that the Chinese Government had initially declined Russian requests to undertake their own sampling of the Songhua River after the spill occurred.[113] UNEP criticised this lack of cooperation by China, noting that 'it is a common practice that in transboundary incidents sampling and analysis are undertaken by all countries involved and affected as well as by an independent internationally recognized laboratory'.[114] It therefore recommended that both China and Russia provide access to independent and impartial sampling and chemical analysis in relation to the Songhua River accident.[115]

The UNEP Report recognised that the recently established programme between China and Russia for joint monitoring of transboundary waters was 'an encouraging step in furthering multilateral cooperation on shared water resources'. However, it also suggested that the riparian states of the Amur River Basin (China, Russia, Mongolia and North Korea) should consider establishing an international commission for the sustainable development of the river system. According to UNEP, activities of the proposed commission could include joint monitoring and information

---

[111] Ibid, 12–13. UNEP describes 'APELL' as 'a local process of hazard communication and coordination', and states that 'UNEP and national and international bodies have programmes to promote and facilitate this local level process'.

[112] United Nations Environment Programme, *Commemorating 25 Years of Awareness and Preparedness for Emergencies at Local Level: Achievements and Way Forward* (UNEP 2012), 4. The APELL system was implemented by Thailand in 1993, and APELL-related activities have also been carried out in China, India, Sri Lanka, Vietnam, Cambodia and the Philippines over the past decade: see Ruth Coutto, 'UNEP's Portfolio of Safer and Responsible Production', presentation to International Council of Chemical Associations, 20 October 2010.

[113] Above n. 98.

[114] Above n. 106, 16.

[115] Above n. 106, 16.

sharing, implementation of work programmes, geographic information systems, risk inventories and clear procedures for early warning and response.[116] These are all elements that are addressed under the *Industrial Accidents Convention*, to which Russia (but not China) is a Party.

Whilst the observations and recommendations made in the UNEP report are valid, membership of the Convention by China and its Asian neighbours may offer greater protection against the transboundary effects of any future industrial accidents. One major advantage of the Convention is its multilateral, multi-stakeholder approach to preventing and responding to transboundary industrial accidents. The notification system used by Parties necessarily involves the prompt sharing of information between agencies at the local, regional, national and international level. By contrast, the APELL Programme developed by UNEP is specifically designed for the local level only, and therefore it cannot ensure that other levels of administration are adequately informed or involved. The many technological advances and political changes that have occurred since the Programme was first devised in 1988 may also undermine its modern-day currency.

Specific issues such as sampling and analysis procedures would form part of the emergency response measures that are required under the Convention. For example, Article 11(2) requires that the transboundary effects of an industrial accident should be assessed jointly by concerned Parties (where appropriate), for the purpose of taking adequate and coordinated response measures. Annex XI also requires Parties to exchange information on a wide range of matters, including the implementation and surveillance of monitoring programmes, and the measures they have taken in response to transboundary industrial accidents. Importantly, the Convention does not preclude Parties from reaching bilateral or multilateral agreements on these matters, so China's agreement with Russia in 2006 on joint monitoring of transboundary waters would not necessarily be compromised.[117]

In 2008, China and Russia signed an agreement on the 'rational use and protection of transboundary waters', extending their cooperative approach to the broader issue of shared water resources. Such bilateral agreements are a tool commonly used by China to cooperate with its neighbours on environmental issues. However, it is unlikely that bilateral agreements like these could provide an adequate means for addressing

---

116 Above n. 106, 17.

117 Environment News Service, 'China and Russia Sign River Monitoring Pact', 21 February 2006, accessed 18 November 2014 at http://www.ens-newswire.com/ens/feb2006/2006-02-21-02.asp.

transboundary industrial accidents in a systematic or detailed manner. Moreover, as UNEP observed in 2005 in the context of the Amur River basin, all the relevant riparian countries need to be involved in the monitoring and management of a transboundary river, thus requiring a multilateral (or regional/cross-regional) approach.[118] The *Industrial Accidents Convention* could therefore complement existing bilateral agreements by providing an overarching legal framework for cooperation on the transboundary effects of industrial accidents.

The example of China powerfully illustrates the need for, and potential role of, the *Industrial Accidents Convention* – and indeed the *Civil Liability Protocol* – in the Asian context. If membership of the Convention were to be opened up, China and other Asian countries could benefit from acceding to the Convention in several ways. First and foremost, the Convention would provide guidance on developing a legal and institutional framework to address prevention, preparedness and response measures for industrial accidents and their local, regional, national and transboundary effects.[119] Currently, there are no other binding multilateral or regional agreements in Asia that deal with the issue comprehensively. The OECD has compiled a non-binding guidance document which is intended for industry, public authorities, communities and other stakeholders.[120] However, the only Asian members of the OECD are Japan, South Korea and Israel, so the relevance for Asia as a whole is limited.

According to Wyrowski, accession to the Convention would also provide 'a platform for establishing or strengthening cooperation inside and outside countries' on matters relating to transboundary industrial accidents, as it covers areas that are usually managed by different authorities at different levels.[121] New Parties can learn new approaches to resolving complex issues, such as land use planning and industrial safety, from existing Parties to the Convention.[122] Many Asian countries are likely to be eligible for financial and technical help under the Assistance

---

118 Above n. 106, 17.

119 Lukasz Wyrowski, 'Benefits of and national legislation and authorities for UNECE Convention on the Transboundary Effects of Industrial Accidents', presentation to the Joint Seminar on the Espoo Convention and Convention on Transboundary Effects of Industrial Accidents, Ashgabat, Turkmenistan, 5–6 June 2011.

120 OECD, *Guiding Principles for Chemical Accident Prevention, Preparedness and Response* (OECD 2003, 2nd edn).

121 Above n. 119.

122 Above n. 119.

Programme, to overcome any challenges they face in implementing the Convention. Similarly, if the Protocol ever comes into force, the fact that it is open to accession by all UN member states subject to approval of the existing members, would introduce a major new liability tool to contribute to global environmental governance.

V.2 Global

Discussions have already begun on the possible extension of *Industrial Accidents Convention* membership to all countries. In 2013, an informal proposal was made by the WGD for an amendment to Article 29 to allow any UN member to accede to it.[123] The options for introducing global membership were to be discussed in more detail at the eighth COP Meeting in December 2014, with a view to adopting a suitable amendment potentially at the ninth COP Meeting in 2016.[124]

Making the Convention a global instrument is perceived to offer several potential advantages, the main one being that it would raise the standard of industrial safety across the world. Other benefits could include the 'new experience' that other Parties would bring, and the galvanising effect that may have on the work of the Convention; exchange of information with other regions; enhanced 'political relevance and visibility'; and an increase in partnerships and funding prospects.[125] Possible obstacles to global membership are a perception among non-UNECE countries of the Convention as a 'European' instrument; the significant resources and commitment required from Parties; cost implications for the UNECE; and potential confusion with other global instruments.[126]

In relation to the Protocol, as mentioned this is already potentially open to global accession. In 2010, the sixth Convention MOP announced a three-step approach to help UNECE countries, particularly those with economies in transition, to ratify the Protocol.[127] The approach involved the following steps: Step 1 – to strive to better understand what national

[123] Above n. 50, 14, para. 31.

[124] UNECE, Opening of the Convention on the Transboundary Effects of Industrial Accidents to other member states of the United Nations: Considerations and options with regard to a possible amendment, ECE/CP.TEIA/2014/6 (2014).

[125] Above n. 50, 14–15.

[126] Above n. 50, 15.

[127] UNECE, Report of the Sixth Meeting of the Conference of the Parties to the Convention on the Transboundary Effects of Industrial Accidents, The Hague, 8–10 November 2010, ECE/CP.TEIA/22, para. 65.

legislation is required to implement the Protocol in light of differences between the Protocol and other civil liability instruments; Step 2 – to carry out case studies based on realistic potential accidents to understand the implications including the benefits of implementing the Protocol and/or other instruments; and Step 3 (not particularly relevant to Asia) – to identify and recommend specific actions that would enable the Republic of Moldova and Ukraine to implement the Protocol.[128]

The first step in this approach has already been achieved, in the form of the IEEP Report commissioned by the UNECE, which identifies the specific provisions in national legislation that would be needed to implement the *Civil Liability Protocol*.[129] Work on the second step has already begun, with four case studies being described briefly in the IEEP Report. Further, more detailed work on these case studies remains yet to be funded, but the Convention Bureau has indicated that work on Step 3 will not proceed until Step 2 has been completed.[130] It is implicitly hoped that this step-by-step process will clarify any remaining issues that the Protocol signatories have, highlight the importance to the entire UNECE region of ratifying the Protocol, and prompt other countries to take action once the European/Eurasian states selected as part of this process have successfully demonstrated their capabilities in this area.

VI. CONCLUSIONS

The *Industrial Accidents Convention* is the weakest of the five UNECE treaties for four main reasons: first, it is not a global instrument and despite recent efforts of the MOP, there is no immediate pressure for this among the Parties; second, publicly available data in relation to implementation is not currently available, which is completely inconsistent with the open

---

[128] UNECE, Protocol on Civil Liability and Compensation for Damage Caused by the Transboundary Effects of Industrial Accidents on Transboundary Waters – Note by the Bureaux, 7th Meeting of the Conference of the Parties to the Industrial Accidents Convention, Stockholm, 14–16 November 2012, ECE/CP.TEIA/2012/7, 3. Moldova appears to have been selected on the basis of its ongoing support of the Protocol, and Ukraine most likely due to its role as host for the initial adoption of the Protocol in 2003.

[129] Above n. 28.

[130] UNECE, 'Protocol on Civil Liability and Compensation for Damage Caused by the Transboundary Effects of Industrial Accidents on Transboundary Waters – Note by the Bureau', 7th Meeting of the Conference of the Parties to the Industrial Accidents Convention, Stockholm, 14–16 November 2012, ECE/CP.TEIA/2012/7, 4.

culture of environmental law in the 21st century, as driven by the *Public Participation Convention* and *PRTR Protocol* (Chapter 3), although this may change; third, there is no NCP, which weakens the regime considerably, particularly when a state like Russia consistently flouts its obligations; fourth, the *Civil Liability Protocol* is not in force, which as illustrated in the Songhua/Sungari River incident, may ensure compensation is payable in such cases. The fact that the Protocol is potentially open to global membership is, however of negligible significance because this is likely to be a very long way off as there is only as yet one Party to it.

Nevertheless, the Convention contains a reporting procedure with an onus on states Parties to produce NIRs – which is not a current feature of the *Water Convention* – and therefore the *Industrial Accidents Convention* is stronger in respect of this implementation obligation. This is notwithstanding the compliance problem, which is, however, being apparently attended to. The Convention therefore plays an important role in preventing industrial accidents from occurring, and minimising the transboundary effects of those that do occur, across the UNECE region. As seen, the need for a comprehensive approach to the issue became increasingly apparent after a series of high profile incidents, compelling the UNECE to take decisive action. Countries responded to this need and the Convention was negotiated and adopted within a relatively short timeframe. Although at first there were issues regarding implementation of the Convention – and compliance with its obligations – most of these problems have since been resolved. Countries with economies in transition are furthermore being assisted in their efforts to ratify and implement the Convention, to overcome the particular challenges faced by them in the area of industrial safety.

The lack of a binding global instrument on the issue of transboundary effects of industrial accidents has now led to calls by some for the Convention to be opened up to global membership. In the Asian context, there could be tangible benefits for those countries that have heavily industrialised areas, are undergoing rapid economic and urban development, and have shared boundary waters. All countries could, however, benefit from utilising the prevention, mitigation and response procedures established under the Convention, as well as the combined experience of existing Parties to the Convention. Whilst some relevant non-binding guidance principles and codes of conduct exist – together with bilateral agreements on transboundary water management between some Asian countries, they fall far short of providing a comprehensive management system for transboundary industrial accidents that is required.

6. The Water Convention and Water and Health Protocol

I. INTRODUCTION: STATUS, MEMBERSHIP AND INSTITUTIONS (CONVENTION AND PROTOCOL)

The Convention on the Protection and Use of Transboundary Watercourses and Lakes (*Water Convention*) came into force on 6 October 1996, after adoption in Helsinki on 17 March 1992 with 30 signatories then, or soon after.[1] There are currently 39 Parties including the EU. Since 2013 it has been a global treaty,[2] and, outside the UNECE region is hence potentially applicable to other Asian states, subject to further ratifications by existing Parties. This is particularly relevant given the large number of transboundary watercourses in the region and the need to regulate matters of environmental protection, and ensure equitable and reasonable use. Despite this, academic interest to date has focused on the 1997 UN Convention on International Watercourses (*International Water Convention*), which recently entered into force and is discussed in a final section of this chapter.[3]

Parties to the *Water Convention* include one western Asian state (Azerbaijan), three central Asian states (Kazakhstan, Turkmenistan and Uzbekistan) and Russia. It is expected that other states will join shortly.[4]

[1] Convention on the Protection and Use of Transboundary Watercourses and Lakes (Helsinki, 17 March 1992), 31 ILM (1992) 1312, in force 6 October 1996. See Patricia Wouters, 'Global Water Governance Through Many Lenses' (2008) *Global Governance: A Review of Multilateralism and International Organizations* 14(4) 523–34.

[2] United Nations Economic Commission for Europe, Convention on the Protection and Use of Transboundary Watercourses and Lakes, *The Global Opening of the 1992 UNECE Water Convention* (UNECE 2013).

[3] Convention on the Law of Non-Navigable Uses of International Watercourses (New York, 21 May 1997, by UNGA Res. 51/229), 36 ILM (1997) 700, in force August 2014.

[4] With respect to Georgia, and with the intention of strengthening cooperation with Azerbaijan, see United Nations Economic Commission for

Iran for example has recently expressed an interest in joining the Convention,[5] as has Iraq.[6] The Convention has two protocols, the *Water and Health Protocol*,[7] and the *Civil Liability Protocol*,[8] the latter of which is shared with the *Industrial Accidents Convention*.[9] The *Water and Health Protocol* has 36 signatories and 26 Parties, including Azerbaijan and Russia (Parties) and Armenia and Georgia (signatories). It is not open to accession to non-UNECE states other than members of the Regional Committee for Europe of the WHO, to which their member states have transferred competence over matters governed by the Protocol. The *Civil Liability Protocol*, discussed in Chapter 5, has only one (non-Asian) Party to date; Armenia and Georgia are however signatories. References to 'the Protocol' in this chapter are to the *Water and Health Protocol*.

The main institutional bodies under the Convention are the MOP, which meets every few years,[10] the Bureau,[11] Legal Board,[12] and IC.[13] The MOP is the main decision-making body comprising all Parties, with the objective of securing implementation. The main responsibilities of the Bureau are to develop the workplan, strengthen implementation, and carry out any other tasks given to it by the MOP. The Legal Board is not

Europe/OSCE Environment and Security Initiative, *Draft Report of the National Working Group Meeting for Identification of the Legal and Institutional Needs for Accession and Implementation of the UNECE Water Convention by Georgia*, Tbilisi, 26 June 2009.

5 UNECE, 'Iran discusses the benefits of the UNECE Water Convention', press release, 23 January 2013.

6 UNECE, 'Iraq and Tunisia express interest in joining UNECE Water Convention', press release, 16 October 2013.

7 Protocol on Water and Health to the Convention on the Protection and Use of Transboundary Watercourses and Lakes (London, 17 June 1999), UNTS 2331, 202, in force 4 August 2005.

8 Protocol on Civil Liability and Compensation for Damage Caused by the Transboundary Effects of Industrial Accidents on Transboundary Waters (Kiev, 21 May 2003), not in force. This was adopted on the same occasion as the *SEA Protocol*.

9 Convention on the Transboundary Effects of Industrial Accidents (Helsinki, 17 March 1992), UNTS 2105 (1992) 457, in force 19 April 2000.

10 The sixth MOP was held between 28 and 30 November 2012 in Rome.

11 The twentieth meeting of the Bureau was held on 27 June 2014 in Geneva.

12 The tenth meeting of Legal Board was held between 31 January and 1 February 2012 in Geneva.

13 The fourth meeting of the IC will be held on 4 December 2014 in Geneva.

surprisingly focused on the legal aspects when requested by other bodies. There is no comparable body under the other UNECE treaties. It has specifically focused on the development of the authoritative *Implementation Guide* (which is one of only two such UNECE treaty guides, the other prepared on the *Public Participation Convention*),[14] and the formal compliance procedure administered by the IC which commenced operation in 2013.

Under the Convention there are also two working groups (WG) (Integrated Water Resources Management,[15] and Monitoring and Assessment[16]); two task forces (Water and Climate, and Water-Food-Energy-Ecosystems Nexus); and a Joint ad-hoc Expert Group on Water and Industrial Accidents, recognising the connection between the two Helsinki Conventions and their shared *Civil Liability Protocol*. There is furthermore an International Water Assessment Centre established under the Convention. Given the focus of this book on implementation and compliance, the MOP, Bureau, Legal Board and IC will receive the primary attention.

The main institutional bodies under the Protocol are the Protocol MOP, which meets every few years,[17] the Bureau,[18] and the CC,[19] each with similar roles to those under the Convention. The CC is comparable in operation to the IC, for example, (the terms are used interchangeably

[14] United Nations Economic Commission for Europe, Convention on the Protection and Use of Transboundary Watercourses and Lakes, *Guide to Implementing the Water Convention* (United Nations 2013) (*Implementation Guide*). This will be referenced throughout this chapter, the purpose of which is to provide detailed commentary on selected Convention provisions to assist Parties in implementation, non-Parties in decisions on ratification or accession, and to support cooperation and encourage ratification outside the UNECE region. Because of the focus of the book on Asia, the examples of application in a European context are not considered here; however they may be useful for Asian states complying with the Convention. Note that there is no commentary on Articles 4–8, 12, and 17–21 of the Convention.

[15] The ninth meeting of the WG on Integrated Water Resources Management was held between 25 and 26 June 2014 in Geneva.

[16] The thirteenth meeting of the WG on Monitoring and Assessment was held between 3 and 4 July 2012, a joint meeting with the WG on Integrated Water Resources Management.

[17] The third session of the Protocol MOP was held between 25 and 27 November 2013 in Oslo.

[18] The twelfth meeting of the Bureau of the *Water and Health Protocol* was held on 28 November 2014 in Geneva.

[19] The tenth meeting of the CC under the *Water and Health Protocol* was held on 24 November 2014 in Geneva.

under the UNECE NCPs), and this will be the main focus for the same reasons. There is also a WG on Water and Health,[20] two task forces (Target Setting and Reporting,[21] and Surveillance), and a Project Facilitation Mechanism.

As in each of the chapters on the treaties, the structure of Chapter 6 will first provide some historical background to the Convention and Protocol, and explain their legal development. It will then discuss objectives and general procedural provisions of the Convention and Protocol, before analysing legal implementation and practical compliance of each in an Asian context. Application in central Asia, as with each of the other substantive chapters on the five treaties, is again considered in Chapter 8. A section on prospects in Asia and globally will precede the conclusions.

II. HISTORICAL BACKGROUND AND LEGAL DEVELOPMENT (CONVENTION AND PROTOCOL)

As noted in the authoritative *Implementation Guide*,[22] transboundary water management issues assumed a greater significance in the UNECE region in the 1980s, with the publication of two documents: the *Declaration of Policy on Prevention and Control of Water Pollution*, and the *Decision on Principles regarding Cooperation in the Field of Transboundary Waters*.[23] With these documents and the outcomes of the Meeting on the Protection of the Environment of the CSCE,[24] the text of a legally binding water agreement was soon concluded. The timing was fortuitous given the break-up of the former Soviet Union and the need to contend with new European and Asian borders. The Convention has hence 'played a crucial role in the region in supporting the establishment and strengthening of cooperation and serving as a model for a number of

[20] The seventh meeting of the WG on Water and Health was held between 25 and 27 November 2014 in Geneva.

[21] The seventh meeting of the Task Force on Target-Setting and Reporting was held between 3 and 4 July 2014 in Geneva.

[22] *Implementation Guide*, 1.

[23] Adopted by the UNECE at its 42nd session, 1997 in Decision 1(42).

[24] Sofia, 16 October–3 November 1989.

bilateral and multilateral agreements.'[25] Given the geo-politics of Eurasia especially, the Convention has also now wide relevance in Asia.[26]

Although more detailed than the *International Water Convention* (discussed at the end of this chapter and previously mentioned in Chapter 2), the *Water Convention* is still essentially a framework convention, like the *Air Pollution Convention*.[27] It is therefore unlike the *Industrial Accidents*,[28] *EIA*,[29] and *Public Participation*[30] *Conventions* (considered in Chapters 3, 4 and 5) in this regard, each of which contains detailed procedures respectively for protecting people and the environment. While the *Water Convention* establishes an institutional structure to assist with implementation, compliance and further development, realisation of these matters is dependent upon bilateral and multilateral agreements being reached between the riparian states which share the resource, as will be explained in the next section.

Part I duties of the Convention are the more general and apply to all Parties, and Part II duties are more specific and must be implemented via further agreements between the Riparian Parties. Part III provisions also apply to all Parties. After the adoption of the Convention in 1992, the adoption of the two Protocols was furthermore a significant development, and most recently also the potential opening of the Convention to all UN states, the full implications of which are still to be seen. The initiation for the latter began on 28 November 2003, when the Parties amended Articles 25 and 26 – later to come into force on 6 February 2013 – which entitled universal participation subject to further ratifications by existing Parties. The twentieth anniversary the year before – which anticipated the global application of the treaty and heralded other significant reforms over the previous two decades, (including the establishment of the IC) – was therefore a cause for some celebration, while acknowledging the

[25] *Implementation Guide*, 1.

[26] As an example of the current relevance of the treaty in Asia, see 'Workshop on Legal, Institutional and Technical Aspects of Managing Transboundary Groundwaters' held between 29 and 31 May 2012 in Almaty.

[27] Convention on Long-range Transboundary Air Pollution (Geneva, 13 November 1979), UNTS 1302 (1979) 217, in force 16 March 1983.

[28] Above n. 9.

[29] Convention on Environmental Impact Assessment in a Transboundary Context (Espoo, 25 February 1991), 30 ILM (1991) 802, in force 27 June 1997. This is often known as the 'Espoo Convention'.

[30] Convention on Access to Information, Public Participation in Decision-Making and Access to Justice in Environmental Matters, opened for signature Aarhus, 25 June 1998, 2161 UNTS 447 (in force 30 October 2001). This is often known as the 'Aarhus Convention'.

major challenges lying ahead.[31] The programme of events to celebrate the anniversary included presentations on transboundary issues in central Asia and, from Russia, how the Convention supports bilateral agreements.[32]

In relation to the Protocol, in 2006, the year after it came into force, the facts speak for themselves as to why it was needed. More than 170,000 cases of water-related disease were reported, and a lack of sanitation, improper waste treatment, unsafe disposal of chemicals, overuse of fertilizers and irresponsible water management threatened human health and impacted upon watercourses.[33] Collectively, these things represented 'a legacy of environmental degradation and potential health risk that could take decades to reverse'.[34] In 1999 in London therefore, the international community decided to act, and adopted the Protocol at the Third Ministerial Conference on Environment and Health.[35]

III. OBJECTIVES AND GENERAL PROCEDURAL PROVISIONS

III.1 Convention

The *Water Convention* is, like the *EIA Convention*, also concerned with harm prevention and cooperation, but specifically in connection with

---

[31] Meeting of the Parties, Sixth session, Rome, 28–30 November 2012, Item 3 of the provisional agenda, Special session on the twentieth anniversary of the Convention and its opening to all United Nations Member States. From Helsinki to Rome: Messages to the Sixth Session of the Meeting of the Parties from the Water Convention Anniversary Event, MOP-6/2012/INF.2. See also Item 8 of the (same) provisional agenda, Vision for the future of the Water Convention, ECE/MP.WAT/2012/L.2, 18 September 2012.

[32] Ministry of the Environment/Ministry of Agriculture and Forestry/ Ministry of Foreign Affairs (Finland), Federal Office for the Environment (Switzerland), UNECE, *Programme: Anniversary Event to Celebrate 20 Years of the Helsinki Convention and Debate its Future*, 3–4 September, Helsinki.

[33] UNECE/WHO Regional Office for Europe, *Protocol on Water and Health* (UNECE/WHO 2009), 1, accessed 18 November 2014 at http://www.unece.org/fileadmin/DAM/env/water/publications/brochure/Protocol_E_A4.pdf.

[34] Ibid.

[35] For an overview, see also WHO, *The Protocol on Water and Health: Making a Difference* (WHO 2006) accessed 18 November 2014 at http://www.euro. who.int/__data/assets/pdf_file/0003/97833/WaterProtocol_2006upd_web.pdf.

transboundary watercourses and international lakes. The Preamble emphasises the role of the UNECE in 'promoting international cooperation for the prevention, control and reduction of transboundary water pollution and sustainable use of transboundary waters'.[36] As noted above, the text is mainly divided into two parts: Part I (Articles 2–8) applying to all Parties, and Part II (Articles 9–16) applying to Riparian Parties. Part III (Articles 17–28) contains institutional and final provisions, including dispute settlement. The focus of both main parts is, however, on preventing, controlling and reducing transboundary impacts and using transboundary waters in a reasonable and equitable way. Cooperation through specific agreements and establishing joint bodies are key parts of the procedures. Preceding Part I, Article 1 contains definitions of 'transboundary waters',[37] 'transboundary impact',[38] 'Party', 'Riparian Parties', 'joint bodies', 'hazardous substances' and 'best available technology'.[39]

a. Provisions applying to all parties

Article 2 of Part I contains obligations to 'take all appropriate measures to prevent, control and reduce any transboundary impact',[40] including pollution 'with the aim of ecologically sound and rational water management, conservation of water resources and environmental protection'. Although limited to freshwater in the main, Article 2(6) requires Parties

---

[36] For an example of the importance of cooperation, see 'Workshop on Quantifying Benefits of Cooperation', held between 22 and 23 May 2014 in Geneva.

[37] Although the definition of transboundary waters includes both surface and groundwaters, the focus is primarily on surface waters. To redress this imbalance and recognise the key role of groundwaters, the Convention is making additional moves in this area. See for example the work of the Legal Board, especially in its eighth, ninth and tenth meetings, which include the development of model provisions on groundwater in cooperation with the WG on Integrated Water Resources Management, as endorsed both by the WG and the Bureau. A Core Group on Groundwater was subsequently formed, with a first meeting held in 2012, which included Azerbaijan, Kazakhstan and Russia. See also above n. 26 and below n. 56.

[38] Transboundary impact is to be interpreted similarly to the *EIA Convention*, especially for Parties also to that treaty. Note that while the main focus is on the reciprocal obligations of Riparian Parties the common interest of members of the community are also to be protected.

[39] *Implementation Guide*, 13–18.

[40] This is the codification of the 'no harm' customary international law rule and is a due diligence obligation focused on what is appropriate and proportional to the degree of risk and harm; see *Implementation Guide* 19–21.

to protect the environment influenced by their transboundary waters, including the marine environment. Reasonable and equitable use, and conservation and restoration of ecosystems are also required.[41] In taking these measures, the Parties must be guided by the precautionary, cooperation, polluter-pays and intergenerational equity principles.[42]

In Articles 2(7) and 2(8) are found provisions ensuring that application of the Convention will not lead to the lowering of environmental standards, and allow for more stringent measures to be taken by Parties.[43] Articles 3(1)(c) and (f) establish the requirement for waste water discharge limits found in permits to be based on the best available technology for discharges of hazardous substances, and for appropriate measures to be taken to reduce nutrient inputs. Stricter requirements including prohibition are to be imposed dependent upon the receiving environment, further to Article 3(1)(d). Biological treatment is to be used in relation to municipal waste water wherever possible under Article 3(1)(e), and for nutrients and hazardous substances from diffuse sources, especially agriculture, appropriate measures are to be taken further to Article 3(1)(g).[44]

Article 3(1)(h) requires EIA as part of the approach to prevention, control and reduction of transboundary impacts, and specific reference is to be made to the *EIA Convention*, illustrating the combined effect of the agreements. Further provision is found in Part II in relation to the obligations of Riparian Parties, although given the broader focus of the *Water Convention* this does not detail components of the EIA process. Article 9(2) provides for the establishment of joint bodies between the Riparian Parties under the Convention, one of the purposes of which (j) is 'to participate in the implementation of environmental impact assessments relating to transboundary waters, in accordance with appropriate international regulations'.

In regard to Article 3(1)(h) the *Implementation Guide* devotes four pages to discussing the requirement for EIA, which it refers to as 'an important element within the whole range of the "appropriate measures"', because it 'enhances public participation and transparency in the authorization of projects' 'and enables public authorities to adopt better

---

41 *Implementation Guide*, 22–7.

42 *Implementation Guide*, 28–39 for cooperation and polluter pays principles.

43 *Implementation Guide*, 40–7.

44 *Implementation Guide*, 48–52.

informed decisions implementing the substantive obligations of prevention'.[45] It furthermore comments that the adoption of national legislation requiring EIA 'is a necessary condition for the implementation of EIA also at the international level'.[46]

In respect of Article 9(2)(j) (Riparian Parties below) the *Implementation Guide* emphasises that the Convention does not require a joint body to conduct an EIA, rather to 'participate in its implementation'. As to the 'international regulations' deemed appropriate, the *Implementation Guide* makes specific reference to the *EIA Convention*, highlighting significant synergies between these treaties (and the combined contribution of these two treaties to transboundary environmental governance), and comments:

> The Espoo Convention provides a parameter for reference for the implementation of EIA which is directly legally binding for those Parties of the Water Convention that are also Parties to it. It can nonetheless provide legal guidance in the field also for those Parties of the Water Convention that are not Parties to the Espoo Convention. Such guidance is likely to become indirectly binding also for non-Parties to the Espoo Convention insofar as its standards become general practice customarily followed, at least at the pan-European level.[47]

With regard to SEA, the *Implementation Guide* also makes reference to the *SEA Protocol*, and opines correctly that SEA is relevant for the implementation of Article 3(1)(h) of the *Water Convention* as it falls within the scope of the expression 'other means of assessment'.[48] The relationship between this provision and Article 9(2)(j) and (h) – applying to Riparian Parties – is also considered by the *Implementation Guide*.[49] The participation of joint bodies in the implementation of EIA relating to transboundary waters must therefore be read in the light of the earlier obligation. Article 9(2)(h) provides that joint bodies shall serve as a 'forum for the exchange of information on existing and planned uses of water and related installations that are likely to cause transboundary impact'.

The *Implementation Guide* furthermore considers the minimum requirements needed to comply with the EIA provision in the Convention. A legislated national consent regime for activities likely to cause harm to transboundary waters is required, with EIA a precondition before

---

45 *Implementation Guide*, 53.
46 *Implementation Guide*, 53.
47 *Implementation Guide*, 53.
48 *Implementation Guide*, 54.
49 *Implementation Guide*, 54.

any authorisations.[50] SEA should also be considered as part of any such regime in respect of plans and programmes relevant to the *Water Convention*.[51] Annex II of the *SEA Protocol* makes reference to water specific projects for which plans and programmes may set the context. Designation of competent authorities is needed for such a regime and documentation considered should comply with minimum content and standard requirements, as outlined by the relevant Annexes in the *EIA Convention* and *SEA Protocol*. Notification and consultation should follow the procedures of these agreements and information and public participation obligations should also be informed by the *Public Participation Convention*.[52] All of these other linkages are also illustrative of the combined contribution of the agreements to transboundary environmental governance.

Article 3(1)(j) requires the development of contingency planning measures to prepare an effective response to emergencies impacting upon water quality and the ecosystem. The need to ensure cooperation during all phases – prevention, preparedness, response and restoration – are emphasised. Emergencies can relate to a range of issues which the *Implementation Guide* identifies: technical failure, accidents concerning hazardous substances, natural disasters and extreme weather events, and sabotage.[53] The relationship with Article 14 of the Convention – concerning the obligation to notify other Parties about critical situations that may have a transboundary impact – is also noted, as is the relevance of the *Industrial Accidents Convention*. This highlights a further synergy between these UNECE treaties.[54]

Article 3(2) contains the obligation to set emission limits for discharges from point sources into surface waters based on the best available technology. This may include partial or total prohibition of the production or use of hazardous substances, and reference is to be made to other (non-UNECE) treaties where they contain lists of these substances applicable to the area covered by the Convention. Given the potential global application of the Convention since the adoption of this text, such lists – and the reach of the other treaties – will also be global, although this is not mentioned in the *Implementation Guide*, which focuses on other agreements in the UNECE region.[55] Article 3(3) requires each Party

---

[50] *Implementation Guide*, 54.
[51] *Implementation Guide*, 54.
[52] *Public Participation Convention*, above n. 30.
[53] *Implementation Guide*, 55.
[54] *Implementation Guide*, 55.
[55] *Implementation Guide*, 58–9.

to define water quality objectives and adopt criteria for them, to prevent, control and reduce transboundary impact, with guidance for developing them set out in annex II of the Convention. These objectives and criteria are additional to the setting of emissions limits for discharges, and are expanded on further in the setting of targets for water quality in surface and ground waters in the *Water and Health Protocol*, as noted in the section below.[56] The *Implementation Guide* notes that several countries in the Caucasus and central Asia are currently revising their systems for water quality classification.[57]

Articles 4–8 of the Convention conclude Part I applying to all Parties, and although brief (and not discussed in the *Implementation Guide*), are nonetheless of some significance. Article 4 requires the establishment of monitoring programmes for transboundary waters, primarily to collect baseline data rather than to evaluate the outcomes of approved development proposals. Article 5 obliges cooperation in research efforts by the Parties to develop effective techniques to prevent, control and reduce transboundary impact. Article 6 provides for the 'widest exchange of information, as early as possible' in relation to issues of concern, and the related Article 8 provides for protection of information 'related to industrial and commercial secrecy, including intellectual property, or national security'. Article 7 states that 'Parties shall support appropriate international efforts to elaborate rules, criteria and procedures in the field of responsibility and liability', clearly relevant to the development of the *Civil Liability Protocol* that, if and when in force, will apply to both this Convention and the *Industrial Accidents Convention*.

b. Provisions applying to Riparian Parties

Further to the provisions applicable to Riparian Parties and the framework nature of the Convention, Article 9, supplementing Article 2(6) on cooperation in general, requires the preparation of bilateral and multilateral agreements between them.[58] Agreements are intended to include matters covered by the Convention and other issues the Riparian Parties

---

[56] *Implementation Guide*, 60. In relation to groundwaters, see UNECE, *Model Provisions on Transboundary Groundwaters* (UN 2014).

[57] *Implementation Guide*, 61. Footnote 77 of the Guide refers to 'maximum allowable concentrations' of substances in water used as water quality objectives, a 'no risk' criteria for a single form of water use.

[58] These can be located in the document: Economic Commission for Europe Convention on the Protection and Use of Transboundary Watercourses and International Lakes, *Second Assessment of Transboundary Rivers, Lakes and Groundwaters* (United Nations 2011).

wish to include for the catchment area they specify within. The mandatory obligation for such agreements to be prepared distinguishes, as the *Implementation Guide* comments: 'the Water Convention from other international instruments in the field and is considered to be the main added value of the Convention'.[59] Outside of this mandatory obligation between Riparian Parties, the *Implementation Guide* opines that agreements between a Riparian Party and a non-Riparian Party – in particular states not Party to the Convention – is a means of exchanging information in accordance with Article 17(2)(b).[60]

Russia is singled out as an example of a Riparian Party to have implemented the obligation to enter into agreements under this important provision. It shares transboundary waters with both Asian Parties (Azerbaijan and Kazakhstan) and Asian non-Parties (China, North Korea, Georgia and Mongolia). It also shares transboundary waters with European Parties and non-Parties. In the 1990s Russia entered into bilateral agreements with Kazakhstan (1992, replaced by an agreement in 2010), Mongolia (1995), China (2008) and Azerbaijan (2010). There is no bilateral agreement between Russia and Georgia.[61]

Article 9(2) provides that agreements entered into must ensure the establishment of joint bodies, which are given numerous tasks including: identification of pollution, monitoring, exchange of information, detailing emissions limits and analysing control effectiveness, detailing water quality objectives and criteria, developing programmes to reduce pollution, setting up warning processes, operating as a forum for information exchange of uses likely to result in transboundary effects, promoting cooperation on the best available technology, and participating in the implementation of EIA.[62] Detailed guidance on the form of any joint body is elaborated in the *Implementation Guide*, with the example of

---

[59] Other requirements to establish joint bodies and for institutional cooperation are also emphasised. See *Implementation Guide*, 63–4.

[60] *Implementation Guide*, 63.

[61] *Implementation Guide*, 68. It also notes here that Russia is furthermore a Party to the Agreement on General Principles of Interaction in Rational Use and Protection of Transboundary Water Bodies in the States-Participants of the Commonwealth of Independent States.

[62] For examples of current work, see Joint Bodies workshop held between 9 and 10 April 2014 in Geneva, and press release, 'UNECE Water Convention holds global workshop for river basin commissions', 23 September 2013. This was held in the International Year of Water Cooperation, the same year in which the *Water Convention* became a global treaty, and included discussion on reform in the Mekong River Commission and emerging Afghan-Tajik cooperation on hydrology and environment in the upper Amu Darya Basin.

plenipotentiaries for transboundary waters – facilitation by an official on behalf of a riparian state – in the context of the Caucasus and central Asia provided.[63]

In the UNECE/UNEP publication: *Water Management: Guidance on Public Participation and Compliance with Agreements*[64] – which is referred to the *Implementation Guide* as another issue upon which the Riparian Parties deem it necessary to cooperate[65] – there is a set of recommendations to apply the provisions of the *Public Participation Convention* to water management, including transboundary waters.[66] In particular, the document includes the following recommendations to enhance public participation in relationships with Riparian States and joint bodies:

- Riparian States and joint bodies should provide for the participation of NGOs as nonvoting participants in the meetings of joint bodies and in the meetings of subsidiary organs of joint bodies. Conditions for inviting NGOs to participate as observers must be based on reasonable criteria, which should be clear to the public.
- Riparian States and joint bodies should establish procedures so that the public can have an oversight role in the conduct of transboundary cooperation.
- Riparian States shall ensure public participation in the development of international documents, plans and programmes for specific catchment areas.
- Riparian States are encouraged to provide for public participation, including NGOs, in the preparation of the international water agreements. NGOs could be invited to participate in intergovernmental negotiations.
- Joint bodies should have the opportunity to receive and consider information from the public. The public should be given the opportunity to submit inquiries in writing to the joint body. Joint bodies should develop a public communication strategy and establish a focal point for liaison with NGOs.[67]

---

63 *Implementation Guide*, 71.

64 UNECE/UNEP, Network of Experts on Public Participation and Compliance, *Water Management: Guidance on Public Participation and Compliance with Agreements* (2000).

65 Such matters include 'non-confrontational, non-judicial and consultative procedures for reviewing compliance', which are discussed in a section in this chapter below. See *Implementation Guide*, 65.

66 United Nations and United Nations Economic Commission for Europe, *River Basin Commissions and Other Institutions for Transboundary Water Cooperation: Capacity for Water Cooperation in Eastern Europe, Caucasus and Central Asia* (United Nations 2009) 29–30.

67 Above n. 64.

Consultation is furthermore the subject of Article 10 of the Convention and is a more specific obligation than that found in Article 2(6). The *Implementation Guide* elaborates on the customary international law nature of this obligation and its core role in the *EIA Convention*.[68] Joint monitoring and assessment obligations further to Article 11 provide information to guide action, as will be discussed in the section on implementation below. As with the *EIA Convention*, Parties may adopt and implement more stringent measures. Article 12 provides for research common to the Riparian Parties to be carried out, and Article 13 provides specifically for information to be exchanged between them further to the agreements they enter into with one another. Such information is to include: baseline data on transboundary waters, experience in relation to best available technology and research results, emission and monitoring data, measures taken and planned to prevent, control and reduce pollution, and any relevant permits issued.[69]

Article 14 concerns the establishment of warning and alarm systems in relation to critical situations arising with potential transboundary impact, whether natural phenomena or based on human activity.[70] Relating to Article 14 (together with which it should be read), Article 15 provides for mutual assistance in the case of critical situations arising, with details to be elaborated between the Riparian Parties.[71] Article 16 requires that information in relation to transboundary waters is made available to the public, specifically in relation to water quality objectives, permits and related conditions, and the results of monitoring and assessment. Although the public is not defined, the *Public Participation Convention* and *Water and Health Protocol* (considered below), should be referred to in this regard. So also should the *EIA Convention* when EIA is being carried out.[72] Reference should also be made to the consultation provision considered above and related guidance on public participation on water management also examined above.

Dispute settlement provisions are found in Article 22 of the Convention. As with the other UNECE treaties, these provisions are typically of

---

[68] *Implementation Guide*, 77–8.

[69] *Implementation Guide*, 82–4.

[70] For European examples, see *Implementation Guide*, 85–9. Note the Water Convention is referred to in the EU Water Framework Directive; see Directive 2000/60/EC of the European Parliament and of the Council of 23 October 2000 establishing a framework for Community action in the field of water policy, [2000] OJ L327/1–73.

[71] *Implementation Guide*, 90–2.

[72] *Implementation Guide*, 93–7.

last resort, to be utilised where the dispute avoidance procedures (typically NCPs) are unsuccessful. Article 22(1) applies in relation to the interpretation or application of the Convention text, and negotiation or other acceptable means are provided for. At any time, including after signature or ratification, a Party may declare its acceptance of matters to be determined by the ICJ and/or by arbitration in accordance with the procedure laid down in Annex IV. If both methods are accepted by a Party, unless the Parties in dispute agree, Article 22(3) provides that the matter may only be submitted to the ICJ.[73] The *Implementation Guide* emphasises that the general international law of water is considerable, including the *Lac Lanoux* arbitration (1957), and more recently the *Danube Dams* (1997) and *Pulp Mills* (2010) cases concluded before the ICJ.[74] The *Implementation Guide* notes, however, that while arbitration and adjudication are not compulsory under the *Water Convention*, this is in part overcome by the dispute avoidance procedures found now in the compliance procedure.[75]

III.2 Protocol

The objective of the Protocol in Article 1 is to promote the protection of human health and well-being in national and transboundary contexts. Improving water management, protection of ecosystems and the prevention, control and reduction of disease are key parts of this. Article 2 is the definition section, Article 3 establishes the scope of the Protocol, and Article 4 contains the general provisions. All appropriate measures are to be taken to ensure adequate supplies of wholesome drinking water (Article 4(2)(a)), adequate sanitation (Article 4(2)(b)), effective protection of drinking water from pollution (Article 4(2)(c)), sufficient safeguards for human health against disease (Article 4(2)(d)), and effective monitoring of potential disease (Article 4(2)(e)). All proposed measures must be assessed for their implications upon human health, water

[73] For detailed elaboration, see *Implementation Guide*, 98–100.

[74] See *Implementation Guide*, 99. For consideration of these cases see Philippe Sands and Jacqueline Peel, *Principles of International Environmental Law* (3rd edn, Cambridge University Press, Cambridge 2012). In relation to the duty of cooperation in particular, see Ruby Moynihan and Bjørn-Oliver Magsig, 'The Rising Role of Regional Approaches to International Water Law: Lessons from the UNECE Water Regime and Himalayan Asia for Strengthening Transboundary Water Cooperation' (2014) *Review of European, Comparative and International Environmental Law* 43, 44.

[75] Ibid.

resources and sustainable development (Article 4(4)). Where Parties to the Protocol are also Parties to the *EIA Convention*, compliance by public authorities with requirements of that Convention satisfy the requirement in the Protocol for due account to be taken of significant impact of proposals (Article 4(6) and (7)).[76]

Principles and approaches are set out in Article 5, including the precautionary, polluter pays, equitable and reasonable utilisation, harm prevention, inter and intra-generational equity, subsidiarity and public participation[77] principles. A guidance document has been published in relation to public participation, which plays a major role in various aspects of the Convention.[78] A catchment management approach is to be applied (Article 5(j)). Article 6 is concerned with publication and periodic revision of national and local levels of performance targets and target dates, to ensure access to drinking water and sanitation provision for all. Public participation is a key part of establishing targets, which are also to take into account a range of factors including *WHO Guidelines*[79] (Article 6(2)(a)). Targets and dates are to be published within two years of becoming a Party to the Protocol (Article 6(3)). To promote the achievement of targets, arrangements for coordination between authorities are to be established (Article 6(5)(a)); water management plans in local, national and transboundary contexts are to be prepared (Article 6(5)(b)); a framework for monitoring and enforcing drinking water quality is to be established (Article 6(5)(c)); and standards set out in targets are also to be capable of monitoring, promotion and enforcement (Article 6(5)(d)).

Comprehensive surveillance and early warning systems must be established by the Parties to identify incidents of disease and significant risks in accordance with Article 8(1)(a), providing prompt and clear information to authorities and the potentially affected public, and making recommendations to authorities and the public about preventive and remedial action. Article 8(1)(b) requires contingency plans to be prepared in response, and under Article 8(1)(c), public authorities must have the

---

[76] Note the additional requirements of the *SEA Protocol* to the *EIA Convention* in respect of health concerns. See Chapter 4.

[77] This principle (Article 5(i)) derives from the three pillar structure of the *Public Participation Convention*, see Chapter 3.

[78] United Nations Economic Commission for Europe, *Guide to Public Participation under the Protocol on Water and Health* (United Nations 2013), ECE/MP.WH/9.

[79] See http://www.who.int/publications/guidelines/en/, accessed 18 November 2014.

capacity to respond. Within three years of becoming a Party, response systems must be in place (Article 8(3)). Article 9 is concerned with public awareness, education, training, research and development and information, requiring Parties to take measures to raise levels of public awareness, promote understanding, encourage education and training and research and development in respect of water and health related matters. Article 10 contains detailed provisions for public information, which for those Parties also Party to the *Public Participation Convention* and *PRTR Protocol* should be read in conjunction with those other requirements. This is of course another indication of the potential combined effect of the agreements.

Article 11 (discussed further below) briefly requires international cooperation to support the objectives of the Protocol and assist in implementing national and local plans. Article 12 contains more detailed requirements for joint and coordinated international action, Article 13 for cooperation in relation to transboundary waters, and Article 14 international support for national action. In relation to Article 12(a)–(c), Parties are required to promote international cooperation further to Article 11 by developing commonly agreed targets for matters in Article 6(2), develop indicators for purposes of Article 7(1)(b), and establish joint or coordinated surveillance systems, contingency plans and response capacities further to Article 8. Other provisions in Article 12(d)–(g) include: providing mutual assistance to respond to disease and threats, developing integrated information systems, providing prompt and clear notification of disease and significant threats to authorities, and exchanging information on effective means of public notification.

Concerning Article 13, Parties are required to exchange information in relation to transboundary waters, establish joint or coordinated management plans, surveillance and early warning systems and contingency plans, adapt any existing agreements to ensure adherence to the Protocol, and consult on the adverse effect on public health of any diseases (Article 13(1)(a)–(d)). In relation to Article 14, promotion of water management plans and schemes to improve water supply and sanitation, improved infrastructure projects to facilitate finance and related matters required by other provisions of the Protocol are emphasised.

Dispute settlement provisions in the Protocol are found in Article 20 and make reference to Article 22 under the Convention to the effect that where Parties to the Protocol are also Parties to the Convention, acceptance of compulsory means of dispute settlement will be the same. For Parties to the Protocol who are not Parties to the Convention, the default provision is that any dispute will be submitted to the ICJ unless the Parties decide otherwise.

IV. PRACTICE

IV.1 Convention

a. Implementation

In contrast with other UNECE agreements, which require the preparation of NIRs to analyse implementation, there is no obligation for this; this process is, however, subject to current deliberations by the IC, as discussed in the next section. The Article 11 obligation in the *Water Convention* therefore only enables the collection of baseline data to evaluate practice, although this has been supported by Article 13, as noted above and explained below. Article 11 includes 'the effectiveness of measures taken for the prevention, control and reduction of transboundary impact' (Article 11(3)). The WG on Monitoring and Assessment has an important role to play regarding this provision, assisting Parties with joint programmes for monitoring the conditions of transboundary waters, including floods and ice drifts, as well as transboundary impacts. It also has a leading role in preparing periodic assessments of the status of transboundary waters to enable progress with implementation to be measured. It promotes the exchange of data on environmental conditions, encourages Parties to inform each other about critical situations with transboundary impact, including making publicly available the results of water and effluent sampling, and the verification of compliance with water-quality objectives and permit conditions.

Two assessments of transboundary rivers, lakes and groundwaters have been completed to date. The first was completed in 2007, and released at the sixth 'Environment for Europe' ministerial conference in Belgrade;[80] with the second completed in 2011, as a contribution to the seventh ministerial conference in Astana.[81] Contributions were received from numerous states, not only Parties to the Convention, but also UNECE members who are not Parties, and experts from countries outside the UNECE region who share waters with UNECE states, in particular Afghanistan, China, Iran and Mongolia. The *Second Assessment* notes generally that although efforts have been made to reduce transboundary impacts, water resources are still under considerable pressures. It also

---

[80] See United Nations Economic Commission for Europe, *Our Waters: Joining Hands Across Borders – First Assessment of Transboundary Rivers, Lakes and Groundwaters* (United Nations 2007). The 'First Assessment'.

[81] Above n. 58.

finds that although the UNECE region is the most advanced in terms of cooperation on transboundary waters, results are still mixed.[82]

The *First Assessment* consists of three parts: Part I objectives and scope; Part II transboundary surface waters; and Part III transboundary groundwaters. Of particular interest are chapters 1–4 of Part II, which outline the drainage basins of the White, Barents and Kara Seas; the Sea of Okhotsk and the Sea of Japan; the Aral Sea and other transboundary surface waters in central Asia; and the Caspian Sea. Additionally, chapters 1–6 of Part III concern transboundary groundwaters in the Caucasus and central Asia. The report emphasises the reasonable and equitable use of transboundary waters, and the particular challenges to those countries with arid or semi-arid climates in EECCA. However, it notes that only 20 per cent of transboundary rivers in the Caucasus and central Asia are in a 'high or good chemical status'.[83] Findings for central Asia are analysed in Chapter 8.

In regard to western Asia, a number of assessments were completed for the major transboundary rivers discharging into the Caspian Sea, their major transboundary tributaries, and associated lakes. These included the Kura Basin (shared between Armenia, Azerbaijan, Georgia, Iran and Turkey). This was found to be polluted by poorly treated or untreated wastewater from the 11 million people living in the area; and mining, metallurgical and chemical industries; declines in industrial pollution due to the collapse of many industries in the 1990s was, however, noted.[84]

In eastern Asia, assessments were completed for the Amur River Basin, (shared between China, Mongolia and Russia); and the Tumen River Basin, (China, North Korea and Russia).[85] In relation to the latter, the assessment comments: 'The drawing up of a multilateral agreement between China, the Democratic People's Republic of Korea and the Russian Federation is of utmost importance. It should provide for joint measures on monitoring and assessment… in order to decrease the overall human impact on the waters in the Tumen River basin.'[86] The establishment of joint working groups was therefore noted as having led to positive results, even in the Amur River basin (China and Russia) and

---

82 Above n. 58, Foreword, Ján Kubiš.

83 Above n. 80, 28.

84 Above n. 80, 99.

85 Above n 80, 62–67. Regulation under the *Water Convention* overlaps to some extent with the *Tumen Agreements* (see Chapter 2 of this book). See also p. 65, which comments on the status of the Songhua/Sungari River Basin (analysed in Chapter 5 of this book).

86 Above n. 80, 67.

the Tumen River basin (China, North Korea, and Russia), which in the past had had a high water-related conflict potential among the riparian countries.[87]

The *Second Assessment* had a stronger focus on integrated water resources management, with the Preface noting another significant feature, a focus on national frameworks, which is presumably directed at addressing the current absence of a Party-led reporting requirement through NIRs. It states:

> Legal, institutional and socio-economic issues have a prominent place in the Second Assessment, given their crucial importance for transboundary water cooperation. As national frameworks strongly influence water management and cooperation at the transboundary level, the Second Assessment also provides information on national institutional settings for water management. The legal basis for transboundary cooperation is also examined: bilateral and river basin agreements on transboundary waters, as well as relevant multilateral environmental agreements entered into by UNECE countries and their neighbours, are inventoried.[88]

Part I of the *Second Assessment* contains an overview, and Part II outlines the objectives and scope of the assessment. Part III contains the major findings, with the Caucasus the subject of chapter 4 and central Asia chapter 5.[89] In Part IV, the drainage basins of the White, Barents and Kara Seas are examined in detail in chapter 1; and the Sea of Okhotsk and the Sea of Japan in chapter 2. These include shared basins of the Amur River (China, Russia and Mongolia); the Argun/Hailaer River (China, Russia and Mongolia); the Ussuri/Wusuli River (China and Russia); the Khanka/Xingkai Lake (China and Russia); the Sujfun/Razdolnaya River (China and Russia); and the Tumen/Tumannaya River (China, Russia, and North Korea).[90] The Caspian Sea is examined in chapter 4.[91]

As an example of some of the findings in northern Asia, Part IV chapter 1 discusses the Yenisey River, which flows entirely within Russian territory, although the upper part of the basin is transboundary,

---

[87] Above n. 80, 34.

[88] Above n. 58, as per Lea Kauppi.

[89] Drainage basins of the Aral Sea and other transboundary waters in central Asia are considered in Part IV, chapter 3. Chapter 8 of the current book analyses the status of these waters.

[90] See above n. 58, 99–106.

[91] For a summary of the numerous transboundary watercourses and international lakes in this sub-region which cross nine riparian states, see above n. 58, 131.

as it includes parts of the Selenga River, shared with Mongolia.[92] This also consists of the Selenga River, Lake Baikal and the Angara River, where heavy metals and petroleum products have impacted water quality, which in the Selenga is concluded to be 'heavily polluted'.[93] The Russian-Mongolian Joint Commission on the Protection and Use of Transboundary Waters is, however, in existence, which operates on the basis of the intergovernmental 1995 Agreement on the protection and use of transboundary waters, and meets regularly.[94] To address current pressures, there are 19 surface water monitoring stations observing daily in the Selenga Basin in Mongolia. In the framework of the 'Strengthening Integrated Water Resources Management in Mongolia' project, 17 groundwater-monitoring wells are proposed to be established within the Selenga River Basin area.[95] In another example in western Asia, deterioration of water quality and degradation of ecosystems is bringing Georgia and Azerbaijan together to develop a bilateral agreement on the shared water resources of the Kura River Basin as part of a joint UNECE-OSCE project under the Environment and Security Initiative.[96]

As indicated above, in the current absence of a NIR requirement on the Parties as a means of evaluating implementation, the Article 11 provision is however strengthened by the obligation imposed on Riparian Parties to, in the context of agreements between them, exchange information. This must be done in relation to environmental conditions, experience gained, various data, measures taken and planned to address transboundary effects, and permitting information (Article 13(1)). National regulations must also be exchanged (Article 13(2)), and if requested, other data not currently available on payment of a fee (Article 13(3)). Finally, various activities are required '[f]or the purposes of the implementation of this

---

[92] Other shared basins include the Ob River (China, Kazakhstan, Mongolia and Russia); the Irtysh/Ertis (Russia, Kazakhstan, and, with a very small part shared by China and Mongolia); the Tobol and Ishim/Esil sub-basins (Russia and Kazakhstan). See above n. 58, 91–98.

[93] *Second Assessment*, above n. 58, 90. While it also concludes that Lake Baikal serves as a natural barrier for the transboundary flow of pollutants, preventing their impact on the downstream part of the watercourse, it is, however, significantly impacted by mining activity and as such is being considered for inscription on the List of World Heritage in Danger. See Chapter 2 for discussion of the *World Heritage Convention*.

[94] The provisions of the Agreement include an exchange of information on transboundary waters.

[95] See above n. 58, 90, and note the other governance mechanisms in place.

[96] See press release: 'Water and Biodiversity: UNECE Water Convention puts ecosystems at the heart of water management', 22 May 2013.

Convention', including joint ventures, provision of technical assistance, joint training programmes and organisation of events (Article 13(4)).

b. Compliance

In relation to compliance, the *Water Convention* has only recently established a NCP, which is not required under the original Convention text, but which has been initiated by the Legal Board at its seventh meeting based on experiences with the other UNECE treaties.[97] The mandate of the Legal Board as established by the fifth MOP includes development of a mechanism to facilitate and support implementation and compliance. The Chair of the Legal Board recommended such a body be of an 'advisory, consultative and facilitative nature and as such would serve as a dispute prevention mechanism',[98] although some delegations supported the view that non-compliance was significant and that the establishment of a formal reporting procedure under the Convention would be helpful in measuring implementation and compliance.[99] Participants from central Asia added that reporting could also serve as a benchmark for implementation.[100] Following the agreement of members of the Legal Board, it was accepted that non-state actors, especially the public, should have a role in indirectly bringing issues to the IC.[101]

At the eighth meeting of the Legal Board, discussions of the drafting group established to prepare the compliance procedure were considered.[102] A distinctive feature of the mechanism was to be the advisory procedure, emphasising the assistance side of non-compliance where there was a lack of deliberate failure to adhere to the Convention. Under this, a Party or Parties could request advice from the IC about efforts to attempt to secure compliance.[103] Agreement was reached about Parties themselves or those affected triggering the procedure, or by the secretariat referring submissions,[104] and that the IC itself on its own initiative

---

[97] Meeting of the Parties, Legal Board, Seventh meeting Geneva, 15 and 16 April 2010; Report of the Legal Board on its Seventh Meeting, ECE/MP.WA/AC.4/2010/2, 28 June 2010, para. II, 'Mechanism to facilitate and support implementation and compliance'.

[98] Ibid, para. II.9.

[99] Ibid, para. II.12–14.

[100] Ibid, para. II.15.

[101] Ibid, para. II.25.

[102] Meeting of the Parties, Legal Board, Eighth meeting Geneva, 24 and 25 February 2011; Report of the Legal Board on its Eighth Meeting, ECE/MP.WAT/AC.4/2011/2, 17 June 2011, para. II.

[103] Ibid, para. II.13.

[104] Ibid, para. II.14.

could trigger the procedure – including based on information received from the public[105] – however, it was not proposed that the public directly make submissions, unlike under the *Public Participation Convention* CC. In relation to the measures that may follow any non-compliance, these were confirmed to be facilitative rather than punitive, ranging from assistance requests to action plans and progress reports. More serious measures could only follow after MOP deliberations, comprising issuing statements of concern, declarations of non-compliance, cautions or suspension of rights and privileges under the Convention.[106]

The ninth meeting of the Legal Board endorsed most of the previous recommendations, although referrals by the secretariat were considered unnecessary.[107] The need for a formal reporting mechanism was also discussed further, with the need to avoid duplication with other mechanisms, (such as in the EU), emphasised, and the need to separate the discussion of a reporting mechanism from the compliance procedure.[108] The tenth meeting approved the text of such a procedure and determined that the MOP would examine it further in November 2012,[109] when a draft decision was prepared for adoption.[110] This was duly done, and the IC commenced its work soon thereafter.[111]

The IC has since held three meetings, with another due soon;[112] members serve in a personal capacity rather than as state representatives. The first meeting was held in June 2013 and the agenda included discussion of lessons learnt from other implementation and compliance mechanisms. In addition to procedures under various MEAs these also

105 Ibid, para. II.15.

106 Ibid, para. II.17.

107 Meeting of the Parties, Legal Board, Ninth meeting Geneva, 1 and 2 September 2011, Report of the Legal Board on its Ninth Meeting, ECE/MP.WAT/AC.4/2011/5, 23 November 2011, para. II.10.

108 Ibid, para. II.14.

109 Meeting of the Parties, Legal Board, Tenth meeting Geneva, 31 January and 1 February 2012, Report of the Legal Board on its Tenth Meeting, ECE/MP.WAT/AC.4/2012/2, 16 May 2012, para. II.9. Annex I contains the text of the 'Mechanism to support implementation and compliance', and Annex II the 'Core rules of procedure of the Implementation Committee'.

110 Meeting of the Parties, Sixth session, Rome, 28–30 November 2012, Item 4(a) of the provisional agenda, Draft decision on support to implementation and compliance, ECE/MP.WAT/2012/L.4, 14 September 2012.

111 Meeting of the Parties, Sixth session, Rome, 28–30 November 2012, Report of the Meeting of the Parties on its sixth session, ECE/MP.WAT/37, Ad.2, 23 July 2013.

112 To be held on 4 December 2014.

included those established under the *Public Participation* and *EIA Conventions* (and *SEA Protocol*), as well as the *Water Convention* (and *Water and Health Protocol*).[113] The relationship between compliance procedures and domestic remedies, periodic reporting and compliance procedures, the non-adversarial nature of the procedures, the role of the Secretariat, together with other issues, received particular attention.[114] Concerns raised with the *EIA Convention* Secretariat by the European Commission in relation to disputes between EU member states Parties to the Convention were also considered.[115]

The first meeting discussed at length the need for a formal reporting mechanism under the Convention.[116] The secretariat informed the IC of the discussions of the Legal Board from 2010–2012 during the establishment of the IC, when several Parties emphasised the significance of a reporting mechanism to evaluate progress and assist with implementation. The work programme adopted at the 2012 MOP included 'Consideration of the need for reporting under the Convention', to be led by the Convention Bureau as supported by the secretariat. The WG on Integrated Water Resources Management in consultation with the IC was tasked to analyse the need for a reporting mechanism.[117] The first meeting of the IC therefore exchanged views on the need for such a mechanism and found as follows:

> The Committee stressed that a reporting mechanism would help promote implementation by identifying gaps in implementation and compliance and therefore stimulating specific measures directed at improving implementation. In addition, reporting would provide a basis for evaluating the effectiveness of the Convention and for the exchange of experiences between Parties on the implementation of the Convention.[118]

---

[113] Meeting of the Parties, Implementation Committee, First meeting Geneva 5 June 2013, Report of the Implementation Committee at its first meeting, ECE/MP.WAT/IC/2013/2, 29 October 2013, para. II.7.

[114] Ibid, para. II.8.

[115] Ibid, para. II.10; for further information, see Simon Marsden, '*MOX Plant* and the Espoo Convention: Can Member State Disputes Concerning Mixed Environmental Agreements be Resolved outside EC Law?' (2009) 18(3) *Review of European Community and International Environmental Law* 312–27.

[116] Above n. 113, para. III.13.

[117] Above n. 113, para. III.13.

[118] Above n. 113, para. III.14.

Concentrating on policy issues rather than data, such a reporting mechanism would therefore distinguish itself from related reporting procedures,[119] which had caused concern among certain Parties (particularly EU member states), and threatened the prospect of the establishment for other Parties (in particular those outside the EU, such as in Asia). The second meeting of the IC began by examining issues raised by an environmental NGO in relation to an Asian state, Kazakhstan, (discussed in Chapter 8), and among other matters exchanged views on the possibility of detailing general criteria or factors to guide the determination of when an IC initiative might be started, and how best to publicise the availability of the new NCP.[120]

The third meeting of the IC took place in May 2014 and first considered information provided in relation to transboundary water cooperation in the Irtysh and Ili River Basins, and decided to ask Kazakhstan and Russia for their views and further information, after consultations with China.[121] Among other things, the IC was of the view that reporting should be thematic which would more effectively support implementation by Parties and the work of the Committee. The reporting cycle should take into account other international or regional reporting obligations to avoid duplication where possible.[122] Whether this is so remains to be seen, as decisions are taken and experience is gained.

IV.2 Protocol

a. Implementation

Article 7 is concerned with review and assessment of progress. On the basis of the collection and evaluation of data (Article 7(1)), Parties are required to publish the results (Article 7(2)) and make them publicly available (Article 7(3)). A review of progress in meeting the targets set is required, an assessment must be published (Article 7(4)), and a summary report must be provided to the secretariat for circulation to the other Parties (Article 7(5)). This provides the basis for evaluating progress with implementing the Protocol by the MOP (Article 7(6)). Guidelines on the

---

119 Above n. 113, para. III.15.

120 Meeting of the Parties, Implementation Committee, Second meeting Geneva 12 December 2013, Report of the Implementation Committee on its second meeting, ECE/MP.WAT/IC/2013/4, 13 January 2014, paras. II and IV.

121 Meeting of the Parties, Implementation Committee, Third meeting Bologna 15 May 2014, Report of the Implementation Committee on its third meeting, ECE/MP.WAT/IC/2014/2, 18 June 2014, paras. 5–9.

122 Ibid, paras. 13 and 14.

setting of targets, evaluation of progress and reporting have been prepared by the WG on Water and Health for use by the Parties.[123] Guidelines have also been prepared on the preparation of summary reports.[124]

The Protocol has furthermore been experimenting with a pilot reporting exercise, designed to improve reporting while reducing excessive burdens. A first regional report on the implementation of the Protocol has also recently been concluded, with Armenia, Azerbaijan, Georgia, Russia and Uzbekistan all submitting reports (in Russian[125]). In relation to both exercises, it has been found that although most Parties submitted reports, they were of varying quality.[126] Information on common indicators was believed to be 'data-rich, but information poor',[127] not related to targets set and progress towards them. Parties had also had significant problems target setting and reporting on water quality issues.[128] There is also an acknowledged need for cooperation between the Protocol and Convention in relation to target areas.[129]

A second reporting exercise under Article 7 was completed in 2013 based on the 2012–2013 period. The outcomes of the reporting cycle demonstrated increased compliance with the guidelines and template for summary reports, and improved overall quality of submitted reports as compared with the pilot reporting exercise conducted from

---

[123] Meeting of the Parties to the Protocol/World Health Organization Regional Office for Europe, Working Group on Water and Health, second meeting Geneva, 2–3 July 2009, Item 5 of the provisional agenda, Setting of targets, evaluation of progress and reporting, *Guidelines on the Setting of Targets, Evaluation of Progress and Reporting*, ECE/MP.WH/WG.1/2009/4, EUR/08/5086340/9, 4 June 2009.

[124] http://www.unece.org/fileadmin/DAM/env/water/meetings/TFIR/Third%20 meeting/guidelines_for_reporting_english.pdf, accessed 18 November 2014.

[125] An unofficial English version of the Georgian report is, however, accessible on the website, see http://www.unece.org/fileadmin/DAM/env/water/Protocol_reports/reports_pdf_web/Georgia_summary_report_en_unofficial.pdf, accessed 18 November 2014.

[126] Meeting of the Parties, Second session, Bucharest, 23–25 November 2010, Item 6(a) of the provisional agenda, Procedure and mechanisms facilitating the implementation of the Protocol: national summary reports on implementation, Regional report on the status of implementation of the Protocol, ECE/MP.WH/2010/2–EUDHP/1003944/4.2/1/8, 16 September 2010.

[127] Ibid, para. III.11.

[128] Ibid.

[129] Ibid, para. III.12.

2009–2010.[130] One of the findings was that the Task Force on Target Setting and Reporting was crucial in the implementation of the Protocol, by serving as a regional hub for the exchange of experience and expertise on setting targets, adopting measures towards their implementation and assessing and reporting on progress.[131] Another was that in the light of the important role of the public both in the setting of targets and reporting, it was proposed to incorporate activities on public participation into the new programme area related to setting targets and reporting entitled, 'Improving governance for water and health: support for setting targets and implementing measures'.[132] In the Caucasus, it was found that the targets under the Protocol had not yet been set in Azerbaijan, where implementation was based mostly on the realisation of national programmes; in Georgia draft targets had been established in eight areas in 2011 as the result of an assistance project, but had not yet been officially adopted; in Armenia an ongoing project on target setting was expected to be completed by 2014.[133] A third cycle of reporting will commence in 2016.

b. Compliance

The Protocol compliance procedure was established by Article 15 and is managed by the CC with its own rules of procedure.[134] This is based on the reviews and assessments provided under Article 7. Multilateral arrangements 'of a non-confrontational, non-judicial and consultative nature' for reviewing compliance were established by the Parties at the first Protocol MOP. The procedure is advanced in that, like the *Public Participation Convention* CC and the Human Rights Committee[135] – to

---

130 Meeting of the Parties, Third session, Oslo, 25–27 November 2013, Item 7(a) of the provisional agenda, Review of past activities and discussion of future activities in the different areas of work: target setting and reporting, Lessons learned and future work on target setting and reporting, ECE/MP.WH/2013/2–EUDCE/1206123/3.1/2013/MOP-3/09, 12 September 2013.

131 Ibid, para. 20(a).

132 Ibid, para. 20(d).

133 Ibid, annex, para. 14.

134 Meeting of the Parties/World Health Organization Regional Office for Europe, Compliance procedure, Rules of procedure of the Compliance Committee. See also Decision I/2 Protocol MOP on review of compliance. Note that as with the Convention IC, members serve in a personal capacity.

135 See Alan Boyle, 'Human Rights or Environmental Rights – A Reassessment' (2006–2007) 8 *Fordham Environmental Law Review* 471.

which guidance refers[136] – public submissions can be made, although the text only requires 'appropriate public involvement'.

Following the first reporting exercise under the Protocol held from 2009–2010 (which highlighting difficulties faced in implementing the Protocol, in particular setting targets and dates), in response the CC decided at its fifth meeting in June 2010 to enhance its facilitation and assistance functions, and agreed to enter into consultations with a number of Parties. At its sixth meeting in March 2011,[137] the CC outlined the main features for a new consultation process geared to help Parties implement their obligations under the Protocol.[138] To help Parties in implementing the provisions of the Protocol, the CC will, therefore, assist Parties in developing an accurate analysis of their situation (enabling them to set targets under the Protocol), provide recommendations to the Parties on how to improve their situation, and assist Parties in seeking support from donors, specialised agencies and other competent bodies.

The CC has met a further three times since then and made significant progress. At the seventh meeting, among other things the CC discussed how to involve NGOs in the work under the Protocol and in CC, the training needs of NGOs and possible synergies with the CC under the *Public Participation Convention*;[139] it also noted its recognition of the close relationship between the Protocol and the human right to water and sanitation, inviting the Office of the UN High Commissioner for Human Rights to seek possibilities for cooperation,[140] and considered that the participation of the Chair of the CC in the regular meetings of the seven human rights treaty bodies would be an effective means to foster mutual awareness and cooperation.[141]

---

136 Meeting of the Parties/World Health Organization Regional Office for Europe, Compliance procedure, Guidelines on communications from the public.

137 Meeting of the Parties, Compliance Committee, Sixth meeting Geneva 1 and 2 March 2011, Report of the Sixth meeting of the Compliance Committee, ECE/MP.WH/C.1/2011/2-EUR/DHP100394/4.2/2011/2, 11 April 2011.

138 http://www.unece.org/fileadmin/DAM/env/water/meetings/CC/ToR_Consultation_Process.pdf, accessed 18 November 2014.

139 Meeting of the Parties, Compliance Committee, Seventh meeting Geneva 3 November 2011, Report of the Seventh meeting of the Compliance Committee, ECE/MP.WH/C.1/2011/4-EUR/DHP1003944/4.2/2011/4, 20 December 2011, para. III.12.

140 Ibid, para. IV.14.

141 Ibid, para. IV.16.

At the eighth meeting there was further discussion on both of these matters as well as the consultation process,[142] and at the ninth meeting it noted with pleasure that the Consultation Process under the Protocol had been the inspiration for the advisory procedure under the *Water Convention*'s IC, whereby a Party could request advice from the IC about its difficulties in implementing the Convention.[143] It also discussed in detail the contents of its report to be submitted to the third session of the Protocol MOP, in particular with regard to the Consultation Process and Parties' compliance with reporting requirements.[144] The tenth meeting is due to be held in November 2014.

V. PROSPECTS

V.1 Asia

Prospects for the *Water Convention* in Asia are good, based on the large number of transboundary watercourses and lakes, and growing experience in the region; it is however limited by the absence of key players, notably China and India, who are not UNECE members, although this will not prevent them joining the Convention in the future once it is in practice open to all UN states. Because of shared watercourses between the two continents, cooperation between Europe and Asia has, however, been significant regarding this treaty.[145] An example of potential Asian application of the *Water Convention* is in the 'Third Pole' region, the Himalayas, as noted in Chapter 1.[146] This is also an excellent example of the relationship between the *Water Convention* and the other UNECE agreements. After providing an overview of the international law of cooperation, Moynihan and Magsig discuss the relationship between the *Water Convention* and the other UNECE agreements, in particular the

142 Meeting of the Parties, Compliance Committee, Eighth meeting Geneva 3 November 2011, Report of the Eighth meeting of the Compliance Committee, ECE/MP.WH/C.1/2012/2-EUDCE/1206123/3.1/2012/3, 30 November 2012.

143 Meeting of the Parties, Compliance Committee, Ninth meeting Geneva 3 November 2011, Report of the Ninth meeting of the Compliance Committee, ECE/MP.WH/C.1/2013/2–EUDCE/1206123/3.1/2013/06, 21 November 2013.

144 Ibid, para. III.6.

145 See for example, International Conference 'Europe-Asia transboundary water cooperation', held between the 15 and 16 December 2011 in Geneva. This promoted dialogue and cooperation on the management and protection of transboundary waters along the border of the two continents.

146 Above n. 74.

Public Participation, *EIA*, *Industrial Accidents Conventions* and related protocols. They comment on the future role of the Convention within and beyond the UNECE region as follows:

> There is momentum to share the experiences of this regional approach with transboundary water cooperation at the global, other regional and basin levels. The UNECE Secretariat recently held workshops on transboundary water cooperation in Latin America; and the Workshop 'River Basin Commissions and Other Joint Bodies for Transboundary Water Cooperation: Legal and Institutional Aspects' held in Geneva was attended by numerous non-UNECE States from Latin America, the Middle East, Africa and – of particular relevance to this article – Himalayan Asia (including Afghanistan, Thailand, Bangladesh and Burma), which participated in discussions on the transferability of the UNECE water regime beyond the UNECE region.[147]

Involving China and India in the work of the Convention is clearly vital to improving Asian prospects, not only in relation to the Third Pole, but also in relation to the other numerous watercourses crossing borders that they, along with Russia, share with their Asian neighbours. The development of large scale infrastructure for economic development (which are very often large dams), impacting watercourses and the environment more broadly, is a major concern. This significantly impacts upon downstream states and shared river basins. In relation to the Third Pole, Moynihan and Magsig note that China voted against the adoption of the *International Water Convention*; Afghanistan, Bhutan, Burma, India and Pakistan abstained or were absent; and Bangladesh, Cambodia, Laos, Nepal, Thailand and Vietnam voted in favour. However, to date, none of the latter – who are the most impacted as a result of the actions of the more powerful upstream state(s) – has ratified the Convention.[148]

In relation to the Protocol, there is much work still to be done to secure effective implementation and compliance among existing Parties, and to encourage others to become Parties, although there is no prospect for UN members more generally to accede to the Protocol. Nonetheless, there is evidence of progress in Asia as noted above. In the Caucasus, the UNECE has recently assisted Azerbaijan and Georgia in regard to joint sustainable management of the Kura River Basin.[149] As mentioned

---

[147] Above n. 74, 51–2.

[148] Above n. 74, 52. For discussion of China's position, see Patricia Wouters, 'The Yin and Yang of International Water Law: China's Transboundary Water Practice and the Changing Contours of State Sovereignty' (2014) 23(1) *Review of European, Comparative and International Environmental Law* 67, 71–2.

[149] http://www.unece.org/index.php?id=32826, accessed 18 November 2014.

briefly above, on 30 April 2013, representatives of Azerbaijan and Georgia met in Tbilisi to discuss a draft bilateral agreement as part of a joint UNECE-OSCE project under the Environment and Security Initiative (ENVSEC).[150] Consultations were constructive with only a few unresolved issues. Both states rely on the water in the Kura Basin as a key source of drinking water, as well as for sanitation, municipal and industrial water use, hydropower and irrigated agriculture, among other uses. Increased variation in and reduction of water flow, deterioration of water quality, ecosystem degradation, flooding and bank erosion are some of the issues that need to be addressed jointly by the two Riparian states.

The draft agreement provides a framework for cooperation between the two countries on water pollution prevention and control, conservation of biodiversity, emergency situations, data and information sharing and public participation. It also envisages the establishment of a joint commission for the protection and rational use of water resources of the Basin. The project has furthermore provided technical assistance to Georgia in identifying its legal and financial needs for accession to, and implementation of, the *Water Convention*.[151]

In another recent project, the UNECE has also helped Armenia set targets on water and health.[152] The tenth meeting of the Steering Committee of the Armenian National Policy Dialogue on water resources was held in Yerevan on 26 September 2013.[153] At the meeting, an expert group presented a draft baseline analysis of Armenia's health and

---

[150] ENVSEC (www.envsec.org, accessed 18 November 2014) was established in 2003 and includes the OSCE, the Regional Environmental Centre for Central and Eastern Europe (REC), UNDP, UNECE and UNEP. It works to assess and address environmental problems that threaten or are perceived to threaten security, societal stability and peace, human health and/or sustainable livelihoods, within and across national borders in conflict-prone regions.

[151] See above n. 4.

[152] http://www.unece.org/unece-main/info-resources/presscurrent-press-h/environment/2013/unece-helps-armenia-to-set-targets-on-water-and-health/unece-helps-armenia-to-set-targets-on-water-and-health.html, accessed 18 November 2014.

[153] National Policy Dialogues (NPDs) on Integrated Water Resources Management (IWRM) and Water Supply and Sanitation are the main operational instrument of the EU Water Initiative Component for EECCA. The UNECE is the strategic partner for support to the policy dialogue processes on IWRM. NPDs are under way in the following countries of the region: Armenia, Azerbaijan, Georgia, Kazakhstan, Kyrgyzstan, Moldova, Tajikistan, Turkmenistan and Ukraine. More information is available at www.unece.org/env/water/npd, accessed 18 November 2014.

environmental situation and legal framework on water, a first step towards setting national targets under the Protocol. Thirty representatives of different stakeholders and donors attended the meeting, with the UNECE helping to establish a national expert group which presented the draft baseline analysis. This comprises an in-depth study of the environmental and health situation in Armenia, as well as the existing national and international legal frameworks. It will be followed by identification and prioritisation of problems needing particular attention. Targets were expected to be finalised and adopted by mid 2014.

V.2 Global

There are many examples of how the *Water Convention* contributes to improved global environmental governance. The second meeting of the global network of basins working on climate change adaptation for instance, was held between 13 and 14 February 2014 in Geneva.[154] The creation of this global network was an outcome of the sixth World Water Forum with results to be presented at the next Forum in the Republic of Korea in 2015. The global network aims to enable the comparison of methodologies and approaches, foster exchange of experience and promote a shared vision between the participating basins. It is also part of the *Water Convention*'s programme of work for 2013–2015, which also includes a global platform for water and climate change adaptation in the form of annual workshops. These are all significant contributions.

Advocacy for the *Water Convention* setting a global model has been strong for some time, for example by the current chair of the IC.[155] The global outlook may be closely linked with the success of the *International Water Convention* now it is in force following accession by Vietnam, the 35th required Party.[156] From western to eastern Asia, Jordan, Lebanon, Syria, Iraq, Qatar, Uzbekistan and Vietnam are Parties

---

154 See 'UNECE convenes first workshop of the global network of river basins on climate change adaptation', press release, 3 July 2013.

155 See Attila Tanzi, 'Regional Integration and the Protection of the Environment: The UNECE Process on Water Law as a Model for the Global Dimension', in T Scovazzi (ed.) *The Protection of the Environment in a Context of Regional Economic Integration* (Giuffrè, Milan 2001).

156 For further analysis of environmental aspects, see Owen McIntyre, *Environmental Protection of International Watercourses under International Law* (Ashgate Publishing, Farnham 2007), and Christina Leb, *Cooperation in the Law of Transboundary Water Resources* (Cambridge University Press, Cambridge 2013).

to the *International Water Convention* and Yemen is a signatory; there are also a dozen Parties in Africa and one in South America (another is a signatory), with European states making up the remainder. Whether non-UNECE states in Asia choose to ratify the *Water Convention*, the *International Water Convention* or both, therefore remains to be seen. The provisions of the *Water Convention* are generally more specific, with the exception of the principle of equitable and reasonable utilisation in the *International Water Convention*.[157] However, whatever the effect of these two instruments coming into force almost together, Moynihan and Magsig emphasise the overall global outlook for the *Water Convention* in positive terms, particularly given its connection with the other UNECE agreements:

> The potential role of the UNECE regime is significant in terms of its scope to apply the highly developed procedural rules and institutional mechanisms to strengthen international water law at the global, other regional and basin levels, and thereby enhance political support for transboundary water cooperation worldwide. The UNECE water regime also sits within the broader UNECE regional governance framework, thus benefiting from integrated cross-sectoral regional dialogues, which lead to concrete forms of integrated cooperation and capacity-building activities on a whole range of transboundary environmental issues concerning energy, water and other natural resources.[158]

VI. CONCLUSIONS

The *Water Convention* is – perhaps with the *EIA Convention* – arguably the most significant of all of the UNECE treaties in the Asian context. Given the large number of transboundary watercourses and international lakes in the region and positive engagement with the Convention by many Parties, especially in central Asia (as discussed in Chapter 8), it has been a major contribution to the sustainable development and improved global governance of the region. The Protocol has, additionally, much to celebrate in the time since coming into force, and the issues addressed in the agreement are also of fundamental concern in the Asian region. The

---

[157] See Joseph W Dellapenna and Joyetta Gupta (eds), *The Evolution of the Law and Politics of Water* (Springer, Berlin 2009), which makes only passing mention of the Helsinki Water Convention. For differences between these regimes, see 'The Global Opening', above n. 2, 9–10; Sands and Peel, above n. 74, 310 (*International Water Convention*) and 322 (*Water Convention*); and Wouters, above n. 148, 68–71.

[158] Above n. 74, 52.

need to increase ratifications by highlighting the benefits of both agreements has been a key focus and will remain so until the Convention is in practice open to all UN states.[159]

Notable achievements of both agreements have been the establishment of the Convention IC and the Protocol CC. Both benefit from members sitting in a personal capacity, effective governance and, in the case of the CC, the public submission process. The work of the Legal Board in facilitating the former has of course been considerable, and the publication of the *Implementation Guide* to the Convention, explaining in a clear and authoritative manner the requirements of the treaty is a major assistance to existing and potential Asian Parties in fulfilling their obligations. In relation to the Convention, the detailed provisions for joint bodies and enabling bilateral and multilateral agreements are key ingredients for successful application.

The absence of a reporting mechanism for each Party while a cause for concern, is currently under discussion. Unlike the other UNECE agreements which require Parties to prepare periodic NIRs, the Convention at present relies on information from the periodic assessments conducted by the WG. While this is an independent means of obtaining information, the lack of a detailed questionnaire to be completed by each Party must also be introduced. These are operating effectively in relation to the other UNECE agreements, and need to be also part of the *Water Convention* requirements. When this is the case and the number of Parties steadily increases, there are ample grounds for optimism about the Asian and global outlook. In relation to the first, the close linkages with the other UNECE agreements is a key part; in relation to the second, the synergies and momentum generated by the *International Water Convention* will very likely benefit the future for the *Water Convention* also.

[159] For procedure, see Treaty Section of the Office of Legal Affairs, United Nations, *Treaty Handbook* (United Nations 2012).

7. The Air Pollution Convention and Associated Protocols

I. INTRODUCTION: STATUS, MEMBERSHIP AND INSTITUTIONS (CONVENTION AND PROTOCOLS)

The Convention on Long-range Transboundary Air Pollution[1] (*Air Pollution Convention*) is remarkable for its longevity and success, in tackling one of the most challenging global environmental problems, the production and long-distance migration of harmful air pollutants. Since its adoption, Parties to the Convention have also negotiated eight Protocols dealing with specific aspects of air pollution. The Convention opened for signature on 13 November 1979 and entered into force four years later on 16 March 1983; it now has 51 Parties, including the USA and Canada.[2] Two of the original signatories and Parties to the Convention were Russia and Turkey, whose territories cross Europe and Asia; since then the Caucasian and central Asian states of Armenia, Azerbaijan, Georgia, Kazakhstan and Kyrgyzstan have all also ratified. Neither the Convention nor the Protocols are currently open to accession to states outside the UNECE.

The eight Protocols to the Convention are the Protocol on Long-term Financing of the Cooperative Programme for Monitoring and Evaluation of the Long-range Transmission of Air Pollutants in Europe (*EMEP Protocol*),[3] the Protocol on the Reduction of Sulphur Emissions or their

---

[1] Convention on Long-Range Transboundary Air Pollution (Geneva, 13 November 1979) 1302 UNTS 217, in force 16 March 1983. It is often abbreviated as 'CLRTAP' or 'LRTAP'.

[2] See generally, Johann Sliggers and Willem Kakebeeke (eds), *Clearing the Air: 25 Years of the Convention on Long-range Transboundary Air Pollution* (United Nations Economic Commission for Europe 2004).

[3] Protocol on Long-term Financing of the Cooperative Programme for Monitoring and Evaluation of the Long-range Transmission of Air Pollutants in Europe (Geneva, 28 September 1984) 1491 UNTS 167, in force 28 January 1988.

Transboundary Fluxes by at least 30 Per Cent (*Sulphur Protocol*),[4] the Protocol on the Control of Emissions of Nitrogen Oxides or their Transboundary Fluxes (*NOx Protocol*),[5] the Protocol on the Control of Emissions of Volatile Organic Compounds or their Transboundary Fluxes (*VOCs Protocol*),[6] the Protocol on Further Reduction of Sulphur Emissions (*Second Sulphur Protocol*),[7] the Protocol on Heavy Metals (*Heavy Metals Protocol*),[8] the Protocol on Persistent Organic Pollutants (*POPs Protocol*),[9] and the Protocol to Abate Acidification, Eutrophication and Ground-level Ozone (*AEO Protocol*).[10] The *EMEP Protocol* has attracted the most Parties (44), whilst the *VOCs Protocol* and the *AEO Protocol* have the fewest (24 and 25 Parties, respectively).

According to Article 10, the Executive Body, (like the COPs and MOPs of other UNECE agreements), is the main governing body of the Convention, and is comprised of representatives of the Parties. Its primary functions are to ensure the implementation of the Convention and establish relevant subsidiary working groups to deal with specific matters. The four main subsidiary bodies are currently the EMEP Steering Body, Implementation Committee (IC), Working Group on Effects (WGE) and Working Group on Strategies and Review (WGSR). Meeting annually, the Executive Body considers annual reports from the subsidiary bodies, reviews ongoing work, plans future activities and approves the associated budget.[11]

---

[4] Protocol on the Reduction of Sulphur Emissions or their Transboundary Fluxes by at least 30 Per Cent (Helsinki, 8 July 1985) 1480 UNTS 215, in force 2 September 1987.

[5] Protocol on the Control of Emissions of Nitrogen Oxides or their Transboundary Fluxes (Sofia, 31 October 1988) 1593 UNTS 287, in force 14 February 1991.

[6] Protocol on the Control of Emissions of Volatile Organic Compounds or their Transboundary Fluxes (Geneva, 18 November 1991) 2001 UNTS 187, in force 29 September 1997.

[7] Protocol on Further Reduction of Sulphur Emissions (Oslo, 14 June 1994) 2030 UNTS 122, in force 5 August 1998.

[8] Protocol on Heavy Metals (Aarhus, 24 June 1998) 2237 UNTS 4, in force 29 December 2003.

[9] Protocol on Persistent Organic Pollutants (Aarhus, 24 June 1998) 2230 UNTS 79, in force 23 October 2003.

[10] Protocol to Abate Acidification, Eutrophication and Ground-level Ozone (Gothenburg, 30 November 1999) 2319 UNTS 81, in force 17 May 2005.

[11] UNECE, 'Introduction – Executive Body', accessed 19 November 2014 at http://www.unece.org/env/lrtap/executivebody/welcome.html.

The EMEP Steering Body and the WGE are the main subsidiary bodies providing scientific and technical support for the Convention. The EMEP Steering Body holds annual meetings and submits reports on its activities to the Executive Body. The work of the Steering Body is undertaken by five programme centres and four taskforces, which report back to the Steering Body. The Bureau of the Steering Body meets with representatives from the programme centres and taskforces regularly regarding the EMEP workplan and budget. In addition, the Bureau meets with the WGE to ensure that the work of both bodies is complementary and avoids duplication.

The IC for the Convention was set up in 1997 to deal with implementation and compliance matters.[12] In 2012, the Executive Body made a decision on 'Improving the Functioning of the Implementation Committee', which contains the new terms of reference for the IC.[13] The IC is comprised of nine Parties to the Convention, each elected for a term of two years. Each member of the IC must be Party to at least one Protocol, and the Committee meets twice a year.[14] The IC reports annually to the Executive Body, which retains ultimate decision-making power on implementation matters.

The WGE was established in 1980 to develop international cooperation on the research and monitoring of pollutant effects. The WGE produces detailed information on the degree and geographical extent of the impacts on human health and the environment caused by major air pollutants. It oversees six International Cooperative Programmes (ICPs) and a Task Force on Health, which work to 'identify the most endangered areas, ecosystems and other receptors by considering damage to human health, terrestrial and aquatic ecosystems and materials'.[15] The WGE meets annually to review the results of the ICPs, assess the ongoing needs of the Convention, and prepare a workplan for future activities; it reports to the Executive Body and publishes substantive reports presenting its

---

[12] Decision 1997/2 Concerning the Implementation Committee, Its Structure and Functions and Procedures for Review of Compliance.

[13] Executive Body, Decision 2012/25 On Improving the Functioning of the Implementation Committee, ECE/EB.AIR/113/Add.1.

[14] Ibid, Section I and II of the Annex. From 1 January 2017, all members of the IC must be a Party to at least one of the following: the *Heavy Metals Protocol* (1998), the *POPs Protocol* (1998) or the *AEO Protocol* (1999): ibid, para. 9.

[15] UNECE, 'Introduction – Working Group on Effects', accessed 19 November 2014 at http://www.unece.org/env/lrtap/workinggroups/wge/welcome.html.

findings. The Bureau of the WGE undertakes the detailed planning, coordination and reporting of workplan activities.

The WGSR is the main negotiating body for the Convention, assisting the Executive Body with various policy-related matters and working closely with both the EMEP Steering Body and the WGE. The tasks of the WGSR include assessing scientific and technical activities in the preparation and revision of protocols; negotiating revisions to existing protocols and the preparation of new ones; promoting the exchange of technology; and preparing proposals for any strategic development under the Convention.[16] Several specific taskforces and expert groups, together with a network of experts, have been created under the auspices of the WGSR, which meets annually.

The role of Secretariat of the Convention is fulfilled by the Executive Secretary of the UNECE (Environment Division). As required by Article 11, the Secretariat performs functions such as convening and preparing meetings of the Executive Body, distributing reports and other relevant information to the Convention Parties, and any other tasks assigned to it by the Executive Body.

II. HISTORICAL BACKGROUND AND LEGAL DEVELOPMENT

II.1 Convention

The *Air Pollution Convention* is the first UNECE agreement to be adopted. As such it is worth discussing the history and legal development in rather more detail than the previous agreements as it illustrates the cooperative approach taken to treaty making which was built on in the development of the other treaties and protocols. The origins of the Convention can be traced back to the early 1960s, when scientists' suspicions of a connection between sulphur emissions (in continental Europe) and acidification (of Scandinavian lakes) came to the attention of European lawmakers.[17] In 1961, the Council of Europe's (CoE) Parliamentary Assembly recommended that a European conference on air

---

[16] UNECE, 'Introduction – Working Group on Strategies and Review', accessed 19 November 2014 at http://www.unece.org/env/lrtap/workinggroups/wgs/welcome.html.

[17] Government of Canada, *Convention on Long-range Transboundary Air Pollution* (2008) 1.

pollution be held to clarify the issue and to discuss the potential for a binding agreement.[18]

By 1964, the Committee of Ministers of the CoE had realised the gravity and complexity of the issue and convened the European Conference on Air Pollution in Strasbourg.[19] The conference attracted experts from the fields of science, law, medicine, technology, industry and economics, together with government officials and representatives from international organisations. The agenda included topics such as the impacts of air pollution on health, the environment and economic factors; 'danger' thresholds; methods for measuring and reducing air pollution, factors influencing air pollution, the potential for a European convention on air pollution, and others.[20] To examine the issue in more detail after the conference, the CoE created the Committee of Experts on Air Pollution, which held its first session in 1966.[21] The main task of this Committee was to prepare draft recommendations and agreements on air pollution.[22] A contemporary commentator, Adinolfi, noted that:

> … everybody is convinced that in a technical field, such as that of air pollution control, each country has something to gain through a collective analysis of the problems and through collective decisions. Therefore, although the results are not yet spectacular, the governments seem to attach great importance to the work of this Committee.[23]

In 1968, the CoE's Committee of Ministers approved a Draft Declaration of Principles on Air Pollution Control.[24] It also asked member countries to submit a report every three years on measures taken to reduce and

---

[18] Recommendation 290 (61); this was reiterated in a further recommendation made in 1962: S Ercman, 'Activities of the Council of Europe and the European Economic Communities related to Transboundary Air Pollution', in C Flinterman, B Kwiatkowska, J G Lammers, *Transboundary Air Pollution: International Legal Aspects of the Co-operation of States* (Martinus Nijhoff, Leiden 1986), 131–40, 132.

[19] G Adinolfi, 'First Steps toward European Cooperation in Reducing Air Pollution – Activities of the Council of Europe', (1968) 33 *Law and Contemporary Problems* 421.

[20] Ibid, 421–2.

[21] Resolution (66) 23 on Air Pollution, Committee of Ministers of the Council of Europe; see also ibid, 422.

[22] Above n. 19, 422.

[23] Above n. 19, 426. At the time, Adinolfi was working for the President of the Consultative Assembly of the CoE.

[24] Resolution (68) 4: see Ercman, above n. 18, 132.

prevent air pollution.[25] Several further resolutions were made over the next few years on specific issues related to air pollution, such as sulphur dioxide emissions.[26]

When the link between air pollution and acidification was confirmed in the 1970s, and the various damaging effects of long-range pollutants became better understood, momentum grew towards taking decisive international action. The UNECE formed a Working Party on Air Pollution Problems and began conducting an annual review and analysis of the air pollution issue.[27] As Gehring notes, this project 'was officially intended to keep member governments informed of developments in this field. However, it provided a communicative channel designed to facilitate the regular exchange of information about national policies that could generate international pressure on polluting countries'.[28]

In late 1974, air pollution experts met in Moscow and then Oslo, to identify the basic elements of a cooperation programme on long-range transboundary air pollution.[29] This proposal was specifically referred to in a recommendation made in the same year by the CSCE that the UNECE should 'develop through international co-operation an extensive programme for monitoring and evaluation of the long-range transport of air pollutants, starting with sulphur dioxide and with possible extension to other pollutants'.[30] The need for cooperation in environmental matters was emphasised by the CSCE in the *Helsinki Final Act* (1975), although the UNECE's work on the air pollution issue had already commenced by that stage.[31] It is important to note that the CSCE continued to work on the transboundary air pollution issue in parallel to the UNECE, in a

---

[25] Ercman, above n. 18, 132.

[26] Ercman, above n. 18, 132–3.

[27] *Programme of Work of the Commission*, E/ECE/911/Add.2, 22; Thomas Gehring, *Dynamic International Regimes: Institutions for International Environmental Governance*, Studies of the International Environmental Law Network, vol. 5, (Peter Lang, Frankfurt 1994) 90–1.

[28] Gehring ibid, 91, citing the *Programme of Work of the Commission*, E/ECE/911/Add.2, 22.

[29] B Fjeld and B Ottar, *Preliminary Report on Existing Knowledge with regard to SO_2 Emission Sources* (Norwegian Institute of Air Research, Kjeller 1975) 3; Gehring above n. 27, 86.

[30] *Conference on Security and Cooperation in Europe – Final Act*, Cooperation in the Field of Economics, of Science and Technology and of the Environment, Helsinki (1975) 30.

[31] Ibid.

complementary rather than obstructive manner, throughout the 1970s until the adoption of the Convention.[32]

Work started on developing a UNECE monitoring programme in 1974, through the Working Party on Air Pollution Problems. By early 1975, the Working Party had finalised the 'Cooperative Programme for the Monitoring and Evaluation of the Transmission of Air Pollutants in the ECE Region'.[33] At this time, rapporteurs nominated by the Soviet Union and Norway also began working on a methodology for an inventory of sulphur dioxide emissions from stationary sources in the UNECE region.[34] Gehring notes that the preference given to the Soviet Union and Norway reflected their dominant roles at the time in east-west cooperation and air pollution respectively.[35] It is said that, whilst the Soviet-Norwegian collaboration on air pollution was not a source of contention within the UNECE, it highlighted the inaction of major western countries on the issue.[36]

In early 1976, a Task Force was formed by the UNECE to begin implementing the Cooperative Programme by collecting information on the quantity and deposition of pollutant emissions.[37] With Norway as the lead country, 11 European countries – all highly industrialised with the exception of the Soviet Union – participated in the Task Force and agreed to supply data on their emissions.[38] Neither the USA nor Canada was involved in the work of the Task Force. Later that year it adopted a work plan, setting out responsibilities and procedures for collecting and evaluating emissions data.[39] It recommended that the Norwegian Institute for Air Research be responsible for coordinating data measurement and analysis, and that two meteorological institutes in different parts of Europe be chosen to conduct the final evaluation of the data.[40] Close cooperation between all three institutes was envisaged.[41] The UNECE

---

[32] Whilst a detailed description of the work undertaken by the CSCE is beyond the scope of this book, it is provided in Gehring, above n. 27

[33] Above n. 27, 87.

[34] See generally, Fjeld and Ottar, above n 29; Gehring, above n. 27, 87.

[35] Above n. 27, 87.

[36] Above n. 27, 87.

[37] Above n. 27, 87.

[38] Above n. 27, 88. The countries were Denmark, Finland, France, Italy, the Netherlands, Norway, Sweden, Switzerland, the UK, West Germany and Russia.

[39] Above n. 27, 88.

[40] Above n. 27, 88.

[41] Above n. 27, 88.

Working Party on Air Pollution Problems accepted these recommendations in 1977.[42] A Steering Committee was also established at this time, to deal with all matters relating to the effective implementation of the Cooperative Programme, which by then had also become known as EMEP.[43] The Working Party took on a supervisory role for the work carried out by the EMEP Steering Committee.

The momentum towards a regional framework for transboundary air pollution continued to grow. The Soviet Union made several attempts to initiate a regional meeting on environmental issues more broadly, but these were opposed for political reasons by some European and North American countries.[44] Norway and Sweden also pursued the idea of an international conference, but one that would specifically address transboundary air pollution. Norway stated that 'the time was ripe for [a high-level] meeting on environmental problems, particularly those relating to the long-range transport of air pollutants'.[45] Both Nordic countries were strongly motivated to address transboundary air pollution, having already been affected by pollution from other parts of Europe for some time. Eventually the proposals of both the Soviet Union and the Nordic countries converged somewhat, forming the basis of the UNECE's recommendation that the matter be discussed constructively at its session in 1978.[46]

At this stage, however, the UNECE had still not settled on a particular environmental issue as the subject of the proposed multilateral conference. It had agreed that a high-level meeting on environmental matters was necessary, and that it should preferably focus on one issue only, but it was obliged to consult with the Member States and discuss the matter in depth prior to making a final decision. The UNECE therefore compiled a list of several significant environmental issues, based on proposals by individual governments. In late 1977, discussions held during a Consultative Meeting of the Senior Advisers to UNECE Governments on the Environment (SAEP) revealed that 'transboundary air pollution was the only topic that received wide support and virtually

---

42 ENV/WP.1/8, para. 36; above n. 27, 89.
43 ENV/WP.1/8, para 36; and ECE/ENV/15, para. 92; above n. 27, 89.
44 Above n. 27, 95–6.
45 E/ECE (XXXII)/SR. 4, para. 22; cited in Gehring, above n. 27, 96.
46 Above n. 27, 96.

no resistance'.[47] It appears that the only disagreement between the countries may have been in relation to the appropriate scope of the topic.[48]

Yet the selection process was still not complete. The UNECE Secretariat submitted a report to the Commission on the outcome of the consultation process, identifying transboundary air pollution and four other issues as possible candidates for the high-level meeting.[49] Although it appears that transboundary air pollution was the only real contender among the Member States from this point onwards, there was considerable political disagreement over the way in which the matter should proceed. Some western European countries wanted to take a 'go slow' approach, and opposed a binding framework; the USA indicated its possible support for the issue; and some Nordic countries and the Soviet Union advocated prompt action. Neutral countries, such as Switzerland, played an important role in helping the opposing sides reach a compromise at this stage.[50] They were able to defuse the political aspects of the process and emphasise the need for regional cooperation on environmental matters.[51]

A special workgroup on transboundary air pollution was established to undertake more detailed preparations for the high-level meeting.[52] At the first meeting of the Special Group on Transboundary Air Pollution in mid 1978, the five Nordic countries put forward two instruments for consideration: a 'Draft Convention for the ECE Region on Reduction of Emissions Causing Transboundary Air Pollution', and a memorandum setting out the key elements of a proposed mandatory annex on sulphur emissions.[53] According to Gehring 'these Nordic proposals reflected the general approach toward an international regime supported by the pollution prone Nordic countries and were de facto accepted as the basis for future negotiations'.[54]

---

47 Above n. 27, 98.

48 Above n. 27, 98.

49 E/ECE/936; above n. 27, 99: the four other topics were low- and non-waste technology, transboundary water pollution, control of toxic substances and toxic wastes, and protection of native fauna, flora and habitats.

50 Above n. 27, 102–3.

51 Above n. 27, 102–3.

52 Above n. 27, 105.

53 Above n. 27, 106. The five countries were Denmark, Sweden, Norway, Finland and Iceland.

54 Above n. 27, 106.

However, some western European countries continued to resist the push for a binding agreement in the near future, arguing that more research first needed to be done on the effects of transboundary air pollution.[55] Eventually it became evident that a compromise was again needed, and the USA put forward a draft document designed to achieve this. The USA proposal involved separating the main instrument on transboundary air pollution from any further 'optional' protocols that may be agreed later.[56] In response, the Nordic countries conceded that any protocol on sulphur emissions would have to be postponed until after the framework agreement on air pollution had been concluded.[57] The agreement would, however, still contain provisions ensuring 'a continuing process of multilateral consultations and negotiations'.[58] For its part, the Soviet Union was keen for the matter to be resolved through compromise, though it remained ambivalent as to whether the eventual outcome should be a binding or non-binding instrument.[59]

Another significant development in the evolution of the Convention occurred at this stage. France proposed the establishment of an institutional body that 'would have operational responsibility for the implementation of [the] agreement', including the development of policies and strategies, coordination of envisaged activities, and review and revision functions.[60] These institutional provisions were later incorporated into Articles 2 to 8 of the final text of the Convention.[61]

The drafting and discussion of the proposed instrument continued at the fourth special session of SAEP in March 1979.[62] The preamble and certain clauses of the draft instrument were drawn up, although key issues still had to be resolved: the form that the instrument should take and the degree of commitment to take action (for instance whether mandatory or merely exhortatory language should be used).[63] These issues were left to the Commission itself to decide at its 1979 session.[64] At this session, the Commission prioritised the task of finalising the draft text in readiness for the high-level meeting later in the year. Whilst some

55 Above n. 27, 116.
56 Above n. 27, 117.
57 Above n. 27, 118.
58 Above n. 27, 120.
59 Above n. 27, 119–120.
60 Above n. 27, 117.
61 Above n. 27, 117.
62 Above n. 27, 120.
63 Above n. 27, 121.
64 Above n. 27, 121.

western European countries initially maintained their opposition to the concept of a binding agreement, Norway and Sweden warned that a failure to agree on the issue of form could jeopardise the success of the high-level meeting, and this seems to have had the desired effect.[65]

Two weeks of closed-door negotiations by the Commission resulted in the final proposed text of a binding instrument on transboundary air pollution, together with an agenda for the long-awaited High-Level Meeting on the Protection of the Environment, scheduled for November 1979.[66] The Meeting was attended by almost all EC Member States, who endorsed the text of the proposed Convention early in the proceedings and without further negotiation.[67] Another document was also accepted at the Meeting: a Resolution on Long-range Transboundary Air Pollution, which was a statement of intent to cooperate further to resolve certain issues that had been too controversial to be included in the main Convention text.[68] The Resolution also served, by way of an interim mechanism, to bridge the gap in time between the High-Level Meeting and ratification of the Convention by the Signatories.[69] According to Gehring, the story of the Convention was one of mixed success, yet it represented a significant development in international environmental cooperation:

> In terms of substance, the regime as established in 1979 was comparatively weak because of the complete lack of reduction targets. However, it reflected a certain agreement *that* transboundary air pollution should be controlled, limited and prevented, and *that* the best technology available and economically feasible should be employed. Apparently, these obligations were not detailed enough to create tangible and concrete duties, but they indicated the direction in which the regime would develop in the future and permanently established the issue of long-range transboundary air pollution on the international agenda.[70]

II.2 Protocols

When the Convention was first adopted in 1979, its primary purpose was to provide a framework for addressing the problem of acidification,

---

65 Above n. 27, 123.

66 Above n. 27, 127.

67 Above n. 27, 128. However, as the author points out, the Convention was signed not at the Meeting itself, but at a later date in Geneva.

68 ECE/HLM.1/2/Annex II; Gehring, above n. 27, 120 and 129.

69 Above n. 27, 129.

70 Above n. 27, 130 (original emphasis).

which was primarily caused by sulphur dioxide and nitrogen oxide emissions. However, at that time, the Parties also anticipated that the Convention would be extended to other major pollutants with transboundary effects in due course. The terms of the Convention were made sufficiently broad to cater for this eventuality, and as a result, eight Protocols have been adopted over the intervening period.

The first of the eight Protocols, the *EMEP Protocol*, was intended to ensure the long-term financial viability of the Convention's scientific programme, EMEP. Since 1977, it had been collecting data on pollutant emissions, and by the early 1980s the importance of its work to the objectives of the Convention was already evident. The Protocol currently has 44 Parties and entered into force in 1988.[71] According to the UNECE, EMEP has, since its inception over three decades ago, 'taken an international leadership role in supporting air pollution policy development and its implementation within its domain and also globally'.[72] More specifically, it has 'developed a unique and specific capacity to quantify long-range transport of air pollution including source-receptor relationships for calculation of transboundary fluxes as well as a widely accepted system for quality assurance of methods and results'.[73] These science-based results are relied upon by the Convention bodies in the preparation of policy responses to long-range air pollution problems.

Early data obtained by EMEP had already confirmed the belief by Nordic countries that sulphur dioxide emissions from other UNECE countries were causing them harm. Once the Convention had been concluded, renewed calls were made for the issue to be addressed through a binding agreement, and the matter was prioritised at the first session of the Executive Body in 1983.[74] Although a proposal to reduce sulphur emissions by a third was initially opposed strongly by France, the UK, USA and some other UNECE countries, in 1984 the tide turned in favour of such an agreement.[75] As a result, the *Sulphur Protocol* was signed in 1985, becoming the first protocol to contain specific measures

---

[71] Above n. 3.

[72] UNECE, *Revised Strategy for EMEP for 2010–2019*, 17 September 2012, ECE/EB.AIR/2009/16/Rev.1, at 2.

[73] Ibid.

[74] Above n. 13, 14.

[75] Yves Berthelot and Paul Rayment, *Looking Back and Peering Forward – A Short History of the United Nations Economic Commission for Europe, 1947–2007* (United Nations Economic Commission for Europe, Geneva 2007) 72; Sliggers and Kakebeeke above n. 2, 14–16 and 19.

to address a particular pollutant.[76] Although at least two major opponents, the UK and USA, never signed the Protocol, it entered into force in 1987 and now has 25 Parties.

In response to rising concerns about the contribution of nitrogen oxides to acidification, greater efforts were made by the UNECE to understand the scientific basis of the issue and reach a consensus on measures to address it. The *NOx Protocol* was concluded in 1988.[77] It focuses on reducing emissions of nitrogen oxides, which are known to cause respiratory illness in humans and environmental problems such as excess nutrients, poor water quality, lack of biodiversity and ground-level ozone formation.[78] It incorporates the important concept of the 'critical load' (in this context, referring to the level of nitrogen in the soil), which has since been used as the basis of emissions control strategies for other protocols. It entered into force in 1991 and currently has 34 Parties.

Shortly after the *NOx Protocol* came into being, negotiations began for a protocol on another cause of ground-level ozone formation, VOCs. These are emitted through vehicular and industrial combustion processes, as well as through dry-cleaning and other activities, and are suspected of causing serious human health problems such as leukemia.[79] The *VOCs Protocol* was concluded in Geneva in 1991.[80] It entered into force in 1997 and has 24 Parties.

Within a few years of signing the 1985 *Sulphur Protocol*, the UNECE Parties recognised that sulphur emissions were continuing, and that 'further and more effective action' was needed to control and reduce them.[81] The result was the *Second Sulphur Protocol* which introduces an 'effects-based approach', which involves setting long-term targets for reductions in sulphur emissions with reference to 'critical loads' of pollution.[82] The term 'critical load' refers to the point above which exposure to a pollutant begins to have significant harmful effects on a sensitive element of the environment. It is also the first of the protocols to specifically mention the precautionary principle in its preamble, reflecting the growing global acceptance of the concept following the

---

[76] Above n. 4.
[77] Above n. 5.
[78] Above n. 2, 7.
[79] Above n. 2, 7.
[80] Above n. 6.
[81] Preamble to the Protocol.
[82] Above n. 7.

1992 *Convention on Biological Diversity* (see Chapter 2).[83] The Protocol entered into force in 1998, and currently has 28 Parties. It complements, and mostly supersedes, the first *Sulphur Protocol*. However, some Parties which did not accede to the *Second Sulphur Protocol* remain bound by the original Protocol.

In 1998, the UNECE concluded two protocols in Aarhus: the *Heavy Metals Protocol*[84] and the *POPs Protocol*.[85] The *Heavy Metals Protocol* creates a reduction and elimination scheme for three of the most harmful pollutants – lead, mercury and cadmium. It entered into force in 2003 and currently has 33 Parties. Amendments to the Protocol were made in 2012 to introduce more stringent controls of heavy metal emissions, and to enhance the flexibility of the Protocol for new Parties (such as those in central Asia). The existence of the *Heavy Metals Protocol* helped to stimulate and inform negotiations for the global *Mercury Convention*, which was eventually adopted in 2013.[86]

The *POPs Protocol* targets 28 substances that have toxic characteristics, are likely to cause significant harm to humans or the environment, may be carried over long distances, and are persistent and capable of bioaccumulation. These primarily comprise pesticides, industrial chemicals and by-products. It entered into force in 2003, and now has 33 Parties. Similarly to the *Heavy Metals Protocol*, the *POPs Protocol* played an important role in elevating the POPs issue to the international arena in the late 1990s. It provided a reference point for the UNEP in the negotiation and drafting of the global *POPs Convention* adopted in Stockholm in 2001 (see Chapter 2).[87] In 2009 and 2010, amendments were made to the *POPs Protocol* to add more substances to the original list of 16 POPs, and to relax some of its provisions so as to facilitate accession by economies in transition. However, these amendments are not yet in force. In recent years, the widespread effectiveness of the *POPs Convention* has resulted in the *Air Pollution Convention* Executive Body redirecting its efforts from POPs to other, more urgent issues.[88]

---

[83] Convention on Biological Diversity (Rio de Janeiro, 22 May 1992), 31 ILM 822, in force 29 December 1993.

[84] Above n. 8.

[85] Above n. 9.

[86] The Minamata Convention on Mercury (Kumamoto, 10 October 2013) unreported, not in force; by August 2014 it had attracted 101 signatures and one ratification (the USA). It requires 50 ratifications to enter into force.

[87] Above n. 75, 96.

[88] See for example *Conclusions of the Working Group on the Future Development of the CLRTAP*, Conference on Air Pollution and its Relations to

The most recent addition to the Convention, the *AEO Protocol*, addresses four pollutants: ammonia, sulphur, volatile organic compounds and nitrogen oxides.[89] The Protocol entered into force in 2005, and has 25 Parties. It was amended in 2012 to include national commitments to reduce emissions by 2020 and beyond, to update the emission limits in its technical annexes, and – in keeping with similar amendments to the two Aarhus Protocols – to introduce greater flexibility for accession by new Parties. The 2012 amendments have been given provisional application pending formal entry into force.[90]

III. OBJECTIVES AND GENERAL PROCEDURAL PROVISIONS

III.1 Convention

The Convention serves two main functions: it sets out general principles for international cooperation on reducing and monitoring air pollution, and it provides an institutional framework for research and policy on the issue. The central aim of the Convention is to protect people and the environment from air pollution, and more specifically, 'to limit and, as far as possible, to gradually reduce and prevent air pollution including long-range transboundary air pollution' (Article 2).

The Convention urges its Parties to develop 'without undue delay' policies and strategies to combat the discharge of air pollutants, through exchanges of information, consultation, research and monitoring (Article 3). Parties are expected to review their own policies, scientific activities and technical measures aimed at tackling the discharge of potentially harmful air pollutants (Article 4). 'Best practice' policies and strategies should include air quality management systems, incorporating control measures that are compatible with balanced development, and the best available technology that is economically feasible (Article 6).

An important feature of the Convention is the emphasis on consultation and cooperation between its Parties. It requires that early consultations be held between affected Parties and emitting Parties (Article 5). Parties are

---

Climate Change and Sustainable Development ('Saltsjöbaden 3'), Sweden, 12–14 March 2007, 2.

[89] Above n. 10.

[90] Decision 2012/4, Provisional Application of Amendment to the Protocol to Abate Acidification, Eutrophication and Ground-level Ozone, ECE/EB.AIR/111/Add.1.

also directed to collaborate in research on, and development of, emissions reduction technologies, monitoring and modelling techniques, effects of pollutants, assessment of alternative measures, and educational and training programmes (Article 7). Information exchanges between Parties should include emissions data, data on the transmission and effects of pollutants, control technologies and costs, relevant national, subregional and regional policies and strategies, and any major changes to national policies and industrial development that are likely to cause significant changes in long-range transboundary air pollution (Article 8).

The success of the Convention and Protocols is often attributed to their solid scientific basis, in particular the work done through the Cooperative Programme for Monitoring and Evaluation of Air Pollutants in Europe (or 'European Monitoring [and] Evaluation of Pollutants' – EMEP).[91] The foundations for EMEP, which has been referred to as the 'backbone' of the Convention,[92] are provided in Article 9. The main objective is to provide Parties with scientific information relating to the long-range movement, deposition, concentration, extent and impacts of air pollutants covered by the Convention.

The remainder of the Convention deals with the role of the Executive Body (Article 10) and the Secretariat (Article 11); and procedural provisions relating to amendments to the Convention (Article 12) and settlement of disputes (Article 13). In regard to dispute settlement, the Convention and each of its Protocols contains a specific provision.[93] Article 13 of the Convention is brief and states:

> If a dispute arises between two or more Contracting Parties to the present Convention as to the interpretation or application of the Convention, they shall seek a solution by negotiation or by any other method of dispute settlement acceptable to the parties to the dispute.

III.2 Protocols

The *EMEP Protocol* creates a financial mechanism to support the scientific work carried out under the Convention, through a flexible contributions scheme. Under Article 3, Parties to the Protocol which are

---

91 Above n. 17, 4.

92 Above n. 2, 31.

93 See Article 13 of Convention; Article 8 of the *Sulphur Protocol*; Article 12 of the *VOCs Protocol*; Article 12 of the *NOx Protocol*; and Article 9 of the *Second Sulphur Protocol*. The later protocols contain the following non-compliance provisions: Article 12 of the *POPs Protocol*; Article 11 of the *Heavy Metals Protocol*; and Article 11 of the *AEO Protocol*.

within the EMEP area must make annual mandatory contributions to the EMEP work programme, in accordance with a cost-sharing scale set out in the Protocol's Annex. Mandatory contributions may be in currency or in kind, and are to be supplemented by voluntary contributions, which can be made by any country, organisation or individual.

Article 2 of the *Sulphur Protocol* calls on Parties to reduce their national annual sulphur emissions by almost a third (as measured against 1980 levels), as soon as possible or at the latest by 1993. To achieve this, Parties were required by Articles 4 and 6 to develop relevant national programmes, policies and strategies, and report annually on their progress to the Executive Body. Where necessary, and warranted by environmental conditions, Parties were also obliged to consider making further reductions beyond the 30 per cent target in accordance with Article 3.

The *NOx Protocol* requires Parties to take effective measures to control and/or reduce their annual emissions of nitrogen oxides to 1987 levels or below, by 1994 in accordance with Article 2(1). Within two years of the Protocol entering into force, Articles 2(2) and (3)(a) also required them to apply national emissions standards to any major new stationary sources of emissions and new mobile sources in major categories, and introduce pollution control measures for major existing stationary sources. In the period from 1990 to 2006, NOx levels dropped by 35 per cent within the EU, and by 23 per cent in the USA.[94]

Article 2(3)(a) of the *VOCs Protocol* requires the control and reduction of national emissions of VOCs by 30 per cent (based on 1988 levels) by 1999, and a commitment by Parties to apply, within two years of the Protocol's entry into force, appropriate national or international emissions standards and measures to sources of VOCs within their jurisdiction. The promotion of non-VOC products and public awareness of VOC emissions are among other obligations. According to the UNECE, non-methane VOC emissions decreased by 41 per cent in the EU, between 1990 and 2006.[95]

Article 2(4) of the *Second Sulphur Protocol* requires Parties to use the most effective measures that are appropriate to their circumstances, to achieve emissions reductions. Under Articles 4 and 5 they are also to adopt national strategies, policies, programmes, and measures to implement the Protocol, and to report periodically to the Executive Body in this regard. In addition, Articles 3 and 6 require Parties to facilitate the

---

94 Above n. 2, 7.

95 United Nations Economic Commission for Europe, 'UNECE's Convention on Long-range Transboundary Air Pollution celebrates 30th Anniversary', http://www.unece.org/env/lrtap/30anniversary.html, accessed 19 November 2014.

exchange of relevant technologies and techniques, and promote research, development, monitoring and cooperation relating to sulphur emissions. According to the UNECE, sulphur dioxide levels dropped by 70 per cent within the EU, and by 36 per cent in the USA, between 1990 and 2006.[96] These figures far exceed the original 30 per cent target set by the 1985 *Sulphur Protocol*, and demonstrate the success of sustained efforts by Parties to reduce emissions under both of the protocols.

The *Heavy Metals Protocol* requires each Party to reduce its emissions of lead, mercury and cadmium to 1990 levels or below, by taking effective measures that are 'appropriate to its particular circumstances' in accordance with Article 3(1). It identifies industrial and combustion processes as the main sources of heavy metal emissions, and accordingly requires specific changes to be made to these processes to achieve emissions reductions under Article 3(2). Clear limits are to be placed on emissions from stationary sources, and the best available techniques are to be applied as part of emission reduction strategies. As with the other protocols, Parties are required under Article 7(1) to report periodically to the Executive Body on their levels of heavy metal emissions, and the specific measures they have taken to implement the Protocol. Amendments in 2012 introduced more stringent measures for reducing emissions of heavy metals and particulate matter, and expanded the categories of industrial activity covered by the Protocol.

The *POPs Protocol* aims to control, reduce or eliminate discharges of POPs (Article 2), through an immediate ban on the production and use of the most harmful substances (for instance the substances listed in Annex I, including aldrin, chlordane and dieldrin) (Article 3(1)(a)), strict limits on the use of DDT, HCH and PCBs (Annex II) (Article 3(1)(c)), and a gradual reduction in emissions of polycyclic aromatic hydrocarbons (PAHs), dioxins, furans, and hexachlorobenzene (HCB) (Annex III) (Article 3(5)(a)). Emissions of Annex III substances are to be reduced to 1990 levels or below, through 'effective measures' that take into account the relevant Party's 'particular circumstances'. Annex IV specifies limit values for dioxins and furans from major stationary sources, Annex V provides guidance on the use of best available techniques to control POPs emissions from major stationary sources, Annex VI sets timeframes for the application of limit values and best available techniques to new and existing stationary sources, Annex VII describes recommended control measures for reducing POPs emissions from mobile sources, and Annex VIII specifies categories of major stationary sources.

---

[96] Above n. 2, 7.

Article 3(1) of the *AEO Protocol* establishes emission ceilings for ammonia, sulphur, volatile organic compounds and nitrogen oxides; Articles 3(2) to (5) place restrictions on specific emission sources; and Article 3(6) requires best available techniques to be used to achieve reductions. Amendments made in 2012 set targets for national emissions reductions by the year 2020 and thereafter. Emission limit values for both stationary and mobile sources were also revised, and ceilings were set for emissions of fine particulate matter. Between 1990 and 2006, levels of ammonia fell by 20 per cent and levels of primary particulate matter decreased by 28 per cent in the EU.[97]

Whilst all of the Protocols adopted prior to 1997 have a similarly brief clause to the Convention, those entering into force after 1997 include a detailed provision on the settlement of disputes.[98] The more detailed provision requires that disputes be resolved through negotiation or other peaceful means wherever possible; if settlement cannot be achieved in this way, then the matter is to be referred for conciliation or arbitration, or to the ICJ (if both Parties have expressly accepted its jurisdiction).[99] It appears that few Parties to the later Protocols have recognised the competence of the ICJ in this regard, leaving any disputes to be settled through the remaining avenues.[100]

IV. PRACTICE (CONVENTION AND PROTOCOLS)

IV.1 Implementation

One of the primary roles of the Executive Body is to undertake reviews of the Parties' implementation of the Convention in accordance with Article 10(2)(a). It delegated much of this role to the IC when it was established in 1997, and now makes decisions based on the reports and recommendations of the Committee. Taken together, the Convention and Protocols have for the most part been effective in reducing emissions of

---

97 Above n. 95.

98 See above n. 93.

99 See Article 9 *Second Sulphur Protocol*, Article 11 *Heavy Metals Protocol*, Article 12 *POPs Protocol*, and Article 11 *AEO Protocol*.

100 See generally, Andreas L Paulus, 'Dispute Resolution' (at 362), and specifically in the context of the Convention, Tuomas Kuokkanen, 'The Convention on Long-range Transboundary Air Pollution' (at 165), both in Geir Ulfstein, Thilo Marauhn and Andreas Zimmermann (eds), *Making Treaties Work: Human Rights, Environment and Arms Control* (Cambridge University Press, Cambridge 2007).

certain pollutants, thereby lowering the overall amount of air pollution in the UNECE region. As the Executive Body, the main governing body of the Convention noted in 2010:

> The Convention on Long-range Transboundary Air Pollution has delivered demonstrable improvements in reducing acidification of the environment, in reducing the highest peak levels of ozone and photochemical smog, and has begun to make improvements in atmospheric levels and deposition of nitrogen – one of the most important global environmental problems in addition to climate change. The Convention has also shown itself to be flexible and dynamic in responding to new challenges and problems in the area of transboundary air pollution.[101]

The main functions of the IC are to conduct periodic reviews of compliance by Parties with their reporting obligations (based on emissions data submitted to EMEP and responses to a questionnaire on strategies and policies); investigate possible cases of non-compliance by individual Parties; consider any systemic issues that have been identified in relation to compliance; and undertake in-depth reviews of specific obligations under individual Protocols at the request of the Executive Body.[102] The IC consists of representatives from nine Parties to the Convention, elected for a term of two years.[103] It meets twice a year and makes recommendations as part of its annual report to the Executive Body.[104]

Although the Convention itself makes no mention of a duty of Parties to report on implementation, all of the Protocols (except for the *EMEP Protocol*) impose obligations to report on strategies, policies and other measures to implement their provisions.[105] The questionnaire on strategies and policies is generally sent out to Parties by the IC every two

---

[101] Decision 2010/18, Long-Term Strategy for the Convention on Long-range Transboundary Air Pollution and Action Plan for Its Implementation, ECE/EB.AIR/106/Add.1, at 1.

[102] Decision 2012/25 on Improving the Functioning of the Implementation Committee, ECE/EB.AIR/113/Add.1, Annex (Section IV).

[103] From 2017, each Committee member must also be a Party to at least one of the three most recent Protocols.

[104] Above n. 102, Annex (Section X).

[105] Article 6 of the *Sulphur Protocol*; Article 8 of the *NOx Protocol*; Article 8 of the *VOCs Protocol*; Article 5 of the *Second Sulphur Protocol*; Article 7 of the *Heavy Metals Protocol*; Article 9 of the *POPs Protocol*; and Article 7 of the *AEO Protocol*.

years, although the most recent one was distributed in 2010.[106] It is designed to allow Parties to meet all of the reporting requirements regarding implementation of the Protocols in one document, and to facilitate the exchange of national and local information. The IC also undertakes a general policy review every four years, to give the Secretariat an overall picture of the current situation regarding reduction of air pollution within the UNECE region.[107] In addition to reporting requirements on implementation measures, Parties are required under the Protocols to submit reports on their emissions data.[108]

In 2013, the Secretariat published the results of the 2010 questionnaire in a report titled 'Strategies and Policies for Air Pollution Abatement'.[109] The document presents a review of the progress being made in the implementation of the Convention and its substantive Protocols. Many country-specific examples of implementation for each Protocol are provided in the report, although it is difficult to obtain from this a broad overview of the progress being made. The report is generally positive, noting briefly that the overall targets for most of the pollutants in the Protocols are being met, although the performance of each Party varies.[110] The Executive Body noted in 2013 that the Parties to the two *Sulphur Protocols*, the *NOx Protocol* and the *VOCs Protocol* had not reported any significant changes to their strategies, policies and measures in recent years.[111] Considerable emphasis is now being placed on implementation of the three most recent, the *Heavy Metals*, *POP*s, and *AEO Protocols*.

---

[106] None of the states reviewed were Asian Parties. The IC noted that the Executive Body did not approve a new questionnaire to be distributed in 2012, so distribution did not take place. Instead, the IC has focused on following up on queries as to the 2010 questionnaire: Fifteenth Report of the Implementation Committee, ECE/EB.AIR/2012/16 (2 October 2012), 17.

[107] UNECE, Strategies and Policies of Parties and Signatories to the Convention for the Abatement of Air Pollution: 2010 Draft General Policy Questions, ECE/EB.AIR/2009/13 (5 October 2009), 1.

[108] Reporting on emissions data is not discussed in more detail here, although it is noteworthy that 14 Parties were found not to have complied with their reporting requirements for the 2012 reporting round: above n. 106, 17.

[109] ECE/EB.AIR/123.

[110] Ibid, 9.

[111] Executive Body, Decision 2013/2: Reporting on Strategies, Policies and Other Measures to Implement Obligations under the Convention and its Protocols, ECE/EB.AIR/122/Add.1.

The Executive Body decided in 2013 to incorporate the compliance review process into the sessions of the WGSR.[112] According to this decision, Parties will now be invited to submit details of their implementing policy and strategies annually, prior to its sessions. The WGSR has been instructed to include a summary of the Parties' reports and any relevant policy discussions in its annual report to the Executive Body. The effectiveness of this method of reviewing compliance with reporting obligations is to be evaluated at the 34th Session of the Executive Body.

IV.2 Compliance

Despite the existence of basic dispute settlement provisions in the Convention and early Protocols, it was in practice, 'considered unlikely that a dispute settlement procedure would be applied in relation to non-compliance of the provisions of individual protocols'.[113] By establishing the IC, the Executive Body hoped to address non-compliance matters more effectively,[114] based on the example of a similar mechanism under the 1987 *Ozone Protocol*[115] (see Chapter 2).[116] The intention of the Executive Body was 'to bypass the confrontational and judicial nature of dispute settlement procedures and place more emphasis on getting Parties to fulfil their commitments'.[117] In general, as noted in Chapters 3–6

---

[112] Ibid.

[113] Tuomas Kuokkanen, 'Putting Gentle Pressure on Parties: Recent Trends in the Practice of the Implementation Committee under the Convention on Long-range Transboundary Air Pollution', in Jarna Petman and Jan Klabbers (eds), *Nordic Cosmopolitanism: Essays in International Law for Martti Koskenniemi* (Martinus Nijhoff, Leiden 2003) 315–26, 318.

[114] Above n. 12.

[115] Protocol on Substances that Deplete the Ozone Layer (Montreal, 16 August 1987), 1522 UNTS 3, in force 1 January 1989.

[116] Decision II/5 (Non-Compliance), Report of the Second Meeting of the Parties to the 1987 Montreal Protocol on Substances that Deplete the Ozone Layer, UNEP/OzL.Pro.2/3, 29 June 1990; Decision IV/5 and Annexes IV and V, Report of the Fourth Meeting of the Parties, UNEP/OzL.Pro.4/15, 25 November 1992, 32 ILM (1993) 874.

[117] UNECE Committee on Environmental Policy, Report on the First Meeting of the Task Force on Compliance Mechanisms to the Second Meeting of the Signatories to the Convention on Access to Information, Public Participation in Decision-Making and Access to Justice in Environmental Matters, Dubrovnik, Croatia, 3–5 July 2000, CEP/WG.5/2000/4, Annex IX, 21–22.

above, the compliance regimes developed by the UNECE have 'deliberately focused on avoiding complexity and being non-adversarial, transparent and cooperative'.[118]

According to Kuokkanen, another reason for establishing a mechanism that could extend beyond bilateral dispute settlement was the difficulty in proving a causal link between non-compliance by one Party and the impacts of that non-compliance on another.[119] In addition, there was recognition that 'a compliance mechanism would serve the general interests of the parties whilst a dispute settlement procedure appears to be inherently bilateral in nature'.[120] For these reasons, the Executive Body chose to establish a non-compliance procedure that could be applied to all existing, pending and future Protocols.[121]

The NCP under the IC can be triggered either through submissions by Parties or referrals by the Secretariat (for instance the Executive Secretary of the UNECE) or the IC where it becomes aware of a case of possible non-compliance.[122] A Party may also make a submission to the Secretariat if the Party concludes that it is unable to fully comply with its obligations despite its best efforts.[123] The IC has various information-gathering powers and functions.[124] After deliberating on a particular instance of alleged non-compliance, it must make recommendations to the Executive Body.[125] Based on the IC's report and recommendations, the Executive Body may then decide on 'non-discriminatory measures' to ensure full compliance by the relevant Party.[126] These are usually specified in the formal decisions of the Executive Body, and the IC is instructed to review the Party's compliance with the required measures and report back at a certain time.

The IC regularly considers matters of non-compliance by Parties to the Convention and Protocols and refers them to the Executive Body for a final decision. Initially, beginning in 2000–2001, the Committee only dealt with a couple of cases per year, but this number rose steadily over the ensuing decade. In 2012, for example, 14 countries were found not to

---

118 Ibid, Annex IX, 21–22.

119 Above n. 113, 318.

120 Above n. 113, 318; see also above n. 117, Annex IX, 21.

121 Above n. 113, 317.

122 Above n. 113, 319; above n. 102, Section V.4(a), Section VI.5 and Section VII.5 of the Annex.

123 Above n. 102, Section V.4(b) of the Annex.

124 Above n. 102, Section VIII.6 of the Annex.

125 Above n. 102, Section X.9 of the Annex.

126 Above n. 102, Section XII.11 of the Annex.

have complied with their emissions data reporting obligations under various Protocols.[127] A similar number of non-compliance cases have been handled every year for at least the past several years. According to Goeteyn and Maes, the decisions in these non-compliance cases have tended to be facilitative in nature, with the aim of assisting Parties to reach full compliance rather than imposing punitive measures.[128] They contend that 'it is clear that the installation of the Implementation Committee has had a positive impact on compliance with the reporting obligations'.[129]

Following the 2010 questionnaire on strategies and policies, the IC identified five countries that had not fully complied with their reporting requirements.[130] In its 2013 decision, the Executive Body noted the partial non-compliance of Russia and 'urged' it to provide the missing information to bring it into full compliance.[131] Apart from expressing its dissatisfaction, setting out a timetable and encouraging these countries to respond, there is little else that the Executive Body or IC can do to secure compliance.

In 2011, as part of the Action Plan for the Implementation of the Long-term Strategy, the IC was tasked with identifying and evaluating systemic and other barriers to achieving compliance with the Convention and Protocols.[132] The term 'systemic barriers' generally refers to issues that can affect more than one Party and that may be beyond the control of individual Parties. In its report to the Executive Body in late 2012, the IC identified several types of systemic barriers, including: inaccurate obligations in the Protocols, or obligations for which there are no measures that can be taken or no cost-effective measures that can be taken; linkage of obligations to old base years that can no longer be calculated; the insufficiency of the reporting guidance; and outdated or obsolete emissions factors where there is no or insufficient information to improve

[127] Above n. 106, para. 100.

[128] Nils Goeteyn and Frank Maes, 'Compliance Mechanisms in Multilateral Environmental Agreements: An Effective Way to Improve Compliance?', (2011) 10(4) *Chinese Journal of International Law* 791–826 (para. 36).

[129] Ibid.

[130] France, Latvia, Luxembourg, Russia and the EU: above n. 106, 17.

[131] Decision 2013/17 Concerning compliance by the European Union, Latvia and the Russian Federation with their obligations to report on strategies and policies, ECE/EB.AIR/122/Add.1, paras. 3 and 6.

[132] ECE/EB.AIR/106/Add.1.

estimates or their reliability.[133] The IC recognised that cases of non-compliance attributed solely, or mainly, to a systemic barrier were best referred to the Executive Body for resolution.[134] However, where the reason for non-compliance is primarily within the control of the individual Party or Parties involved, the IC is regarded as the appropriate forum.[135]

V. PROSPECTS

V.1 Asia

In the Asian context, there remains much work to be done on a comprehensive regime for managing transboundary air pollution, whether or not that regime is eventually provided by the Convention. Almost two decades ago, transboundary air pollution in southeast Asia was identified as a 'significant environmental issue' by Townsend-Gault et al.[136] More recently Schwela et al described the growing problem of transboundary air pollution in Asia generally:

> Urban air quality in Asia is becoming increasingly affected by pollution resulting from neighbouring jurisdictions. Transboundary air pollution in the form of atmospheric brown cloud, acidification and dust and sandstorms all contribute directly or indirectly to effects on human health, environment and the economy in the region.[137]

---

[133] Above n. 106, para. 115. The IC is currently undertaking an evaluation of all the identified systemic barriers and will report to the Executive Body in the near future.

[134] The IC can also refer its own recommendations on such a matter to the Executive Body: para. 116.

[135] ECE/EB.AIR/2012/16, para. 116.

[136] Ian Townsend-Gault, David VanderZwaag, and Robert Adamson, 'Transboundary Ocean and Atmospheric Pollution in Southeast Asia: Prospects for Regional Cooperation', in Amitav Acharya and Richard Stubbs (eds) *New Challenges for ASEAN – Emerging Policy Issues* (UBC Press, Vancouver 1995) 28.

[137] Dietrich Schwela, Gary Haq, Cornie Huizenga, Wha-Jin Han, Herbert Fabian and May Ajero, *Urban Air Pollution in Asian Cities – Status, Challenges and Management* (Earthscan, Abingdon, UK and New York, USA 2006) 19. According to the authors (14), the regional and global impacts of atmospheric brown cloud are likely to intensify over the next 20–25 years as the population of the Asian region and sources increase.

With reference to acidification, Schwela et al contend that 'the deposition of sulphur in some areas of Asia is now equal to or higher than in the most polluted areas of Europe and North America'.[138] Indeed, it appears that most parts of Asia are affected in some way by at least one transboundary air pollution issue. In western Asia,[139] air pollution has increased significantly over the past few decades, mainly in the form of high levels of sulphur dioxide and nitrogen oxide caused by rapid industrialisation, in addition to naturally occurring dust storms.[140] The rise in air pollution in this region shows no signs of slowing, a problem that is compounded by a decreasing rainfall.[141]

Another major problem is the use of uncontrolled burning to convert forest into agricultural land in some countries, particularly Indonesia. The transboundary air pollution caused by these fires:

> ... remains a perennial problem. [...] The impacts of the haze [caused by the fires] include major disruption of travel and transport, increasing risk of traffic accidents, public health risks through the transboundary transport of fine and ultrafine PM [particulate matter] and environmental damage.[142]

There is significant variation in the level of awareness of the transboundary air pollution problem throughout Asia. This is unsurprising, given the variability in economic development, cultural backgrounds and geographical features among Asian countries. In many of these countries, air pollution is inadequately recorded and poorly understood, and other problems may legitimately be considered more pressing.

However, a few countries that have long suffered the effects of air pollution from their neighbours are already well aware of the problem.[143]

---

[138] Ibid, 15–16.

[139] Also sometimes referred to as 'west Asia', this region includes Iraq, Jordan, Lebanon, Palestine, Syria, Bahrain, Kuwait, Oman, Qatar, Saudi Arabia, the United Arab Emirates and Yemen.

[140] United Nations Environment Programme, 'Air Quality and Atmospheric Pollution in the Arab Region', (Regional Office for West Asia 2007).

[141] J Lelieveld et al, 'Model Projected Heat Extremes and Air Pollution in the Eastern Mediterranean and Middle East in the Twenty-First Century' (2013) March *Regional Environmental Change* 7. The 2007 UNEP report (above n. 140) also states (at 5) that 'projections indicate that potentially large increases in emissions may occur during the next twenty to fifty years if current development patterns persist'.

[142] Above n. 137, 14.

[143] See for example in relation to Japan and Korea, Inkyoung Kim, 'Environmental Cooperation of Northeast Asia: Transboundary Air Pollution' (2007) 7(3) *International Relations of the Asia-Pacific* 439–62.

For example, there is awareness of the issue among policymakers, scientists and even citizens in some parts of northeast Asia[144] – primarily Japan, South Korea and China – but a significant lack of consensus on the environmental impacts of transboundary air pollution at both the domestic and regional levels.[145] Recent reports on the adverse effects on North America and weather patterns in the Pacific Ocean, generated by high levels of particulate pollution in countries such as China, India and Japan,[146] highlight two trends: a recognition that transboundary air pollution in Asia remains a persistent challenge, and that the effects of this pollution may be more widespread and complex than was earlier thought.

There is also a high level of awareness of air pollution in Singapore and Malaysia, but this is confined to the issue of haze generated by Indonesian fires.[147] ASEAN successfully negotiated a binding agreement on a specific air pollution issue in 2002, the *Haze Pollution Agreement* (see Chapter 2).[148] However, in the broader Asian region, there has so far been a lack of dialogue on the most effective approach to tackling all aspects of transboundary air pollution. There have been no high-profile calls from within Asia for a concerted regional response to address the issue, in marked contrast to the situation preceding the adoption of the Convention in Europe. According to Kim, 'the development of the Convention was largely due to the fact that scientists and specialists were

---

144 Inkyoung Kim (ibid at 443) defines 'northeast Asia' as including six countries: Russia (primarily the Russian Far East), Mongolia, China, South Korea, North Korea and Japan.

145 For example, as Inkyoung Kim (above n. 143, 439) notes, 'the Korean Peninsula and Japan have felt the brunt of China's "export" through acid rain, mercury, and other airborne contaminants as Siberian winds and dust storms flush out China's pollution every spring, severely damaging forests and watersheds.' See also, Juli S Kim, 'Transboundary Air Pollution – Will China Choke on its Success?' (2007) *China Environmental Health Project Fact Sheet*, 2.

146 For example 'Air pollution in Asia intensifies cyclones', *The Japan Times*, 1 February 2014; 'Study: Pollution from Chinese factories is harming air quality on US West Coast', *The Washington Post*, 21 January 2014.

147 There were particularly high levels of haze in 1997 and, most recently, in 2013: see, for example 'Singapore's Haze Hits Record High from Indonesia Fires', 21 June 2013, BBC News online service, http://www.bbc.co.uk/news/world-asia-22998592, accessed 19 November 2014. The Pollutant Standards Index reportedly reached 401, the highest in Singapore's history.

148 Association of South East Asian Nations, *Agreement on Transboundary Haze Pollution* (Kuala Lumpur, 10 June 2002), unreported, in force 2003.

"fully aware" of the need for the joint cooperative efforts of all countries in Europe to solve urgent problems'.[149]

In the Asian context, the failure to consider a binding regional response to transboundary air pollution may be attributed to a range of factors, including political sensitivities, a preference for 'voluntary' rather than mandatory instruments, economic challenges, lack of technical expertise, and the lack of scientific consensus referred to above. Examples of non-binding agreements on air pollution include the *Malé Declaration on Control and Prevention of Air Pollution and its Likely Transboundary Effects for South Asia* (1998)[150] and the *Tripartite Joint Action Plan on Environmental Cooperation between Korea, China and Japan* (2010).[151] Policy and science-related initiatives, such as the East Asia Network on Acid Deposition (EANET),[152] Joint Forum on Atmospheric Environment in Asia and the Pacific,[153] Regional Forum on Environment and Health in Southeast and East Asian Countries (Thematic Working Group on Air Quality) and Clean Air Asia, are also helping to raise awareness through scientific monitoring, information exchange, conferences, and capacity building activities. These initiatives may eventually help to overcome the obstacles to a potential Asia-wide agreement on air pollution, or accession to the Convention.

Although the Convention itself does not currently apply to Asia (with the exception of central Asia), initiatives led or instigated specifically by the Executive Body are already underway in the region. In 2004, the Task Force on Hemispheric Transport of Air Pollution (HTAP Task Force) was created, under the auspices of the Convention, to improve understanding of the intercontinental movement of air pollution across the northern hemisphere. The findings of the Task Force are partly intended to inform the review process for Protocols to the Convention. The long-term project involves the collaboration of scientists across the world in compiling emissions inventories and projections, conducting monitoring and data

---

[149] Above n. 143, 443, citing Sliggers and Kakebeeke, above n. 2, 13.

[150] Covering the countries of Bangladesh, Bhutan, India, Iran, Maldives, Nepal, Pakistan and Sri Lanka. See http://cleanairinitiative.org/portal/node/755, accessed 19 November 2014.

[151] Between Japan, South Korea and China. For the latest developments, see https://www.env.go.jp/press/file_view.php?serial=22137&hou_id=16621, accessed 19 November 2014.

[152] Participating countries are China, Vietnam, Cambodia, Laos, Thailand, Indonesia, Malaysia, Philippines, Japan, Mongolia, South Korea and Russia.

[153] This initiative began in 2010, with the release of the *Joint Plan for Joint Activities on Air Pollution in Asia and the Pacific*.

analysis, undertaking global and regional modelling, and assessing the wide-ranging impacts of hemispheric pollution transport.[154]

In 2010, following the successful completion of the Task Force's first major assessment report, its mandate was renewed.[155] One of the key aims of the Task Force remains to 'assess potential emission mitigation options available inside *and outside* the UNECE region' by working with other groups both within and outside the Convention.[156] The 2010 HTAP Report made several significant observations in relation to Asia:

- there are significant air quality and environmental impacts of the long-range transport of particulate matter (PM), in the outflow of the Asian continent;
- Asian emissions of PM have a stronger tendency to be lifted and transported aloft than do European emissions;
- East Asia currently contributes more than any other region to the hemispheric transport of mercury;
- only a slow decline, or indeed an actual increase, in the rate of emissions of NOx, VOCs and carbon is predicted in East Asia by 2050, compared with a steeper and earlier decrease in Europe and North America;
- sulphur dioxide emissions from East Asia are expected to continue increasing for some time, before declining dramatically by 2050; and
- emissions of black carbon from East Asia are likely to decline dramatically by 2050.[157]

Another initiative in Asia with Convention origins is the Greenhouse Gas and Air Pollution Interactions and Synergies (GAINS-Asia) scientific model, which has been specially adapted from the original European/North American model for application in Asia. The GAINS-Asia model was developed by experts in China and India in association with the International Institute for Applied Systems Analysis (IIASA). It identifies the local health impacts of various transboundary air pollutants, and analyses the cost-effectiveness of potential tools for reducing emissions.[158] The GAINS-Asia model is being applied extensively in China,

[154] HTAP Task Force website, http://www.htap.org/, accessed 19 November 2014.

[155] Hemispheric Transport of Air Pollution 2010, Executive Body, 28th Session, Informal Document No. 10, ECE/EB.AIR/2010/10.

[156] 'Phase 2: Background and Rationale', HTAP Task Force website, accessed 19 November 2014 at http://www.htap.org/ (emphasis added).

[157] Above n. 155, 6.

[158] One key finding to date has been that the application of advanced emission control technologies could reduce health impacts in China by 43% by the year 2030: IIASA website, 'The GAINS Model', accessed 19 November

India and Pakistan, and is freely accessible online for use by other countries.[159] The key policy messages that have come out of GAINS-Asia include the following:

- Economic growth will exacerbate the current air quality problems in Asia unless existing pollution control laws are significantly upgraded;
- Compared to a conventional strategy, the GAINS cost-effectiveness approach can find ways to reduce costs for improving air quality by 80%; and
- By selecting a mix of measures to simultaneously cut air pollution and greenhouse gas emissions, countries can also further reduce air pollution control costs.[160]

A third initiative led by the Convention is the collaboration with the NEASPEC,[161] which is part of UNESCAP. A NEASPEC project currently being undertaken by Russia aims to study existing sub-regional and international mechanisms for transboundary air pollution and to identify gaps in knowledge, prioritise needs, and propose options for a strengthened multilateral approach.[162] According to Ballaman, it is 'expected that the developments in North-East Asia might lead to the establishment of a policy-type umbrella framework that would cover the existing monitoring and modelling programmes like the Joint Research Project on Long-Range Transboundary Air Pollutants and the Acid Deposition Monitoring Network in East Asia'.[163]

V.2 Global

Celebrating its 35th anniversary in 2014, the Convention seems to have already achieved, or be on the way to achieving, most of the air pollution reduction goals set out in its Protocols. Although the Secretariat has

---

2014 at http://www.iiasa.ac.at/web/home/research/modelsData/GAINS/GAINS.en.html.

[159] Richard Ballaman, 'Comparing Regional Environmental Governance in East Asia and Europe – Air Pollution', Paper presented at Workshop on *Comparing Regional Environmental Governance in East Asia and Europe*, Kyoto, 24–25 January 2013, 4.

[160] IIASA website, 'GAINS-Asia', accessed 22 November 2014 at http://gains.iiasa.ac.at/gains/ASN/index.login?logout=1.

[161] See Chapter 2, Tumen programme.

[162] Above n. 159, 3.

[163] Above n. 159, 3–4.

expressed satisfaction at the overall progress being made, it has identified several important areas in which work remains to be done. In 2013, it noted that:

> Increased ratification, implementation and compliance with existing protocols will continue to be a high priority in the Convention. In particular, the Executive Body reaffirmed that a more active participation of countries in Eastern Europe, the Caucasus and Central Asia and South-Eastern Europe was one of the key priorities, stressing the need for support directed to assist these countries in ratifying and implementing the three most recent protocols to the Convention.[164]

New and emerging challenges in relation to the sources, movement and effects of long-range transboundary air pollution will also need to be addressed within the context of the Convention and Protocols in coming years. Issues such as particulate matter, links between air pollution and climate change, hemispheric transport of air pollution and reactive nitrogen in the environment have already been identified as areas of ongoing interest.[165]

The Secretariat has stated that 'the goal is for the Convention to be a leading regional framework, working with other bodies, in addressing the remaining and emerging transboundary air pollution challenges in the twenty-first century'.[166] However, the success of the Convention in Europe and North America has led some – both within and outside of the Convention – to informally advocate its use in reducing long-range transboundary air pollution globally.[167] This could potentially be achieved either by making membership of the Convention open to all countries – which is currently not the case – or by using it as a leading example for a future multilateral or regional agreement on the issue.[168] The former option is canvassed further by Brachtl, who contends that 'LRTAP and its eight protocols, though originally regional in scope, offer

---

[164] UNECE, Strategies and Policies for Air Pollution Abatement, 2013, ECE/EB.AIR/123, 13.

[165] Ibid. See also n. 2.

[166] Ibid.

[167] See for example Martin Williams (Chair of the Executive Body), 'Future Role and Challenges for CLRTAP', Presentation to Saltsjöbaden 5 Workshop, Gothenburg, Sweden, 24–26 June 2013, 20.

[168] See for example, Megan Brachtl, 'Working Group 4 – Background Note for the Session on Air Pollution Agreements – Going for Global Governance of the Troposphere', Saltsjöbaden 5, Gothenburg, Sweden, 24–26 June 2013, 1–2.

adequate structure to address transboundary air pollution on a global scale'.[169] The second option is identified by Sands and Peel:

> While the treaty has a restricted regional scope (Europe and North America), it has nevertheless served as a model for subsequent treaties adopted at the global level [...] and provides a precedent for other regions in their efforts to address acid rain and related transboundary atmospheric problems.[170]

There is some recognition of the need for an international agreement on transboundary air pollution that goes beyond the current scope of the Convention:

> Now, at the beginning of the 21st century, a more extensive agreement to combat transboundary air pollution is needed in order to manage pollutant emissions from nations who are not party to LRTAP. Developing countries in particular are not only less likely than their more industrialized counterparts to be able to deal effectively with transboundary pollution, but are also more likely to suffer domestically from the ill effects of polluting emissions.[171]

Using the Convention – whether directly or indirectly – as the basis for global action on long-range transboundary air pollution has, Brachtl argues, several advantages.[172] First, it offers an opportunity to avoid the substantial costs and delays associated with negotiating a new global instrument 'from scratch'.[173] Second, the Convention has a proven track record in setting reduction targets for specific pollutants, taking new scientific research into account for emissions standards, and recognising the need for long-term monitoring and analysis.[174] Ballaman also acknowledges that the Convention and Protocols have much to offer

---

[169] Megan Brachtl, 'Capitalizing on the Success of the Long-Range Transboundary Air Pollution (LRTAP) Regime to Address Global Transboundary Air Pollution', in Lawrence E Susskind and William R Moomaw (eds), XIV *Papers on International Environmental Negotiation* (PON Books, Cambridge, MA, USA 2005) 1. She also identifies two other options: calling on the UNECE 'to institute cooperative projects with other organizations and countries without imposing binding obligations', and establishing 'a new umbrella oversight structure under which LRTAP would fall, [...] [to] oversee the development of other regional treaties to address transboundary air pollution'.

[170] Philippe Sands and Jacqueline Peel, *Principles of International Environmental Law* (Cambridge University Press, Cambridge 2012) 246–7. This corresponds approximately to the third option identified by Brachtl, above n. 169.

[171] Above n. 169, 3. See also, Brachtl, above n. 168, 1–2.

[172] Above n. 169, 3.

[173] Above n. 169, 3.

[174] Above n. 169, 3.

non-UNECE countries, including well-developed tools for emissions monitoring and reduction.[175]

An extension of the current scope of the Convention to all countries could be achieved by removing the geographical restrictions from membership, as has already been done for the *Water Convention*.[176] Individual countries – beginning with the major polluters – could then be invited by the UNECE to sign the Convention, in the hope that neighbouring countries would then follow suit.[177] Alternatively, groups of countries may be encouraged to become signatories to the Convention through collaboration with regional UN organisations.[178] Either way, certain inducements could be offered to bring non-UNECE countries 'on board'. These could include flexible reduction or phase-out timeframes, new technology transfer provisions, and extra financial assistance.[179] The 2013 'Saltsjöbaden 5' Workshop on the future direction of the Convention recommended that steps be taken to open it up to countries outside the UNECE.[180]

The option of using the Convention as the basis for a new global 'umbrella' instrument on transboundary air pollution, under which the Convention would be but one of several regional sub-agreements, is another possibility. Most likely overseen by UNEP, such a framework treaty would 'allow for the creation of other regional agreements similar, but not necessarily identical, to LRTAP while keeping the LRTAP regime intact'.[181] These regional agreements would be negotiated separately from the Convention, but could incorporate its most successful and appropriate features.[182] One benefit of this approach is that it would 'promote regional cooperation to address environmental problems that have both national and regional impact[s], which is especially important

---

175 Richard Ballaman, 'Personal views on future work for a better air quality', Presentation to the 'Saltsjöbaden 5' Workshop, Gothenburg, Sweden, 24–26 June 2013, 7.

176 Brachtl, above n. 169, 2.

177 Ibid, 3.

178 Above n. 169, 4.

179 Above n. 169, 4.

180 'Taking International Air Pollution Policies into the Future: Main Conclusions from the Saltsjöbaden V Workshop 24–26 June 2013', 4. The Workshop was organised jointly by Swedish government agencies, the Executive Body, European Commission, Global Atmospheric Pollution Forum and Nordic Council of Ministers.

181 Above n. 169, 7–8.

182 Above n. 169, 8.

for developing countries experiencing increased levels of pollution as a result of economic growth and industrialization'.[183] The Saltsjöbaden 5 Workshop recommended that the Convention initiate discussions with other regional networks on the appropriate elements of an apparently non-binding global framework for cooperation on air pollution, which would provide an agreed process for information sharing and policy coordination.[184]

A third option that would capitalise on the success of the Convention, but without resulting in any binding obligations, would be to promote cooperative projects with non-UNECE countries on long-range transboundary air pollution.[185] As mentioned above, such cooperative work is already being undertaken in the central Asian region, by the UNECE's EECCA Coordinating Group. Based on that model, similar initiatives could potentially be extended to other (non-UNECE) regions. Essentially, the goal would be 'to share the experience and expertise of members of LRTAP to achieve voluntary reductions in pollution emissions in other regions of the world'.[186] Voluntary cooperation may be more attractive to non-UNECE countries than binding obligations, although it is also possible that good progress in the former may eventually lead to the latter.[187] There are also fewer obstacles to achieving voluntary cooperation on transboundary air pollution than more formalised action.[188]

Despite the calls made at the Saltsjöbaden 5 Workshop for a proactive approach to global outreach for the Convention, as yet there have been no formal proposals by either the UNECE or the Executive Body to open up the Convention to all countries.[189] An element of caution, combined with a lack of resources, may be the cause of this apparent reluctance.[190] The Convention's 2010 Long-Term Strategy does, however, emphasise the

---

183 Above n. 169, 9.

184 Above n. 180, 4.

185 Above n. 169, 5–7.

186 Above n. 169, 5.

187 Above n. 169, 7.

188 See for example, above n. 169, 5.

189 With the exception of the recommendations made by the Saltsjöbaden 5 Workshop in June 2013.

190 For example Ballaman (above n. 175, 7) suggests that collaboration with countries outside the UNECE region generally would be welcomed only if they came 'knocking at the door' and were prepared to commit themselves.

importance of pursuing various informal outreach activities, particularly those relating to science. It sets out a ten-year work program, as well as identifying potential work up to 2050. It states that 'extensive geographical scientific cooperation' with non-UNECE countries, which has already begun through the work of several Convention working groups, is to be 'strongly encouraged' in the future.[191]

The increasing emphasis of the Convention on stimulating policy change, in addition to the already established level of scientific cooperation, is evident in the Long-Term Strategy. It recognises that scientific and political outreach activities by the Convention 'will become increasingly important, particularly to foster cooperation between regional agreements around the world, and also as a bridge between regional and global action'.[192] In response, one strategic priority of the Convention is to actively pursue greater cooperation at the strategic and policy levels on intercontinental air pollution issues with other regions,[193] and the global community.[194] More generally, the Long-Term Strategy envisages that the Convention will strengthen its relevance as a leading regional agreement on transboundary air pollution, and 'maintain visibility on the international scene through unique and relevant work which can serve as an inspiring model for other regions in the world'.[195]

Studies undertaken by the Global Air Pollution (GAP) Forum on the future options for global action on transboundary air pollution have warned that any collaborative efforts on the issue, even if they are only voluntary in nature, are destined to be complex. According to the GAP Forum, such efforts:

> … must take account of deep-seated and long-standing differences among regions and states in cultural values and priorities; in their stage of economic development; and, particularly, in their governance. This means that any one current approach – such as the approach of the LRTAP Convention – is unlikely to be fully and directly transferable to other regions, or – if it is – is

---

191 Above n. 101, para. (h).

192 Above n. 101, para. 16(k).

193 As an example see Jason Buhi and Lin Feng, 'Honoring the International Joint Commission's Role in the United States-Canada Transboundary Air Pollution Control Regime: A Century of Experience to Guide the Future' (2009) 11 *Vermont Journal of Environmental Law* 107.

194 Above n. 101, para. 16(k).

195 Above n. 101, paras. 17(a) and 17(c).

unlikely to achieve its objectives and be viable for the longer term without significant regional adaptation.[196]

VI. CONCLUSIONS

The *Air Pollution Convention* provides a framework for countries to reduce and monitor their emissions, whilst the Protocols contain the detailed provisions that must be implemented to achieve these goals, with reference to particular pollutants or groups of pollutants. The Convention and Protocols now cover most of the major air pollutants, including SO_2, NOx, VOCs, ammonia, POPs and heavy metals. In addition to setting specific reduction targets for these pollutants, the Protocols provide for further research and development on pollutants, exchange of scientific and technical information, and environmental monitoring programmes.

The effectiveness of the Convention and Protocols in reducing and eliminating most of the world's worst transboundary air pollutants is widely recognised. Covering most of Europe and north America, the Convention has achieved success primarily due to its strong scientific and technical basis, represented by EMEP and the work of subsidiary bodies such as the WGE. The Convention has, for the most part, evolved to reflect changing knowledge regarding the causes and effects of specific air pollutants. It has also helped to lay the foundations, and provide guidance, for the negotiation of global treaties on POPs and mercury. The Convention appears to be well-placed to continue its role in addressing new air pollution issues as they emerge, whilst maintaining its supervision of Parties' compliance with earlier obligations. Current issues such as particulate matter and black carbon are likely to be incorporated into the work of the Convention, and the close links between climate change and air pollution will be an important factor shaping its future.

Given the present lack of a comprehensive global treaty on air pollution, it is conceivable that pressure will grow for the expansion of the Convention beyond the confines of the UNECE. If so, Asia stands to benefit substantially from such an expansion, as many parts of the region continue to suffer the combined effects of industrialisation and rapidly growing economies. The various policy-oriented initiatives to tackle air pollution that are already underway in Asia are a promising start, but they cannot provide the overarching legal framework and specific obligations that are needed. Opening up the membership of the Convention, if it does

---

[196] Above n. 169, 5.

occur, could be a slow process, if the more than decade-long delay of the coming into force of both amendments to the *Water Convention* and *EIA Convention* is any indication.[197] In the meantime, the progress of the central Asian countries in ratifying and implementing the Convention will provide an insight into its broader application in the Asian context, and perhaps in time, globally.

[197] Although the relevant amendment to the membership provision of the *Water Convention* was made in 2003, (as seen in Chapter 6), it only entered into force in 2013; similarly the amendment to the *EIA Convention* was made in 2001 (as seen in Chapter 4), but it only entered into force in 2014; for both, further ratifications are, however, needed from existing Parties.

PART III

Combined effect and outlook

8. Practice and capacity building in Central Asia

I. INTRODUCTION

This chapter is focused on practice: the implementation of and compliance with the five UNECE Conventions, and the 12 associated Protocols in central Asia; it also addresses issues of capacity building which are a key part of assisting Parties to meet their obligations. While evidence of this in relation to individual agreements may be limited, the combined contribution of those that do apply will be analysed as a case study of how they are collectively relevant to central Asia specifically. The chapter will draw together the application of each of the agreements in this subregion where, together with the Caucasus (and partly Russia), the take up of these treaties and protocols outside of Europe has been the greatest. It will evaluate their combined significance in order to help answer the central research question posed in Chapter 1: what is the current and potential contribution of the UNECE environmental agreements to transboundary environmental governance in Asia? This will be developed further in Chapter 9 in relation to other parts of Asia, not just the Caucasus or Russia as discussed in Chapters 3–7, but also in the non-UNECE member states in western and eastern Asia where limited interest in the agreements has been expressed to date, but where, in discussing prospects prior to the conclusions in Chapters 3–7, there is significant potential for future application.

Where possible, implementation of the agreements will be examined with reference to domestic implementing law – or the constitutional framework for this – and review by the implementation reporting mechanisms (primarily NIRs) and compliance procedures in the UNECE Conventions. Domestic law in central Asian states follows the typical structure known as 'state ecological expertise', the former Soviet assessment and decision making process, that, while similar to EIA procedures in the UNECE treaties, is, however, distinct in several fundamental ways. Because of this, many aspects have been found to be non-compliant with the *EIA* and *Public Participation Conventions* in particular,[1] and this is therefore considered in some detail. Similarly, the constitutional legal framework of the central Asian states has also been called into question by NCPs. The direct application of the agreements – which is the basis of their monist legal frameworks – requires compliance despite the absence of transposition into domestic law, and this, it has been argued, is evidence of implementation of the agreements. This will also be discussed in some detail below. Finally, the role of MDBs/IFIs in requiring implementation of and compliance with the UNECE agreements prior to lending will also be highlighted in relation to the *EIA Convention*. Although states may not be Party to the agreements, they may therefore nonetheless be obliged to implement their obligations as a condition of lending.

To begin with and to set the scene for what is to follow, the chapter will consider the claims that central Asia is a distinct geo-political subregion based on recent historical events. It will then examine the role of the UNECE in central Asia, especially since independence from the former Soviet Union in 1991. The state ecological expertise system will next be outlined in some depth as it is relevant to the implementation and compliance of several of the agreements, and not only to central Asia but also in the Caucasus (and parts of eastern Europe). Thereafter practice and potential for implementation and compliance will be reviewed, with reference to membership of each of the agreements, domestic legal arrangements and public international law. The final and largest part of the chapter will consider the application of each of the five treaties and associated protocols in central Asia, before drawing together the findings in a concluding section.

II. CENTRAL ASIA IN CONTEXT

II.1 A Distinct Geo-political Subregion

Central Asia is made up of the states of Kazakhstan, Kyrgyzstan, Tajikistan, Turkmenistan and Uzbekistan, each which (like Pakistan and Afghanistan), is named after the people that live there. Kazakhstan has a

[1] Convention on Environmental Impact Assessment in a Transboundary Context (Espoo, 25 February 1991), 30 ILM (1991) 802, in force 27 June 1997; Convention on Access to Information, Public Participation in Decision-Making and Access to Justice in Environmental Matters (Aarhus, 25 June 1998), 38 ILM (1999) 517, in force 30 October 2001.

population of 17 million, Kyrgyzstan 6 million, Tajikistan 8 million, Turkmenistan 5 million and Uzbekistan 30 million. Due to energy exports, Kazakhstan is the wealthiest with an average annual income of just under US$10,000 per year; Tajikistan is the poorest with under US$1,000 per year. The other states have had mixed fortunes, with some – such as Turkmenistan – also benefiting from energy exports, notably natural gas, in recent years.

The subregion came into existence following the dissolution of the Soviet Union in 1991, and while elections have been held in all of the states since independence, none have been regarded as free or fair and several have reputations for corruption and humans rights abuses.[2] This is also the case with respect to the other post-Soviet states in the Caucasus,[3] where ongoing conflict has been noted previously (see Chapter 4).[4] Since independence, each of these states and the region has needed to forge an identity with other actors in a now globalised world. This has not been an easy path, as noted by Lloyd:

> … independence appeared to be *thrust upon* the hesitant regional states with little warning. The tenuous experience as Soviet republics did not seem to offer the Central Asian countries the required 'political, economic, and psychological' preparedness for independent participation in and interactions with the global society of states.[5]

As a result, Kavalski notes that not only was central Asian statehood 'awkward', but the newfound freedom of the five states also suggested a power vacuum in the region,[6] with Russia unable to assert its position thereafter and maintain the previously dominant, or absolute, position of

---

[2] See for example, Haroon Siddique, 'Tony Blair advises Kazakh President on Publicity after Killing of Protesters', *The Guardian*, 24 August 2014.

[3] See for example, M J del Valle, 'Azerbaijan Detains Prominent Human Rights Activists in Fresh Crackdown', *The Guardian*, 15 August 2014.

[4] Although this is the case primarily with regard to the relationship between Armenia and Azerbaijan, conflict between Russia and Georgia is also of ongoing concern, and, mostly recently in eastern Europe, between Russia and the Ukraine. In relation to Russia and Georgia, see James A Green and Christopher P M Waters (eds), *Conflict in the Caucasus: Implications for International Legal Order* (Palgrave Macmillan, Basingstoke, UK and New York, USA 2010). In relation to resource specific conflicts, see also Thomas Bernauer and Tobias Siegfried, 'Climate Change and International Water Conflict in Central Asia' (2012) 49(1) *Journal of Peace Research* 227.

[5] S J Lloyd, 'Landlocked Central Asia' (1997) 2(1) *Geopolitics* 97, 97.

[6] Emilian Kavalski, 'Uncovering the "New" Central Asia: The Dynamics of External Agency in a Turbulent Region', in Emilian Kavalski (ed.), *The New*

the Soviet Union as effectively a coloniser. During Soviet times therefore, the central Asian states' economies were deliberately structured as providers of agricultural raw materials such as cotton and wheat; they also produced substantial amounts of oil, gas and other minerals for the Soviet Union, which following independence enabled exploitation for others under a capitalist market.

Of particular note and relevance for this book, however, was the vacuum subsequently filled not just by other states (such as China, the USA, Turkey, Iran, India and Japan), but the significant role played by IGOs. Given security issues, these have of course included NATO and the OSCE. The EU and UN institutions, including UNESCAP and the UNECE, have also importantly been in a position of increased influence since independence, which has been beneficial in enabling capacity building in the subregion in relation to gaining a greater understanding and acceptance of the environmental agreements.

II.2 Environmental Issues and Governance

Once Russian control was established in central Asia in the mid-19th century, agricultural policies encouraged the expansion of irrigated areas and cotton production. In 1924 Stalin nationalised Soviet water resources, and from 1925 to 1936 the former Tsarist administrative units of central Asia were divided into the five republics. The desire for control of watercourses, which crossed the boundaries of the five republics, led to water management in central Asia being directed by central planning organisations and ministries in Moscow.[7] The Soviet allocation regime favoured cotton production in the downstream states of Uzbekistan and Turkmenistan, and benefits were shared with the former Soviet Union at the expense of the two upstream states, Tajikistan and Kyrgyzstan. The upstream countries received payments for lost hydropower generation

---

Central Asia: The Regional Impact of International Actors (World Scientific, Singapore 2010) 6.

[7] Michelle Lim, 'Effective Governance across Central Asian Boundaries: What Lessons does the Central Asian Transboundary Watercourse Management Experience Provide for Mountain Biodiversity Conservation across the Kyrgyz-Tajik Boundary?', in Robin Warner and Simon Marsden (eds), *Transboundary Environmental Governance: Inland, Coastal and Marine Perspectives* (Ashgate Publishing, Farnham 2012) 111; and Daene C McKinney, 'Cooperative Management of Transboundary Water Resources in Central Asia', in Daniel Burghart and Theresa Sabonis-Helf (eds), *In the Tracks of Tamerlane: Central Asia's Path to the 21st Century* (National Defense University, Washington DC 2004) 187.

and provided upstream storage; large dams and reservoirs were constructed in the mountainous areas of Tajikistan and Kyrgyzstan, although the development of irrigated lands was limited. Region-wide basin water organisations (bvos) were established in 1986 in the Amu Darya and Syr Darya basins to manage water resources according to Soviet approved plans, to ensure compliance with inter-republican water allocations. Use of water from these basins has been a major contributing factor to the shrinking of the Aral Sea since the late 1950s.[8]

After the breakup of the Soviet Union the central Asian republics knew that stabilising transboundary water relations on independence was vital, given their heavy dependence on irrigated agriculture. Although the downstream riparians were still benefiting from generous water allocations, they now became dependent on their upstream neighbours for these, increasing the possibility of conflict. To avoid this, on 12 September 1991, the water ministers of each republic declared that joint water resources management would be established on the basis of equity and mutual benefit and shortly afterwards, the *Agreement on Cooperation in the Field of Joint Management and Conservation of Interstate Water Resources* was concluded to replace the former centralised system.[9]

Article 7 established the Interstate Commission for Water Coordination (ICwC), which enabled control, rational use and protection of interstate water resources. It was responsible for the management, allocation and development of regional management policies to ensure the rational utilisation of water resources; it also governed the activities of the two regional bvos. From 1992, the ICwC and the two regional bvos were responsible for development and allocation planning, quality control, conservation and environmental protection. The central Asian states agreed to maintain the basic principles of water allocation that prevailed in Soviet times, with the Agreement acknowledging the equal rights of member states to use the interstate resources and their responsibility to

---

8 See for example: Hu Wen Jun, 'Regional Cooperation Issues in Water Utilization of Aral Sea Basin' (2009) 32(6) *Arid Land Geography* 821; Bo Libert, Erkin Orolbaev and Yuri Steklov, 'Water and Energy Crisis in Central Asia' (2008) 6(3) *China and Eurasia Forum Quarterly* 9.

9 Agreement on Cooperation in the Field of Joint Management and Conservation of Interstate Water Resources (Almaty, 18 February 1992), accessed 20 November 2014 at http://www.caee.utexas.edu/prof/mckinney/papers/aral/agreements/ICWC-Feb18-1992.pdf. See Jason Bart, 'Weaponizing Water: Water and Energy as Sources of Conflict among the Central Asian Soviet Successor States' (2013) 22(1) *Michigan State International Law Review* 409; and Christine Bichsel, 'Liquid Challenges: Contested Water in Central Asia', (2011) 12(1) *Sustainable Development Law and Policy* 24.

protect them. It, however, also affirmed the continuation of existing Soviet structures and principles of interstate water allocation. The issues of concern are addressed to a large extent by the *Water Convention*,[10] which is particularly relevant in the subregion. Lim explains the problems with which this has to contend:

> The inheritance of Soviet water allocation regimes is the main reason for transboundary water disputes in present-day central Asia. The inherited Soviet water management rules prioritize irrigated agriculture and do not take into account the current power generation needs of the upstream states of the Kyrgyz republic and Tajikistan. These upstream states often claim that water allocation based on Soviet era rules limits the development of irrigation on their lands. Downstream countries, on the other hand, complain that poor water quality in the middle and lower reaches of the basins is reducing agricultural production and damaging public health.[11]

Further to the *Agreement on Cooperation in the Field of Joint Management and Conservation of Interstate Water Resources*, and before considering the role of the UNECE in central Asia and its treaty making efforts, it is also of note that the central Asian states have concluded another subregional environmental agreement, the *Framework Convention on Environmental Protection for Sustainable Development in Central Asia.*[12] Adopted in 2006, the purpose of this in Article 3 is 'to ensure the effective protection of the environment for sustainable development in Central Asia, including the improvement of ecological environment, rational use of natural resources, as well as reduce and prevent transboundary environmental damage through the harmonization and coordination of environmental policies and actions of the Contracting Parties and by establishing reciprocal rights and responsibilities'.

Article 4 sets out general principles of international environmental law; Article 5 general obligations; Article 6 concerns environmental protection and sustainable development; Article 7 monitoring and evaluation; Articles 8–13 protection and management of air, water, land, waste, mountain ecosystems and biodiversity; Article 14 is concerned with

---

[10] Convention on the Protection and Use of Transboundary Watercourses and Lakes (Helsinki, 17 March 1992), 31 ILM (1992) 1312, in force 6 October 1996.

[11] Above n. 7, 119.

[12] Framework Convention on Environmental Protection for Sustainable Development in Central Asia (Ashgabat, 22 November 2006) TRE-143806, not in force. accessed 20 November 2014 at http://www.ecolex.org/server2.php/libcat/docs/TRE/Full/En/TRE-143806.pdf.

cooperation in emergencies; Article 15 national authorities; Article 16 scientific and technical cooperation; Article 17 exchange and access to information; Article 18 public participation; and Article 19 implementation and compliance. Other general provisions related to treaty management and dispute settlement follow. Although this treaty is a comprehensive instrument potentially applicable to all of the central Asian states, it has yet to come into force with no indication of when this may occur.

II.3 The UNECE and Sustainable Development

After the breakup of the Soviet Union, the transition from centrally planned to market economies, and the integration of countries in transition into the global economy was a major concern of the UNECE. It began actively engaging in capacity building to help countries implement recommendations, standards and, of particular relevance to this book, international agreements. These activities were extended to central Europe and the countries of EECCA where states chose to become members. Since adapting to the changing geopolitical landscape, the UNECE has undergone major reforms (in 1997 and 2005) to better tailor its activities to the needs of its member states.[13]

It has in recent times actively worked with organisations in central Asia to develop the environmental agreements further. In 2013 for example, it signed a MoU with the Eurasian Economic Commission, a supranational governing body of the Customs Union of Belarus, Kazakhstan and Russia, and a key institution of the Eurasian Economic Community (EEC). The Commission aims at strengthening cooperation between the Parties in various areas. In the area of transport, a major contributor to cross border environmental concerns, the two organisations plan to collaborate under the framework of what are known as 'Euro-Asian Transport Linkages', promoting border crossing facilitation and implementation monitoring. In respect of these efforts, the Chair of the Commission commented:

> Cooperation with UNECE is very important for EEC since UNECE produces and collects best national and international practices in a number of areas. Its knowledge and experience are highly estimated, as we intend to base our

[13] See Yves Berthelot and Paul Rayment, *Looking Back and Peering Forward – A Short History of the United Nations Economic Commission for Europe, 1947–2007* (United Nations Economic Commission for Europe, Geneva 2007).

> legislation on the best international practices. This is the reason why we need this dialogue with UNECE.[14]

A specific example of the UNECE's engagement with central Asia in connection with the environment is cooperation with the Interstate Commission on Sustainable Development (ICSD) to strengthen implementation of the UNCSD Rio+20 outcomes. The ICSD is in charge of coordinating regional cooperation on the environment and sustainable development in central Asia, coordinating implementation of the five states commitments under environmental conventions with transboundary dimensions. An expert meeting took place in 2013 under the framework of the UNECE Programme 'Regional Dialogue and Cooperation on Water Resources Management in Central Asia'.[15] This programme – which is considered in more depth below in relation to the *Water Convention* – was coordinated by both the UNECE and the ICSD. It agreed on the mandate of a task force to develop an in-depth study and recommendations on how the ICSD could contribute efficiently to the implementation of the outcomes of the Rio+20 Conference at the regional level.

The meeting included an in-depth discussion of how to increase the ICSD role in promoting green development. It was clear that the new challenges and opportunities brought about by Rio+20 required closer cooperation between the ICSD and other organisations and institutions under the umbrella of the ICSD parent body, the International Fund for Saving the Aral Sea (IFAS).[16] The IFAS was established to manage the effects on this inland sea caused by the long history of exploitation by cotton production in the area in particular. Participants reviewed implementation of the Regional Environmental Action Plan and discussed updates. They also considered the participation of ICSD in the implementation of the Third Aral Sea Basin Programme,[17] and how the ICSD could improve access to international and donor assistance for

---

[14] See Press release, 26 June 2013, accessed 20 November 2014 at http://www.unece.org/index.php?id=33072.

[15] See http://www.unece.org/env/water/cadialogue/cadwelcome.html, accessed 20 November 2014.

[16] For an overview, see presentation by Saghit Ibatullin, 'International Fund for Saving the Aral Sea (IFAS) as a basis for regional cooperation in Central Asia' March 2010, accessed 20 November 2014 at http://www.unece.org/fileadmin/DAM/env/cep/ExtBureau16-17Mar2010/IFAS_EC_ppp_e.pdf.

[17] See UNECE, 'Central Asian States finalize the Third Aral Sea Basin Program', press release 17 December 2010, accessed 20 November 2014 at http://www.unece.org/press/pr2010/10env_p43e.html.

green development. Phase II of the UNECE Programme, entitled 'Regional Dialogue and Cooperation on Water Resources Management in Central Asia',[18] aims to improve the capacity of IFAS, including its organisations and institutions and continue the strengthening of their legal basis. This project is a component of the 'Transboundary Water Management in Central Asia' programme which ran from 2009–2014 and was carried out on behalf of the German Federal Foreign Office.[19]

II.4 The Legacy of State Ecological Expertise Systems

As a result of Soviet occupation, along with Russia and the other countries in eastern Europe and the Caucasus, the central Asia states inherited a different EIA system to that generally practised by western nations. The *EIA Convention* IC has therefore noted a 'general systemic inconsistency between the Convention and environmental assessment within the framework of state ecological expertise systems'.[20] It is necessary to understand this inconsistency to evaluate implementation of the obligations of the *EIA Convention*, and subsequent compliance with them, in the five states that make up central Asia;[21] it is also relevant with respect to states in the Caucasus and Russia itself. It is furthermore necessary to understand this framework of state ecological expertise for purposes of the *Public Participation Convention*, the pillar II provisions of which in particular have also been difficult to implement and comply with by the central Asian states.[22]

---

[18] See http://www.unece.org/env/water/cadialogue/2ndphase.html, accessed 20 November 2014.

[19] See https://www.giz.de/en/worldwide/15176.html, accessed 20 November 2014.

[20] United Nations Economic and Social Council, Meeting of the Parties to the Convention on Environmental Impact Assessment in a Transboundary Context, Sixth session, Geneva, 2–5 June 2014. Item 11(a) of the provisional agenda, Adoption of decisions: decisions to be taken by the Meeting of the Parties to the Convention. General Guidance on Enhancing Consistency between the Convention and Environmental Impact Assessment within State Ecological Expertise in Countries of Eastern Europe, the Caucasus and Central Asia, ECE/MP.EIA/2014/2, 20 March 2014, 3.

[21] See Jerzy Jendrośka, 'Challenges of the Espoo Convention application in Eastern Europe, the Caucasus and Central Asia', Seminar on legislation and procedures for implementation of the Espoo Convention in Eastern Europe, the Caucasus and Central Asia, Geneva, 17 May 2010.

[22] See section on *Public Participation Convention* below, and note in particular Tatiana R Zaharchenko and Gretta Goldenman, 'Accountability in

State ecological expertise, which is also known as State Environmental Review (SER), is the environmental evaluation of a decision-making process by special expert committees linked with government bodies. An analysis of potential environmental impacts is first carried out by either the competent authority or external experts nominated for this purpose. Only after the SER conclusions are reached – if supportive – can the proposal be carried out. The SER process is usually formalised by a national SER law or a general environment protection law.

The SER process is preceded by a procedure which is also designed to analyse the assessment of environmental impacts and known as 'OVOS'. Screening for both OVOS and the SER processes is usually triggered with reference to a list of activities. Unlike the SER process however, OVOS is usually regulated by lower level regulation such as construction standards or other instruction, which often cannot be enforced. Significantly also the proponent is responsible for preparing the OVOS Statement which – like an EIA report in western-type EIA processes – is the basis for public consultation. In contrast to western EIA however, regardless of whether the proponent is a public or private entity, the proponent also carries out the public consultation. While it is this aspect of the state ecological expertise system that is primarily in conflict with the requirements of the *EIA* and *Public Participation Conventions* and which have required states to introduce changes to existing law or a brand new legal framework, there are indeed quite a few other general issues, as set out below.

The list approach to screening for OVOS is first too narrow, not including activities such as deforestation or intensive animal rearing; there are also no criteria or thresholds for other activities. Second, the scoping process is usually not distinguished as a specific procedure and documentation requirements are limited. Third, and most importantly of all, public participation is only mandatory at the OVOS stage if at all, and the process is not detailed in any such law. The public are usually also only given access to very limited parts of documentation, and the proponent – whether public or private – carries out the consultation. Fourth, although a decision is made following the SER process, it is not clear whether this is the final decision, or whether subsequent permitted decisions are the final decision. There is also no requirement for due

---

Governance: The Challenge of Implementing the Aarhus Convention in Eastern Europe and Central Asia', (2004) 4 *International Environmental Agreements: Politics, Law and Economics* 229.

account to be taken of the OVOS documentation or outcomes; furthermore, the reasons and considerations for any decision are not available to the public, the decision is not publicly announced, and authorities do not keep adequate records.

State ecological expertise systems are finally typically triggered too late in the process for timely transboundary consultations between origin and affected states. Given that the documentation may be finalised and the consultations may already have been concluded under the OVOS part of the procedure, it would be too late to begin transboundary consultations unless the public participation was to begin again. Restrictions on access to information and the fact that private developers conduct the procedure are also not compliant with expectations.

III. PRACTICE AND CAPACITY BUILDING

III.1 Overview

General issues of implementation and compliance were considered in some detail in Part V of Chapter 1. Here it is helpful to emphasise the factual position with respect to current membership of the environmental agreements, which indicate exactly which Asian states are required to implement and comply with any obligations within them; the different domestic arrangements that pertain to implementation in the monist states of central Asia as raised above (and which is of relevance to other states in the UNECE region), the position under international law concerning states that are signatories to MEAs generally but not Parties, and associated matters of treaty law; and to note the approach of the UNECE as a result of many of these circumstances, most particularly the focus on encouraging ratification and building capacity for implementation in the subregion.

Geographically speaking, there are 11 Asian states who are members of the UNECE. These are located in western Asia, including the Caucasus (Turkey, Israel, Armenia, Azerbaijan and Georgia); central Asia (Kazakhstan, Kyrgyzstan, Tajikistan, Turkmenistan and Uzbekistan); and northern Asia (Russia). Some of these states may also be classified as European as their territory intersects Asia and Europe (Turkey, Russia and Georgia in particular). In Table 8.1, membership of the UNECE agreements is indicated by each of these states.

From the table, it can therefore be seen that, leaving aside legal questions of domestic application of international law (discussed below), implementation of treaty and protocol obligations into domestic law is

Table 8.1 Asian membership of UNECE treaties (1–5) and protocols (6–10) (at 23 August 2014)

UNECE member ↓ / Agreement & no. of Parties →	1. Public partic (7)	2. EIA (4)	3. Industrial accidents (4)	4. Water (5)	5. Air Poll. (7)	6. PRTR (1)	7. SEA (1)	8. Civil Liab. (0)	9. Water & health (2)	10. Air (all*) (5)
Kazakhstan	√	√	√	√	√					
Kyrgyzstan	√	√			√					
Tajikistan	√					X				
Turkmenistan	√			√						
Uzbekistan				√						
Armenia	√	√	√		√	X	√	X	X	√ (EMEP) X (AEO, POPs, Heavy metals)
Azerbaijan	√	√	√	√	√				√	
Georgia	√				√	X	X	X	X	√ (EMEP)

Russia	X	√	√	√		√	√ (Sulph, N0x, EMEP) X (2nd Sulph)
Turkey				√			
Israel					√		

Notes:
Asian states (**central Asian states in bold**)
Conventions (1–5) and protocols (6–10)
√ = ratified; X = only signed
* There are eight protocols to the Air Pollution Convention, but only three of these have been ratified by Asian states (1st Sulphur, NOx, EMEP)

Source: UN Treaty Collection https://treaties.un.org/Home.aspx?lang=en

only relevant to Kazakhstan in relation to all five treaties. In regard to the other central Asian states, Kyrgyzstan must implement the requirements of three treaties (*Public Participation, EIA* and *Air Pollution*[23]); Turkmenistan two (*Public Participation* and *Water*); and Tajikistan (*Public Participation*) and Uzbekistan (*Water*), one each. Only one of the states, Tajikistan has formally accepted any of the protocols (*PRTR*[24]). Another way of expressing this factual information is that the *Public Participation Convention* has the most central Asian Parties (four, all except Uzbekistan); with, in descending order of number of ratifications, the *Water Convention* (three, Kazakhstan, Turkmenistan and Uzbekistan); the *EIA Convention* (two, Kazakhstan and Kyrgyzstan); the *Air Pollution Convention* (two, Kazakhstan and Kyrgyzstan); and the *Industrial Accidents Convention* (one, Kazakhstan).

The UNECE has outlined the status, application and relevance of each of the agreements in central Asia in a significant recent publication.[25] This introduces the conventions and protocols, and explains their place in international law (including customary international law, considered in relation to the *EIA* and *Water Conventions* below); discussing how they address key issues of water management; reporting, implementation and compliance; and assistance and capacity building.[26] The document concludes: 'The UNECE environmental instruments are an authoritative and coherent legal framework – in other words, common "rules of the game" – which could be applied as an appropriate overarching legal framework for water management and transboundary water cooperation in Central Asia.'[27] The status, application and relevance of the (amendments to) the *Water Convention* and *EIA Convention* in relation to the coming into force of these treaties for non-UNECE states, was considered in Chapters 6 and 4.

---

[23] Convention on Long-Range Transboundary Air Pollution (Geneva, 13 November 1979) 1302 UNTS 217, in force 16 March 1983.

[24] Protocol on Pollutant Release and Transfer Registers to the Convention on Access to Information, Public Participation in Decision-Making and Access to Justice in Environmental Matters (Kiev, 21 May 2003), unreported, in force 8 October 2009.

[25] United Nations Economic Commission for Europe, *Strengthening Water Management and Transboundary Water Cooperation in Central Asia: The Role of UNECE Environmental Conventions* (United Nations 2011), ECE/MP.WAT/35.

[26] Ibid, chapters 3, 4 and 5.

[27] Ibid, 133.

III.2 Domestic and International Legal Frameworks

In relation to transboundary matters specifically, domestic law in the central Asian states has often not incorporated provisions for this, relying on the doctrine of the 'direct application' of public international law that is part of the constitutional status of the monist central Asian states. Direct application concerns the incorporation of treaties into states and IGOs (like the EU), which do not require implementing legislation. These are termed 'monist' as distinct from 'dualist' jurisdictions, the latter which require transposition into national law before the international obligation is given effect to.[28]

While direct application can be beneficial in some circumstances where domestic law fails to implement international treaties, there are disadvantages in the central Asian context as elsewhere. These include the vagueness of many treaty provisions which means that national transposition will still be needed, and some treaty bodies, such as the *EIA Convention* IC, has recommended national transposition even where a state is monist. The IC hence has commented: 'The provision in the Constitution to directly apply international agreements is considered by the Committee as being insufficient for proper implementation of the Convention without more detailed provisions in the legislation.'[29]

In relation to international conventions and protocols, public international law is focused upon what is known as *pacta sunt servanda*, which is related to the above, and conflicts with the municipal law of monist states which do not perform treaty obligations. This has been termed the 'fundamental rule of treaty law',[30] whereby 'Every treaty in force is binding upon the parties to it and must be performed by them in

---

[28] See Simon Marsden, 'Invoking Direct Application and Effect of International Treaties by the European Court of Justice: Implications for International Environmental Law in the European Union' (2011) 60(3) *International and Comparative Law Quarterly* 737, 738–9.

[29] See Economic Commission for Europe, Meeting of the Parties to the Convention on Environmental Impact Assessment in a Transboundary Context, Implementation Committee, Twentieth Session, Geneva, 11–13 January 2011, Opinions of the Implementation Committee, Note by the Implementation Committee, ECE/MP.EIA/IC/2011/INF.1, paras 7 and 8 (decision IV/2, annex II, para. 28).

[30] Wendy Lacey, 'The Law of Treaties', in S Blay, R Piotrowicz and M Tsamenyi, *Public International Law: An Australian Perspective* (2nd edn, Oxford University Press, Melbourne 2005) 99.

good faith'.[31] A related rule provides that 'A party may not invoke the provisions of its internal law as justification for its failure to perform a treaty'.[32] This related rule has been an issue where federal states have introduced reservations to treaties arguing their constitutions give competence to regional governments (such as a province or internal state),[33] or argued that decisions of the judicial branch of government prevent compliance.[34] International law is therefore not concerned with the status of the treaty within the legal system of the contracting Party, only that it is binding upon its Parties.[35] For non-Parties who are, however, signatories, there is also the obligation not to take any measures thereafter that would 'defeat the object and purpose' of the Convention.[36] This is important because even though a number of central Asian states (and other UNECE states) may be only signatories to certain agreements, this does not mean that there are no obligations to perform in relation to them.

III.3 Encouraging Membership and Capacity Building

Notwithstanding the above, because the UNECE agreements have yet to be comprehensively or substantially ratified by the majority of states in the subregion, efforts by and for non-Parties (particularly by the UNECE itself), have in many cases been focused upon encouraging ratification in the states which have yet to do so. As such, in each of the parts below dealing with the agreements, there is a similar focus on capacity building activities to compensate for the fact that implementation and/or compliance may not be relevant (or be of less relevance), if states are not Parties

---

[31] Article 26, Convention on the Law of Treaties (Vienna, 23 May 1969) 1155 UNTS 331, in force 27 January 1980 (VCLT). The VCLT is widely accepted to contain obligations which are also customary international law, which means for states which are not Parties to it these are still binding upon them unless they have 'persistently objected' to them; see Ted L Stein, 'The Approach of the Different Drummer: The Principle of the Persistent Objector in International Law' (1985) 26 *Harvard International Law Journal* 457.

[32] Article 27 VCLT.

[33] See Canada's reservation to the *EIA Convention*; discussed in Marsden above n. 28, 741.

[34] See Belgium's argument before the ACCC which was roundly denied; discussed in Marsden below n. 35, 202.

[35] Simon Marsden, 'Direct Public Access to EU Courts: Upholding Public International Law via the Aarhus Convention Compliance Committee' (2012) 81(2) *Nordic Journal of International Law* 175, 202–3.

[36] Article 18 VCLT.

or signatories. Support for UNECE members to join the treaties and protocols was discussed in each of the Chapters 3–7 above. It, together with capacity building in states which are already Parties to the agreements, is a key aspect of the work of the UNECE in central Asia and elsewhere.

The other issue to note in relation to implementation is that some of the agreements to which the central Asian states are bound, either currently lack requirements for NIRs (*Water Convention* and *Air Pollution Convention*), for them to be publicly available (*Industrial Accidents Convention*[37]), or for a NCP (*Industrial Accidents Convention*). In these circumstances, information and awareness about implementation and compliance may be more difficult to assess. In the sections that follow therefore, where relevant or possible implementation and compliance issues are first addressed in relation to the five conventions, and the *PRTR Protocol* – the only one with any members – for Tajikistan, a signatory. Second, the efforts of the UNECE and related bodies to encourage further ratifications and understanding of the agreements are discussed at length. This is important to be in a position to comment on the potential combined significance of the agreements where membership may be lacking. Third, in the case of some agreements (in particular the *EIA Convention*), the absence of a signature or ratification to an agreement may not necessarily be fatal to analysis of implementation issues where this is required by a MDB/IFI, and this is discussed where relevant.

IV. PUBLIC PARTICIPATION CONVENTION AND PRTR PROTOCOL

IV.1 Convention

a. Implementation

In relation to the *Public Participation Convention*, other than Uzbekistan which has neither signed nor ratified the convention, the other four central Asian states are all Parties to this treaty. There have been four rounds of NIRs to date, on a three-yearly cycle (2005, 2008, 2011 and 2014). Of the four central Asian Parties in the most recent round, Kazakhstan and Tajikistan have produced reports in English, Kyrgyzstan

---

[37] Convention on the Transboundary Effects of Industrial Accidents (Helsinki, 17 March 1992) 2105 UNTS 457, in force 19 April 2000.

in Russian, with no report from Turkmenistan. Given limited access, the two NIRs in English are discussed below at some length (notably Kazakhstan's), which highlight some of the issues with the state ecological expertise system operating in central Asia in particular, and which is of relevance to the other states. As Kazakhstan is, however, also the only central Asian state to have ratified all of the UNECE treaties, its NIR is analysed in particular detail as its collective experience with the *Public Participation* and the other four treaties is the only factual basis on which to respond to the research question posed in Chapter 1, in the sense of drawing lessons of relevance to the other central Asian states and potentially Asia more broadly, and beyond.[38]

In relation to Kazakhstan's 2014 NIR therefore, this is based on analysis of previous reports and various documents and events. The latter include environmental and civil procedure laws; jurisprudence of the Supreme Court; the Report of Kazakhstan on implementation of Decision IV/9c on its compliance (see section below); and websites of state agencies, the National Aarhus Centre, the ecological association 'Green Salvation' and other NGOs. The draft NIR was sent to these NGOs on 2 August 2013, posted on the government and Aarhus Centre websites as part of a consultation process with the public; and on 9 October 2013, the Report was discussed at the round table entitled 'Legal and regulatory aspects of the implementation of the AC in Kazakhstan'.[39]

The process furthermore included an analysis of laws that contain provisions on the rights of natural persons, public associations and other legal persons in the fields of environmental protection, protection and efficient use of natural resources, public health and radiation safety, and architectural, town planning and construction activities. Examples include

---

[38] This is in part also possible given the detailed nature of its NIR in relation to Tajikistan's. Although now a decade old, see the findings of Zaharchenko and Goldenman, above n. 22, in relation to Kazakhstan, which highlight the culture of secrecy and professionalism which has hindered effective implementation of this treaty. See for example at 235 in relation to the public right to know, 239 concerning the maintenance of public order, and 244 concerning the meaning of the Russian word 'consolidation' in relation to consultation efforts. See also generally, Bende Toth, 'Public Participation and Democracy in Practice – Aarhus Convention Principles as Democratic Institution Building in the Developing World' (2010) 30(2) *Journal of Land Resources and Environmental Law* 295; this discusses the deliberations of the CC in relation to Kazakhstan at 304–5 and 314–15, and Turkmenistan at 314.

[39] Republic of Kazakhstan, Ministry of Environment Protection, *Format for the Aarhus Convention implementation report in accordance with Decision IV/4* (ECE/MP.PP/2011/2/Add.1), undated.

the *Environmental* and *Water Codes*, and *Acts on Public and Radiation Safety*, and *Architectural, Town Planning and Construction Activities*.[40] The NIR also notes that a special working group was created within the Supreme Court to prepare a summary of cases heard in the Supreme Court and local courts, and that a practical manual was prepared to assist implementation of the third pillar.[41]

In relation to the first pillar (access to information), obstacles encountered concerning the implementation of Article 4 of the Convention are that Article 161(4(5)) of the *Environmental Code* (EC) contains restrictions on access to EIA and SER materials further to the existing system of state ecological expertise (as noted in Part II.4 above). The NIR states that a proposal for the removal of this restriction is introduced in the draft *Law on the Aarhus Convention*.[42] Other obstacles reported on in relation to Article 4 are the '[d]issociation of environmental information on the various state agencies, the lack of exchange of this information … [and the absence of] basic information publicly available in electronic form …'.[43] Revision of the *draft Law on the Aarhus Convention* is again noted as needed to implement Article 5 of the Convention.[44]

In relation to the second pillar (public participation), and implementation of Article 6 (specific activities), it is reported that there are various procedures which are currently not compliant with the Convention. For example public hearings to discuss the EIA documentation are organised by the developer, who 'agrees the time and place of the public hearing with local government authorities and publishes a notice in the media about the hearing, specifying the place and time'.[45] In relation to public participation in decision making at the stage of approving EIA projects, Kazakhstan reports that it is not always possible to name the earliest stage in environmental decision-making procedures for some legislation;[46] and furthermore, there is no clear regulation about the information to be presented to the public for discussion.[47] The *draft Law on the Aarhus Convention* is again intended to deal with these issues.

It is therefore acknowledged that the current rules on the conduct of SER do not contain procedural rules on public participation, although the

---

40 Ibid, 2–3.
41 Ibid, 5.
42 Ibid, 14.
43 Ibid, 14.
44 Ibid, 19.
45 Ibid, 22–3.
46 Ibid, 23.
47 Ibid, 24.

rules concerning the conduct of public hearings were updated by the Ministry of Environmental Protection on 26 March 2013.[48] In relation to the implementation of Article 7 (public participation in plans and programmes) it is furthermore acknowledged that despite recent reforms:

> Rules of conduct of public hearings [do] not fully cover the full variety and criteria for effectiveness (timeliness, fullness and adequacy) of public participation in making environmentally-significant decisions while developing state, sectoral and regional development programmes for sectors of the economy and schemes for locating the forces of production … [and] As yet there has been no experience of conducting strategic environmental assessments of plans, policies and programmes.[49]

The experience with the implementation of Article 8 (public participation in law-making) is also not without implementation challenges. Kazakhstan notes therefore, that while natural and legal persons can participate in the 'discussion and preparation of suggestions about draft legislation', there are numerous problems in practice, including that the:

> Mechanism for implementing public participation in law-making is not set. It is not mandatory to include public suggestions in comparative tables of amendments to draft laws. There are practically no mechanisms to provide feedback on public suggestions … As a result, the public often does not have a real opportunity to participate in the lawmaking process except for some isolated cases.[50]

Finally, in relation to the third pillar, and implementation of Article 9 (access to justice), Kazakhstan refers to the Constitution and numerous statutes of relevance.[51] Recent developments reported on include a new Law 'On state-guaranteed legal aid' which was passed in 2013; the approval of a comprehensive plan of action to increase the level of legal culture of citizens for 2012–2014; and the *draft law on the Aarhus*

---

[48] Ibid, 27, and Order #50, where the definition of 'public hearing' is given in accordance with Convention norms (p.3 (3) of the Rules).

[49] Ibid, 30.

[50] Ibid, 31.

[51] Ibid, 33–4. These include the Civil Procedure Code (CPC), EC, Forest Code, Water Code, Act on Specially Protected Natural Territories, Act on the Protection, Replenishment and Use of Animals, Act on Architecture, Town Planning and Construction, Sanitation and Disease Prevention Act, Act on Natural and Anthropogenic Emergencies, Public Associations Act as well as in Supreme Court Plenary Decision on the application by judges of environmental protection legislation.

Convention, which includes additions to the definition of clear and specific remedial procedures for determining the jurisdiction of civil cases on claims of environmental NGOs in both substantive and procedural law.[52] Reference is made to the manual for judges on the application of the Convention in Kazakhstan, which was prepared by OSCE/Supreme Court and which provides a complex analysis of national laws. The round table entitled 'Compliance with AC and national legislation in the solving of disputes relating to the protection of the environment' (held on 10 April 2013) is also noted in reporting on implementation challenges, which include that:

> The Public Associations Act giving NGOs the right to initiate court proceedings to protect the rights and legitimate interests of their own members, needs to be brought into line with the AC and EC, under which NGOs have the right to apply to court with environment-related claims to protect the interests of an unspecified group of people, and not just their own members … In order to meet their obligations in an adequate and tangible fashion and to prevent adverse impacts on the environment and human health, public environmental associations must have the necessary scope of rights, including the right of access to justice not just through actions to defend the rights and interests of specific citizens when specific damage has been caused … The legal standing of public associations in the situations described is [also] limited by several criteria.[53]

In relation to the NIR of Tajikistan, which unlike Kazakhstan is only Party to the *Public Participation Convention*, in summary the report expresses similar obstacles to implementation as Kazakhstan.[54] Not being as detailed as Kazakhstan's report, perhaps befitting the fact that the former is the wealthiest and Tajikistan the poorest central Asian state,[55] reference is again made to similar matters as forming the basis of the report. These include previous NIRs, legislation,[56] other documents, and

---

52 Ibid, 36.

53 Ibid, 37–8.

54 Committee on the Environmental Protection under the Government of the Republic of Tajikistan, *National Report on Implementation of the Aarhus Convention in the Republic of Tajikistan for 2011–2013*, 1 November 2013.

55 This is indicated in the response to questions 4, 12 and 16 of the NIR, ibid, 9, 16–17, and 20 for example.

56 Ibid, 7–8. These are stated as laws and codes on Environmental Protection, Atmospheric Air Protection, Ecological Expertise, Biological Safety, Protection of Soils, Wildlife, Specially Protected Natural Areas, Environmental Monitoring, Environmental Education of the Population, Environmental Information, Production and Consumption Waste, Radiation Safety, Protection and

materials of seminars and trainings and forums. It is confirmed also that the Report is made with the support and active participation of ecological NGOs and society more broadly. The purpose of the NIR is expressed by Tajikistan to be as follows, interestingly making reference to the OSCE as much as the UNECE; this is perhaps in recognition of the importance of resource security, cooperation and environmental protection to regional stability:

> … to introduce the OSCE, the Secretariat of Convention and through them the society of our country a[n]d other countries to the basic ecological challenges in Tajikistan, in addition to report about how successful the Convention is being realized in Tajikistan and how the implementation of the Convention promotes to protect the rights of citizens and the present and the next generation for having a worthy life in the conditions of the environment, meeting his interests of his health and welfare.[57]

The NIR confirms the legal system of Tajikistan to be very similar to Kazakhstan's, with MEAs effective via the doctrine of direct application.[58] The major ecological challenges are specified as climate change, deforestation, and waste and water management. The reference to waste is notable given that Tajikistan is the only central Asian state to be a member of the *PRTR Protocol* (as a signatory). In summary, the major implementation challenges are identified as follows: a lack of technical expertise and knowledge on environmental protection including the judiciary; a lack of cooperation with the media; a weakness of specialised institutions generally; poor awareness of citizens and NGOs about the need to protect their environmental rights; and a lack of practice and precedent of citizens' appeals, and concerning the conduct of public hearings.[59]

Use of Flora, Hydro Meteorological Activity, Water, Land, Forest[s], State Sanitary Supervision, Informatization, State Secrets, Appeals of Citizens, State Statistics, Press and Other Mass Media, and Public Associations.

[57] Ibid, 2.

[58] The NIR reports in response to question 2, (ibid, 7) that: 'According to Article 10 of the Constitution of the Republic of Tajikistan, international legal acts recognized by Tajikistan are a constituent part of the legal system and are [accorded] a priority over national legislation.'

[59] Ibid, 7 (in response to question 2 of the NIR).

b. Compliance

In relation to submissions from the public to the CC, there have been a number in respect of Kazakhstan.[60] In 2004, in the very first cases to be considered by the CC, the first against Kazakhstan concerned access to information and justice in relation to a proposal to import and dispose of foreign radioactive waste (ACCC/C/2004/1); the second concerned the participation of local residents in the permitting procedure for the construction of high-voltage overhead powerlines (ACCC/C/2004/2); and the third concerned a failure to enforce domestic environmental law concerning the operation of an industrial facility to store cement and coal and produce cement (ACCC/C/2004/6).[61]

In the first case Kazakhstan was found to be non-compliant with Article 4(1) and (2) and Article 9(1); in the second, it was found to be non-compliant with a number of provisions in Article 6; and in the third it was found non-compliant with Article 9(3) and (4).[62] In following up each of these cases during the 2005–2008 intersessional period, the CC found that Kazakhstan had subsequently taken measures to bring about compliance with all of the findings with the exception of the provision in Article 9(4).[63] This remained outstanding during the 2008–2011 intersessional period, and the MOP subsequently issued a caution to Kazakhstan based on its endorsement of the CC findings.[64]

More recently, the CC has been called upon to consider a case in relation to public participation in decision making for the construction of the Western Europe-Western China transit corridor (ACCC/C/2011/59). It again found non-compliance by Kazakhstan, with Article 6(2), (6), (7) and (9). The CC recommended various actions, including a plan for implementation, which was due to be submitted by 30 November 2013.[65] Since 2011, a statement was received by the CC indicating that despite the caution in relation to ACCC/C/2004/6, Kazakhstan had still failed to bring itself into compliance with the relevant Decision IV/9c.

---

[60] See 2004/1, 2, 6, 10; 2007/20; 2011/59; and 2013/88 accessed 20 November 2014 at http://www.unece.org/env/pp/pubcom.html.

[61] These are summarised with the other cases against Kazakhstan in: Meeting of the Parties Fifth session, Maastricht, the Netherlands, 30 June and 1 July 2014. Item 5(b) of the provisional agenda, Procedures and mechanisms facilitating the implementation of the Convention: compliance mechanism, Compliance by Kazakhstan with its obligations under the Convention, Report by the Compliance Committee, ECE/MP.PP/2014/17, 8 May 2014.

[62] Ibid, paras. 2 and 4.

[63] Ibid, paras. 6–7.

[64] Ibid, para. 9.

[65] Ibid, paras. 10 and 11.

When it met at the fifth session of the MOP in 2014, the CC considered varied information received from Kazakhstan in relation to the outstanding matter from the third 2004 case and in regard to the 2011 case.[66] Because of a failure of Kazakhstan to provide evidence that it had met the requirements of Decision IV/9c or the recommendations in relation to the 2011 case, the CC concluded that in relation to both Kazakhstan was still in non-compliance.[67] It recommended the MOP to endorse these findings and invite Kazakhstan to continue its efforts and submit further detailed information in years to follow.[68] The MOP subsequently noted the efforts made, while also noting that further work was needed to fully address the outstanding points, and a draft decision prepared by the Bureau was subsequently adopted.[69]

Claims have also been made against Turkmenistan following a case in relation to the *Act on Public Associations* (ACCC/C/2004/5); the CC subsequently found Turkmenistan non-compliant with Articles 3(4) and (9) and consequently Article 3(1).[70] The second session of the MOP endorsed the CC findings via Decision II/5c,[71] but during the inter-sessional period 2005–2008 the CC concluded that Turkmenistan had failed to implement the required measures, 'apparently because it contested the finding of non-compliance'.[72] It recommended that the MOP confirm its earlier finding of non-compliance. This was duly done via Decision III/6e, with a caution issued to become effective unless various steps were taken, in particular amending the *Act on Public Associations*.[73]

---

66 Ibid, Part II, 'follow-up action'.
67 Ibid, paras. 42 and 43.
68 Ibid, para. 44.
69 Meeting of the Parties Fifth session, Maastricht, the Netherlands, 30 June and 1 July 2014. Item 5(b) of the provisional agenda, Procedures and mechanisms facilitating the implementation of the Convention: compliance mechanism, Draft decision V/9i concerning Compliance by Kazakhstan with its obligations under the Convention, prepared by the Bureau, ECE/MP.PP/2014/L.18, 6 May 2014.
70 Meeting of the Parties Fifth session, Maastricht, the Netherlands, 30 June and 1 July 2014. Item 5(b) of the provisional agenda, Procedures and mechanisms facilitating the implementation of the Convention: compliance mechanism, Compliance by Turkmenistan with its obligations under the Convention, Report by the Compliance Committee, ECE/MP.PP/2014/21, 17 June 2014, para. 2.
71 Ibid, para. 3.
72 Ibid, para. 4.
73 Ibid, para. 5.

During the following intersessional period 2008–2011 it was clear that no efforts had been taken in this regard,[74] and at the MOP fourth session it was decided that the caution should re-enter into effect on 1 January 2013, failing appropriate measures being taken.[75] It became clear over the following months that there was a difference of opinion between the CC and Turkmenistan concerning compliance,[76] and although a new *Act on Public Associations* was finally introduced ensuring that most of the obligations were complied with, Article 7(2) remained unfulfilled.[77]

With respect to Turkmenistan, the MOP welcomed the constructive efforts made to address recommendations made to bring legislation and practice into compliance, while recognising that further work was needed by each to fully address the outstanding points; a decision was subsequently adopted.[78]

c. Capacity building

To further implementation efforts, a subregional meeting for the central Asian states was recently organised jointly by the UNECE and OSCE.[79] The meeting was a response to the call made by the Parties at the fourth session (Chisinau, 29 June–1 July 2011), which highlighted capacity-building needs. While ensuring access to justice was acknowledged to be the most challenging issue, a lack of expertise related to the procedural requirements for effective implementation was also highlighted in this context.

---

74 Ibid, para. 7.

75 Ibid, para. 8.

76 Ibid, para. 30.

77 Ibid, para. 58. Another statute, the *Law on Nature Protection*, was also found to be non-compliant with this provision, see paras. 53–55.

78 Meeting of the Parties Fifth session, Maastricht, the Netherlands, 30 June and 1 July 2014. Item 5(b) of the provisional agenda, Procedures and mechanisms facilitating the implementation of the Convention: compliance mechanism, Draft decision V/9m concerning Compliance by Turkmenistan with its obligations under the Convention, prepared by the Bureau, ECE/MP.PP/2014/L.22, 18 June 2014.

79 Meeting of the Parties to the Convention on Access to Information, Public Participation in Decision-making and Access to Justice in Environmental Matters, Working Group of the Parties, fifteenth meeting, Geneva, 3–5 September 2012, item 3(c) of the provisional agenda, substantive issues: access to justice. Report of the subregional meeting 'Implementing the Aarhus Convention Today: Paving the Way to a Better Environment and Governance Tomorrow' held in Almaty, Kazakhstan, 22–23 May 2012, AC/WGP-15/Inf.1.

Two parallel workshops and several joint sessions were held. The first workshop, entitled 'Greening Justice and the role of the Judiciary in this Process' brought together senior judges and representatives from judicial training institutions, as well as environmental law experts, to discuss the legal aspects of access to justice and the role of the judiciary in implementing and enforcing the Convention.[80] The second workshop, entitled 'How to Implement the Aarhus Convention: Learning Practical Experiences' provided a platform for dialogue between representatives from Aarhus Centres and government, NGOs and IGOs to discuss challenges in the practical implementation of all three pillars and to learn good practices.[81]

IV.2 Protocol

a. Implementation

In regard to the *PRTR Protocol*, no central Asian countries have yet ratified this, although Tajikistan has signed. As such, Tajikistan has an obligation not to defeat the object and purpose of the treaty generally. However, implementation still remains relevant, as the questionnaire for the 2014 NIRs contains the requirement to comment on implementation of Article 4(9) of the Convention which concerns PRTRs. In response to question 15, Tajikistan therefore notes that seminars promoting the *PRTR Protocol* have been held to create the registers, but that again funding has been an issue to further implementation.[82]

Kazakhstan, although neither a Party nor a signatory to the Protocol, reports in its Convention implementation response, that further to Article 161 (4(2)) of the *Environmental Code*, the State Environmental Information Archive includes PRTRs and other registers of environmental information. It also notes that an Action Plan for the implementation of the Sectoral Program 'Zhasyl damu' for 2010–2014 includes a paragraph about the ratification of the *PRTR Protocol*, and that at present proposals for the ratification are being prepared.[83]

b. Capacity building

In relation to capacity building, in 2011 within the framework of the OSCE project a local pilot version of the PRTR of Kazakhstan was developed. On 8 September 2011 in Astana a round table on 'Prospects

---

[80] Ibid, Part III.1.
[81] Ibid, Part III.2.
[82] Above n. 54, 19.
[83] Above n. 39, paras. 18–19.

for the introduction of the National PRTR system in Kazakhstan' was held within the UNITAR project, which examined the results of projects to implement PRTR and recommendations for PRTR development in Kazakhstan.[84] In 2014 it was planned to continue the work on PRTR within the budget of the State Environmental Information Archive.[85]

The Protocol has much to offer in terms of enhancing the transparency of environmental information and providing a disincentive for polluters, so it is imperative to consider the obstacles that have prevented Asian countries from ratifying the Protocol to date, and how they may be overcome. These obstacles to ratification were identified in the early days of the Protocol:

> Establishing national PRTR systems would be a difficult task in many countries of [...] Central Asia, taking into account the wide range of point-source activities, as well as diffuse sources, on which reporting would be required under the protocol. Even if obstacles at the national level could be overcome, achieving harmonization between countries at different levels of economic development would pose a major challenge.[86]

A decade later, the Global Round Table on PRTRs in 2013 recognised that challenges remained for countries with economies in transition, particularly at the implementation stage, in terms of establishing an appropriate regulatory framework, either through amending existing legislation or adopting new national legislation on PRTRs.[87] In developing new institutional structures and capacities, these countries face difficulties caused by a lack of coordination and information-sharing between institutions; technical issues concerning data management, access and dissemination; and education and awareness-raising among stakeholders.[88]

According to the Global Round Table, there is some cause for optimism despite these issues. Pointing to 'remarkable examples' of

---

[84] See http://www.unitar.org/cwm/prtr, accessed 20 November 2014.

[85] UNECE, *Promotion of the Protocol on Pollutant Release and Transfer Registers in countries in Eastern Europe, the Caucasus and Central Asia*, ECE/MP.PRTR/2014/L.6.

[86] Report of the First Extraordinary Meeting of the Parties [to the Convention on Access to Information, Public Participation in Decision-making and Access to Justice in Environmental Matters], ECE/MP.PP/4, 5 August 2003, per Ms Chkhobadze (representative from Georgia), 4.

[87] Joint report by the secretariat of the Protocol on Pollutant Release and Transfer Registers and the Organisation for Economic Co-operation and Development, ECE/MP.PRTR/2014/7, 9.

[88] Ibid.

regional, harmonised PRTRs in central America and elsewhere, it contends that 'multiple experiences from a variety of countries and subregions [...] show that accession to the PRTR Protocol and implementing PRTR systems are both feasible. However, the time frame for PRTR implementation depends on political good will. Willingness to invest in human and technical resources remains key for successful implementation.'[89]

None of the other central Asian countries have submitted a NIR to the UNECE, as they are not required to do so until accession occurs. Apart from co-hosting the Global Round Table, the UNECE has taken other recent measures to raise awareness of the *PRTR Protocol* – both in central Asia and beyond the UNECE region – to try and increase the number of Parties to the Protocol.[90] A proposal for activities to promote the Protocol in the countries of EECCA was adopted by the Second Protocol MOP in July 2014.[91] The aim is to accelerate accession through activities such as setting up a regional PRTR expert group, developing national PRTR strategies and projects, providing access to European and UNECE experts, convening international meetings and holding training sessions, and facilitating financial support.[92] It is hoped that:

> ... implementation of the activities will help to build the countries' capacities for the establishment of national PRTRs and make the role of PRTRs more understandable and transparent to key stakeholders [...], which, in turn, will serve as an additional incentive for countries in Eastern Europe, the Caucasus and Central Asia to join the Protocol.[93]

V. EIA CONVENTION AND SEA PROTOCOL

V.1 Convention

a. Implementation and compliance

In central Asia this agreement is applied by Kazakhstan and Kyrgyzstan as Parties. Both submitted NIRs as part of the most recent Review of

---

89 Ibid, 13.

90 ECE/MP.PRTR/2010/2/Add.1, Decision I/6 on Work Programme for 2011–2014, Annex I.

91 Above n. 85; Decisions and Major Outcomes [as adopted by the Meeting of the Parties at its second session], ECE/MP.PRTR/2014/CRP.3, 3–4 July 2014, Maastricht, 3.

92 Above n. 85, 5–6.

93 Above n. 85, 6.

Implementation in 2013. The Kyrgyzstan NIR is in Russian with an informal translation in English, which is considered here together with Kazakhstan's NIR. As outlined in Chapter 4, there have been four implementation reviews to date: the first to mid-2003;[94] the second from mid-2003 to the end of 2005;[95] the third from the start of 2006 to the end of 2009;[96] and the most recent, from the start of 2010 to the end of 2012.[97] Compliance issues in relation to these Parties are also discussed below. Responses by the other Asian Parties to this treaty (Armenia and Azerbaijan) were briefly noted in Chapter 4.

The application of the Convention in central Asia, as with the Caucasus, derives from its membership and decisions reached at the Second and Third MOPs in Sofia and Cavtat. In Sofia in February 2001, Decision II/8 entitled 'Strengthening subregional cooperation' emphasised the need to encourage the development of bilateral and multilateral agreements through subregional cooperation to better implement the Convention.[98] Building on pilot workshops in the Balkan and Black Sea regions, subregional cooperation was aimed at countries in transition, in particular those formerly part of the Soviet Union, including the central Asian states, with a view to improving the ratification process. In Cavtat in June 2004, Decision III/5 also entitled 'Strengthening subregional cooperation', developed this further following experience gained in

---

94 United Nations Economic Commission for Europe, *Convention on Environmental Impact Assessment in a Transboundary Context: Review of Implementation 2003,* Advance Copy, 30 August 2004 ('first review').

95 United Nations Economic Commission for Europe, *Review of Implementation of the Convention on Environmental Impact Assessment in a Transboundary Context* (United Nations 2008), ECE/MP.EIA/11 ('second review').

96 United Nations Economic Commission for Europe, *Review of Implementation of the Convention on Environmental Impact Assessment in a Transboundary Context (2006–2009)* (United Nations 2011), ECE/MP.EIA/16 ('third review').

97 Meeting of the Parties, Sixth session, Geneva, 2–5 June 2014, Item 6 of the provisional agenda, Review of compliance, implementation and work done by the Implementation Committee, Draft fourth review of implementation of the Convention, note by the Secretariat, ECE/MP.EIA/2014/3, 20 March 2014. The final 2013 report is currently not available on website, although completed questionnaires can be viewed; accessed 20 November 2014 at http://www.unece.org/env/eia/implementation/review_implementation.html.

98 See ECE/MP.EIA/4, Annex VIII, 128–30.

central and eastern Europe and southeastern Europe, as detailed in associated guidance.[99]

The first review of implementation raised a specific compliance matter with respect to Kyrgyzstan, which was dealt with shortly afterwards with the Secretariat satisfied with the response;[100] further brief details are outlined in the compliance section below. In the second review Kyrgyzstan gave as examples of application a project that was close to a border or a cross-border river, or where it required transport of toxic chemicals through the affected Party.[101] In the third review Kyrgyzstan referred to subregional guidance on transboundary EIA as a helpful tool.[102] In relation to clarity, it observed the need for thresholds for all activities listed in Appendix I, and for specific distance to be confirmed in relation to international borders in Appendix III.[103] It also recognised the need to adopt a new regulation on EIA, and eventually an environmental code.[104]

In relation to Kazakhstan's most recent NIR, in response to the fourth review, a limited amount of information is provided in response to the standard questionnaire, with many answers simply that there is 'no practice'. What is of interest however is information provided by the state Party that further to Article 2(2) of the Convention, Kazakhstan planned to develop and adopt instructions for carrying out transboundary EIA of intended economic activities with significant environmental impacts;[105] and that it planned to amend the Rules for conducting public hearings, with the draft of the revised Rules posted on the website of the Aarhus Center of the Republic of Kazakhstan.[106] Consistent with the current application of the system of state ecological expertise, Kazakhstan also comments as an example: 'Starting with the date of the announcement on organization of accounting of public opinion on the EIA draft the customer (developer) ensures the access of the public to the EIA draft,

---

[99] See ECE/MP.EIA/6, Annex V, 76–91.

[100] Above n. 94, 9.

[101] Above n. 95, para. 127(h).

[102] Above n. 96, 34.

[103] Above n. 96, 35.

[104] Above n. 96, 35.

[105] Ministry of Environment Protection of the Republic of Kazakhstan, *Report on Implementation of the Espoo Convention on Environmental Impact Assessment in a Transboundary Context* (2012) 2.

[106] Ibid. These were approved by the order of the Minister of Environment Protection dated on May 7, 2007, No. 135-p.

reception and registration of the comments and suggestions.'[107] The response to the questions on Article 6 also provide further information relevant to this SER approach. Other information of interest in Kazakhstan's NIR relates to research efforts under Article 9, which makes reference to transboundary collaboration with Russia, China and other states in central Asia:

- 'The research of the ecological status of cross-border regions of Kazakhstan to solve the problems of transboundary nature'. The object of the study was the border with the Russian Federation territory;
- 'Investigation of ecological condition of the border with China and Kazakhstan's districts of Central Asian countries to solve the problems of transboundary nature'. *The aim of the project* – development of measures to solve the problems of sustainable nature management of the border areas of Kazakhstan and adjacent territories of China, Kyrgyzstan, Uzbekistan and Turkmenistan and the development of environmental proposals for the regulation of cross-border environmental management based on the landscape-ecological assessment.

In relation to Kyrgyzstan's most recent NIR, similar conclusions emerge.[108] The adoption and registration of a 'draft Instruction on the Procedure for the Proposed Activity Environmental Impact Assessment (EIA)' is therefore noted as a planned development.[109] Appendix I is confirmed as not fully transposed into the current national legislation, which, for example, does not include paragraphs 9, 15, and 17 of Appendix I.[110] Kyrgyzstan makes extensive reference to the *Guidelines on Environmental Impact Assessment in a Transboundary Context for Central Asian Countries* (the 'Guidelines' – discussed below);[111] in response to questions about notification for example, it cites these in

---

[107] Above n. 105, 9.

[108] State Agency of Environmental Protection and Forestry under the Government of the Kyrgyz Republic, *Report of the Kyrgyz Republic on the Implementation of the Convention on Environmental Impact Assessment in a Transboundary Context in the period 2010–2012,* May 2013, informal translation.

[109] Ibid, 2.

[110] Ibid, 3.

[111] See UNECE, MOP to the Espoo Convention, Working Group on EIA, Tenth Meeting, Geneva, May 2007, Activities related to the Convention listed in the workplan (Decision III/9), Capacity-building in Eastern Europe, Caucasus and Central Asia (EECCA), Guidelines on Environmental Impact Assessment in a Transboundary Context for Central Asian Countries, Prepared by Kazakhstan, Kyrgyzstan, Tajikistan, Turkmenistan and Uzbekistan. See ECE/MP.EIA/WG.1/2007/6, 12 March 2007.

regard to the format and timeframe for notifications.[112] Extensive reference is also made to the system of state ecological expertise.[113] Some practical experience is noted with respect to a project concerning Kazakhstan (the development of the Jerooy gold deposit, discussed below 'pilot project' in relation to capacity building), which, despite being suggested as an example of good practice, it appears was itself aborted.[114] Other comments made by Kyrgyzstan were that with respect to the clarity of the Convention, the terms 'major', 'large', and 'close to an international frontier', were not clear.[115]

Contextualising the Convention in central Asia are the *Guidelines*. The objective is to detail the procedural mechanisms, although they are only recommendatory. Any legal basis is hence derived from national EIA laws unless, in the case of the two central Asian Parties to the Convention, they have also ratified its provisions and deposited their instruments of ratification. The *Guidelines* consist of five independent but interrelated parts: review of national EIA legislation and practice; recommendations for the country or Party of origin; recommendations for the affected country or Party; recommendations for the project proponent; and other matters, which include SEA. Most of the *Guidelines* in the first part detail the steps taken by the central Asian Parties and others up to mid-2005 to implement the Convention where applicable.

As noted in Chapter 4 and above, the only compliance manner arising under the *EIA Convention* with respect to central Asia was a specific matter with respect to Kyrgyzstan. This was initiated by a letter from the secretariat to Kyrgyzstan, dated 26 August 2005, similarly requesting clarification of Kyrgyzstan's response to the questionnaire,[116] which raised concerns about procedures for notification and government decision making. This was responded to by Kyrgyzstan, in a letter dated 23 November 2005,[117] indicating that full consultations had in fact taken place with NGOs and that in fact the timing of all of the concerns was prior to ratification of the Convention. A letter from the secretariat to

---

112 Above n. 108, 4–5, 7–9.

113 Above n. 108, 6–9.

114 Above n. 108, 10–13.

115 Above n. 108, 14.

116 Accessed 20 November 2014 at http://www.unece.org/fileadmin/DAM/env/eia/documents/ImplementationCommittee/eia.ic.sci.1/eia.ic.sci.1.3/IC_Kyrgyzstan_compliance2005_question_from_secretariat.pdf.

117 Accessed 20 November 2014 at http://www.unece.org/fileadmin/DAM/env/eia/documents/ImplementationCommittee/eia.ic.sci.1/eia.ic.sci.1.3/IC_Kyrgyzstan_compliance2005_response_from_Kyrgyzstan_en.pdf.

Kyrgyzstan, dated 18 July 2006, stated that the IC was satisfied with the information provided and would not consider the matter further.[118]

Finally, the *EIA Convention* in particular has, like the *Industrial Accidents* and *Water Convention* as noted below, significance beyond treaty law. This is because the principle, if not the content, of EIA has been acknowledged by the ICJ to be part of customary/general international law.[119] Even where central Asian and other states may not be Party to this agreement, and be obliged to carry out its detailed requirements as Parties, they will still therefore be obliged to follow the principle of cooperation and the no harm rule underlying this agreement and others. This has been applied in the context of international rivers, as expressed in the *Pulp Mills* case between Uruguay and Argentina as follows:

> In this sense, the obligation to protect and preserve, under Article 41(a) of the Statute, has to be interpreted in accordance with practice, which in recent years has gained so much acceptance among States that it may now be considered a requirement under general international law to undertake an environmental impact assessment where there is a risk that the proposed industrial activity may have a significant adverse impact in a transboundary context, in particular, on a shared resource. Moreover, due diligence, and the duty of vigilance and prevention which it implies, would not be considered to have been exercised, if a party planning works liable to affect the regime of the river or the quality of its waters did not undertake an environmental impact assessment on the potential effects of such works.[120]

V.2 Convention and Protocol

a. Capacity building

While only two central Asian states are Parties to the Convention (Kazakhstan and Kyrgyzstan), others have decided to follow its procedures in relation to the development of proposals with potential transboundary significance. Together with these Parties, Tajikistan has passed domestic implementing legislation,[121] and Uzbekistan is preparing to

---

[118] Accessed 20 November 2014 at http://www.unece.org/fileadmin/DAM/env/eia/documents/ImplementationCommittee/eia.ic.sci.1/eia.ic.sci.1.3/IC_Kyrgyzstan_compliance2005_follow_up_from_secretariat.pdf.

[119] See *Case Concerning Pulp Mills on the River Uruguay (Argentina v. Uruguay),* Judgment of 20 April 2010.

[120] Ibid, para. 204.

[121] Tajikistan ratified the *EIA Convention* in 2004 but has still to deposit its instrument of ratification with the UN, which is needed for it to become a Party. See *Guidelines* para. 39. See also Dmytro Skrylnikov, *Review of Legislation on*

ratify the Convention.[122] To demonstrate the application of the *Guidelines*, a UNECE pilot project was begun soon afterwards.[123] It proceeded between 2006–2009, and involved international as well as local experts. The objective was to demonstrate effective implementation of the Convention in Kazakhstan and Kyrgyzstan through conducting a full transboundary EIA procedure on a specific planned project in Kyrgyzstan, with the involvement of Kazakh authorities and the public.[124]

The project was a new copper and gold mining operation proposed by a mining company which required a licence in Kyrgyzstan, and was situated very close to the Kazakh border. Downstream water pollution was a significant potential impact. On the basis of this experience, national implementation mechanisms were developed and human capacities increased through training sessions in Kazakhstan and Kyrgyzstan. Two major EIA laws were also amended to clarify procedures and include public participation. The later phases of the project concentrated on updating the 2005 *Guidelines*.

Most recently, a series of capacity building workshops were held in 2010 in the central Asian states.[125] These have included an expert workshop to enhance understanding of the Convention and Protocol with a focus on domestic land-use and sectoral planning in Uzbekistan.[126] The objective was to raise awareness of what would be involved if Uzbekistan chose to accede to the Protocol, and the workshop was designed to improve the actors' capacities to transpose and implement international principles, standards and good practice in SEA based on practical exercises. Although none of the central Asian states are currently Parties or signatories to the Protocol, the *Resource Manual on the SEA Protocol*

Environmental Impact Assessment of the Republic of Tajikistan with Regard to Introduction and Implementation of the Espoo Convention (2010); this detailed guide was prepared as part of the UNECE-GTZ programme 'Regional Dialogue and Cooperation on Water Resources Management' and includes discussion of the OVOS/SER procedures.

[122] None of the central Asian states are signatories or Parties to the *SEA Protocol*.

[123] Organisation for Security and Cooperation in Europe/UNECE, *Environmental Impact Assessment in a Transboundary Context: Pilot Project in Central Asia Project Report* (2009).

[124] See above n. 108.

[125] See http://www.unece.org/env/eia/subregions/central_asia.htm, accessed 20 November 2014.

[126] See http://www.unece.org/index.php?id=27140, accessed 20 November 2014.

provides an example of a detailed capacity assessment which can be used in EECCA.[127]

VI. INDUSTRIAL ACCIDENTS CONVENTION AND PROTOCOL ON CIVIL LIABILITY

VI.1 Convention

a. Implementation and compliance

Kazakhstan is the only Party to the *Industrial Accidents Convention*. However as indicated in Chapter 5, individual NIRs are not publicly available under this treaty and it is therefore not possible to discuss Kazakhstan's NIR in detail. Notwithstanding this, Kyrgyzstan, Tajikistan and Uzbekistan made a commitment at the High-Level Commitment Meeting in 2005 to report on their progress towards acceding to the Convention.[128] However, progress since that time appears to have been slow, with only Uzbekistan and Kyrgyzstan approaching some form of readiness.[129] Turkmenistan has recently expressed a strong interest in acceding to all of the UNECE environmental agreements, including this Convention.[130] In 2011, at the UNECE International Conference on Europe-Asia Transboundary Water Cooperation, it was noted that:

> Cooperation in disaster risk reduction and prevention, preparedness and response to accidental water pollution is especially important in the Europe-Asia border region due to the existence of many old outdated infrastructure and industrial facilities close to the border which can have significant transboundary impacts in case of accidents.[131]

---

[127] UNECE, *Resource Manual to Support Application of the SEA Protocol* (United Nations 2012), ECE/MP.EIA/17, Annex B1.1, 191; and Annex B1.2, 195 (which contains terms of reference for national capacity development strategies).

[128] Report of the High-Level Commitment Meeting, Conference of the Parties to the Convention on the Transboundary Effects of Industrial Accidents, 14–15 December 2005, Doc. CP.TEIA/2005/12. The High-Level Meeting is discussed further below.

[129] Minutes of the Meeting, 23rd Meeting of the Working Group on Implementation, Doc. CP.TEIAB/2013/INF.9, 27–28 November 2013.

[130] East Time News Agency, 'Turkmenistan to join international environmental conventions', 8 April 2014, http://easttime.info/news/turkmenistan/turkmenistan-join-international-environmental-conventions, accessed 20 November 2014.

[131] UNECE, 'International Conference Europe-Asia Transboundary Water Cooperation, Geneva, 15–16 December 2011 – Report', 4.

Kazakhstan submitted a NIR prior to the Sixth Report by the WGI, which covered the period 2010–2011.[132] While the detail of this is not available, the information provided by the WGI's Report indicates that, overall, Kazakhstan had made a reasonable effort to put necessary measures in place under the Convention. Over time, the UNECE has acknowledged the numerous challenges presented by the implementation of the Convention:

> The Convention is complex and requires for its implementation the coordinated involvement of a number of competent authorities at the national level. Certain tasks under the Convention also require vertical coordination between national authorities and regional and local authorities as well as industry and the public. Finally, implementing the Convention fully requires bilateral cross-border cooperation with neighbouring countries.[133]

These complexities have been particularly difficult for some countries in the UNECE region – such as those in the EECCA – to overcome. Early obstacles to accession and/or implementation for most EECCA countries were an inadequate institutional framework and limited human and financial resources, primarily due to ongoing political and economic problems.[134] Moreover, the majority of industrial facilities in these countries were outdated and poorly maintained, using obsolete technologies. In many cases, emergency response and notification systems were either not in place, or fell far short of the requirements of the Convention. The inability of EECCA countries to properly implement the Convention had become more apparent within the first few years of its entry into force, through the regular implementation reviews that were undertaken.

Reflecting its considerable frustration over implementation difficulties, particularly with respect to Russia's non-compliance concerning reporting as outlined in Chapter 5, the 7th COP Meeting tasked the WGD with considering possible remedies for non-compliance with the reporting requirement.[135] The WGD has since recommended informally that the

---

[132] UNECE, Sixth Report on the Implementation of the Convention (2010–2011), ECE/CP.TEIA/2012/3, 23 August 2012.

[133] UNECE, 'Draft Internationally Supported Assistance Programme for the East European, Caucasian and Central Asian and the South-east European Countries to Enhance their Efforts in Implementing the Convention', CP.TEIA/2004/2, 2.

[134] Ibid, 4.

[135] UNECE, Report of the Conference of the Parties on its Seventh Meeting, Stockholm, 14–16 November 2012, ECE/CP.TEIA/24, 4 (para. 16).

obligation to report under Article 23 of the Convention be further clarified.[136] It has also suggested that the mandate of the WGI could be reviewed to include compliance matters.[137] Lastly, the WGD has recommended that remedies for non-compliance with reporting requirements should be contained within an overall compliance mechanism, as is common practice in other multilateral environmental agreements.[138] It remains to be seen what steps will be taken to strengthen the reporting obligation, and to introduce remedies for non-compliance.

b. Capacity building

Various international workshops, seminars and training exercises were held by the UNECE in 2001–2002 to help countries address problems of implementation.[139] At the 2nd COP Meeting, in 2002, the Parties took the more formal step of recognising 'the need to assist some countries with economies in transition in their efforts to apply the Convention in practice'.[140] The 'Sub-Regional Workshop on the Convention's Implementation in the Caucasian and Central Asian Countries', held in 2003 in Armenia, subsequently played an important role in identifying the specific obstacles and needs of the EECCA countries.[141] It reached three main conclusions: that EECCA countries had to undertake considerable work to accede to and implement the Convention, and show their commitment; that a strong commitment by all actors involved in industrial accidents was essential to applying the Convention successfully; and an internationally supported assistance programme should be drawn up to enhance the efforts of these countries in acceding to and implementing the Convention, taking into account their difficult economic and financial situation.[142] The Sub-Regional Workshop also identified several key elements of its proposed assistance programme, all of which were considered during the final drafting process.

On the basis of implementation reviews and these workshop activities, the WGI recommended to the Convention Bureau in 2004 that an

---

136 Background paper on possible amendments to the Convention – Note by the secretariat, Informal Document, WG.1-2014.Inf.1 (February 2014) (at 10).

137 Ibid.

138 Ibid.

139 Above n. 133, 5.

140 UNECE, Conference of the Parties to the Convention on the Transboundary Effects of Industrial Accidents – Report of the Second Meeting, ECE/CP.TEIA/7, 30 January 2003, 1.

141 Above n. 133, 6.

142 Above n. 133, 6.

internationally-funded assistance programme be devised.[143] The Bureau endorsed the recommendation, stating that the programme would be 'needs-driven' and comprise partnership arrangements, workshops, training sessions and/or exchange of experts to help countries implement the Convention. It would also aim to assist countries that were not already parties to the Convention, particularly those in Caucasus and central Asia, to accede to and implement it.[144] The outcome was the 'Internationally Supported Assistance Programme for the East European, Caucasian and Central Asian and the South-east European Countries to Enhance their Efforts in Implementing the Convention' (Assistance Programme), which was adopted by the 3rd COP Meeting later in 2004.[145]

The Assistance Programme sets out the measures to be taken by beneficiary countries to demonstrate their commitment to implementing the Convention, and capacity-building activities and other services to be provided or financed by donor countries. It also provides an action plan, defining further steps to be taken by the COP and beneficiary countries to implement the Assistance Programme. There are currently 15 beneficiary countries participating in the Assistance Programme,[146] with an invitation to Turkmenistan proposed.[147] It is based on the principle that assistance can only be effective if a recipient country is capable of receiving the assistance, and is committed to taking full advantage of it.[148] The measures to be taken by beneficiary countries, and the relevant assistance to be provided by other UNECE members, are divided into ten sections that correspond approximately to the main obligations under the Convention. They include the following:

- making the Convention text available in the relevant national language … ;
- reviewing all relevant national legislation and identifying gaps and inconsistencies … ;
- identifying and designating competent authorities that will be responsible for implement[ation] … ;
- identifying all hazardous industrial facilities within their territory;

---

143 Above n. 133, 6.

144 Above n. 140, Annex I, 18.

145 Budapest, 27–30 October 2004, CP.TEIA/2004/2.

146 In Asia these include: Armenia, Azerbaijan, Georgia, Kazakhstan, Kyrgyzstan, Tajikistan, and Uzbekistan.

147 UNECE, 'Minutes of the Meeting', 25th Meeting of the Bureau of the Industrial Accidents Convention, Geneva, 11–12 June 2013, ECE/CP.TEIA/B/2013/INF.9, 5.

148 UNECE, *The Assistance Programme – The Convention on the Transboundary Effects of Industrial Accidents* (UNECE 2010) 2.

- designating a competent authority to notify potentially affected parties … ;
- establishing specific terms of reference for relevant authorities to ensure … operational safety … ;
- designating or establishing one or two points of contact for industrial accident notification … ;
- preparing a detailed document describing the implementation of the industrial accident notification system at the national level … ;
- determining whether adequate on-site and off-site contingency plans have been prepared … ; and
- launching an effective campaign to raise public awareness of the importance of the Convention … [149]

The Assistance Programme sets out a strategy for achieving the above tasks in its two-phase Action Plan, which comprises a preparatory phase (for most participating countries, this took place during 2004–2006) followed by an implementation phase. The preparatory phase involved releasing the draft Assistance Programme for comment (and, if appropriate, revision) by the Convention Parties; convening a high-level meeting to secure a firm commitment by EECCA countries regarding the practical application of the Convention; and sending an expert team to review implementation, identify further needs, and report findings in beneficiary countries.[150]

During the preparatory phase, the relevant countries were required to satisfy the fact-finding missions that they were able to receive assistance, and to demonstrate their needs.[151] In the first round of fact-finding missions in 2006, only half of the countries visited had met these requirements.[152] Three out of another four countries visited in the next round of fact-finding missions (2007–2008) were ready to enter the implementation phase.[153] Progress continued steadily in the remaining EECCA countries, with only one country, Turkmenistan, still receiving assistance in the preparatory phase in 2011–2012.[154]

---

[149] Above n. 133, 7.

[150] Above n. 133, 10.

[151] Above n. 148, 2.

[152] UNECE, Report on the Results of the Preparatory Phase of the Assistance Programme, 9 October 2006, ECE/CP.TEIA/2006/3, 5.

[153] UNECE, Progress Report on the Assistance Programme, 12 September 2008, ECE/CP.TEIA/2008/4, 4.

[154] UNECE, Progress Report on the Assistance Programme – Note by the Bureau and the Working Group on Implementation, 7th Meeting of the Conference of the Parties, Stockholm, 14–16 November 2012, 13. This assistance was in the form of an information workshop on the Convention.

Meeting all the basic requirements of the preparatory phase is a pre-condition to a country entering the implementation phase. The implementation phase allows beneficiary countries to participate in capacity-building activities (for example workshops, training sessions and exchange programmes), transboundary pilot projects and joint exercises, and to obtain advisory services where needed. The Assistance Programme states that 'assistance will be provided in such a way as to fully use existing mechanisms and international institutional arrangements, e.g. the Regional Environmental Centres for the Caucasus, for Central Asia and for Eastern Europe'.[155] The Convention Secretariat is responsible for organising and managing activities under the Assistance Programme, with the guidance of the Bureau. The Programme is funded through contributions to the Convention's trust fund from donor countries (primarily western European UNECE member countries and the EU), IFIs, IGOs and other programmes.

In 2005, a High-Level Commitment Meeting was held in Geneva, fulfilling a key requirement of the preparatory phase of the Assistance Programme.[156] Representatives of 17 countries, including from the EECCA regions adopted a declaration,[157] committing their governments to implementing the Convention, whilst central and western European countries pledged their strong support for the Assistance Programme. The Declaration notes that most of the EECCA countries had already implemented the majority of the basic tasks required under the Assistance Programme, and that these countries would 'ensure that the remaining tasks will be carried out without delay'.[158] The countries committed themselves to submitting NIRs and demonstrating their progress to fact-finding teams.[159] They promised to actively participate in needs-driven assistance activities, receive advisory services and put forward proposals for transboundary pilot projects. Lastly, they called on the countries of central and western Europe and north America, and IFIs and programmes, to 'support further the assistance programme financially and in kind in order to facilitate its full implementation'.[160]

---

155 Above n. 133, 11.

156 Above n. 128.

157 These included in Asia, the following states: Armenia, Azerbaijan, Georgia, Kazakhstan, Kyrgyzstan, Russia, Tajikistan and Uzbekistan.

158 Above n. 128, 9.

159 Above n. 128, 9.

160 Above n. 128, 10.

In 2008, a Strategic Approach was introduced to guide all future activities under the Assistance Programme.[161] This aims to help countries to identify their challenges in implementing the Convention, and to design measures to address those challenges.[162] Since 2010, it has used a cyclical mechanism[163] that involves three steps: first, an analysis of the country's level of implementation under six work areas (identification and notification of hazardous activities, prevention, preparedness, response and mutual assistance, and public information and participation), and identification of challenges faced; second, the development of a national action plan (including assistance projects) to address the identified challenges; and third, measurement of the results achieved using specific indicators and criteria. If this process reveals any additional challenges, a new 'cycle' begins.[164] During 2011–2012, three projects were underway as part of the implementation phase, and were primarily based on prevention, preparedness and response measures.[165] Two of these projects were set to continue into 2013–2014.[166]

At the 6th COP Meeting in 2010, all beneficiary countries were requested to provide a self-assessment of their progress in implementing the Convention by September 2011, and to continuously update the document thereafter. In addition, they were to submit a national action plan based on the results of their initial self-assessment by early 2012, and update it when needed.[167] Only two-thirds of the beneficiary countries submitted a self-assessment by the deadline, and overall these were considered by the WGI to be unsatisfactory, displaying a poor understanding of both the Strategic Approach and the Convention itself.[168]

To add to the growing concern of the Bureau, only four (all European) countries had sent a national action plan to the Convention Secretariat by late 2012. Accordingly, the COP at its 7th Meeting reminded all beneficiary countries of their obligation to carry out self-evaluations and

---

[161] The Strategic Approach was adopted at the Fifth Meeting of the Conference of the Parties, 25–27 November 2008, Geneva, ECE/CP.TEIA/2008/5.

[162] Above n. 148, 2.

[163] The cyclic mechanism was adopted at the Sixth Meeting of the Conference of the Parties in The Hague, 8–10 November 2010, ECE/CP.TEIA/2010/6, and ECE/CP,TEIA/22.

[164] Above n. 148, 3.

[165] These involved national training sessions for identification of hazardous activities under the Convention (Kyrgyzstan, Tajikistan and Uzbekistan); see Progress Report on the Assistance Programme, above n. 154, 8.

[166] The on-site inspection training project and the Danube Delta project.

[167] Above n. 154, 3.

[168] Above n. 154, 5.

to submit action plans.[169] However, 'recognizing that countries still encountered difficulties using the indicators and criteria, the Conference entrusted the Bureau and the WGI with an evaluation of the criteria and indicators and with finding ways to assist countries with their application'.[170] The Bureau decided to monitor progress on these matters more closely in future, and to divide the monitoring workload for the Assistance Programme more effectively between itself and the WGI.[171] The COP continues to place a high priority on the work of the Assistance Programme.[172]

Whilst the overall understanding and awareness of the Convention's requirements has undoubtedly increased[173] in some countries of central Asia – partly due to the Assistance Programme – challenges remain in enforcing national policies on the issue. Training workshops and regional conferences are helping to sustain interest in the Convention and accumulate knowledge in relevant areas, so as to prepare for eventual accession and implementation. Countries in central Asia are now able to learn from the early experiences of a handful of their own countries in implementing the Convention. As more information is exchanged, and awareness of the need for regulation of transboundary industrial accidents grows, those countries yet to accede may be further encouraged to do so.

VI.2 Protocol

a. Capacity building

In relation to capacity building efforts connected with the Protocol, as this agreement is not in force these have been limited to encouraging ratifications. This was discussed in detail in the 'global outlook' section of Chapter 5, where the three-step approach to ratify was announced by the sixth Convention MOP.

---

[169] Above n. 135, 10.
[170] Above n. 135, 10.
[171] Above n. 154, 5–6.
[172] Above n. 135, 6.
[173] Fifth Report on the Implementation of the Convention (2008–2009), ECE/CP.TEIA/2010/3 (at 4).

VII. WATER CONVENTION AND WATER AND HEALTH PROTOCOL

VII.1 Convention

a. Implementation

Kazakhstan, Turkmenistan and Uzbekistan are all Parties to this Convention. As indicated in Chapter 6, however, there is no current provision for NIRs to be submitted by Parties under this treaty and therefore it is not possible to effectively evaluate the implementation efforts of these three central Asian Parties. It is therefore necessary to refer to the assessments conducted by the WG, particularly the most recent.[174] Despite this, in the same manner that non-signatories or Parties are obliged to follow the principle of EIA as noted above, so there are duties in water law in relation to cooperation and equitable utilisation that have been accepted as customary international law.[175] This means that even though Kyrgyzstan and Tajikistan are neither Parties nor signatories,[176] these obligations would still need to be followed as if they were Parties.

International water law has been studied extensively, including in central Asia.[177] While it is not the intention to repeat what has been said elsewhere, recent work by Ziganshina is noteworthy for its focus on central Asia, transboundary water problems and applicable treaty law; this also reviews implementation and compliance, with procedures and institutional measures outlined.[178] Subregional agreements identified include the *Almaty Agreement*,[179] and a range of other measures.[180] Four of the five UNECE agreements are cited as relevant (the exception is the

---

174 See Economic Commission for Europe Convention on the Protection and Use of Transboundary Watercourses and International Lakes, *Second Assessment of Transboundary Rivers, Lakes and Groundwaters* (United Nations 2011), Pt III, chapter 5 (central Asia), Pt IV, chapter 3 (Aral Sea/central Asia).

175 See Patricia Wouters, 'The Yin and Yang of International Water Law: China's Transboundary Water Practice and the Changing Contours of State Sovereignty' (2014) 23(1) *Review of European, Comparative and International Environmental Law* 67, 69–71.

176 Signatories must not defeat the object and purpose of the treaty, see above n 36.

177 See in particular, Dinara Ziganshina, 'International Water Law in Central Asia: Commitments, Compliance and Beyond' (2009) 20 *Water Law* 96.

178 Ibid, 103–5.

179 Above n. 9.

180 Above n. 177, 99.

Air Pollution Convention), and globally, the *International Water Convention*;[181] other MEAs are also indicated, which were outlined in Chapter 2.[182] The author ends by emphasising the need for further research on compliance and the broader effect of international water law in central Asia in particular.[183] This is beyond the contribution of this chapter, which is focused on addressing the UNECE agreements individually and in relation to each other where relevant.

In the *First Assessment*, it was noted that effects of climate change on the ecological regime of rivers are also becoming visible in transboundary basins in central Asia,[184] where the rise in air temperatures leads to significant melting of glaciers, resulting in noteworthy changes of the rivers' hydrological and ecological regimes.[185] Furthermore, water sharing among countries in the same basins to satisfy demands of national economic activities (irrigation, manufacturing, energy production), continues to cause upstream-downstream conflicts, including adverse effects on the environment (e.g. the destruction of water-related ecosystems). Most affected are the basins in central Asia (particularly the Amu Darya, Syr Darya, and Ili), and the Samur basin.[186] It was also noted that in a transboundary context, one area of conflict is between hydropower production and irrigational agriculture, which is particularly obvious in the basins of the Amu Darya and Syr Darya.[187]

In the *Second Assessment*, Pt III, chapter 5 summarises the cooperation efforts of the central Asian states following independence, implementation and updating efforts, and the problem of regulating hydro-power development.[188] In relation to the discussion of 'legal, policy and institutional frameworks' which is found in this chapter of the report, of particular note is that: 'One of the shortcomings of the existing legal

---

[181] Convention on the Law of Non-Navigable Uses of International Watercourses (New York, 21 May 1997, by UNGA Res. 51/229), 36 ILM (1997) 700, in force August 2014.

[182] Above n. 177, 100–1.

[183] Above n. 177, 105–7.

[184] See Ariel Dinar, Shlomi Dinar, Stephen McCaffrey, and Daene McKinney, 'Case Study 4: The Aral Sea Basin' in *Understanding Transboundary Water Conflict, Negotiation and Cooperation* (2nd edn, World Scientific, Washington, DC 2013) 339–62.

[185] See United Nations Economic Commission for Europe, *Our Waters: Joining Hands Across Borders – First Assessment of Transboundary Rivers, Lakes and Groundwaters* (United Nations 2007) 29.

[186] Ibid.

[187] Ibid, 32.

[188] Above n. 174, 66.

framework is the insufficient links between the various legal instruments.'[189] This refers to the *Almaty Agreement* and related agreements discussed by Ziganshina above, the *Caspian Sea Convention* (discussed in Chapter 2),[190] and the fact that the *Framework Convention*[191] has not come into force. It also adds force to the argument for the *Water Convention* to potentially provide a coordinating framework within the context of the UNECE treaty regime more broadly in the region, which the UNECE has itself advocated.[192] Current JC arrangements are cited (see also Chapter 6), and deficiencies are noted as follows, for example: 'with regard to the Ili and the Irtysh, it is a shortcoming that there is no permanent executive body of the Kazakh-Chinese or Kazakh-Russian Joint Commission'.[193]

The *Second Assessment* also comments on national law reform of Parties to the *Water Convention*, which is especially significant as evidence of implementation efforts. The *Water Codes* of Kazakhstan are for example outlined. The 2003 Code provided for extensive NGO consultation; the 2005 Code introduced an integrated approach, and established a National Water Council. Reforms to legislation in Uzbekistan highlight the introduction of new basin water administrations. In Tajikistan (a non-Party), it was expected that reform would result in water management being transferred from administrative units to river basin authorities, to be created during 2011–2013.[194] Implementation efforts have been slowed by a typical 'lack of resources and weakness of institutions' and 'frequent lack of intersectoral coordination'.[195] However:

> A positive development is the setting up of basin councils to facilitate participation of all the concerned stakeholders. At the national level, advisory basin councils have been set up already in Kazakhstan and on the Talas in 2009 in Kyrgyzstan. Kyrgyzstan is expecting to complete the establishment of river basin management authorities and basin councils required by the Water Code in 2011.[196]

---

[189] Above n. 174, 67.

[190] *Framework Convention for the Protection of the Marine Environment of the Caspian Sea* (Tehran, 4 November 2003), unreported, in force 12 August 2006.

[191] Above n. 12.

[192] Above n. 25.

[193] Above n. 174, 67.

[194] Above n. 174, 67–8.

[195] Above n. 174, 68.

[196] Above n. 174, 68.

The findings relevant to central Asia from the *Second Assessment* have been extensively analysed since the work concluded. Libert and Lipponen note that while the *Second Assessment* covered the waters shared by the five central Asian states and their neighbours (Afghanistan, China, Iran, Mongolia and Russia), the central Asian states depend heavily on the main transboundary rivers in the Aral Sea basin, the Amu Darya and the Syr Darya. They emphasise that the conflict between water use for irrigation and hydro-power generation has raised political tension in the subregion,[197] and that the 'legal framework for regional cooperation in the management of shared water resources, developed in the 1990s and based on practices from the Soviet Union, is not working well'.[198]

The first of four case studies they review concerns the Aral Sea Programme 3 and the legal and institutional strengthening of water cooperation. This began in December 2010 with IFAS considering the third Aral Sea programme, a regional action plan for 2011–2015 to mitigate impacts, progress towards IWRM and sustainable development, including contributions towards the MDGs, and improving resilience to contend with climate change (see section IV above for context). With respect to institutional and legal aspects, which were a key component, they comment that this 'is politically a very difficult area … a step-by-step, evolutionary rather than revolutionary, approach … has been selected by the countries'.[199]

The third of the case studies is concerned with the safety of hydro-technical installations, which emphasises the link between the *Water* and *Industrial Accidents Conventions*,[200] supported by the Joint Ad Hoc Expert Group on Water and Industrial Accidents, and the *Civil Liability Protocol*. Dam safety has been a significant concern for many years in central Asia, where there are more than 100 facilities, most located on transboundary watercourses. Apart from Uzbekistan, all of the other central Asian states lack adequate institutional and legal frameworks. The

---

197 Bo Libert and Annukka Lipponen, 'Challenges and Opportunities for Transboundary Water Cooperation in Central Asia: Findings from UNECE's Regional Assessment and Project Work' (2012) 28(3) *Water Resources Development* 565, 566–7; see also generally, Bo Libert, 'Water Management in Central Asia and the Activities of the UNECE' in M M Rahaman and O Varis (eds), *Central Asian Waters: Social, Economic, Environmental and Governance Puzzle* (Helsinki University of Technology 2008) 35.

198 Libert and Lipponen, above n.197, 568.

199 Libert and Lipponen, above n.197, 570.

200 See http://www.unece.org/environmental-policy/treaties/water/areas-of-work-of-the-convention/water-and-industrial-accidents.html, accessed 20 November 2014.

first phase of a UNECE project was therefore begun in 2006, with the second commencing at the end of 2007, subsequently completed in 2011. This phase focused on supporting the introduction or revision of national legislation, developing a regional cooperative framework and capacity development.[201]

As an example of the conflict over water in central Asia, the development of the Rogun hydro-electric dam by Tajikistan[202] is a major concern of Uzbekistan's. It was begun during Soviet times, although halted in the 1990s. Neighbouring Uzbekistan's withdrawal from the regional power grid in 2009 ended Tajikistan's electricity supply from Russia, which prompted its need for hydroelectricity. As the downstream state, Uzbekistan is concerned about its water supply for irrigation of its cotton industry. Tajikistan is also planning to construct a reservoir and hydropower station in the upper reaches of the Zeravshan River which may affect the quantity of water downstream, again impacting upon Uzbekistan. The project was assessed under WB procedures, as the WB is potentially a major financier.[203] The Environmental-Social Assessment included consideration of riparian issues and cross-border impacts.[204] Since Tajikistan is neither a member of the *EIA Convention* nor the *Water Convention* it does not have to comply with either, so the application of the WB's procedures is significant.

b. Compliance

The second meeting of the IC received information from an environmental NGO based in Astana, Kazakhstan. Concern was expressed regarding difficulties in transboundary water cooperation in the Irtysh River Basin, shared by Russia, Kazakhstan, China and Mongolia, and the situation in the Ili River Basin which is shared by China and Kazakhstan was also referred to. The IC, without prejudice to any future decision and within the framework of its information gathering function, requested its

---

201 See http://www.unece.org/env/water/damsafety.html, accessed 20 November 2014.

202 See for example David Trilling, 'Tajikistan: World Bank Begins Rogun Data Dump, Recommends Repairs' 2 October 2013, accessed 20 November 2014 at: http://www.eurasianet.org/node/67575.

203 See generally Salman Salman, *The World Bank Policy for Projects on International Waterways: An Historical and Legal Analysis* (The World Bank, Washington DC 2009).

204 See World Bank E2476 V5, Terms of Reference for the Preparation of an Environmental and Social Impact Assessment.

Chair to write a letter to the concerned Parties, Kazakhstan and Russia, enclosing the information provided and the analytical report on the matter presented by the Vice-Chair of the Committee. The letter asked the two Parties for their views on the matter and for any further information that they might consider appropriate, and requested a reply if possible prior to the IC's next meeting.[205]

The third meeting of the IC took place in May 2014 and first considered information provided in relation to transboundary water cooperation in the Irtysh and Ili River Basins. This information was to include technical characteristics of the development in the upstream part of the basins; related monitoring activities and results addressing water quality and quantity, and ecosystems; the impact, if any, of the development on the socioeconomic conditions of the local population; the contribution of related bilateral agreements to addressing the potential impact of development; and the related mitigation measures actual or intended. The IC decided to request Kazakhstan and Russia for their views and further information, after government consultations with China.[206]

c. Capacity building

The first item on the work plan for 2013–2015 for the *Water Convention* is support to implementation and accession. This is stated to include legal and technical assistance to build on guidance documents already produced. It will also include support to Parties and non-Parties to 'prevent or manage existing or potential conflicts regarding transboundary waters, and support to implementation and compliance through the Implementation Committee'.[207] Activities include those in central Asia/Aral Sea Basin (water quality, dam safety, institutional development and capacity building), in the Chu and Talas Basins, and Afghan-Tajik transboundary

---

[205] Meeting of the Parties, Implementation Committee, Second meeting Geneva 12 December 2013, Report of the Implementation Committee on its second meeting, ECE/MP.WAT/IC/2013/4, 13 January 2014, paras. 4–6.

[206] Meeting of the Parties, Implementation Committee, Third meeting Bologna 15 May 2014, Report of the Implementation Committee on its third meeting, ECE/MP.WAT/IC/2014/2, 18 June 2014, paras. 5–9.

[207] Meeting of the Parties Sixth session Rome, 28–30 November 2012, Items 4 and 9 of the provisional agenda, Review of past activities and discussion of future activities in the different areas of work. Programme of work for 2013–2015, terms of reference of bodies established to implement it and resources needed for its implementation. Draft programme of work for 2013–2015, prepared by the Bureau, ECE/MP.WAT/2012/L.1, 19 September 2012, 8.

waters (monitoring and assessment).[208] The second item on the work plan is the EU Water Initiative and the NPDs,[209] with the objective of strengthening governance and applying IWRM. Apart from Uzbekistan, all central Asian states are included.

One of the most significant capacity building activities in recent years has been organised jointly by the UNECE and the German Agency for International Cooperation (GIZ), and is the programme known as the 'Regional Dialogue and Cooperation on Water Resources Management in Central Asia'.[210] The first phase was completed at the end of 2011, with synergies developed between activities and the NPDs. An important outcome of this work was the significant UNECE publication discussed above: *Strengthening Water Management and Transboundary Water Cooperation in Central Asia: The Role of UNECE Environmental Conventions*.[211] The second phase of the project continued between 2013 and 2014. This aimed to improve the capacity of IFAS and modernise its legal basis, enhance the capacity of central Asian governments to apply international water law, and to improve the application of the principles of IWRM) at the river basin and regional levels.

Examples of specific recent capacity building efforts in the region include the UNECE helping Kyrgyzstan to improve its understanding of international water law,[212] supporting the modernisation of water legislation in Tajikistan,[213] and supporting Afghan-Tajik cooperation on

---

208 Ibid, 8–9.

209 United Nations Economic Commission for Europe, *The European Union Water Initiative: National Policy Dialogues – Achievements and Lessons Learned* (United Nations 2013), ECE/MP.WAT/38.

210 German Agency for International Cooperation, *Programme Documentation 2009–2011 – Transboundary Water Management in Central Asia Programme* (undated). This contains details of the three pilot project clusters that formed the programme.

211 Above n. 25.

212 Accessed 20 November 2014 at http://www.unece.org/unece-main/info-resources/presscurrent-press-h/environment/2013/unece-helps-kyrgyzstan-to-improve-understanding-of-international-water-law/unece-helps-kyrgyzstan-to-improve-understanding-of-international-water-law.html.

213 Accessed 20 November 2014 at http://www.unece.org/unece-main/info-resources/presscurrent-press-h/environment/2013/unece-supports-moderniza tion-of-water-legislation-in-tajikistan/unece-supports-modernization-of-water-legis lation-in-tajikistan.html.

environment and hydrology in the Amu Darya Basin.[214] Finally, in relation to Kazakhstan as an example of the current relevance of the treaty in Asia, a Workshop on Legal, Institutional and Technical Aspects of Managing Transboundary Groundwaters was held in late May 2012.[215] This was significant given the later promulgation of the non-binding guidance for the implementation of the Convention with regard to groundwater and facilitating the application of the principles of the Convention to transboundary groundwaters. The guidance aims to improve transboundary water cooperation with regard to groundwater and strengthen integrated management of transboundary surface waters and groundwaters.[216]

VII.2 Protocol

a. Capacity building

None of the central Asian states are Parties to the *Water and Health Protocol*, so this very brief paragraph focuses attention on capacity building in this area. As a recent example, on 21 June 2013 the first meeting of the high-level Steering Committee of the NPD on water was held in Kazakhstan. As a result of this, it was agreed to form an expert group to begin an analysis into the benefits of joining the *Protocol on Water and Health,* as a first considered step towards accession.[217]

---

[214] Accessed 20 November 2014 at http://www.unece.org/unece-main/info-resources/presscurrent-press-h/environment/2012/unece-supports-afghan-tajik-cooperation-to-address-severe-floods-vulnerable-ecosystems-and-climate-change-impacts-in-amu-darya-basin/unece-supports-afghan-tajik-cooperation-to-address-severe-floods-vulnerable-ecosystems-and-climate-change-impacts-in-amu-darya-basin.html.

[215] Accessed 20 November 2014 at http://www.unece.org/index.php?id=29751.

[216] UNECE, *Model Provisions on Transboundary Groundwaters* (United Nations 2014), ECE/MP.WAT/40.

[217] Accessed 20 November 2014 at http://www.unece.org/unece-main/info-resources/presscurrent-press-h/environment/2013/unece-launches-national-policy-dialogue-on-water-in-kazakhstan/unece-launches-national-policy-dialogue-on-water-in-kazakhstan.html.

VIII. AIR POLLUTION CONVENTION AND ITS PROTOCOLS

VIII.1 Convention

a. Implementation and compliance

Kazakhstan and Kyrgyzstan are the only Parties to this Convention. As indicated in Chapter 7, there is no provision for NIR data generally to be submitted by the Parties, which makes evaluation of implementation efforts difficult, as this is therefore limited to emissions data. In 2013 Kyrgyzstan indicated that it had introduced measures to implement the Convention,[218] and also submitted its EMEP emissions data on time.[219] In 2014 Kazakhstan reported that some measures had been taken to reduce air pollution under the Convention,[220] including policies to implement best available technology use, promote a 'green economy', and limit vehicle emissions.[221] However, Kazakhstan's emissions reporting has been less satisfactory, as the required data has not always been submitted on time or in complete form.[222]

Ongoing implementation efforts in Kazakhstan are being hampered by a lack of understanding of Convention requirements and objectives by government officials, the complexity of the implementation requirements, low levels of expertise in the area, a lack of funding, and frequent

---

[218] A V Romanov, 'Facilitating implementation and ratification of CLRTAP Protocols in the Eastern Europe, Caucasus and Central Asian countries (EECCA Project)', *Report to Workshop to promote the ratification of the protocols under the LRTAP Convention across the entire UNECE region*, 4–5 March 2014, Oslo.

[219] European Environment Agency/Centre on Emission Inventories and Projections (2013), 'Inventory Review 2013: Review of emission data reported under the LRTAP Convention and NEC Directive', Fig. 1, Status of official submissions to the CLRTAP in 2013, 12.

[220] Irina Eserkepova, 'Review of a Situation on Heavy Metals and Plans on Ratification of CLRTAP Protocols in Kazakhstan', Report to Workshop to promote the ratification of the protocols under the LRTAP Convention across the entire UNECE region, 4–5 March 2014, Oslo.

[221] Ibid.

[222] In 2013, Kazakhstan failed to submit its emissions data: European Environment Agency/Centre on Emission Inventories and Projections (2013), 'Inventory Review 2013: Review of emission data reported under the LRTAP Convention and NEC Directive', 34. Subsequently, Kazakhstan, Azerbaijan and others were 'encouraged to make efforts to improve the regularity and completeness of their reporting'.

departmental restructuring.[223] These problems are common to those being experienced by other central Asian countries, where environmental considerations are displaced by a strong focus on economic development. In 2013, Kazakhstan and Kyrgyzstan both requested further support from the UNECE in developing national emission inventories and in other areas, such as revising existing legislation and policy.[224]

As neither Kazakhstan nor Kyrgyzstan has ratified any of the protocols (below), their compliance obligations are limited to the Convention itself. No formal submissions in relation to non-compliance by Kazakhstan or Kyrgyzstan have been made to the Secretariat to date. As mentioned above, where Kazakhstan has failed to submit emissions data on time as required under the Convention, this has resulted only in an exhortation to comply fully with the requirement in future.[225]

VIII.2 Convention and Protocol

a. Capacity building

Whilst both Kazakhstan and Kyrgyzstan acceded to the Convention over a decade ago, Tajikistan, Turkmenistan and Uzbekistan chose not to. In 2011 Tajikistan indicated that it had ‘long term plans for accession to the LRTAP Convention’,[226] and Uzbekistan stated that the issue of the Convention was ‘being discussed with relevant Ministries and Agencies’.[227] In 2009 Turkmenistan also indicated an interest in becoming a Party, although this is yet to happen.[228] Uzbekistan has been conducting preparatory work for accession, and has participated in activities, including attending recent sessions of the Executive Body and hosting a workshop on national emission inventories in 2013.[229] Uzbekistan has requested future assistance from the UNECE in analysing the conformity

---

223 Above n. 220.

224 Report of the Executive Body on its thirty-second session, ECE/EB.AIR/122, 9–13 December 2013, 11.

225 Above n. 219, 34.

226 Report of the 1st Session of the EECCA Coordinating Group, to the 48th Session of the Working Group of Strategies and Review, 11–15 April 2011, Geneva, 2–3.

227 Ibid.

228 United Nations, *Clearing the Air: 30th Anniversary of the Convention on Long-range Transboundary Air Pollution* (2009) 14.

229 Above n. 224, 11.

of its legislative, institutional and financial frameworks with the standards under the Convention, assessing the need to revise existing legislation, and conducting a cost-benefit analysis.[230] These efforts appear to reflect a genuine commitment on the part of Uzbekistan to accede to the Convention and its protocols in the short- to medium-term.

Until very recently there has been a general lack of involvement in Convention activities by central Asian countries, going back over the past three decades. This may reflect a degree of indifference by the UNECE to the role of the region in managing transboundary air pollution. However, in recent years the UNECE has recognised that 'the active involvement of the countries of Eastern Europe, the Caucasus and Central Asia [EECCA] [...] is imperative to the regional cohesiveness and effectiveness of the Convention on Long-range Transboundary Air Pollution'.[231] It notes that these countries 'occupy extensive territories and substantially contribute to the overall atmospheric air pollution of the UNECE region'.[232]

To address these difficulties, the UNECE has now prioritised measures to ensure the implementation and ratification of the Convention and Protocols by its member states in central Asia and the rest of the EECCA area. To this end, the UNECE's Action Plan for Eastern Europe, Caucasus and Central Asia (EECCA Action Plan) contains four key objectives:

- To raise the political profile of the Convention and its activities in the region;
- To promote ratification of the Convention and key Protocols (the EMEP Protocol, the two 1998 Aarhus Protocols and the 1999 Gothenburg Protocol);
- To increase cooperation and the exchange of information through an expansion of modelling and monitoring activities; and
- To support the involvement of Central Asian countries in the activities of the Convention.[233]

---

230 Above n. 224, 11.

231 See United Nations Economic Commission for Europe, *Capacity Building Activities*, accessed 20 November 2014 at: http://www.unece.org/environmental-policy/treaties/air-pollution/capacity-building-activities.

232 Executive Body, Establishment of a Coordinating Group on the Promotion of Actions Towards Implementation of the Convention in Eastern Europe, the Caucasus and Central Asia, Decision 2010/17, ECE/EB.AIR/106/Add.1 (2010) 1.

233 United Nations Economic Commission for Europe, Working Group on Strategies and Review, Revised Action Plan for Eastern Europe, Caucasus and

The Coordinating Group on Promotion of Actions towards Implementation of the Convention in the EECCA (EECCA Coordinating Group) was created by the Executive Body in 2010, and is led by Russia. The purpose is to assist EECCA countries with preparations to accede to the Convention and its Protocols. Measures that are being used to achieve this goal include helping individual countries to develop national action plans,[234] carry out emissions monitoring and reporting, and conduct pilot studies that apply emissions reduction technology in particular industrial sectors.[235]

In addition to these specific projects in individual central Asian countries, the Executive Body has instigated significant revisions to the *AEO Protocol* and both Aarhus Protocols in recent years,[236] to encourage more extensive ratification and implementation, in particular by those Parties with economies in transition. A concerted effort has been made to make these Protocols more 'attractive' to such Parties, by introducing more flexible emissions reduction targets and implementation measures that allow for different economic circumstances.[237] Greater provision has also been made for financial, technical and scientific assistance by established Convention Parties, particularly through the efforts of the EECCA Coordinating Group.[238]

In relation to the protocols specifically, none of the central Asian countries have signed any of them. In 2011 Kyrgyzstan admitted that it

---

Central Asia, ECE/EB.AIR/WG.5/2007/17, 6 July 2007. The original Action Plan was drawn up in 2005.

[234] For example, the UNECE project, Capacity Building for Air Quality Management and the Application of Clean Coal Combustion Technologies in Central Asia, 2004–2007, 9–10. The project involved defining the 'major requirements and legislative measures for meeting obligations under the [CLR-TAP] protocols' for a selected Central Asian country (Kazakhstan), and drawing up a detailed National Programme for meeting obligations under those protocols, together with an Implementation Plan containing specific steps and a timetable for implementing the National Programme.

[235] Ibid.

[236] See for example Decision 2011/1 on Review and revision of protocols, ECE/EB.AIR/109/Add.1; Decision 2012/1 (AEO Protocol amendments), ECE/EB.AIR/111/Add.1, Decision 2012/5 (Heavy Metals Protocol amendments), ECE/EB.AIR/113/Add.1.

[237] See for example, Report of the 1st Session of the EECCA Coordinating Group, to the 48th Session of the Working Group of Strategies and Review, 11–15 April 2011, Geneva, 4–5.

[238] See for example, Executive Body, Report on Activities of the EECCA Coordinating Group in 2012, Informal Document No. 16, 31st Session of the Executive Body, Geneva, 11–13 December 2012.

had 'no certain plans on accession to the protocols'. By contrast, Kazakhstan declared that 'efforts [had] been made on preparation and accession to [the LRTAP] protocols',[239] and accession to four Protocols was being planned for 2014.[240] In general, and with the important exception of Kazakhstan, the initial response of the central Asian countries to the Convention and its Protocols has been muted and largely non-committal.

In 2010, a joint project was launched by Kazakhstan, Belarus and Russia to implement and ratify the *Heavy Metals Protocol*, *POPs Protocol* and *AEO Protocol*.[241] Key aims of the project were to develop national air pollution strategies, as well as introduce best available technologies, emissions inventories and an emissions reduction policy framework for the most harmful pollutants.[242] The project was completed in 2013, although further capacity-building activities, such as the provision of technical assistance, are being undertaken to enhance the ability of central Asian countries to implement the Convention and key protocols.[243] In 2014, Kazakhstan's representative reported to the UNECE that a proposal to accede to the *AEO Protocol* would be made to the Government.[244]

It is possible to make some early observations in relation to the current influence of the Convention and Protocols in central Asia, and to draw some cautious conclusions on the potentially wider application in the Asian region generally. First, the work being undertaken by the EECCA Coordinating Group to prepare central Asian countries for ratification and implementation of the Convention and key Protocols represents a significant step in awareness-raising and capacity-building. If the initiatives are successful in central Asia, they will provide a useful blueprint for possible extension of the Convention to other countries in the region. Although the adaptation of the Convention's complex legal structure to

---

239 Above n. 237, 2–3.

240 Nadia Karmanova, 'The EECCA Coordinating Group', Presentation to the 27th Meeting of the ICP Materials Task Force, Prague, 6–8 April 2011, 4. As at mid-2014, these accessions were yet to be made.

241 UNECE, 'The Russian Federation, Belarus and Kazakhstan launch joint project to combat air pollution', Press release, 14 April 2010, accessed 20 November 2014 at http://www.unece.org/press/pr2010/10env_p13e.html.

242 Ibid.

243 Above n. 224.

244 Above n. 220.

central Asian countries is proving difficult,[245] those countries have indicated some willingness to agree to binding obligations.[246]

IX. CONCLUSIONS

Central Asia is in many ways an ideal subregion to test the application of the UNECE agreements. It contains numerous environmental and resources issues, which are both significant and transboundary in nature; it also contends with a legacy of inadequate domestic environmental law, and outdated environmental planning and management processes. The states of the subregion are also varied in population, resources and development; while at the same time (whatever improvements may have been made) broadly homogeneous in relation to a prevailing culture of secrecy, corruption and political authoritarianism, under which opposition to the various regimes has often been brutally suppressed.

Water is unquestionably the most significant issue in each of the states, with both supply and quality components. Tension between the upstream states of Tajikistan and Kyrgyzstan on one hand, and the downstream states of Uzbekistan and Turkmenistan on the other, relates to the dam building activities of the former for hydro-electricity generation, at the expense of the latter for irrigated agriculture. This explains why most of the interstate relations outside the UNECE regime have concerned water. If it comes into force, the *Framework Convention* would potentially be a means of addressing other environmental concerns in the region, including land degradation.

Many of the UNECE agreements relate to transboundary waters, particularly the *Water* and *Industrial Accidents Conventions*, and also the *EIA Convention*, so the UNECE is well placed to contribute its treaty-making endeavours in the subregion. The *Public Participation Convention* has a similarly close relationship with the *EIA Convention*, as the *Water* and *Industrial Accidents Conventions* do with one another. It is therefore – potentially at least – additionally a very powerful instrument in the subregion; first, given the link between environmental and human rights it provides, and second, because it is the key to overcoming the historical inadequacies of the OVOS/SER systems in central Asia that

245 See for example 'Taking International Air Pollution Policies into the Future: Main Conclusions from the Saltsjöbaden V Workshop 24–26 June 2013; and 'Report of the Working Group on Strategies and Review on its fifty-first session', 30 April–3 May 2013, ECE/EB.AIR/WG.5/110 (Annex III).

246 For example Kazakhstan, see above.

have required much domestic law to be overhauled. Last but not least, the *Air Pollution Convention*, while more of a stand-alone treaty than the other four, and more principles-based, does have a relationship with the others. As the first of the UNECE conventions, and with a heavy emphasis on consultation and information exchange between the Parties, its governance structures have been a precedent for the other agreements that have chosen to emulate them, which include its working groups and task forces addressing various matters.

Finally, in connection with being able to contribute to answering the central research question: 'What is the current and potential combined contribution of the UNECE environmental agreements to the development of transboundary environmental governance in Asia and globally?' there are major hurdles as indicated. A glance at Table 8.1 above indicates that Kazakhstan is the only central Asian state that is Party to all five treaties, so it is only possible to comment on the combined significance of all of the treaties in Kazakhstan, potentially to draw lessons with respect to the other states in the subregion. Of the treaties themselves, none have been universally ratified by all five states, with the *Public Participation Convention* (four Parties) and the *Water Convention* (three Parties) the most acceded to. None of the protocols has yet secured any ratifications at all.

As to what Kazakhstan's experience is able to offer the other four states, the major limitation comes from Kazakhstan's untypical position as clearly the wealthiest state in the subregion, with its interests increasingly in the energy sector, and in the Caspian Sea. As such, its experience, while also connected with water issues and the Aral Sea (which it shares with Uzbekistan), has also been motivated by different concerns to the other states. Chapter 9, the final chapter in this book, looks more broadly at the central research question. It explores what the treaties and protocols can offer other Asian states, and examines the significance of the global application of many of the agreements. The experience of the central Asian states with implementation, compliance and capacity building that have been a key feature of Chapter 8 will also be considered in the concluding chapter. This is because their effectiveness has been found to depend as much on whether a NIR process or NCP is present, as on the willingness of the state concerned to abide by the requirements in question. These are broader structural issues that are relevant to all states, although the experience described and analysed in this chapter will be part of the considerations that follow and conclude the book.

9. Conclusions

I. INTRODUCTION

This book has analysed the potential and actual contribution of the UNECE environmental agreements to the development of transboundary environmental governance in Asia, and, as a result of the global application of many of the agreements, beyond. This final chapter summarises the findings of each of the preceding chapters; first in relation to each of the parts of the book, transboundary environmental governance, treaties and protocols, and combined effect and outlook; second regarding the relationship between the UNECE agreements and other Asian and MEAs considered in Chapter 2 and Chapter 8 (central Asia specifically); and third sketching an outline of what areas of transboundary environmental governance are absent from these regimes, which could be considered for future UNECE treaty development.

II. TRANSBOUNDARY ENVIRONMENTAL GOVERNANCE

In Part I transboundary environmental governance was defined, distinguished from related concepts, and situated in the framework of analysis – the Asian region. The relevance of Asia to the UNECE is because parts of Asia are geographically within the UNECE region (Russia and the eight states of the Caucasus and central Asia, and also Turkey and Israel in western Asia). It is also because the dominant environmental issues and governance concerns in Asia are of clear relevance to the content of the agreements; for example the potential for water and air pollution, and industrial accidents as a result of rapid development.

Chapter 1 provided examples of typical environmental issues in the region and explained how the development of transboundary environmental governance has been the focus. Through illustrating the application of the UNECE transboundary environmental agreements in Asia, there is no question that governance has developed – and improved – as a result, whatever political setbacks continue to dog progress. The agreements have become embedded in the domestic law of the Parties to them, and in turn, through giving effect to the obligations they contain, the law has triggered behavioural change. This is seen for example with respect to making inroads into the former Soviet culture of secrecy and notions of expertise; it is also demonstrated through the application of decision-making procedures to transboundary environmental issues, and improved outcomes with respect to the environment itself.

The first chapter explained why Asia, the UNECE and implementation and compliance are the focus of the book. In each of Chapters 3–8 (in particular in Chapter 8), these foci were demonstrated by examining the status of the agreements for the Asian UNECE members, non-members who have expressed an interest in acceding the agreements, and others who may benefit from the ability to do so. The actions of the UNECE in promulgating the benefits of membership, encouraging application in domestic law, adherence to the treaty obligations and through a wide range of capacity building activities, has been emphasised throughout.

It also defined transboundary environmental governance in Asia with respect to current scholarship and via topical examples. This highlighted the richness of approaches to which the UNECE agreements are a valuable contribution, not only in Asia, but also in Europe and Eurasia, where most UNECE members are located. These approaches range from strictly legal interpretations to links between disciplines, the relationship between different sectors and interests, and between varied stake- and rights-holders. The first chapter also traced developments in transboundary environmental governance – as reported in the literature – that have originated from, and been driven by, various UN bodies, IGOs and other non-state actors.

The role of the UNECE was furthermore outlined in Chapter 1, to be explored again in Chapter 8 specifically with regard to central Asia. It was found that from a history of post-war reconstruction, it has in recent decades – alongside the other regional commissions – focused its efforts upon questions of sustainable development, including environmental policy and protection. It was also emphasised that the CEP plays a key role in enhancing environmental governance and transboundary cooperation, and strengthening implementation of regional commitments, which are made in accordance with the five-pronged approach outlined. It was found that the role of NGOs, both generally as observers of CEP and other treaty meetings, and as reporters and instigators of Parties' failings under treaty NCPs, has been clearly acknowledged and supported over this time.

Finally, the significance of implementation and compliance was emphasised, with the connection between legal application and practical effect outlined. The NIR processes and NCPs in the agreements were identified, and their purpose and function previewed in general terms, regarded as an essential part of any modern treaty regime. The former Soviet states were highlighted as presenting challenges for the application of particularly the *EIA Convention*[1] and *Public Participation Convention*,[2] to be seen further in the case study in Chapter 8. Parallels with other authoritarian states in Asia beyond the UNECE region noted, suggest the experience of the former Soviet states that are part of EECCA is likely to be shared elsewhere. For example in strict Islamic states, China or North Korea this will certainly be so if a reluctance to reform and allow access to information, public participation and access to justice continues.

In Chapter 2, the analysis turned specifically to institutions and regimes outside the UNECE. The purpose was to enable comparisons between the responsibilities of other bodies and treaties in Asia on one hand, and the role of the UNECE on the other. Following a summary of the findings here, comparisons of note are commented upon in section V below. Institutions and regimes were distinguished because while the latter also include the former, the former often exist on a stand-alone basis. UNEP for example, is a sponsor of numerous MEAs, but it is not a 'regime' in itself; however, the MEAs outlined, or collections of them, are very much environmental regimes. For example the *Convention on Biological Diversity*,[3] or the conservation conventions as a whole, contain not only the text of an agreement with supporting guidelines, but also detailed institutional structures for their effective operation, typically a COP or MOP with subsidiary institutions thereunder.

In relation to the role of the UNECE, it was noted that despite the focus of this book upon the environmental agreements it is responsible for, the UNECE is also involved in many other (often, but not always) related areas. These include economic integration and cooperation in environmental policy, forests, housing and land management, statistics, energy, trade and transport. It was found that there are a few other IGOs – both global and regional – that also have this breadth to their activities, notably UNESCO and ASEAN. While the *breadth* of operation of the

---

1 Convention on Environmental Impact Assessment in a Transboundary Context (Espoo, 25 February 1991), 30 ILM (1991) 802, in force 27 June 1997.

2 Convention on Access to Information, Public Participation in Decision-Making and Access to Justice in Environmental Matters (Aarhus, 25 June 1998) 2161 UNTS 447, in force 30 October 2001.

3 Convention on Biological Diversity (Rio de Janeiro, 22 May 1992), 31 ILM 822, in force 29 December 1993.

UNECE is not unique in its involvement in these areas therefore, it is, however, true to say that the *depth* of its efforts is certainly so, with no comparable institutions able to make such claims. The evidence of producing five detailed environmental treaties and 12 related protocols confirms this to be the case. This is an impressive, unparalleled record of treaty making and regime building bar none.

The institutions highlighted in the second chapter include numerous UN bodies: primarily UNEP, UNDP, GEF, WHO, and the ICJ; also the two regional commissions operating in Asia, UNESCWA and UNESCAP. They also include specialist environmental institutions, in particular the IUCN which is itself a substantial treaty sponsor; and the MDBs/IFIs, of which the ADB is focused on Asia. In regard to the MDBs/IFIs, there is clearly considerable potential and practice for these bodies to contribute to improved transboundary environmental governance where, as noted in Chapter 8, states may not be obliged to adhere to treaty commitments, simply because they are not Parties and the commitments do not apply to them directly. This was considered by the *EIA Convention* MOP at its sixth session, and the *SEA Protocol*[4] MOP at its second session, for example. Discussions held there indicated that countries beyond the UNECE:

> … shared similar challenges in assessing and mitigating the environmental impacts of economic activities, in particular when they extended beyond national boundaries. The presentations also showcased the experience of IFIs in applying environmental assessments within and beyond the ECE region. Participants found the exchange between the regions to be a mutually enriching experience, paving the way for the future globalization of the Convention and the Protocol. They also appreciated the discussion on the role that the IFIs could play in promoting the application of the treaties beyond the ECE region through capacity-building activities.[5]

---

[4] Protocol on Strategic Environmental Assessment to the Convention on Environmental Impact Assessment in a Transboundary Context (Kiev, 21 May 2003) unreported, in force 11 July 2010.

[5] Economic Commission for Europe Meeting of the Parties to the Convention on Environmental Impact Assessment in a Transboundary Context Sixth session, Meeting of the Parties to the Convention on Environmental Impact Assessment in a Transboundary Context serving as the Meeting of the Parties to the Protocol on Strategic Environmental Assessment Second session Geneva, 2–5 June 2014, Report of the Meeting of the Parties to the Convention on its sixth session and of the Meeting of the Parties to the Convention serving as the Meeting of the Parties to the Protocol on its second session, para. 42.

In regard to the non-UNECE transboundary environmental regimes currently applicable in Asia, Chapter 2 highlighted the distinction between MEAs that apply in Asia as just one region of operation, and the subregional agreements that are applicable to Asian subregions. The chapter grouped these into the conservation, waste, and climate change/ ozone protection conventions. The example of the *Convention on Biological Diversity* – the key conservation convention in relation to the first category – is cited above alongside numerous other related treaties beginning as early as 1971 with the adoption of the *Wetlands Convention.*[6] In relation to the second, the example of the *Caspian Sea Convention*[7] is notable for the breadth of Asian states Parties (Azerbaijan, Iran, Kazakhstan, Turkmenistan and Russia). This is essential given the strategic location of this inland sea at the intersection of western, central and northern Asia. The *Mekong*,[8] *ASEAN*[9] and *Tumen*[10] Agreements were identified as the other subregional agreements operating in Asia, and section V below draws comparisons between these and the UNECE agreements that relate to them.

III. TREATIES AND PROTOCOLS

Part II of the book examined in detail the UNECE treaties and protocols individually while noting the close connections between them (which are

---

[6] Convention on Wetlands of International Importance, especially as Waterfowl Habitat (Ramsar, 2 February 1971), 11 ILM 963, in force 21 December 1975.

[7] Framework Convention for the Protection of the Marine Environment of the Caspian Sea (Tehran, 4 November 2003), unreported, in force 12 August 2006.

[8] Agreement on the Cooperation for the Sustainable Development of the Mekong River Basin (Chiang Rai, 5 April 1995), unreported, in force 5 April 1995.

[9] Association of South East Asian Nations, Agreement on the Conservation of Nature and Natural Resources, opened for signature 9 July 1985, 15 EPL 64 (1985), not in force; and Association of South East Asian Nations, Agreement on Transboundary Haze Pollution (Kuala Lumpur, 10 June 2002), unreported, in force 2003.

[10] Agreement on the Establishment of the Tumen River Area Development Coordination Committee (New York, 6 December 1995), unreported, in force 6 December 1995; and Agreement on the Establishment of the Consultative Commission for the Development of the Tumen River Economic Development Area and Northeast Asia (New York, 6 December 1995), unreported, in force 6 December 1995.

discussed in section IV below). Chapter 3 analysed the most recent of the treaties, with cross-cutting provisions for access to information, public participation in decision making and access to justice in environmental matters. As noted there and in Chapter 8, the *Public Participation Convention* has more Asian Parties than any of the other treaties (seven of 47 in total), with all of the states of the Caucasus and central Asia other than Uzbekistan Party to it; Russia has also indicated a willingness to accede. This is highly significant because of the bridge between environmental and human rights that it provides, and in an Asian context this is more so given the challenges for improving current human rights norms as discussed. The treaty is also open to accession by all UN member states, and contains an important obligation to promote the application of its principles within international decision-making processes and international organisations, which is a significant contributor to global environmental governance more broadly.

Reflecting the environment/human rights connection, this treaty contains not only an effective NIR process – as noted by the Secretariat in mid-2013[11] – but it also has the strongest NCP of all of the agreements, with only the *Water and Health Protocol* also providing for public submissions.[12] With detailed, transparent procedures, including the reporting of decisions and their precedent effect, it is to this NCP to which the others in the UNECE agreements look for guidance as they develop or apply procedures of their own. Other procedures of note include the application of the convention's provisions on public participation to GMOs, with the adoption of guidelines to this effect. In relation to the *PRTR Protocol*[13] – which is also open to all UN states – only Israel has acceded to it, in 2013. However, it has been signed by Armenia, Georgia and Tajikistan with other signatories outside Asia, and as noted it adds an important private dimension to the operation of this treaty regime.

---

[11] Aarhus Convention Secretariat, *The Aarhus Convention Reporting Mechanism National Implementation Reports: Experiences and Lessons Learned*, Geneva, 19 June 2013.

[12] See Article 15, Protocol on Water and Health to the Convention on the Protection and Use of Transboundary Watercourses and Lakes (London, 17 June 1999), UNTS 2331, 202, in force 4 August 2005.

[13] Protocol on Pollutant Release and Transfer Registers to the Convention on Access to Information, Public Participation in Decision-Making and Access to Justice in Environmental Matters (Kiev, 21 May 2003), unreported, in force 8 October 2009.

Chapter 4 evaluated what has become the international treaty regime for transboundary EIA, the *EIA Convention*. While currently there are only four Asian Parties, Armenia, Azerbaijan, Kazakhstan and Kyrgyzstan (out of 45), it is now potentially open to a global membership, following the ratification and entry into force of the first amendment which has enabled this. Significant consideration has already been given in the literature to the potential for a global agreement on transboundary EIA. Although there were acknowledged political challenges, the *EIA Convention* was always the most likely candidate.[14] Added to this is the general international law of the ICJ (and the jurisprudence of other international courts) which has confirmed that the principle – if not the content – of transboundary EIA is now accepted.

Notable provisions for the effectiveness of this treaty are the NIR process and the NCP. The reporting process will only become obligatory upon sufficient ratifications and entry into force of the second amendment, which is still awaited. However, as there are currently 24 Parties, (the same number that preceded the entry into force of the first amendment), it is extremely likely that the second amendment will follow close on the heels of the first. Nonetheless, outcomes of the current reporting process – which puts the onus on the MOP to require Parties to continuously review progress – indicates progress with implementation. This is despite issues remaining with definitions, the distinct nature of transboundary consultations and post-project analysis. Concerning the NCP, submissions can be made by Parties against one another or on the initiative of the IC; the lack of a public submissions procedure is, however, a weakness. Other procedures of interest include the inquiry procedure for determining whether significant environmental effects are likely, and the *SEA Protocol* which, however, currently has just one Asian Party, Armenia (from a total of 26). As with the

---

[14] John H Knox, 'Assessing the Candidates for a Global Treaty on Transboundary Environmental Impact Assessment' (2003) 12 *New York University Environmental Law Journal* 153; Kees Bastmeijer and Timo Koivurova, 'Conclusions: Globalisation of Transboundary Environmental Impact Assessment', in Kees Bastmeijer and Timo Koivurova (eds), *Theory and Practice of Transboundary Environmental Impact Assessment* (Martinus Nijhoff, Leiden 2008) 376; and Timo Koivurova, 'Could the Espoo Convention become a Global Regime for Environmental Impact Assessment and Strategic Environmental Assessment?', in Robin Warner and Simon Marsden (eds), *Transboundary Environmental Governance: Inland, Coastal and Marine Perspectives* (Ashgate Publishing, Farnham 2012) 323.

Convention, however, interest has been expressed by a handful of Asian states in also joining the Protocol, which is open to all UN states.

Chapter 5 analyses the *Industrial Accidents Convention* which like the *EIA Convention* has just four Asian Parties (out of 41), and is not open to members outside of the UNECE. Unlike other treaties, the potential for this is also limited, with little pressure from existing Parties for this to happen. However, this is open for consideration at the forthcoming MOP,[15] which has been no doubt triggered by the fact that three of the five treaties, (and three of the linked protocols), are now global. It was seen from the conclusions in the fifth chapter that this treaty is the weakest of the UNECE treaties, with lack of a potential global membership being one of the reasons.

Further reasons why the *Industrial Accidents Convention* is relatively weak in comparison with other UNECE treaties are that while there is a NIR process, data is not publicly available; and of great importance, the lack of a NCP is a major weakness of this treaty, towards which the MOP is now directing its attention.[16] Another matter which will improve this treaty is with respect to public participation, which is also flagged for consideration at the forthcoming MOP, again no doubt in response to the first amendment of the *EIA Convention* now ensuring this is so.[17] Finally, the *Civil Liability Protocol*,[18] while potentially a vital global legal instrument to address compensatory issues under both this treaty and the *Water Convention*,[19] also appears likely to take some considerable time to be accepted and come into force.

Chapter 6 is focused on the *Water Convention*. There are five Asian Parties to this treaty: Azerbaijan, Kazakhstan, Russia, Turkmenistan and

---

15 The Eighth Meeting of the Conference of the Parties to the Industrial Accidents Convention will be held from 3–5 December 2014 in Geneva. A key decision to be taken is stated to be 'Consideration with regard to the possible opening of the Convention to UN member States beyond the ECE region.' See http://www.unece.org/env/teia/cop8.html, accessed 20 November 2014.

16 Ibid, where it is stated that 'Decisions on which issues to prepare elements for guidance by the Conference of the Parties, comprising compliance and land-use planning'.

17 Ibid, where it is stated that 'Decisions with regard to the provisions and issues on which work shall proceed to draft an amendment to the Convention, comprising public participation'.

18 Protocol on Civil Liability and Compensation for Damage Caused by the Transboundary Effects of Industrial Accidents on Transboundary Waters (Kiev, 21 May 2003), not in force.

19 Convention on the Protection and Use of Transboundary Watercourses and Lakes (Helsinki, 17 March 1992), 31 ILM (1992) 1312, in force 6 October 1996.

Uzbekistan (out of a total of 39); several other Asian states have, however, indicated an interest in joining. This is now potentially possible as – like the *EIA Convention* following the ratification of an amendment – it is open to all UN member states subject to further ratifications by existing Parties. As noted in the conclusions to Chapter 6, the presence of so many transboundary watercourses and international lakes in Asia makes this treaty particularly significant, and despite the coming into force of the *International Water Convention* in 2014,[20] this is likely to become more so given the more detailed nature of the obligations in the UNECE treaty. These obligations include requirements for the establishment of joint bodies, and bilateral and multilateral agreements detailing obligations between transboundary watercourse states.

Nonetheless both of these water treaties are, like the *EIA Convention*, additionally significant given the customary international law for cooperation and equitable utilisation that underlies the treaty law. They are also very important because they add value and potential frameworks to the existing water agreements reached between numerous states within the region, for example in central Asia as considered in Chapter 8. In connection with implementation, the failure to include a NIR process in the *Water Convention* is a weakness, although this is currently being considered. The NCP is a recent innovation under this treaty also, although not required under the treaty text. It has rapidly drawn the link between implementation and compliance efforts, in discussing the need for a reporting mechanism and giving consideration to specific allegations of alleged non-compliance. The *Protocol on Water and Health* is, while focused on domestic concerns, furthermore a major contributor to the effectiveness of the water regime. Importantly, it contains a NCP triggered by public submissions as noted above, and it has made significant progress in drawing links with other procedures concerned with health and human rights.

Chapter 7 analyses the *Air Pollution Convention*[21] which, like the *Public Participation Convention*, also has the most Asian Parties (seven), from a total of 51. The Asian Parties are: Armenia, Azerbaijan, Georgia, Kazakhstan, Kyrgyzstan, Russia and Turkey. The first of the UNECE agreements, this is a framework treaty for the reduction and monitoring of emissions, with the associated protocols containing detailed provisions

[20] Convention on the Law of Non-Navigable Uses of International Watercourses (New York, 21 May 1997, by UNGA Res. 51/229), 36 ILM (1997) 700, in force August 2014.

[21] Convention on Long-range Transboundary Air Pollution (Geneva, 13 November 1979), 1302 UNTS 217, in force 16 March 1983.

for the reduction of specific pollutants; additionally providing for research and development, the exchange of information and environmental monitoring. This treaty has been widely acknowledged as a major contributor to transboundary environmental governance in reducing and eliminating these pollutants, with the scientific and technical underpinning a key factor in its success. The protocols contain reporting obligations, and a NCP is also in operation, although the presence of 'systemic barriers' to its effectiveness has recently been highlighted. The major weakness of this treaty is, like the *Industrial Accidents Convention*, a lack of a potential global membership, which is also the case with respect to its associated protocols.

IV. COMBINED EFFECT AND OUTLOOK

Part III of the book – including this concluding Chapter 9 – is focused upon the combined effect and outlook of the agreements. Chapter 8 considered the combined effect of the agreements in central Asia in relation to existing practice, where it was noted that the limited current membership of the agreements, despite voluntary assumption of obligations in the specific instances noted, imposes strict limits upon the evidence that is available of this. While Kazakhstan is the only Party to all of the treaties, drawing lessons from its experience for the other central Asian states, it is, it is suggested, generally unreliable given the difference in its position in relation to the other states. However, the shared experience of the Soviet OVOS/expertise system is one notable aspect that the other states can learn from given the experience of Kazakhstan. This experience is also reported by a few of the others in relation to implementation and compliance with the *Public Participation Convention* and *EIA Convention* in particular.

In relation to the combined effect of the agreements generally, the connections between them are clear evidence of this. The *Public Participation Convention* and *EIA Convention*, for example, have clear links in various aspects of procedure, notably provisions in the former for public participation regarding specific decision-making processes (which are often EIA). The coming into force of the first amendment to the *EIA Convention* – which also strengthens public participation – adds to this linkage; the current consideration being given to strengthening public participation in the *Industrial Accidents Convention* is another example. Similarly, the *Water Convention* and *Industrial Accidents Convention*, which were both adopted at the same time, maintain connections between them, because of the greater likelihood of accidents impacting upon transboundary watercourses, which is often where industrial facilities are located. The fact that these two treaties also share the *Civil Liability Protocol* strengthens this further. The health connection is also easily seen between several of the agreements, notably the *SEA Protocol* and *Water and Health Protocol*, and in the *Air Pollution Convention*.

Another example of the combined effect of the agreements, are the provisions for implementation and compliance, which were a major part of the analysis. These are a key part of the majority of the agreements and enable synergies between the agreements to be enhanced where, for example, more than one agreement may apply to a development project to be regulated by domestic law implementing the agreements. Practice was a significant part of Chapters 3–7, with separate sections noting the role of NIR processes and NCPs. The similarities and differences between the NIR process to evaluate implementation on one hand, and NCP to analyse and report on compliance on the other, have therefore been explained, considered and emphasised in the Asian context.

As indicated, it was noted in these chapters that provision for NIR and NCPs is not comprehensive or uniform. NIR processes are therefore found in only three of the treaties: *Public Participation*, *EIA*, and *Industrial Accidents*, with the reports connected with the latter not being publicly available. In relation to the protocols, the *PRTR*, *SEA* and *Water and Health Protocols* have provision for this, although practice varies. Similarly NCPs are found in four of the treaties currently: *Public Participation*, *EIA*, *Water* and *Air Pollution,* together with the *PRTR*, *SEA* and *Water and Health Protocols*. Procedures however differ, with the public only able to initiate procedures directly in two cases, the *Public Participation Convention*, and under the *Water and Health Protocol*; practice is again also varied, typically depending on length of experience.

Links between the NCPs have recently been established, with the first meeting of the Informal Network of the Chairs of compliance/implementation bodies under the agreements held in Geneva on 25 March 2013.[22] This is a significant development in strengthening the combined effect of the agreements in the area of practice, and has been noted with respect to the work of other MEAs, in particular the example

22 Economic Commission for Europe/Environment, Informal Network of the Chairs of compliance/implementation bodies under the Multilateral Environmental Agreements, First Meeting, Geneva, 25 March 2013, Note prepared by the Chair of the Aarhus Convention Compliance Committee with the assistance of the secretariat.

of the Bystroe Canal development in the Danube Delta.[23] They have also been subject to considerable scholarly inquiry in recent years as noted in Chapter 1 in particular. This coordination between these mechanisms, and focus on dispute avoidance rather than settlement, is consistent with the preferred approach of many states, particularly in the Asian developing world.

Chapter 8 gave some brief thoughts on this in the context of the membership of the agreements in central Asia, and deferred discussion of implementation and compliance more broadly to this chapter. What can be said with some conviction in this regard, is that without a detailed mandated procedure for Parties to report on the implementation of their obligations, the effectiveness of any regime will be found wanting; similarly the absence of an accessible, linked NCP to a reporting process will also seriously impede the ability to follow-up failures of Parties to MEAs, including the UNECE agreements. It is, however, noteworthy that the majority of the UNECE agreements have either chosen at the outset to include these procedures, have subsequently introduced them by amendment, or are actively considering the feasibility of so doing. This is further evidence of the combined effect of the agreements given the precedent value of the experience of one of the agreements for another. For example, the decision of the *Water Convention* to introduce a NCP had close regard to the experience under the other agreements.[24]

In relation to the Asian outlook beyond central Asia, it was seen in Chapters 3–7 that the Caucasus has the greatest experience of the agreements to date. This was noted in the sections on implementation and

---

[23] This concerned a challenge by Romania to Ukraine in relation to Bystroe Canal Project. Three NCPs were invoked: the *EIA Convention* IC, the *Public Participation Convention* CC, and the *Bern Convention* (European Wildlife) Standing Committee. It was a complex case as the site is also listed under *Wetlands* and *World Heritage Conventions* and the UNESCO *Man and Biosphere Programme*. For UNECE involvement see http://www.unece.org/env/eia/implementation/eia_ic_s_1.html (*EIA Convention* IC) and http://www.unece.org/fileadmin/DAM/env/documents/2005/pp/c.1/ece.mp.pp.c1.2005.2.Add.3.e.pdf (*Public Participation Convention* CC), both accessed 20 November 2014. For discussion, see Simon Marsden, 'Non-compliance Procedures in International Environmental Agreements: An Evaluation of Recent Jurisprudence', paper presented to the *Eighteenth Annual ANZSIL Conference, International Law in the Second Decade of the 21st Century: Back to the Future or Business as Usual?* 24–26 June 2010.

[24] Water Convention, Meeting of the Parties, Implementation Committee, First meeting Geneva 5 June 2013, Report of the Implementation Committee at its first meeting, ECE/MP.WAT/IC/2013/2, 29 October 2013, para. II.7.

compliance in these chapters. Also in these chapters, the interest in joining the agreements by various non-UNECE Asian states as well as UNECE states was noted. While the ability of non-UNECE states to accede to several of the agreements is now potentially possible, there remain many challenges to involving other Asian states in the UNECE agreements, and in transboundary environmental governance efforts more broadly. These include the reluctance of many states to cede their national sovereignty to international or regional law,[25] and the significance of engaging China[26] and India – the two major Asian states (in addition to Russia) with large numbers of neighbours. However, the benefits of membership of more than one agreement (within Asia in particular), has been recently commented on by both the UNECE and academic commentators in relation to the *Water Convention*,[27] and firm and persistent advocacy will assist in this task.

In relation to the global outlook, the attractiveness of the UNECE agreements will ultimately depend on whether the issues they address are pertinent to local conditions, and whether there are alternative regimes in place to deal with them. The absence of a requirement for UNECE membership in regard to many of the agreements, however, overcomes a major hurdle for many states. Where practicable and possible, the UNECE promoting the benefits of membership of the agreements via the other regional commissions may be a helpful first step.

---

[25] See Roda Mushkat, 'Creating Regional Environmental Governance Regimes: Implications of Southeast Asian Responses to Transboundary Haze Pollution' (2013) 4 *Washington and Lee Journal of Energy, Climate and Environment* 103, 129, 132.

[26] Patricia Wouters, 'The Yin and Yang of International Water Law: China's Transboundary Water Practice and the Changing Contours of State Sovereignty' (2014) 23(1) *Review of European, Comparative and International Environmental Law* 67; and Simon Marsden, 'Developing Approaches to Transboundary Environmental Impact Assessment in China: Cooperation through the Greater Tumen Initiative and in the Pearl River Delta Region' (2010) 9(2) *Chinese Journal of International Law* 393

[27] United Nations Economic Commission for Europe, *Strengthening Water Management and Transboundary Water Cooperation in Central Asia: The Role of UNECE Environmental Conventions* (United Nations 2011), ECE/MP.WAT/35; and Ruby Moynihan and Bjørn-Oliver Magsig, 'The Rising Role of Regional Approaches to International Water Law: Lessons from the UNECE Water Regime and Himalayan Asia for Strengthening Transboundary Water Cooperation' (2014) *Review of European, Comparative and International Environmental Law* 43.

V. RELATIONSHIP BETWEEN UNECE AGREEMENTS AND OTHER ASIAN MEAS

As discussed in section II of this chapter above, it was noted that Chapter 2 considered other institutions and regimes outside the UNECE regime. In relation to the possibility of non-UNECE states joining the UNECE agreements, and the fact that states will consider all regulatory possibilities available to them, what remains to be considered are the connections between these other institutions and regimes on one hand, and the UNECE treaty regimes on the other. This is important because existing links between them, and familiarity with these regimes, may make it more likely that states will choose to accede to the UNECE agreements in the future. As an example, several Asian agreements concern transboundary EIA or water, and provisions of certain UNECE agreements have in some instances been used as a model for these subregional obligations. There are therefore close links between these requirements and with those found in the *EIA* and *Water Conventions.*

Transboundary EIA procedure in the Mekong, Tumen and Caspian Sea subregions indicates this clearly.[28] The *Mekong Agreement* refers to the 'notifying' or 'notified' states for example, in comparison with the 'Party of origin' and 'affected Party' under the *EIA Convention.* The *Caspian Sea Convention Guidelines* are particularly notable, and explicitly follow the *EIA Convention.* Analysis of experience with the *Mekong Agreement* also recommends adhering to the *EIA Convention* procedures, and future elaboration of the *Tumen Agreement* procedures is very likely to do this, strengthening the case for the *EIA Convention* representing state practice in international law. In relation to water, the *International Water Convention* has, as noted, close links with the *Water Convention.* In a central Asian context, there are also links between the agreements reached between the individual states in the subregion and the *Water Convention.* The *Water Convention* is therefore potentially able to harmonise procedures for the preparation of bilateral and multilateral agreements in this area.

---

28 Simon Marsden, 'Developing Agreements for Transboundary Environmental Impact Assessment and Strategic Environmental Assessment in Asia', in Robin Warner and Simon Marsden (eds), *Transboundary Environmental Governance: Inland, Coastal and Marine Perspectives* (Ashgate Publishing, Farnham 2012) 141.

Since membership of more than one of the conventions by the Parties is common, this also has the advantage of cross-fertilisation of procedures. The *Water Convention* benefits from potentially utilising detailed procedures on transboundary EIA found in the *EIA Convention* for example, which are referred to the *Implementation Guide*.[29] The advantages of building synergies between the treaties, was highlighted in a recent seminar held in central Asia on the *Water Convention*.[30] The status of ratification of selected international agreements relevant to transboundary water management by the countries in central Asia has also recently been summarised to assist with this task.[31]

Kazakhstan is an example of a state with overlapping membership of more than one agreement, and it has experience in relation to all five UNECE treaties and the *Caspian Sea Convention*. Given the recent limitation on membership of the UNECE treaties to UNECE states, it is also most advantageous in an Asian context that membership is being opened to non-UNECE states, many of which are in Asia. With the recent entry into force of the first amendment to the *EIA Convention* for example, states such as Afghanistan, China, Iran, Korea, Mongolia and Vietnam can potentially now accede to this as well as the *Water Convention* should they choose to do so, subject to further ratifications by existing Parties.

VI. FUTURE TREATY MAKING PROSPECTS FOR THE UNECE?

Ensuring existing Parties implement and comply with their obligations under the UNECE agreements, while encouraging further ratifications by UNECE member states, and – where possible and practicable – other UN member states, will remain the priority for the UNECE in the period moving forward. Alongside this, attending to treaty reform to ensure

---

[29] United Nations Economic Commission for Europe, Convention on the Protection and Use of Transboundary Watercourses and Lakes, *Guide to Implementing the Water Convention* (United Nations 2013) 53.

[30] UNECE, Report of the national seminar 'UNECE Water Convention and its Role in International Law', Almaty, Kazakhstan, 18–19 October 2010. See session 3: Building synergies with other legal instruments, 7.

[31] United Nations Economic Commission for Europe Convention on the Protection and Use of Transboundary Watercourses and International Lakes, *Second Assessment of Transboundary Rivers, Lakes and Groundwaters* (United Nations 2011), Annex III, 424. This includes the UNECE treaties and protocols and other MEAs.

regimes meet and achieve best practice – such as establishing effective reporting and compliance procedures – is a necessity. What remains to be done is to note that while the desire for new MEAs may have waned in the international community – with current efforts focused on implementation and compliance (and enforcement) of existing obligations – other problems have not gone away and still need an effective international response.

How to regulate large scale land clearances for example, such as in Malaysia and Indonesia where palm oil plantations have been established, with related burning-off impacting neighbouring states, may be of global significance despite the efforts of ASEAN;[32] in other parts of the world such as the Brazilian Amazon, land has, for example, also been (illegally) cleared to establish livestock industries or grow crops for biofuel rather than domestic consumption.[33] Similarly, the issue of historical pollution/site contamination is one that is common to many states globally, and suggests an international response is outstanding.[34] The review of existing MEAs and subregional arrangements in Asia in Chapter 2 of this book indicates that there are many environmental challenges not addressed by either the UNECE or other bodies. Whether the UNECE chooses to engage in further treaty building efforts in these or other areas is perhaps unlikely. However, effective regulatory responses are still needed if transboundary environmental governance in Asia – or other parts of the world – is to effectively contend with these numerous outstanding challenges.

---

[32] Association of South East Asian Nations, *Agreement on Transboundary Haze Pollution* (Kuala Lumpur, 10 June 2002), unreported, in force 2003.

[33] See, for example, http://www.theguardian.com/environment/2014/oct/19/amazon-deforestation-satellite-data-brazil, accessed 22 November 2014.

[34] Elizabeth Brandon, *Global Approaches to Site Contamination Law* (Springer, Dordrecht 2013).

Bibliography

Adinolfi, G, 'First Steps toward European Cooperation in Reducing Air Pollution – Activities of the Council of Europe' (1968) 33 *Law and Contemporary Problems* 421.

Akiner, Shirin, 'Ten years on: Achievements, Prospects, New Concerns', in Shirin Akiner (ed.), *The Caspian: Politics, Energy and Security* (Routledge, Abingdon, UK and New York, USA 2004) 337.

Alter, Karen, *The New Terrain of International Courts: Courts, Politics, Rights* (Princeton University Press, Princeton, NJ 2014).

Andrusevych, A, T Alge and C Konrad (eds), *Case Law of the Aarhus Convention Compliance Committee (2004–2011)* (2nd edn, RACSE, Lviv 2011).

Badenoch, Nathan, *Transboundary Environmental Governance: Principles and Practice in Mainland Southeast Asia* (World Resources Institute, Washington, DC 2002).

Ballaman, Richard, 'Comparing Regional Environmental Governance in East Asia and Europe – Air Pollution', Paper presented at Workshop on *Comparing Regional Environmental Governance in East Asia and Europe*, Kyoto, 24–25 January 2013.

Ballaman, Richard, 'Personal views on future work for a better air quality', Presentation to the 'Saltsjöbaden 5' Workshop, Gothenburg, Sweden, 24–26 June 2013.

Banner, Charles (ed.), *The Aarhus Convention: A Guide for UK Lawyers* (Hart Publishing, Oxford 2015) in press.

Bart, Jason, 'Weaponizing Water: Water and Energy as Sources of Conflict among the Central Asian Soviet Successor States' (2013) 22(1) *Michigan State International Law Review* 409.

Bastmeijer, Kees and Timo Koivurova (eds), *Theory and Practice of Transboundary Environmental Impact Assessment* (Martinus Nijhoff, Leiden 2008).

Bastmeijer, Kees and Timo Koivurova, 'Conclusions: Globalisation of Transboundary Environmental Impact Assessment', in Kees Bastmeijer and Timo Koivurova (eds), *Theory and Practice of Transboundary Environmental Impact Assessment* (Martinus Nijhoff, Leiden 2008) 376.

Bernauer, Thomas and Tobias Siegfried, 'Climate Change and International Water Conflict in Central Asia' (2012) 49(1) *Journal of Peace Research* 227.

Berthelot, Yves and Paul Rayment, *Looking Back and Peering Forward – A Short History of the United Nations Economic Commission for Europe, 1947–2007* (United Nations Economic Commission for Europe, Geneva 2007).

Bichsel, Christine, 'Liquid Challenges: Contested Water in Central Asia', (2011) 12(1) *Sustainable Development Law and Policy* 24.

Blagov, Sergei, 'Damage control for Russia and China after chemical spill', 23 January 2006, *China Environmental News Digest*.

Bošnjaković, Branko, 'The UNECE Environmental Conventions: Their Role and Potential to Promote Conflict Prevention and Settlement of Disputes in Transboundary Environmental Issues', in Eileen Petzold-Bradley, Alexander Carius and Arpád Vincze (eds), *Responding to Environmental Conflicts: Implications for Theory and Practice* (Kluwer, Dordrecht 2001) 263.

Bošnjaković, Branko, 'Negotiations in the Context of International Water-Related Agreements' (UNESCO 2003).

Boyle, Alan, 'Human Rights or Environmental Rights – A Reassessment' (2006–2007) 8 *Fordham Environmental Law Review* 471.

Boyle, Alan, 'Developments in the International Law of Environmental Impact Assessments and their Relation to the Espoo Convention' (2011) 20 *Review of European Community and International Environmental Law* 227.

Brachtl, Megan, 'Capitalizing on the Success of the Long-Range Transboundary Air Pollution (LRTAP) Regime to Address Global Transboundary Air Pollution', in Lawrence E Susskind and William R Moomaw (eds), XIV *Papers on International Environmental Negotiation* (PON Books, Cambridge, MA, USA 2005) 1.

Brachtl, Megan, 'Working Group 4 – Background Note for the Session on Air Pollution Agreements – Going for Global Governance of the Troposphere', Saltsjöbaden 5, Gothenburg, Sweden, 24–26 June 2013.

Brandon, Elizabeth, *Global Approaches to Site Contamination Law* (Springer, Dordrecht 2013).

Buhi, Jason and Lin Feng, 'Honoring the International Joint Commission's Role in the United States-Canada Transboundary Air Pollution Control Regime: A Century of Experience to Guide the Future' (2009) 11 *Vermont Journal of Environmental Law* 107.

Cardesa-Salzmann, Antonio, 'Constitutionalising Secondary Rules in Global Environmental Regimes: Non-Compliance Procedures and the Enforcement of Multilateral Environmental Agreements' (2012) 24 *Journal of Environmental Law* 103.

Churchill, Robin and Geir Ulfstein, 'Autonomous Institutional Arrangements in Multilateral Environmental Agreements: a Little-Noticed Phenomenon in International Law' (2000) 94 *American Journal of International Law* 623.

Connelly, Robert G, 'The UN Convention on EIA in a Transboundary Context: A Historical Perspective' (1999) 19(1) *Environmental Impact Assessment Review* 37.

Contreras, Antonio P, 'Transboundary Environmental Governance in Southeast Asia', in Amit Pandya and Ellen Laipson (eds), *Transnational Trends: Middle Eastern and Asian Trends* (The Henry L Stimson Center, Washington, DC 2008) 156.

Craik, Neil, *The International Law of Environmental Impact Assessment: Process, Substance and Integration* (Cambridge University Press, Cambridge 2008).

Craik, Neil and Timo Koivurova, 'Subsidiary Decision Making under the Espoo Convention: Legal Status and Legitimacy' (2011) 20 *Review of European Community and International Environmental Law* 258.

de Búrca, Gráinne, Claire Kilpatrick and Joanne Scott (eds), *Critical Legal Perspectives on Global Governance* (Hart Publishing, Oxford 2013).

Dellapenna, Joseph W and Joyetta Gupta (eds), *The Evolution of the Law and Politics of Water* (Springer, Dordrecht 2009).

de Mulder, Jan, 'The Expansion of Environmental Assessment in International Law: the Protocol on Strategic Environmental Assessment to the Espoo Convention' (2006) 18 *Environmental Law and Management* 269.

de Mulder, Jan, 'The Protocol on Strategic Environmental Assessment: A Matter of Good Governance' (2011) 20 *Review of European Community and International Environmental Law* 232.

Dinar, Ariel, Shlomi Dinar, Stephen McCaffrey and Daene McKinney, 'Case Study 4: The Aral Sea Basin', in *Understanding Transboundary Water Conflict, Negotiation and Cooperation* (2nd edn, World Scientific 2013) 339.

Dusik, Jiri, Aleh Cherp, Ausra Jurkeviciute, Henrieta Martonakova and Nick Bonvoisin, *SEA Protocol: Initial Capacity Development in Selected Countries of the Former Soviet Union* (REC/UNDP 2006).

Dusik, Jiri and Jian Xie, *Strategic Environmental Assessment in East and Southeast Asia: A Progress Review and Comparison of Country Systems and Cases* (World Bank, Washington DC 2009).

Eastwood, Lauren, *Negotiating the Environment: Civil Society, Globalisation and the UN* (Routledge, Abingdon, UK and New York, USA 2015).

Ebbesson, Jonas, 'Innovative Elements and Expected Effectiveness of the 1991 EIA Convention' (1999) 19 *Environmental Impact Assessment Review* 47.

Ebbesson, Jonas, 'A Modest Contribution to Environmental Democracy and Justice in Transboundary Contexts: The Combined Impact of the Espoo Convention and the Aarhus Convention' (2011) 20 *Review of European Community and International Environmental Law* 248.

Elliott, Lorraine, 'ASEAN and Environmental Governance: Rethinking Networked Regionalism in Southeast Asia' (2011) 14 *Procedia Social and Behavioural Sciences* 61.

Ercman, S, 'Activities of the Council of Europe and the European Economic Communities related to Transboundary Air Pollution', in C Flinterman, B Kwiatkowska and J G Lammers, *Transboundary Air Pollution: International Legal Aspects of the Co-operation of States* (Martinus Nijhoff, Leiden 1986).

Eserkepova, Irina, 'Review of a Situation on Heavy Metals and Plans on Ratification of CLRTAP Protocols in Kazakhstan', Report to Workshop to promote the ratification of the protocols under the LRTAP Convention across the entire UNECE region, 4–5 March 2014, Oslo.

Falkner, Robert, 'Private Environmental Governance and International Relations: Exploring the Links' (2003) 3(2) *Global Environmental Politics* 72.

Farrall, Stephen, Tawhida Ahmed and Duncan French (eds), *Criminological and Legal Consequences of Climate Change* (Hart Publishing, Oxford 2012).

Fifak, Veronika, 'International Law before English and Asian Courts: Finding the Judicial Role in the Separation of Powers' (2013) 3 *Asian Journal of International Law* 271.

Fischer, T B, 'Health and Strategic Environmental Assessment', in R Fehr, M Martuzzi, J Nowacki and F Viliani (eds), *Health in Impact Assessments* (WHO/EUPHA/IAIA 2014).

Fitzmaurice, Malgosia, 'The International Court of Justice and Environmental Disputes', in Duncan French, Matthew Saul and Nigel White (eds), *International Law and Dispute Settlement* (Hart Publishing, Oxford 2010) 17.

Fjeld, B and B Ottar, *Preliminary Report on Existing Knowledge with regard to SO_2 Emission Sources* (Norwegian Institute of Air Research, Kjeller 1975).

French, Duncan, Matthew Saul and Nigel White, *International Law and Dispute Settlement: New Problems and Techniques* (Hart Publishing, Oxford 2010).

Fujita, Sanae, *The World Bank, Asian Development Bank and Human Rights – Developing Standards of Transparency, Participation and*

Accountability (Edward Elgar, Cheltenham, UK and Northampton, MA, USA 2013).

Gehring, Thomas, *Dynamic International Regimes: Institutions for International Environmental Governance*, Studies of the International Environmental Law Network, vol. 5, (Peter Lang, Frankfurt 1994).

Goeteyn, Nils and Frank Maes, 'Compliance Mechanisms in Multilateral Environmental Agreements: An Effective Way to Improve Compliance?' (2011) 10(4) *Chinese Journal of International Law* 791.

Gonzalez, Ainhoa and Riki Therivel, 'Alternatives in Strategic Environmental Assessment of Plans and Programs', (2014) 7 *FasTips,* International Association for Impact Assessment.

Green, James A and Christopher P M Waters (eds), *Conflict in the Caucasus: Implications for International Legal Order* (Palgrave Macmillan, Basingstoke, UK and New York, USA 2010).

Green, Nat, 'Positive Spillover? – Impact of the Songhua River Benzene Incident on China's Environmental Policy', March 2009, *China Environment Forum*, The Wilson Center, Washington DC.

Gulbrandsen, Lars, Steinar Andresen and Jon Birgir Skjærseth, 'Non-State Actors and Environmental Governance: Comparing Multinational, Supranational and Transnational Rule Making', in Bob Reinalda (ed.), *Non-State Actors in the International System of States* (Ashgate Research Companion, Ashgate Publishing, Farnham 2011) 463.

Hayashi, Kiichiro, Young-il Song, Elvis Au and Jiri Dusik, 'SEA in the Asia Region', in Barry Sadler, Ralf Aschemann, Jiri Dusik, Thomas B Fischer, Maria R Partidario and Rob Verheem, *Handbook of Strategic Environmental Assessment* (Earthscan, Abingdon, UK and New York, USA 2011) 89.

Horberry, J, 'Transboundary Environmental Assessment: The Experience of the Mekong River Commission', presentation to the third MOP to the Espoo Convention, 2004.

Hu Wen Jun, 'Regional Cooperation Issues in Water Utilization of Aral Sea Basin' (2009) 32(6) *Arid Land Geography* 821.

Ibatullin, Saghit, 'International Fund for Saving the Aral Sea (IFAS) as a basis for regional cooperation in Central Asia', presentation, March 2010.

Jacobsen, M and O Brun (eds), *Human Rights and Asian Values. Contesting National Identities and Cultural Representations in Asia* (Curzon Press, Abingdon 2000).

Jayakumar, S, Tommy Koh and Robert Beckman, *The South China Sea Disputes and Law of the Sea* (Edward Elgar, Cheltenham, UK and Northampton, MA, USA 2014).

Jayakumar, S, Tommy Koh, Robert Beckman and Hao Duy Phan (eds), *Transboundary Pollution: Evolving Issues of International Law and*

Policy (Edward Elgar, Cheltenham, UK and Northampton, MA, USA forthcoming).

Jendrośka, Jerzy, 'Public Participation in the Preparation of Plans and Programs: Some Reflections on the Scope of Obligations under Article 7 of the Aarhus Convention' (2009) 6 *Journal for European Environmental and Planning Law* 495.

Jendrośka, Jerzy, 'Challenges of the Espoo Convention application in Eastern Europe, the Caucasus and Central Asia', presentation to Seminar on legislation and procedures for implementation of the Espoo Convention in Eastern Europe, the Caucasus and Central Asia, Geneva, 17 May 2010.

Jendrośka, Jerzy and Stephen Stec, 'The Kyiv Protocol on Strategic Environmental Assessment' (2003) 33 *Environmental Policy and Law* 105.

Jerger, David, 'Indonesia's role in realizing the goals of ASEAN's Agreement on Transboundary Haze Pollution' (2014) 14(1) *Sustainable Development Law and Policy* 35–45.

Johnstone, Rachel Lorne, 'Evaluating Espoo: What Protection does the Espoo Convention Offer the Arctic Marine Environment?' (2013) V *Yearbook of Polar Law* 337.

Jones, Gregory and Eloise Scotford (eds), *The Strategic Environmental Assessment Directive: A Plan for Success?* (Hart Publishing, Oxford 2015) in press.

Kaime, Thoko (ed.), *International Climate Change Law and Policy: Cultural Legitimacy in Adaptation and Mitigation* (Routledge, Abingdon, UK and New York, USA 2014).

Karmanova, Nadia, 'The EECCA Coordinating Group', Presentation to the 27th Meeting of the ICP Materials Task Force, Prague, 6–8 April 2011.

Kato, Kazu and Wakana Takahashi, *Regional/Subregional Environmental Cooperation in Asia* (Institute for Global Environmental Strategies, Kanagawa 2001).

Kavalski, Emilian (eds), *The New Central Asia: The Regional Impact of International Actors* (World Scientific, Singapore 2010).

Kersten, Charles, 'Rethinking Transboundary Environmental Impact Assessment' (2009) 34 *Yale Journal of International Law* 173.

Kim, Inkyoung, 'Environmental Cooperation of Northeast Asia: Transboundary Air Pollution' (2007) 7(3) *International Relations of the Asia-Pacific* 439.

Kim, Juli S, 'Transboundary Air Pollution – Will China Choke on its Success?' (2007) *China Environmental Health Project Fact Sheet* 2.

Kirschner, Lisa A and Edward B Grandy, 'The Songhua River Spill: China's Pollution Crisis', *Natural Resources and Environment* (Spring 2006), American Bar Association.

Knox, John, 'The Myth and Reality of Transboundary Environmental Impact Assessment' (2002) 96 *American Journal of International Law* 291.

Knox, John H, 'Assessing the Candidates for a Global Treaty on Transboundary Environmental Impact Assessment' (2003) 12 *New York University Environmental Law Journal* 153.

Koester, Veit, 'Review of Compliance under the Aarhus Convention: A Rather Unique Compliance Mechanism', (2005) 2(1) *Journal for European Environmental and Planning Law* 33.

Koester, Veit, 'The Compliance Committee of the Aarhus Convention – An Overview of Procedures and Jurisprudence' (2007) 37(2) *Environmental Policy and Law* 83.

Koivurova, Timo, 'The Convention on Environmental Impact Assessment in a Transboundary Context', in G Ulfstein, T Marauhn and A Zimmermann (eds), *Making Treaties Work: Human Rights, Environment and Arms Control* (Cambridge University Press, Cambridge 2007) 227.

Koivurova, Timo, 'Could the Espoo Convention become a Global Regime for Environmental Impact Assessment and Strategic Environmental Assessment?', in Robin Warner and Simon Marsden (eds), *Transboundary Environmental Governance: Inland, Coastal and Marine Perspectives* (Ashgate Publishing, Farnham 2012) 323.

Koivurova, Timo, *Introduction to International Environmental Law* (Routledge, Abingdon, UK and New York, USA 2014).

Kotze, Louis J and Thilo Marauhn (eds), *Transboundary Biodiversity Governance* (Brill/Nijhoff, Leiden 2014).

Kuokkanen, Tuomas, 'The Convention on Long-range Transboundary Air Pollution', in Geir Ulfstein, Thilo Marauhn and Andreas Zimmermann (eds), *Making Treaties Work: Human Rights, Environment and Arms Control* (Cambridge University Press, Cambridge 2007) 165.

Kuokkanen, Tuomas, 'Putting Gentle Pressure on Parties: Recent Trends in the Practice of the Implementation Committee under the Convention on Long-range Transboundary Air Pollution', in Jarna Petman and Jan Klabbers (eds), *Nordic Cosmopolitanism: Essays in International Law for Martti Koskenniemi* (Martinus Nijhoff, Leiden 2003) 315.

Lacey, Wendy, 'The Law of Treaties', in S Blay, R Piotrowicz and M Tsamenyi, *Public International Law: An Australian Perspective* (2nd edn, Oxford University Press, Melbourne 2005) 99.

Lambropoulos, Victoria, 'What can Australia Learn from the Europeans about Public Participation? – Article 6 of the Aarhus Convention and

Environmental Impact Statements' (2010) 27(4) *Environmental and Planning Law Journal* 272.

Langlet, David, 'Transboundary Transit Pipelines: Reflections on the Balancing of Rights and Interests in Light of the Nord Stream Project' (2014) September *International and Comparative Law Quarterly* 1, DOI: 10.1017/S0020589314000232.

Langshaw, Alexander, 'Giving Substance to Form: Moving towards an Integrated Governance Model of Transboundary Environmental Impact Assessment' (2012) 81(1) *Nordic Journal of International Law* 21.

Lawrence, Peter, *Justice for Future Generations: Climate Change and International Law* (Edward Elgar, Cheltenham, UK and Northampton, MA, USA 2014).

Leb, Christina, *Cooperation in the Law of Transboundary Water Resources* (Cambridge University Press, Cambridge 2013).

Lee, Maria, *EU Environmental Law, Governance and Decision-Making* (Hart Publishing, Oxford 2014).

Lee, Robert and Ellen Stokes, 'Environmental Governance: Reconnecting the Global and Local' (2009) 36(1) *Journal of Law and Society* 1.

Lelieveld, J, P Hadjinicolaou, E Kostopoulou, C Giannakopoulos, A Pozzer, M Tanarhte and E Tyrlis, 'Model Projected Heat Extremes and Air Pollution in the Eastern Mediterranean and Middle East in the Twenty-First Century' (2013) March *Regional Environmental Change* 7.

Libert, Bo, 'Water Management in Central Asia and the Activities of the UNECE', in MM Rahaman and O Varis (eds), *Central Asian Waters: Social, Economic, Environmental and Governance Puzzle* (Helsinki University of Technology, Helsinki 2008) 35.

Libert, Bo and Annukka Lipponen, 'Challenges and Opportunities for Transboundary Water Cooperation in Central Asia: Findings from UNECE's Regional Assessment and Project Work' (2012) 28(3) *Water Resources Development* 565.

Libert, Bo, Erkin Orolbaev and Yuri Steklov, 'Water and Energy Crisis in Central Asia' (2008) 6(3) *China and Eurasia Forum Quarterly* 9.

Lim, Michelle, 'Effective Governance across Central Asian Boundaries: What Lessons does the Central Asian Transboundary Watercourse Management Experience Provide for Mountain Biodiversity Conservation across the Kyrgyz-Tajik Boundary?', in Robin Warner and Simon Marsden (eds), *Transboundary Environmental Governance: Inland, Coastal and Marine Perspectives* (Ashgate Publishing, Farnham 2012) 111.

Lloyd, S J, 'Landlocked Central Asia' (1997) 2(1) *Geopolitics* 97.

Marsden, Simon, *Strategic Environmental Assessment in International and European Law: A Practitioner's Guide* (Earthscan/Routledge, Abingdon, UK and New York, USA 2008).

Marsden, Simon, 'Enforcing Non-Discrimination in Transboundary Environmental Impact Assessment: Advantages for EU Citizens from the Transposition of the Espoo and Aarhus Conventions?' (2009) 6 *Journal for European Environmental and Planning Law* 437.

Marsden, Simon, '*MOX Plant* and the Espoo Convention: Can Member State Disputes Concerning Mixed Environmental Agreements be Resolved outside EC Law?' (2009) 18(3) *Review of European Community and International Environmental Law* 312.

Marsden, Simon, 'Developing Approaches to Transboundary Environmental Impact Assessment in China: Cooperation through the Greater Tumen Initiative and in the Pearl River Delta Region' (2010) 9(2) *Chinese Journal of International Law* 393.

Marsden, Simon, 'The Espoo Convention and Kiev Protocol in the European Union: Implementation, Compliance, Enforcement and Reform' (2011) 20(3) *Review of European Community and International Environmental Law* 267.

Marsden, Simon, 'Invoking Direct Application and Effect of International Treaties by the European Court of Justice: Implications for International Environmental Law in the European Union' (2011) 60(3) *International and Comparative Law Quarterly* 737.

Marsden, Simon, 'Direct Public Access to EU Courts: Upholding Public International Law via the Aarhus Convention Compliance Committee' (2012) 81(2) *Nordic Journal of International Law* 175.

Marsden, Simon, 'Public Participation in Transboundary Environmental Impact Assessment – Closing the Gap between International and Public Law?', in Brad Jessup and Kim Rubenstein (eds), *Environmental Discourses in Public and International Law* (Cambridge University Press, Cambridge 2012) 238.

Marsden, Simon, 'Developing Agreements for Transboundary Environmental Impact Assessment and Strategic Environmental Assessment in Asia', in Robin Warner and Simon Marsden (eds), *Transboundary Environmental Governance: Inland, Coastal and Marine Perspectives* (Ashgate Publishing, Farnham 2012) 141.

Marsden, Simon, 'The World Heritage Convention in the Arctic and Indigenous People: Time to Reform?' (2014) 6(4) *Yearbook of Polar Law* in press.

Marsden, Simon and Timo Koivurova (eds), *Transboundary Environmental Impact Assessment in the European Union: The Espoo Convention and its Kiev Protocol on Strategic Environmental Assessment* (Earthscan/Routledge, Abingdon, UK and New York, USA 2011).

McIntyre, Owen, *Environmental Protection of International Watercourses under International Law* (Ashgate Publishing, Farnham 2007).

McKinney, Daene C, 'Cooperative Management of Transboundary Water Resources in Central Asia', in Daniel Burghart and Theresa Sabonis-Helf (eds), *In the Tracks of Tamerlane: Central Asia's Path to the 21st Century* (National Defense University, Washington, DC 2004) 187.

Mercier, Jean-Roger, 'The World Bank and Environmental Impact Assessment', in Kees Bastmeijer and Timo Koivurova (eds), *Theory and Practice of Transboundary Environmental Impact Assessment* (Martinus Nijhoff, Leiden 2008) 291.

Morgera, Elisa, 'An Update on the Aarhus Convention and its Continued Global Relevance' (2005) 14 *Review of European Community and International Environmental Law* 138.

Morin, Jean-Frédéric and Amandine Orsini (eds), *Essential Concepts of Global Environmental Governance* (Routledge, Abingdon, UK and New York, USA 2015).

Moynihan, Ruby and Bjørn-Oliver Magsig, 'The Rising Role of Regional Approaches to International Water Law: Lessons from the UNECE Water Regime and Himalayan Asia for Strengthening Transboundary Water Cooperation' (2014) *Review of European, Comparative and International Environmental Law* 43.

Mushkat, Roda, 'Creating Regional Environmental Governance Regimes: Implications of Southeast Asian Responses to Transboundary Haze Pollution' (2013) 4 *Washington and Lee Journal of Energy, Climate and Environment* 103.

Myint, Tun, *Governing International Rivers: Polycentric Politics in the Mekong and the Rhine* (Edward Elgar, Cheltenham, UK and Northampton, MA, USA 2012).

Myint, Tun, 'Case Study 1: The Mekong River Basin', in Ariel Dinar, Shlomi Dinar, Stephen McCaffrey and Daene McKinney, *Understanding Transboundary Water Conflict, Negotiation and Cooperation* (2nd edn, World Scientific, Singapore 2013) 273.

Pallemaerts, Marc (ed.), *The Aarhus Convention at Ten: Interactions and Tensions between Conventional International Law and EU Environmental Law* (Europa Law Publishing, Groningen 2011).

Pallemaerts, Marc, *Study on National Legislation Needed to Implement the Protocol on Civil Liability and Compensation for Damage Caused by the Transboundary Effects of Industrial Accidents on Transboundary Waters* (Institute for European Environmental Policy, undated).

Paulus, Andreas L, in Geir Ulfstein, Thilo Marauhn and Andreas Zimmermann (eds), *Making Treaties Work: Human Rights, Environment and Arms Control* (Cambridge University Press, Cambridge 2007) 362.

Pederson, Ole, 'An International Environmental Court and International Legalism' (2012) 24 *Journal of Environmental Law* 547.

Poncelet, Charles, 'Access to Justice in Environmental Matters – Does the European Union Comply with its Obligations?' (2012) 24(2) *Journal of Environmental Law* 287.

Razzaque, Jona, 'Information, Public Participation and Access to Justice in Environmental Matters: Rio+20 Appraisal', in S Alam, J H Bhuyian, T M Chowdhury and E J Techera (eds), *Routledge Handbook of International Environmental Law* (Routledge, Abingdon, UK and New York, USA 2012) 137.

Razzaque, Jona, *Environmental Governance in Europe and Asia: A Comparative Study of Institutional and Legislative Frameworks* (Routledge, Abingdon, UK and New York, USA 2013).

Reinalda, Bob (ed), *Non-State Actors in the International System of States* (Ashgate Research Companion, Ashgate Publishing, Farnham 2011).

Romanov, A V, 'Facilitating implementation and ratification of CLRTAP Protocols in the Eastern Europe, Caucasus and Central Asian countries (EECCA Project)', *Report to Workshop to promote the ratification of the protocols under the LRTAP Convention across the entire UNECE region*, 4–5 March 2014, Oslo.

Sadler, Barry, *Strategic Environmental Assessment at the Policy Level – Recent Progress, Current Status and Future Prospects* (Regional Environmental Center for Eastern and Central Europe 2005).

Salman, Salman, *The World Bank Policy for Projects on International Waterways: An Historical and Legal Analysis* (The World Bank, Washington, DC 2009).

Sands, Philippe, and Jacqueline Peel, *Principles of International Environmental Law* (Cambridge University Press, New York 2012).

Schwela, Dietrich, Gary Haq, Cornie Huizenga, Wha-Jin Han, Herbert Fabian and May Ajero, *Urban Air Pollution in Asian Cities – Status, Challenges and Management* (Earthscan, Abingdon, UK and New York, USA 2006).

Scott, Karen, 'Non-compliance Procedures and the Resolution of Disputes under International Environmental Agreements', in Duncan French and Nigel White (eds), *International Law and Dispute Settlement: New Problems and Techniques* (Hart Publishing, Oxford 2010) 225.

Smith, Elizabeth, 'Implementing the Espoo Convention: An International Financial Institutions Perspective', in Kees Bastmeijer and Timo Koivurova (eds), *Theory and Practice of Transboundary Environmental Impact Assessment* (Martinus Nijhoff, Leiden 2008) 313.

Song Ying, 'International Legal Aspect of the Songhua River Incident', in Michael G Faure and Song Ying (eds), *China and International Environmental Liability: Legal Remedies for Transboundary Pollution* (Edward Elgar, Cheltenham, UK and Northampton, MA, USA 2008) 325.

Stec, Stephen, 'EU Enlargement, Neighbourhood Policy and Environmental Democracy', in Marc Pallemaerts (ed.), *The Aarhus Convention at Ten: Interactions and Tensions between Conventional International Law and EU Environmental Law* (Europa Law Publishing, Groningen 2011) 35.

Stein, Ted L, 'The Approach of the Different Drummer: The Principle of the Persistent Objector in International Law' (1985) 26 *Harvard International Law Journal* 457.

Stephens, Tim, *International Courts and Environmental Protection* (Cambridge University Press, Cambridge 2009).

Sukaroek, Worawan, 'The MRC Policy Framework on Transboundary EIA: A Better Cooperation will be Enhanced in the Lower Mekong Basin', paper presented to conference entitled *Role of Water Sciences in Transboundary River Basin Management,* Thailand, 2005.

Suzuki, Eisuke, 'Global Governance and International Financial Institutions' (2011) 19(1) *Asia Pacific Law Review* 13.

Talmon, Stefan and Bing Bing Jia (eds), *The South China Sea Arbitration: A Chinese Perspective* (Hart Publishing, Oxford 2014).

Tanzi, Attila, 'Regional Integration and the Protection of the Environment: The UNECE Process on Water Law as a Model for the Global Dimension', in T Scovazzi (ed.), *The Protection of the Environment in a Context of Regional Economic Integration* (Giuffrè, Milan 2001).

Toth, Bende, 'Public Participation and Democracy in Practice – Aarhus Convention Principles as Democratic Institution Building in the Developing World' (2010) 30(2) *Journal of Land Resources and Environmental Law* 295.

Townsend-Gault, Ian, David VanderZwaag, and Robert Adamson, 'Transboundary Ocean and Atmospheric Pollution in Southeast Asia: Prospects for Regional Cooperation', in Amitav Acharya and Richard Stubbs (eds), *New Challenges for ASEAN – Emerging Policy Issues* (UBC Press, Vancouver 1995) 28.

Treves, Tullio, Attila Tanzi, Cesare Pitea, Chiara Ragni, and Laura Pineschi (eds), *Non Compliance Procedures and Mechanisms and the Effectiveness of International Environmental Agreements* (TMC Asser Press, The Hague 2009).

Ulfstein, G, T Marauhn and A Zimmermann (eds), *Making Treaties Work: Human Rights, Environment and Arms Control* (Cambridge University Press, Cambridge 2007) 189.

van Asselt, Harro, *The Fragmentation of Global Climate Governance: Consequences and Management of Regime Interactions* (Edward Elgar, Cheltenham, UK and Northampton, MA, USA 2014).

Warner, Robin and Simon Marsden (eds), *Transboundary Environmental Governance: Inland, Coastal and Marine Perspectives* (Ashgate Publishing, Farnham 2012).

Warner, Robin, and Simon Marsden, 'Perspectives on Transboundary Environmental Governance', in Robin Warner and Simon Marsden (eds), *Transboundary Environmental Governance: Inland, Coastal and Marine Perspectives* (Ashgate Publishing, Farnham 2012) 1.

Wates, Jeremy, 'The Future of the Aarhus Convention', in Marc Pallemaerts (ed.), *The Aarhus Convention at Ten: Interactions and Tensions between Conventional International Law and EU Environmental Law* (Europa Law Publishing, Groningen 2011) 383.

Wijnstekers, Willem, *The Evolution of CITES: A Reference to the Convention on International Trade in Endangered Species of Wild Fauna and Flora* (9th edn, International Council for Game and Wildlife Conservation 2011).

Williams, Martin, 'Future Role and Challenges for CLRTAP', Presentation to Saltsjöbaden 5 Workshop, Gothenburg, Sweden, 24–26 June 2013.

Wishnick, Elizabeth, 'Why a Strategic Partnership?', in James Bellacqua (ed.), *The Future of China-Russia Relations* (University Press of Kentucky, Lexington 2010) 71.

Wouters, Patricia, 'Global Water Governance through Many Lenses' (2008) 14(4) *Global Governance: A Review of Multilateralism and International Organizations* 523.

Wouters, Patricia, 'The Yin and Yang of International Water Law: China's Transboundary Water Practice and the Changing Contours of State Sovereignty' (2014) 23(1) *Review of European, Comparative and International Environmental Law* 67.

Wyrowski, Lukasz, 'Benefits of and national legislation and authorities for UNECE Convention on the Transboundary Effects of Industrial Accidents', presentation to the Joint Seminar on the Espoo Convention and Convention on Transboundary Effects of Industrial Accidents, Ashgabat, Turkmenistan, 5–6 June 2011.

Zahar, Alexander, *International Climate Change Law and State Compliance* (Routledge, Abingdon, UK and New York, USA 2015).

Zaharchenko, R Tatiana and Gretta Goldenman, 'Accountability in Governance: The Challenge of Implementing the Aarhus Convention in Eastern Europe and Central Asia', (2004) 4 *International Environmental Agreements: Politics, Law and Economics* 229.

Ziganshina, Dinara, 'International Water Law in Central Asia: Commitments, Compliance and Beyond' (2009) 20 *Water Law* 96.

Documents of International Institutions and National Governments

Aarhus Convention Secretariat, *The Aarhus Convention Reporting Mechanism National Implementation Reports: Experiences and Lessons Learned*, Geneva, 19 June 2013.
Asian Development Bank, *Safeguard Policy Statement* (Asian Development Bank 2009).
Asian Development Bank, *Operations Manual: Bank Policies*, 1 October 2013.
Asian Human Rights Commission, *Asian Human Rights Charter, a People's Charter*, 17 May 1998.
Author unknown, *The CSCE/OSCE and the Environment: 1975–2000, Working Paper 5*, Centre for OSCE Research, University of Hamburg.
Author unknown, 'Towards a More Coherent Institutional Framework for the UN System's Environmental Activities: Views and Roles of the Regional Commissions', May 2006.
Author unknown, 'Note on the Regional Dimension of Development within the UN', 15 June 2006.
Berthelot, Yves, and Paul Rayment, *Looking Back and Peering Forward – A Short History of the United Nations Economic Commission for Europe, 1947–2007* (United Nations Economic Commission for Europe 2007).
Brels, Sabine, David Coates and Flavia Loures, *Transboundary Water Resources Management: The Role of International Watercourse Agreements in Implementation of the CBD* (CBD/UNEP/WWF 2008).
Committee on the Environmental Protection under the Government of the Republic of Tajikistan, *National Report on Implementation of the Aarhus Convention in the Republic of Tajikistan for 2011–2013*, 1 November 2013.
Conference on Security and Cooperation in Europe, *Report on Conclusions and Recommendations of the Meeting on the Protection of the Environment of the Conference on Security and Co-operation in Europe* (1990).
Espoo Inquiry Commission, *Report on the Likely Significant Adverse Transboundary Impacts of the Danube-Black Sea Navigation Route at the Border of Romania and the Ukraine*, July 2006.
European Commission, *Fifth Environmental Action Plan (1993–2000): Towards Sustainability.*

German Agency for International Cooperation, *Programme Documentation 2009–2011 – Transboundary Water Management in Central Asia Programme* (undated).

Gierke, Wolfgang, in United Nations Economic Commission for Europe, *The Convention on the Transboundary Effects of Industrial Accidents: Twenty Years of Prevention, Preparedness and Response* (United Nations undated).

Government of Canada, *Convention on Long-range Transboundary Air Pollution* (2008).

Inomata, Tadanori, *Management Review of Environmental Governance within the United Nations System* (United Nations Joint Inspection Unit 2008), JIU/REP/2008/3.

Israel Ministry of Environmental Protection, 'Pollutant Release and Transfer Register (PRTR), undated.

Johnson, Stanley, *UNEP – The First 40 Years: A Narrative* (United Nations Environment Programme 2012).

Ministry of Environment Protection of the Republic of Kazakhstan, *Report on Implementation of the Espoo Convention on Environmental Impact Assessment in a Transboundary Context* (2012).

National Environment Agency, 'Factsheet on Transboundary Haze Pollution' (Government of Singapore, 2014).

Organisation for Economic Co-operation and Development, *The PRTR Guidance Manual for Governments* (1996), OECD/GD(96)32.

Organisation for Economic Co-operation and Development, *Guiding Principles for Chemical Accident Prevention, Preparedness and Response* (2nd edn, OECD 2003).

Organisation for Security and Cooperation in Europe/UNECE, *Environmental Impact Assessment in a Transboundary Context: Pilot Project in Central Asia Project Report* (2009).

Ramsar Convention Secretariat, *The Ramsar Convention Manual: A Guide to the Convention on Wetlands (Ramsar, Iran, 1971)*, (6th edn, 2013).

Republic of Kazakhstan, Ministry of Environment Protection, *Format for the Aarhus Convention implementation report in accordance with Decision IV/4* (ECE/MP.PP/2011/2/Add.1), undated.

Skrylnikov, Dmytro, *Review of Legislation on Environmental Impact Assessment of the Republic of Tajikistan with Regard to Introduction and Implementation of the Espoo Convention* (2010).

Sliggers, Johann and Willem Kakebeeke (eds), *Clearing the Air: 25 Years of the Convention on Long-range Transboundary Air Pollution* (United Nations Economic Commission for Europe 2004).

Stanners, David and Philippe Bordeau (eds), *Europe's Environment: The Dobris Assessment* (European Environment Agency 1995).

State Agency of Environmental Protection and Forestry under the Government of the Kyrgyz Republic, *Report of the Kyrgyz Republic on the Implementation of the Convention on Environmental Impact Assessment in a Transboundary Context in the period 2010–2012,* May 2013, informal translation.

Treaty Section of the Office of Legal Affairs, United Nations, *Treaty Handbook* (United Nations 2012).

United Nations, *Guidance to Implementation of the Protocol on Pollutant Release and Transfer Registers* (United Nations 2007).

United Nations, *Clearing the Air: 30th Anniversary of the Convention on Long-range Transboundary Air Pollution* (2009).

United Nations, *Building More Inclusive, Sustainable and Prosperous Societies in Europe and Central Asia: A Common United Nations Vision for the Post-2015 Development Agenda* (United Nations 2013).

United Nations and United Nations Economic Commission for Europe, *River Basin Commissions and Other Institutions for Transboundary Water Cooperation: Capacity for Water Cooperation in Eastern Europe, Caucasus and Central Asia* (United Nations 2009).

United Nations Economic Commission for Europe, *Promotion of the Protocol on Pollutant Release and Transfer Registers in countries in Eastern Europe, the Caucasus and Central Asia*, undated. Doc. ECE/MP.PRTR/2014/L.6.

United Nations Economic Commission for Europe, *Guidance Document on the Aarhus Convention Compliance Mechanism* (United Nations undated).

United Nations Economic Commission for Europe, *Policies and Systems of Environmental Impact Assessment* (United Nations 1991).

United Nations Economic Commission for Europe, *Application of Environmental Impact Assessment Principles to Policies, Plans and Programmes* (United Nations 1992).

United Nations Economic Commission for Europe, *Guidelines on Public Participation in Environmental Decision Making* (UNECE 1996).

United Nations Economic Commission for Europe, *Convention on Environmental Impact Assessment in a Transboundary Context: Review of Implementation 2003,* Advance Copy, 30/08/2004.

United Nations Economic Commission for Europe, *Guidance on Public Participation in EIA in a Transboundary Context*, (United Nations 2006), ECE/MP.EIA/7.

United Nations Economic Commission for Europe, *Our Waters: Joining Hands Across Borders – First Assessment of Transboundary Rivers, Lakes and Groundwaters* (United Nations 2007).

United Nations Economic Commission for Europe, *Review of Implementation of the Convention on Environmental Impact Assessment in a Transboundary Context* (United Nations 2008) ECE/MP.EIA/11.

United Nations Economic Commission for Europe, *The Assistance Programme – The Convention on the Transboundary Effects of Industrial Accidents* (UNECE 2010).

United Nations Economic Commission for Europe, *Review of Implementation of the Convention on Environmental Impact Assessment in a Transboundary Context (2006–2009)* (United Nations 2011). ECE/MP.EIA/16.

United Nations Economic Commission for Europe, Convention on Environmental Impact Assessment in a Transboundary Context, *Structure and Functions of the Implementation Committee and Procedures for Review of Compliance/Operating Rules of the Implementation Committee* (United Nations 2011).

United Nations Economic Commission for Europe, *Review of Implementation of the Convention on Environmental Impact Assessment in a Transboundary Context (2006–2009)* (United Nations 2011) ECE/MP.EIA/16.

United Nations Economic Commission for Europe, Convention on the Protection and Use of Transboundary Watercourses and International Lakes, *Second Assessment of Transboundary Rivers, Lakes and Groundwaters* (United Nations 2011).

United Nations Economic Commission for Europe, *Strengthening Water Management and Transboundary Water Cooperation in Central Asia: The Role of UNECE Environmental Conventions* (United Nations 2011) ECE/MP.WAT/35.

United Nations Economic Commission for Europe, *Resource Manual to Support Application of the UNECE Protocol on Strategic Environmental Assessment* (United Nations 2012) ECE/MP.EIA/17.

United Nations Economic Commission for Europe, *Simplified Resource Manual to Support Application of the UNECE Protocol on Strategic Environmental Assessment* (United Nations 2012) ECE/MP.EIA/18.

United Nations Economic Commission for Europe, Convention on the Protection and Use of Transboundary Watercourses and Lakes, *The Global Opening of the 1992 UNECE Water Convention* (UNECE 2013).

United Nations Economic Commission for Europe, Convention on the Protection and Use of Transboundary Watercourses and Lakes, *Guide to Implementing the Water Convention* (United Nations 2013).

United Nations Economic Commission for Europe, *Guide to Public Participation under the Protocol on Water and Health* (United Nations 2013) ECE/MP.WH/9.

United Nations Economic Commission for Europe, *The European Union Water Initiative: National Policy Dialogues – Achievements and Lessons Learned* (United Nations 2013) ECE/MP.WAT/38.

United Nations Economic Commission for Europe, *The Aarhus Convention: An Implementation Guide* (2nd edn, United Nations 2014).

United Nations Economic Commission for Europe, *Model Provisions on Transboundary Groundwaters* (UN 2014).

United Nations Economic Commission for Europe/United Nations Environment Programme, Network of Experts on Public Participation and Compliance, *Water Management: Guidance on Public Participation and Compliance with Agreements* (2000).

United Nations Economic Commission for Europe/OSCE Environment and Security Initiative, *Draft Report of the National Working Group Meeting for Identification of the Legal and Institutional Needs for Accession and Implementation of the UNECE Water Convention by Georgia*, Tbilisi, 26 June 2009.

UNECE/WHO Regional Office for Europe, *Protocol on Water and Health* (UNECE/WHO 2009).

United Nations Educational, Scientific and Cultural Organisation World Heritage Centre, *Operational Guidelines for the Implementation of the World Heritage Convention* (UNESCO 2013).

United Nations Environment Programme, *Manual on Compliance with and Enforcement of Multilateral Environmental Agreements* (UNEP 2001).

United Nations Environment Programme, *The Songhua River Spill, China, December 2005 – Field Mission Report* (UNEP 2005).

United Nations Environment Programme, *Air Quality and Atmospheric Pollution in the Arab Region* (Regional Office for West Asia 2007).

United Nations Environment Programme, *Introduction to the Resource Kit: A Stepwise Guide – Rotterdam Convention, Share Responsibility* (UNEP 2009).

United Nations Environment Programme, Secretariat of the Stockholm Convention, *Ridding the World of POPs: A Guide to the Stockholm Convention on POPs* (UNEP 2010).

United Nations Environment Programme, Secretariat of the Basel Convention, *The Basel Convention Mechanism for Promoting Implementation and Compliance: Celebrating a Decade of Assistance to Parties* (UNEP 2011).

United Nations Environment Programme, *Commemorating 25 Years of Awareness and Preparedness for Emergencies at Local Level: Achievements and Way Forward* (UNEP 2012).

United Nations Environment Programme, *Handbook for the Vienna Convention for the Protection of the Ozone Layer* (9th edn, Ozone Secretariat UNEP 2012).

United Nations Environment Programme, *Handbook for the Montreal Protocol on Substances that Deplete the Ozone Layer* (9th edn, Ozone Secretariat UNEP 2012).

United Nations Environment Programme, *Environmental Governance*, Factsheet (UNEP undated).

United Nations Environment Programme and Caspian Environment Programme, *Guidelines on Environmental Impact Assessment in a Transboundary Context in the Caspian Sea Region: Step by Step Procedures* (UNEP 2003).

United Nations Environment Programme, United Nations Economic Commission for Europe, United Nations Development Programme, North Atlantic Treaty Organisation, Regional Environment Centre (REC), Organisation for Security and Cooperation in Europe, *Environment and Security in Europe, Transforming Risks into Cooperation: The Case of the Eastern Caspian Region* (2008).

United Nations Framework Convention on Climate Change, *Uniting on Climate: A Guide to the Climate Change Convention and the Kyoto Protocol* (UNFCCC 2007).

UN Framework Convention on Climate Change, *The Kyoto Protocol Mechanisms: International Emissions Trading Clean Development Mechanism Joint Implementation* (UNFCCC 2010).

World Health Organization, *The Protocol on Water and Health: Making a Difference* (WHO 2006).

World Water Assessment Programme, *The World Water Development Report 2014: Water and Energy* (2014).

Index